# RAISING THE FLAG

**ADST-DACOR Diplomats and Diplomacy Series**

SERIES EDITOR

Margery Boichel Thompson

Since 1776, extraordinary men and women have represented the United States abroad under widely varying circumstances. What they did and how and why they did it remain little known to their compatriots. In 1995, the Association for Diplomatic Studies and Training (ADST) and DACOR, an organization of foreign affairs professionals, created the Diplomats and Diplomacy book series to increase public knowledge and appreciation of the professionalism of American diplomats and their involvement in world history. Peter Eicher's accounts of America's pioneer consuls are thoroughly researched and eminently readable stories full of surprises and challenges.

# Raising the Flag

## America's First Envoys in Faraway Lands

*Peter D. Eicher*

*An ADST-DACOR Diplomats and Diplomacy Book*

Potomac Books

AN IMPRINT OF THE UNIVERSITY OF NEBRASKA PRESS

For the next generations of travelers,
Cam, Nick, and Jeremy
Jake, Alex, Ryan, Zoe, and Bri

# Contents

# Illustrations

# Introduction

This book brings together some of the little-known stories of the first Americans to raise our flag officially in distant lands. It chronicles the experiences of pioneering American envoys in a dozen countries around the world, from China to Chile, Tripoli to Tahiti, Mexico to Muscat. Their tales of adventure, hardship, danger, triumph, and tragedy open a window to the history of American foreign affairs, reflecting how American ideas, values, and power helped to shape the modern world. They also show the impact that individuals, even if long forgotten, have exerted on the course of history.

A handful of prominent Americans—Benjamin Franklin, John Adams, Thomas Jefferson—are well known for their diplomatic work during the earliest days of the republic. A few others were well known in their day, but they no longer appear even in textbooks on diplomatic history. Most, however, were never well known, despite their achievements or the impact they had in faraway places.

The lives of most early American diplomats belie the popular image of diplomacy as a round of elegant receptions, royal courts, decorum, and ceremony. Instead, their stories form a saga that sometimes seems stranger than fiction, replete with intrigues, revolutions, riots, war, shipwrecks, swashbucklers, desperadoes, duelists, and bootleggers. Assigned to represent the United States in remote lands, America's early envoys faced extraordinary challenges. Most went with little fanfare and little support from their government. They sailed in tiny ships across uncharted oceans and pirate-infested waters to isolated outposts. They encountered hostile governments, physical privation, and disease. They had the daunting challenge of introducing the United States and its strange new form of government—democracy—to foreign leaders who had never heard of the country and could not conceive of such a political system. Many faced threats from tyrannical despots. Some were held as hostages. At least two led foreign armies into battle. Several were instrumental in expanding American territory. Some were heroes; a few were scoundrels. Many perished, far from home.

This volume centers on the lives and experiences of a dozen American diplomats in the early decades of the republic. It is not intended to be a comprehensive history of early American diplomacy, but instead recounts individual experiences that illustrate the development of foreign policy and the growth of American influence around the world. Many of the events described were the precursors of today's headlines: Americans at war in the Middle East, intervention in Latin America, trade deficits with China. The personal stories are based largely on American sources, especially official dispatches to the State Department, but also documents, letters, diaries, travel accounts, and memoirs. Most of the sources are unpublished; others are long out of print. The focus on original American accounts is deliberate, offering a special insight into the attitudes that drove Americans at the time and highlighting their uniquely American reactions to the oddities they found in distant lands. A history of foreign reactions to these strange American visitors is a subject for further research.

The lives recounted in this volume are limited to the first seventy-five years of American foreign relations, from the American Revolution to the Civil War. This was the formative period of American diplomacy. It was the initial era of "flag raising," years during which the United States first established an official presence abroad. These were also the years of American expansion across North America and of its first steps as a world power.

The years before the Civil War were also the years of sailing ships. It was not until the 1850s that transoceanic steamers began to transform international travel and diplomacy. Before then, it would routinely take many months for American envoys to reach their posts. Once there, sending home for instructions or policy guidance might take a year or longer. As a result, envoys were left largely to their own devices. Post–Civil War diplomats would have many notable adventures of their own, but they would unfold in a different international context.

The United States had no career foreign service until well into the twentieth century. America's first envoys tended to be either prominent citizens already known to government leaders or Americans who established themselves in foreign countries, usually as traders, and then parlayed their connections into an official appointment as a U.S. representative. By Andrew Jackson's administration in the late 1820s and early 1830s, the spoils system had begun to dominate the appointment process, with hundreds of assignments doled out to political supporters with often dubious qualifications.

Readers of this book will encounter a wide variety of diplomatic titles and ranks, which can be confusing even to those familiar with modern diplomatic usage. The most senior diplomatic rank is ambassador, but Americans in the eighteenth and nineteenth centuries considered that title too pretentious for representatives of a democracy. The United States did not begin to confer the title of ambassador until 1893. Before then, the top American envoys were accorded the rank of minister, which is one tier below ambassador in general international practice. In some countries this made little difference, but in others the reduced rank limited American envoys' access to senior officials and left them chafing at the end of receiving lines and in the least desirable places at diplomatic dinner tables. An office abroad headed by a minister was known as a legation, in contrast to an embassy, which would be headed by an ambassador. Lower-level diplomatic titles, in rank order, included commissioner, chargé d'affaires, agent, and secretary. To further confuse matters, there were also ad hoc titles, including special diplomatic agent, confidential agent, and treaty negotiator.[1] Although there were no American ambassadors until 1893, this did not stop some of the envoys mentioned in this book from calling themselves "ambassador."

All of the ranks and titles mentioned above relate to diplomats, who were formally accredited to represent the United States before foreign governments. In addition, however, there was another category of American foreign affairs officials: consular officers. These included consuls general, consuls, vice consuls, and consular agents, as well as commercial agents. While diplomats focused on relations with governments, consuls were charged with protecting American citizens abroad and promoting American shipping and commerce. Diplomats generally resided only in capital cities, but consuls could be appointed to any major—and increasingly to any minor—port or commercial center. As a result, consuls were far more numerous than diplomats. By the end of the Civil War, there were American consular representatives in 644 cities around the world,[2] far more than there are even today. At the same time, there were only forty-five American diplomats, assigned to legations in thirty-three countries. It was consuls, therefore, who first raised the American flag in many countries. With a few exceptions, consuls—unlike diplomats—received no salaries until 1856, but they were permitted to retain their "consular fees," including charges for registering all American ships touching at their ports, as well as fees for services they provided to American citizens. These fees were not enough to support a consul except in a few of the world's busiest ports. It was therefore accepted practice for consuls to engage in private business activities in addition to their official duties. This sometimes led to conflicts of interest that could affect U.S. policy, a problem that was not fully addressed until the adoption of consular reforms in the early years of the twentieth century.

In theory the functions of diplomats and consuls were separate, but in practice the distinction was not always clear. Diplomats also worked to protect Americans citizens and promote trade, while some consuls became deeply involved in sensitive political issues, especially in places where there was no resident American diplomat. The U.S. diplomatic and consular services were not merged into a single foreign service until 1924.

Both diplomats and consuls reported to and took instructions from the Department of State. The department's supervision, however, tended to be extremely lax. Since communications with remote posts took months, envoys were given general instructions but left to themselves to determine how to deal with developing events. American envoys were thus able to drive policy in directions that may not have enjoyed the support of their government, had their government actually known what was transpiring in distant corners of the globe. Moreover, the State Department simply did not have the resources to supervise its personnel abroad. In the 1850s, when the United States had hundreds of consulates and diplomatic missions around the world, the State Department still had only seven clerks, who spent most of their days laboriously copying correspondence by hand. Many of America's early representatives complained bitterly that their dispatches went unanswered and that they felt abandoned by their government.

The various characters in this book had vastly different experiences, but their stories highlight consistent themes in America's growth as a world power. They show the extent to which commerce drove the initial American outreach to many countries. They recount a continuing, often unfriendly, competition with Great Britain. They depict American expansion, both around the world and across North America. They illustrate increasing American military power and the growing willingness to use it, both in war and through "gunboat diplomacy." They show the extent to which early American diplomatic history is linked to American naval history. They demonstrate the firm American conviction that representative democracy is the best form of government. Some American envoys displayed an almost messianic desire to spread the benefits of democracy; virtually all disdained older autocratic systems. And not least, they demonstrate the frequently neglected role of diplomacy in advancing American ideals, influence, and interests around the globe.

Yet another theme that ties these stories together is the sense of adventure and discovery shared by the protagonists. They knew they were visiting places and doing things that were entirely new for Americans. With this in mind, they left detailed accounts of people, places, and their personal experiences: life as a slave in Algiers, revolutions in South America, the magnificent king of Siam, surviving the plague in Constantinople, the California gold rush, and many more. Their official dispatches and private journals offer eyewitness accounts of historic events and some of the best early descriptions of once-remote places and customs. Although the stories in this book unfold over several decades and continents, their many common threads weave a tapestry of early American diplomacy.

# RAISING THE FLAG

# ONE

# For Tea and Country

*Samuel Shaw and the First American Contacts with China*

On the evening of December 16, 1773, a crowd of angry men armed with tomahawks, axes, and pistols made their way through the darkness to Griffin's Wharf, Boston. The men were dressed as Mohawk Indians, their faces blackened with coal dust. At the wharf, they boarded the ships *Dartmouth*, *Eleanor*, and *Beaver* of the British East India Company. Breaking open the hatches, they methodically hurled the chests of cargo overboard. By 9:00 p.m., their work was finished. The "Indians" had dumped 342 crates of Chinese tea into the cold, dark waters of Boston Harbor.

The Boston Tea Party is the most celebrated event in the long history of tea in America. The British authorities responded by closing the harbor, stoking tensions that soon escalated into the American Revolution. The Tea Party sparked similar, if less known, acts of defiance in New York, Annapolis, and other American cities. The tea protests, however, were just a small part of the momentous drama unfolding in the American colonies. The tumultuous decade that followed saw revolution and war. Tea became scarce, and most Americans learned to live without it.

When the war ended, tea was high on the list of commodities in demand among Americans. The peace with Great Britain had barely been signed when merchants up and down the East Coast began to ponder how to obtain supplies of tea. Among them was Robert Morris, a Philadelphia businessman who was perhaps the richest man in the country. Morris had played a pivotal role in funding George Washington's army, earning a place in history as the "financier of the American Revolution." Soon after the war ended, Morris backed a bold plan to send a ship to China to bring tea back into American homes. The idea seemed audacious because China lay 15,000 miles away, across two vast and dangerous oceans. No American ship had ever made the voyage. There was little accurate information available on China, which was still largely a mysterious and forbidding land. With the China trade heavily dominated by the better financed, better organized, and more experienced British, there was good reason to wonder whether Americans could break into the market at all. A failed attempt could spell financial ruin for its backers.

Morris drew together a small group of businessmen from Philadelphia, New York, and Boston and began to make preparations for the venture, outfitting a ship and selecting John Green, a veteran of the Continental navy, as its captain. Even more important than the captain in such a venture, however, was the "supercargo," or commercial agent, who would sail with the ship and take charge of all trading and business transactions at its destination. For this key role the merchants turned to a young man named Samuel Shaw. Shaw would spend the rest of his life in the China trade and would serve as the first official American representative in China.

Shaw was a surprising choice to lead a trading venture to China. He was just twenty-nine, a landlubber, and not widely traveled. The son of a Boston merchant, Shaw attended school for several years, but had no university education. He turned twenty-one just as General Washington was assembling his army outside Boston in the fall of 1776. Like many other young men of his generation, Shaw immediately rallied to the cause. He was commissioned as a lieutenant of artillery and spent the next eight years in the Continental army.

Shaw's unit helped drive the British from Boston, then marched south to join in the ill-fated defense of Manhattan. This was the first time Shaw had left his native Massachusetts. He wrote home that "the people of this place are a motley collection of all the nations under heaven. Every thing is extravagantly dear."[1] He was almost captured during the army's confused retreat across the city, but made his escape to see further combat at Tappan Bay and White

Plains. He followed Washington across the icy Delaware River into the battle at Trenton and spent the bitter winter of 1777–78 at Valley Forge. Later in the war, he fought at Germantown and helped defend West Point.

Shaw's letters home provide a glimpse of the privations faced by the Continental army. He lost his belongings in the retreat from Manhattan and remained unpaid for months at a time. Almost destitute, he wrote home repeatedly, begging his family to send him shirts. By 1779 he lamented that three years in the army have "brought me to poverty and rags."[2] Even at the bleakest times, however, Shaw never considered abandoning the fight. His letters exuded optimism—verging sometimes on irrational optimism—about the certainty of American victory. He railed against the British, who "manifested a spirit of perverseness scarcely to be equaled." The British were responsible for "Murder, devastation, and every species of violence. . . . Pleasant towns laid in ashes . . . old and defenseless inhabitants slaughtered in their houses, and, shame to humanity, the chastity of . . . women violated. . . . The rascally manner in which our enemies prosecute this predatory war would disgrace savages."[3]

Although Shaw escaped serious injury in the war, his close friend and artillery mate Capt. Thomas Randall, who would later share his adventures in China, was taken prisoner at the Battle of Germantown. When Randall tried to escape, "the enemy prevented it, knocking him down and stabbing him in eight places." Seriously wounded, Randall was released on parole after giving his word of honor that he would not rejoin the American forces; this was a common practice at the time. Randall left the army and went into business in Philadelphia.[4]

As the war progressed, Shaw was promoted to the rank of major. Like many men of his era, he chose to be addressed by his military rank for the rest of his life, becoming commonly known as Major Shaw. In 1779 he was appointed aide-de-camp to Gen. Henry Knox, with whom he remained for the rest of the war. At the war's end, Knox was the second highest ranking officer in the Continental army, after Washington.

When peace finally arrived in 1783, Shaw left the army with a personal commendation from Washington, who wrote, "From my own observation, I am enabled to certify, that through the whole of his service, he has greatly distinguished himself in every thing which could entitle him to the character of an intelligent, active, and brave officer." Knox, in a separate letter, concurred that "he has, in every instance, evinced himself an intelligent, active and gallant officer, and as such he has peculiarly endeared himself to his numerous acquaintances."[5]

Immediately after the war, Shaw helped organize the Society of the Cincinnati, a hereditary brotherhood intended to maintain contacts among former army officers and to provide charitable support for members' families.[6] George Washington served as the Society's first president; Henry Knox was a prominent member; Samuel Shaw was its secretary. Several members of the Society were involved in organizing and financing the trading voyage to China. Five of the ship's company were members.

China was not a complete mystery to Americans of the late eighteenth century, but knowledge was scant, and much of what was available was inaccurate. Although Western countries had been in touch with China for centuries, the depth of contact was extremely shallow. In the modern era, Portuguese navigators were the first Europeans to reach China, early in the sixteenth century. They were allowed to establish a trading base at Macao, through which they shipped tea and other oriental products to Lisbon. Jesuit missionaries reached Peking (now Beijing) in 1601 and won sufficient favor from the emperor—in part through a gift of two clocks and a clavichord—to establish themselves for some time in the city. Missionary writings provided much of what was known in the West about China.

In the seventeenth century, the British and the Dutch eclipsed the Portuguese as the most prominent European trading powers in Asia. The Dutch East India Company began to ship tea to Europe as an exotic drink said to have medicinal qualities. By 1650 tea made its way to the Dutch settlement of New Amsterdam, later renamed New York. Meanwhile, the British East India Company was chartered and given a monopoly over British trade with the East. Although the company's focus was India, the first English ship reached Canton (now Guangzhou), just upriver from Macao, in 1637. The English were the first to establish a "factory," or trading post, at Canton, which was designated by the Chinese as the only port open for foreign trade.

Tea first came to England indirectly when King Charles II married a Portuguese princess, Catherine of Braganza, in 1662. A chest of tea formed part of Catherine's large dowry, and she popularized it at the English court. The British East India Company placed its first order for one hundred pounds of Chinese tea two years after Catherine married Charles. Imports of tea to England rose dramatically from that time onward. As the seventeenth century reached its close, tea outstripped silks and porcelain as the major British import from China. Tea was being shipped to English colonists in Massachusetts as early as the 1690s. It became a major source of revenue for the crown. By the outbreak of the American Revolution, tea was the preferred drink of the public in both England and its American colonies.

Westerners tended to hold romantic notions of China. In the mid-1700s, Chinese items and "chinoiserie" were a rage in Europe and America, influencing art and architecture as well as everyday items such as dinnerware, wallpaper, and furniture. A ten-story pagoda was even erected in London's Kew Gardens in 1763. The great minds of the Enlightenment, among them Voltaire and Benjamin Franklin, tended to glorify China—or at least their image of China—as an ideal society. Franklin's *Pennsylvania Gazette* carried a series of articles on the morals of Confucius as early as 1738.[7]

The Chinese, for their part, had little knowledge of or interest in Europe. China still saw itself as the "Middle Kingdom," the center of the civilized world. Other countries were either barbarian, tributary states, or both. The imperial encyclopedia of 1747 asserted that European tales of the existence of five continents are "nothing more than a wild, fabulous story."[8] Christianity was believed to have derived from Buddhism. Portugal was thought to be somewhere south of Java, and stories circulated that the Portuguese purchased children to cook and eat. The Chinese often confused the various European countries, all the more so because of the changing political landscape in Europe over the centuries. For China, the Europeans nations were tributary states, sometimes consolidated in their records as "countries of the western ocean." China saw no particular value in opening itself to the influence of such outsiders and limited European access strictly to a tiny section of a single city on the southern coast, Canton, far from the imperial capital in Peking. Chinese documents referred to the Canton factories as "devil factories," offering further evidence of their disdain for the foreign visitors.

In 1783, the year the Revolutionary War ended, a remarkable American adventurer arrived back in New York after years of traveling the globe. John Ledyard of Connecticut had sailed the South Seas with Capt. James Cook on the last of his famous voyages of discovery, which included stops in the American Northwest and in China. Ledyard may have been the first American to visit China. His book, *A Journal of Captain Cook's Last Voyage to the Pacific Ocean*, published in 1783, helped rekindle American interest in China.

Most notably for the China trade, Ledyard's *Journal* described the abundance of animal skins along the northwest coast of North America, including "foxes, sables, hares, marmosets, ermines, weazles, bears, wolves, deer, moose, dogs, otters, beavers," and others. Sailors on Cook's expedition purchased beaver and other skins for about sixpence each to use as clothing. Months later, when the ship arrived at Canton, Ledyard found to his astonishment that a good fur sold for the equivalent of one hundred dollars.[9] This was a fantastic profit, more for a single fur than Ledyard earned in a year at sea. Even before his book was published, Ledyard began to make the rounds of merchants in Boston, New York, and Philadelphia, trying to stir up interest in the idea of a triangular trade route that would take American ships to the Northwest to trade for furs, then on to China to exchange the furs for tea. The merchants were intrigued. Robert Morris, in particular, was ready to support a venture. In the end, he could not gather enough backers to launch such an uncertain, multiyear project. Ledyard was just a few years ahead of his time; pelts from the American Northwest would eventually come to dominate America's trade with China.

Morris eventually settled for a simpler but still risky China venture, a direct voyage from New York to Canton. After several false starts, he solidified an ill-fated partnership with Daniel Parker, a Massachusetts businessman who enlisted the backing of other financiers. Parker took charge of outfitting a vessel and obtaining a cargo to trade. Parker was a member of the Society of the Cincinnati and a friend of Samuel Shaw's. He recruited Shaw as supercargo for the planned voyage. Shaw agreed on the condition that his close friend Thomas Randall could also join the venture.

After scouring the East Coast for suitable ships, Parker settled on a vessel newly constructed in Boston, the *Angelica*, which he purchased and rechristened the *Empress of China*. The ship was just more than one hundred feet from stem to stern and twenty-eight feet at its widest point, which was less than half the size of most British merchantmen trading with China. A contemporary account called her "handsome, commodious and elegant . . . deemed an exceedingly swift sailer."[10] The *Empress* had a hull sheathed with copper and carried the figurehead of a woman. Recognizing that the ship would be sailing through potentially dangerous waters, it was outfitted with fourteen cannon and a variety of small arms. The merchants planned to dissolve the partnership and sell the ship on its return from China.

As captain, Parker turned to John Green, a bear of a man, weighing in at more than two hundred pounds (three hundred by some accounts) and well over six feet tall.[11] Green was born in Ireland in 1736; he was fifty-two when given command of the *Empress of China*. He had spent his entire life at sea. Starting out in Ireland as a cabin boy, he eventually found himself in Philadelphia, where he went to work for Robert Morris, at first sailing in the coastal trade between Philadelphia and New York, then taking on transatlantic routes. During the revolution, Green became a captain in the Continental navy, commanding several warships and privateers. He was twice captured by the British but was freed in time to command a ship in the last naval skirmish of the war, off the coast of Cuba. In late 1783 Green was technically still a naval officer, but the entire navy was in the process of being decommissioned, so he was given leave to engage in private business.

In addition to Green, Shaw, and Randall, the ship's company included a "second captain," Peter Hodgkinson, who would take command if Green died or became incapacitated at sea. Hodgkinson was Green's brother-in-law and would later command his own ship in the China trade. There were also two mates, a purser, a surgeon and surgeon's mate, a captain's clerk, and two midshipmen, one of whom was Green's eighteen-year-old son. Besides these "gentlemen," there was a crew of thirty-four seamen, including a gunner, two carpenters, a cooper, and cabin boys.

Choosing a cargo for the *Empress of China* posed a dilemma for Daniel Parker, since there were very few products that the Chinese wanted. Most European traders were reduced to exporting specie— silver coins—to China to buy tea, silks, and other Chinese products. The Americans had a potential advantage, however, since their forests produced two products that the Chinese did want. One was fur. The other was a medicinal plant that grew wild in the Appalachian Mountains, *panax quinquefolius*, or ginseng.

To the Chinese, ginseng was a wonder drug. It was used to treat all manner of ailments, from boils and headaches to wounds. Among its other supposed attributes, ginseng was considered an aphrodisiac and a cure for impotence. The thick root of the ginseng plant could grow into a shape that resembled a human body and was called in Chinese the "root of life."[12] China traditionally imported ginseng from Korea, but the supplies were never sufficient.

Benjamin Franklin was the first to report that ginseng grew wild in the Mid-Atlantic colonies.[13] Well before the revolution, entrepreneurs began to collect American ginseng to ship to England then onward to China. Native Americans in the Appalachians were hired to find and dig for ginseng root, which began to eclipse furs as a trading commodity. Daniel Boone, for one, made his fortune through ginseng, not by trapping furs. With independence, Americans were in a position to cut out the English middlemen and control the ginseng trade.

Daniel Parker believed ginseng would bring a hefty profit in China, especially since the revolution had disrupted the supply. But the proposition was still risky, since he had no idea how broad the demand might be or if a shipload would glut the market. Nonetheless, Parker hired Robert Johnston—who would become the surgeon on the *Empress of China*—to lead the search for ginseng. Johnston spent three months traveling through the Appalachian foothills of Maryland and Virginia seeking suppliers for tons of ginseng root. As he cornered the market, the price almost doubled to sixpence a pound. In the end, Parker and Johnston managed to secure 242 casks of ginseng, weighing almost thirty tons.[14]

In addition to ginseng, the *Empress* carried as cargo almost 50 tons of cordage, 69 kegs of tin sheets, 30 tons of lead, 437 yards of broadcloth, plus planks, turpentine, tar, brandy and wine, and one crate of furs. There were also four chests containing 20,000 silver dollars, since specie was the only item that the Americans were certain would be accepted by the Chinese. The ginseng, however, was by far the most valuable part of the cargo. In all, the cargo and the ship cost the financiers $119,000, split equally between Robert Morris and Daniel Parker.[15] Besides the cargo, the ship was provisioned with sufficient water and food—including live animals—to make the long trip to China without stopping along the way.

With the crew and cargo settled, Parker wrote a detailed letter of instruction to Captain Green on January 25, 1784:

> It being of very great Consequence to arrive in Canton before any other Vessel which can go from Europe with fresh Ginseng, every attention has been paid, as you know, to procure a Ship particularly calculated, both for fast sailing and to encounter rough Weather. . . . It is expected that you will go the whole voyage without putting into port. . . . When in port you will be under the direction of Samuel Shaw Esquire or in case of his death Thomas Randall Esquire, who are appointed supercargoes of the Ship. . . . You will stay at

Macao or proceed onward according to the orders you shall receive from your Supercargoes, to whose direction this is confided, and they are instructed to assist you in the disposition of your property to the best advantage, which we doubt not may be Usefull; as the Chinese are very great Rogues. . . .

You will probably be the first who shall display the American Flag in those distant Regions, and . . . you have delivered to you herewith not only the declaration of Independence, but Copies of the several treaties made with the different European powers. . . .

We heartily wish you a Secure and prosperous Voyage and recommend you to the protection of Heaven.[16]

Since the owners were uncertain what formalities might be required once the *Empress* arrived in China—or en route—they applied to Congress, then sitting in Annapolis, for sea letters, or an official testimonial verifying the ship's provenance and purposes. The extraordinary document drawn up by Congress was addressed in such general terms that it might be used by the ship's captain in any circumstances or any port. It read:

Most Serene, Serene, most puissant, puissant, high, illustrious, noble, honorable, venerable, wise and prudent Emperors, Kings, Republicks, Princes, Dukes, Earls, Barons, Lords, Burgomasters, Councillors, as also Judges, Officers, Justiciaries & Regents of all the good Cities and places whether ecclesiastical or secular who shall see these patents or hear them read, We the United States of America in Congress Assembled make known that John Green Captain of the Ship call'd the *Empress of China* is a Citizen of the United States of America and that the ship which he commands belongs to Citizens of the said United States and as we wish to see the said John Green prosper in his lawful affairs, our prayer is to all the beforementioned, and to each of them separately . . . that they may please to receive him with goodness and to treat him in a becoming manner.[17]

The *Empress* was scheduled to sail in mid-January 1784. Samuel Shaw left the army early that month, as it disbanded in West

Point. He hurried to New York City, writing to his brothers, "I shall sail for China by the 15th of January. . . . I hope to shake you by the hand in two years."[18] Nature, however, did not cooperate. The winter of 1783–84 was one of the worst on record. Storms dumped heavy snow on the Eastern Seaboard throughout January and February. The port of New York froze over.

The *Empress of China* finally weighed anchor and sailed from New York the morning of February 22, 1784. It was a freezing morning, but the ice in the harbor had begun to break up. A crowd was on hand to cheer as the ship passed New York's grand battery. The *Empress* fired a salute of thirteen guns, which was answered by twelve guns from the fort. The practice of saluting forts, other ships, and distinguished individuals by discharging cannons was a common practice at the time and regarded as an appropriate courtesy. The crew of the *Empress* would fire many salutes on the voyage and would witness an event that would show how ill-conceived this custom was.

The voyage was generally a calm one. In a letter to the American secretary for foreign affairs, John Jay, Samuel Shaw called it "a pleasant passage, in which nothing extraordinary happened."[19] Early in the voyage Captain Green noted in his journal: "Several of our seamen seasick. Mr. Randall and the purser both sick but eat very much and throw it up again."[20] Shaw's journal includes anecdotes of life at sea. One day, he wrote, we "caught a fish called by the mariners Albacor, or Bonito. . . . Its appearance resembles that of the tunny. . . . We dressed it two ways, stewed and barbecued, and found it but indifferent food."[21] On March 13, being Saturday night, the officers "according to custom drank sweethearts and wives in 'cherry punch.' Songs by those who could sing. All appeared very happy."[22]

The ship crossed the Tropic of Cancer a few days later, prompting what Shaw called "the usual ceremonies" to initiate sailors who had never before crossed the Tropic. Two crew members dressed ludicrously as the Old Man of the Tropic and his wife arrived in "their chariot," a ship's hatch drawn by other sailors dressed as tritons. The blindfolded initiates were lathered with grease and made to pledge never to drink weak beer when strong was available, nor to eat brown bread when there was white, and "never to kiss the maid when he can kiss the mistress, unless he likes the maid best." Each was then dunked into one of the ship's boats that had been filled with water, "all with great good humor," before being issued an extra ration of grog. Since it also happened to be St. Patrick's Day, "proper attention was paid by the gentlemen to the memory of the patron of Ireland," with the officers sharing a fancy meal of codfish, roast pork with applesauce, and potatoes while they drank heartily to the Saint.[23]

Within a few days of leaving port, the *Empress* began to leak. The sailors were forced constantly to work the pumps. Provisions were damaged, the animals had to be moved onto the open deck, and potatoes, turnips, and corn were spread on deck to dry. The leaks forced an unanticipated stop in the Cape Verde Islands, off the coast of West Africa, to have the ship caulked. They anchored in the harbor and respectfully saluted the port with a cannonade. Shaw took advantage of the stop to visit the main towns. He was not much impressed with the islands or their inhabitants, but found Cape Verde an excellent spot to obtain goats, pigs, poultry, and fruit to reprovision the ship. He called on the Portuguese viceroy, who lived in a house that Shaw described as "in point of elegance nearly equal to a good barn." The young wife of another official they met, Shaw wrote, "did not excite in any of us an idea that would militate with the tenth commandment."[24]

There were four other ships in the small port, including a French brig with a cargo of slaves destined for the sugar plantations of the Caribbean. The slaver's captain came on board the *Empress* and agreed to carry letters to the West Indies for onward transport to the United States. As the captain returned to his brig, Shaw retired to his cabin to write a homily against slavery.

After six days in Cape Verde, the *Empress* was back at sea, on course to sail the rest of the way to the East Indies without a further stop. As the endless days at sea dragged on, Shaw had only a few anecdotes to note in his journal. One day they sighted a whale beating the water forcefully with its tail; the sailors told him that the whale was under attack by swordfish, a bit of marine lore widely believed at the time. Another day, three flying fish landed on board the *Empress*. The ship's log recorded sighting beautiful jellyfish, seals, turtles, and "a large bird made like a gannet in shape and color, named albatross."[25] On several occasions, dolphins leaped around the ship, and the crew tried unsuccessfully to harpoon one. One day they sighted four water spouts, visible in the distance for more than an hour.

The days turned into weeks and then months. It is difficult for a modern traveler even to imagine the hardships and discomforts of months at sea in a tiny, creaking, wooden sailing ship—crowded conditions, poor sanitation, odors from the animals, no fresh fruits or vegetables, endless tedium, and the constant danger of storms and pirates. As an additional concern, they were never entirely certain of their geographic position. Sailors still navigated by the sun, stars, and dead reckoning. They could accurately calculate their latitude, but they were never quite sure exactly how far east they had traveled. Shaw mentions several times in his journal the problem of calculating longitude. They began looking for land on June 17 and finally sighted Java a week later, on June 25. It had been over four months since the *Empress of China* left New York and almost as long since it had touched land.

In the Straits of Sunda, between Java and Sumatra, they had the good fortune to encounter a French ship whose captain had been with the French fleet at Yorktown, the decisive battle of the American Revolution. The ship was on its way to Canton, and the captain offered to guide them there, a proposition they happily accepted. Canton was still more than 1,500 miles and many weeks away, including some difficult sailing through the pirate-infested South China Sea.

On August 23, 1794, six months and one day after leaving New York, the *Empress of China* arrived at Macao. According to the ship's log, the journey was 18,248 miles. They dropped anchor at 4:00 p.m. and fired seven cannon in salute. Shaw, together with the ship's purser, "had the honor of hoisting the first Continental flag ever seen or made use of in those seas."[26] The distinctive

Stars and Stripes caused the Chinese to refer to the Americans as the "flowery flag devils," an adaptation of their more general term "foreign devils."[27]

The Portuguese settlement at Macao was past its best days. Portuguese trade with China had greatly declined over the past century, and according to a contemporary description, "Now they have only a fort, with a small garrison. The houses are built in the same manner as in Europe. The Chinese are more numerous than the Portuguese; and the latter are properly a mixed breed, the Portuguese having taken Asiatic wives. Here is a Portuguese governor, as well as a Chinese mandarin, to take care of the town and neighbouring country."[28] Shaw's first impression was positive: "The situation of Macao is very pleasant, and the gentlemen belonging to the European nations trading at Canton are well accommodated there."[29]

The morning after their arrival, the *Empress* was visited by the French consul and by the supercargoes of French, Swedish, and German ships that were in port. Shaw gave the visitors copies of the treaties between the United States and the European powers. The *Empress*, of course, saluted with its guns as the visitors disembarked. Two days later, August 25, was the feast day of St. Louis, an occasion for another cannonade in the harbor, the French ships saluting with twenty-one guns and the other ships responding with thirteen.

From Macao, the *Empress* sailed up the Pearl River to the island of Whampoa (now Huangpu), fourteen miles below Canton and the furthest point inland that foreign ships were allowed to travel. There were about ten European ships already docked at Whampoa, prompting the inevitable cannonade. The *Empress* saluted with thirteen guns, which were returned by thirteen guns from each ship in the harbor. The salute was repeated when the *Empress* dropped anchor—in all, more than 250 cannon were discharged to welcome the *Empress* to Whampoa.

As the smoke subsided, Chinese officials came on board to measure the ship and to gather details of its cargo and armaments. The "grand mandarin"–the top Chinese official in charge of foreign trade in Canton, also called the *hoppo*—sent on board a gift of two bulls, eight bags of flour and seven jars of country wine.[30] Although the hoppo was officially not permitted to accept gifts in return, presents were nonetheless expected. To skirt the regulations, westerners would "sell" him merchandise, usually fine clocks, for about 5 percent of their real value.[31] Other Chinese officials were even less scrupulous, refusing to let the *Empress* unload until they had received a payoff. Shaw argued with them for several days, finally giving in when they cut off provisions to the ship.[32] As time passed, Shaw complained that virtually all Chinese officials were corrupt, demanding "squeeze," or bribes, at every level.[33]

Shaw and Thomas Randall proceeded by small boat from Whampoa to Canton, the bustling hub of China's foreign trade. One early American visitor described the scene: "Myriads of boats moored in long, regular streets . . . salt junks discharging their cargoes . . . immense rafts of timber and bamboos floating down with the tide, managed by a few miserable little wretches. . . . Revenue cruizers rowing in every direction, painted with the brightest colours. . . . Thousands of small ferry boats. . . . Immense junks of four or five hundred tons, gorgeously embellished with the fascinations of dragons, paint, gold-leaf and ginger-bread-work, with a huge eye painted on either side of the bow, to enable the vessel to see her way."[34]

A French supercargo invited Shaw and Randall to share the French "factory" until their own could be arranged, a process that took about a week. The factories, one for each nation and about a dozen in all, were clustered together in a tiny area along the riverbank. They served as both warehouses and temporary residences for the traders, with the living quarters on the upper levels. Shaw described them as "elegant . . . with every accommodation."[35] Chinese servants took care of cooking, washing, and other chores.

Life for the Europeans was comfortable but tightly restricted. They could not enter the city gates, and their actions were confined by petty regulations. They could not, for example, ride in sedan chairs. Foreigners were subject to Chinese laws and justice, including the possibility of arbitrary imprisonment and torture. Contacts with Chinese people were strictly limited, although on rare occasions a Chinese merchant might invite Western traders to his home for a formal dinner. When this did happen, the Europeans generally supplied the table, chairs, wine, and much of the food.[36] Traders were not allowed to bring their wives or families to Canton and not permitted to remain there permanently. When they completed their business, they were required to return to Macao to await the arrival of their ships the following season. The trade was seasonal due to the monsoons. The prevailing winds in the Indian Ocean blow sailing ships northeast toward China from May to October, then shift direction and blow toward the southwest from December through March.

In Canton, Shaw was introduced to the well-established trading system. Trade was transacted through the *cohong*, or "officially authorized merchants."[37] This was a group of ten or so Chinese merchant firms, known generally as the "hong merchants," who had a monopoly on Western trade. Prices for commodities were fixed by the cohong and fluctuated depending on supplies. Each ship was required to employ several Chinese specialists for various tasks—clearing customs, hiring boats, and providing supplies. Contacts between the Chinese and foreigners were conducted in pidgin, a lingua franca using a limited English vocabulary with Chinese syntax. Accounts of pidgin conversations seem ridiculous today; clocks, for example, were "sing-songs" and perfume was "smellum water." Very few Western traders learned Chinese.

Shaw found an excellent market for his ginseng. He traded primarily for tea, but also accumulated substantial amounts of "Nankeens" (silk cloth) and silk garments, fans, and other Chinese products. He also purchased large quantities of porcelain, some of which he specially commissioned with Chinese artists. Porcelain brought back by the *Empress of China* holds pride of place today in a number of prominent American collections. Notably, Shaw commissioned chinaware depicting an allegorical figure of Fame blowing a trumpet, with the badge of the Society of the Cincinnati suspended by a ribbon.[38] He had difficulty getting Chinese artists to produce what he considered an acceptable image. He preserved a sample of their early efforts, commenting, "It is difficult to regard it without smiling."[39] On subsequent visits to China, Shaw commissioned several sets of Society of the Cincinnati china for himself and fellow members.[40] He sold a set to George Washington; pieces are on display at Mount Vernon and other prominent museums.

The most significant political event during Shaw's first trip to China was the so-called Canton war. This began on the evening of November 25, 1784. The British East India Company ship *Lady Hughes* had entertained a number of foreign guests at dinner. On their departure, the ship's cannon fired the customary salute. Unfortunately, there was a small Chinese boat alongside, and the cannons' discharge killed one boatman and wounded two others. The Chinese refused to accept the English explanation that the incident was an accident and demanded that the ship turn over the gunner. In Shaw's words, "It is a maxim of the Chinese law that blood must answer for blood. . . . To give up this poor man was to consign him to certain death. Humanity pleaded powerfully against this measure."[41]

The English refused and hurried the gunner downstream to Macao. In response, the Chinese arrested the *Lady Hughes*'s supercargo, George Smith, saying he would be released only when the gunner was turned over. The various consuls and supercargoes in Canton held an emergency meeting at which they agreed that the Chinese action posed a threat to all of them and required a firm response. The participants, Shaw included, decided unanimously to respond by having their ships in Whampoa send boats with armed men to the factories as a show of force, to provide protection, and to demand Smith's release. This was a drastic step, not least because possession of firearms was strictly prohibited in the factories. A show of force by the traders could easily lead to open hostilities.

The first shots were not long in coming. As the boats made their way up the Pearl River to Canton, they were fired on by Chinese soldiers along the shore; one sailor was wounded. Meanwhile, the Chinese shut down all trading activities, withdrew all Chinese servants from the factories, and closed the gates of Canton. Chinese men-of-war began assembling in the river outside the factories. Soon more than forty armed junks had appeared. Onshore, Chinese troops collected for what appeared to be an imminent attack on the factories. "Every thing," Shaw wrote, "bore the appearance of war."[42]

With forces gathering and tensions mounting, the Chinese made a conciliatory gesture, offering to open negotiations with all the foreign representatives except the English. Shaw was among the delegation that met with the governor. The Chinese again demanded that the gunner be turned over but gave assurances that he would be brought before a tribunal and released if they were satisfied the shooting was accidental. As a gesture of goodwill, they offered to resume trade with all countries except the British. The Western envoys were sent away with a gift of two pieces of silk each.

Back at the factories, European resolve began to crumble. The Danes, Dutch, and French made clear that they were not inclined to go to war with China on behalf of a British seaman. The Europeans began to send their boats and arms back to Whampoa, each boat under a Chinese flag to ensure its safety. Shaw was dismayed by the collapse of Western resolve and by the Chinese success in their strategy of divide and conquer. The Chinese warships, he wrote, "were not very formidable . . . while their soldiers were armed with swords, bows and arrows, and match-lock muskets. . . . I am certain that three European long-boats, properly equipped, might have forced their way through them, had they been five times as numerous."[43] Shaw did not explain what advantage would have been gained by forcing longboats through the Chinese blockade or what he would have foreseen as the next step.

The English, faced with deserting allies and overwhelming Chinese numbers, yielded and surrendered the gunner. The arrested supercargo, George Smith, was released shortly thereafter. The English were forced to ask pardon of the Chinese officials, after which their trade was also restored. With that, the "Canton war" came to an end.

Although Shaw as yet had no official American position, he reported the events in a letter to U.S. Secretary for Foreign Affairs John Jay. The American longboat, he wrote, was the last to leave the factories and return to Whampoa, and it did not depart until the English advised him that it should go. Moreover, the American boat, unlike those of the Europeans, "was not disgraced with a Chinese flag."[44] Shaw reported that the English had offered profuse thanks for his steadfastness. He wrote in his journal, "Thus ended a very troublesome affair, which commenced in confusion, was carried out without order and terminated disgracefully."[45] The poor gunner remained in Chinese custody. He was later executed by strangulation.

On December 28, 1784, after four months in China, the *Empress of China* sailed for home, laden with tea and other Chinese goods. Thomas Randall stayed behind in Canton to complete a separate deal he and Shaw had concluded, chartering a Dutch ship to take still more Chinese goods back to the United States. The "war" had apparently not caused a rethinking of Western courtesies. As the *Empress* sailed from Whampoa, she saluted the remaining ships with nine guns, which they returned.

The passage home was by a route similar to the outward journey and was largely uneventful, an almost unbroken tedium of five months at sea. The ship stopped for a few days in Cape Town for provisions. Remarkably, there was a letter there awaiting Shaw with sad news, informing him of the death of his father. On May 11, 1785, the *Empress of China* sailed up New York's East River and dropped anchor. Shaw wrote: "We saluted the city with thirteen guns, and finished our voyage."[46] He had been away for fifteen months and, according to the ship's log, sailed 32,458 miles.

The *Empress of China* arrived to great acclaim. Newspapers in all major American cities carried stories of the voyage. Its success was a sensation and inspired other merchants to follow in its wake. The voyage also belied predictions of commercial disaster. An English newspaper, for example, reported just two months before Shaw's return that "the Americans have given up all thought of a China trade, which can never be carried on to advantage without some settlement in the East Indies."[47]

Samuel Shaw took time during his first ten days home to send a letter to John Jay about the first U.S. trading visit to China. He wrote on May 19, 1785, "It becomes my duty to communicate to you, for the information of the fathers of the country . . . the respect with which its flag has been treated in that distant region." The voyage attracted "the attention of the Chinese towards a people of whom they have hitherto had but very confused ideas. . . . It was some time before they could fully comprehend the distinction between us and Englishmen. They styled us the *New People*; and when by the map we conveyed to them an idea of the extent of our country, with its present and increasing population, they were highly pleased at the prospect of so considerable a market for the productions of their own empire." Shaw reported only very briefly on the trading possibilities and provided a description of the Canton war. He sent Jay the two pieces of silk he was given by Chinese officials when he joined the other envoys seeking George Smith's release. He asked Jay to convey these to the Congress, since he considered them a gift to the United States. Shaw added a special mention of how helpful and friendly the French had been in Canton. "The harmony maintained between them and us was particularly noticed by the English, who more than once observed, that it was a matter of astonishment to them that the descendants of Britons could so soon divest themselves of prejudices which they had thought to be not only hereditary, but inherent in our nature."[48] Jay sent the letter on to Thomas Jefferson, the U.S. minister in Paris, who took pleasure in passing it on to the French foreign minister.[49]

A few weeks later Shaw received a letter of thanks from Jay, on behalf of the Congress: "That Congress feel a peculiar satisfaction in the successful issue of this first effort of the citizens of America to establish a direct trade with China, which does so much honor to its undertakers and conductors."[50] Jay also returned the two pieces of silk, which had been sent back to him by the Congress.

During the fifteen months that the *Empress of China* was away, the ship's owners fell out with each other. Daniel Parker, who had recruited Shaw and taken the lead in outfitting the ship, embezzled funds from his partnership with Robert Morris and absconded to Europe. Parker, among his other malfeasances, had secretly stolen 2,300 of the 20,000 silver dollars that were supposed to have been aboard the *Empress*. Shaw, as supercargo, was held accountable for the missing $2,300, a small fortune at the time. As a result, Shaw did not share in the profits of the *Empress*, although he did make a modest profit on the goods he and Randall shipped on their own account. Five years passed before Parker admitted his crime, but he remained a fugitive in Europe.

Despite Parker's perfidy, the venture was a commercial triumph for Morris and the other investors. The *Empress* brought home eight hundred chests of tea, more than twice the amount dumped into Boston Harbor during the Tea Party. In addition, it carried ten thousand pieces of silk and large quantities of porcelain. The cargo was distributed and sold in New York, Philadelphia, Boston, and elsewhere with great fanfare and publicity. Newspapers advertised the sale of "Fresh Bohea tea of the first quality, in Chests, Half and Quarter Chests, China, a great Variety, Sattins, Lute strings, Persians, Taffetas of different Qualities, black and other Colours, for Gentlemen's Summer Wear, Nankeens, Elegant Sattin Shoe-Patterns, Pearl Buttons with Gold Figures, Superfine Lambskins, Ivory and lacquered Ware, Tea-Caddies, A Large Assortment of lacquered Tea-Trays, Waiters, Bottle-stands, &c. &c., Silk Handkerchiefs, Hair Ribbons, Cinnamons and Cinnamon Buds, Black Pepper, 200 Boxes excellent Sugar, &c." As planned, the *Empress of China* was sold. Her new owners sent her on another trading voyage to China.[51]

Samuel Shaw, now jobless and not yet in a position to sponsor his own trading ventures, accepted an offer from his old friend Henry Knox to serve as secretary of the War Department. It was not long, however, before China began to loom again in his future. Robert Morris approached Shaw and Randall about another China venture, but the terms were not to their liking. Shaw was then approached by Isaac Sears on behalf of a group of New York traders, and he agreed to lead a second mission. In December 1785, after just seven months back home, Shaw informed his brothers that he was going back to China. Ever optimistic, he wrote, "If I live to return, I shall be in easy, very easy circumstances."[52]

As Shaw was making his final preparations for the voyage, Secretary Jay recommended to Congress that "as the attention of American merchants begins to turn to the China and India trade," it would be useful to consider appointing a consul and vice consul "for

Canton and other parts of Asia. Such officers would have a degree of weight and respect which private adventurers cannot readily acquire, and which would enable them to render essential services to their countrymen, on various occasions. . . . their commission would give them more ready access to, and greater influence with Princes, Governors, and Magistrates than private merchants can in general expect."[53] The Congress agreed and, shortly before Shaw's departure, elected him as the first American consul at Canton.

Jay sent Shaw his commission in late January 1786, just days before his departure. In his letter of instructions to Shaw, Jay wrote that "neither salary nor perquisites" were attached to the office of consul, but he hoped Shaw could derive commercial advantages from the position, since "so distinguished a mark of the confidence and esteem of the United States will naturally give you a degree of weight and respectability which the highest personal merit cannot very soon obtain for a stranger in a foreign country."[54] At the time there were no established rules for U.S. consuls. Only three or four other consuls had been named by Congress, all to European posts. Shaw was thus one of the very first American businessmen-consuls—private traders expected to support themselves but also to represent the United States in a foreign port. This would become the norm for U.S. consuls in the years ahead. Later consuls would, however, derive a small income from providing services and papers to American ships.

In the absence of any clear precedent, Shaw's duties as consul were vague and were not expected to take much of his time, especially in light of how few Americans he was likely to encounter in China. Still, the appointment of a consul would have the benefit of showing the American flag officially in the Far East, and Shaw would be expected to provide information on little known lands and trading opportunities that would be shared with other Americans. Jay instructed Shaw:

> Permit me, however, to request the favor of your correspondence, and that you will transmit to me, by proper conveyances, whatever intelligence and observations you may think conducive to the pub-

lic good. The mercantile and other regulations at Canton respecting foreigners; the number and size of foreign vessels, and of what nations, which annually enter there; their cargoes and what articles of merchandise answer best; are matters which merit attention.[55]

Shaw replied to Jay the same day (both were in New York), expressing his "most humble and grateful acknowledgements for the honor" conferred on him by the Congress. He proposed to Jay that a vice consul also be named, in case of his death or some other mishap, which "in so long a voyage as that which I am about to undertake, may by no means be improbable." It would also be useful to have a vice consul to take charge in Canton while Shaw traveled in other parts of the Far East, as he hoped to do. Shaw recommended his friend Thomas Randall, "a gentleman properly qualified for the appointment. . . . He has been in China with me and now is about to return there again."[56] Shaw's recommendation was accepted, and the Congress quickly named Randall as vice consul.

On February 4, 1786, Shaw and Randall left New York on their second voyage. They sailed on the *Hope*, a ship about the same size as the *Empress of China*, captained by James Magee.

The *Hope*'s outward journey proved more perilous than Shaw's first voyage. A few weeks out of New York, Shaw was at dinner with the officers when they were alarmed by a cry of "fire!" They ran to the deck to see the main topmast in a blaze, posing a fatal danger to the ship. The crew's efforts to douse the fire were fruitless, and it raged on violently, threatening to spread to other sails. As a last resort, the captain gave orders to cut away the topmast and let it fall into the sea. As fiery debris tumbled to the deck, a burning spar landed on a chest loaded with gunpowder. Miraculously, it bounced overboard without igniting the powder.

A few days later, the *Hope* faced another deadly menace. The lookout sighted an "Algerine," a pirate cruiser out of Algiers. Barbary pirates in the eastern Atlantic had already begun to capture American ships, seizing their cargos and holding their crews for ransom or pressing them into slavery. The *Hope* raised the English flag, thinking this would put the Algerian off, since English ships were protected by a treaty with Algiers. The ruse didn't work, and the Algerian came after them with full sail. The *Hope*, with a damaged mast, was in grave danger. "But it was no time to hesitate," Shaw wrote in his account of the event; "the main tack was got on board, and in the course of three or four hours we had the satisfaction to find that we outsailed her. The next morning, she was not in sight."[57] Two weeks later the ship was chased by another Barbary pirate, but again managed to escape.

The *Hope* sailed nonstop to the East Indies and made port in Batavia (now Jakarta), capital city of the Dutch East Indies. It arrived on July 4, a voyage of five months from New York. Shaw was much taken with the town and offered what may be the earliest description by an American:

> The city of Batavia, on the island of Java, is large, the streets wide, intersecting each other at right angles, and the houses built of brick and very commodious. The country-seats in its environs are far superior in point of elegance to any thing of the kind I have ever seen. The police is excellent, and, in short, I think the whole city in appearance exceeds any description of it which I have met with, and is a striking example of the wealth and energy of the Dutch nation. It is true, this capital of their settlements in India has cost the lives of at least a million of the innocent natives, whom we ought to suppose equally dear to the Supreme Father of all.[58]

Shaw visited the governor-general and received permission to trade. The *Hope* carried iron and naval supplies, which sold well in Batavia. He spent three weeks touring the town and the surrounding area and mingling happily with its European residents, much admiring the town's administration, fortifications, and well-run orphan colleges.

Leaving Batavia behind, the *Hope* sailed on to Macao, arriving on August 10. Captain Magee had fallen ill on the passage and died in Whampoa a few days later. Shaw and Randall proceeded upriver to Canton and secured a factory. One change they found was that in the wake of the "Canton war," Western ships there had prudently given up the custom of saluting each other with cannon.

Trade in Canton was booming, with more Western ships visiting than ever before. Most striking, five American ships, including the *Hope* and the *Empress of China*, on its second voyage, reached Canton in the course of the trading season. While the English continued to dominate the China trade, the Americans already matched the Dutch and Portuguese. Merchants from Philadelphia and Salem had joined New Yorkers in the China trade. Seeing an opportunity, Shaw and Randall decided to establish a mercantile agency in Canton—which they named Shaw and Randall—to provide trading services for American ships.[59]

To Shaw's distress, the rising number of foreign ships sent the price of tea soaring. American ginseng, however, was still in great demand. In a dispatch to John Jay, Shaw waxed eloquent on the value of ginseng: "It must be pleasing to an American to know that . . . the other wise useless produce of her mountains and forests will in a considerable degree supply her with the elegant luxury [tea]. . . . the ginseng of America . . . might perhaps be rendered as beneficial to her citizens as her mines of silver and gold have been."[60] The increased supplies of ginseng did not appear to have affected local demand or its price. Shaw speculated that it might be worth attempting to cultivate ginseng in America rather than relying on wild ginseng for supplies.

Shaw's official report to Jay described the trade with China carried on by each of the nations of Europe. The English, he wrote, bring mainly cotton from India, but also "sandal-wood, putchock-root, ebony, opium, shark fins and birds' nests."[61] The English also carry on a smuggling trade with the Dutch East Indies, exchanging opium and guns for pepper and spices. Other countries' trade was hard hit by an English decision to cut drastically its import duties on tea. French, Danish, and Swedish ships previously depended on smuggling tea to England to make their trips profitable; the sharp drop in English tariffs destroyed much of their commerce. In addition to the Europeans, Shaw found Armenians and Moors at Canton, trading in pearls and other commodities. For the past two years, he reported, individual traders had successfully sent a few small vessels from Canton to the northwest coast of America to bring back furs for trade.

Taking his consular assignment to heart, Shaw explained in detail the procedures for trading in Canton. He listed port duties, inspection procedures for the ships, and expenses that shippers should expect to incur. He also described the operations of the cohong merchants who controlled foreign trade. He gave examples of Chinese "knavery"—demands for bribes from officials—and warned that many of the small Chinese traders are "indisputably rogues, and require to be narrowly watched." The cohong itself, however, "are a set of as respectable men as are commonly found in other parts of the world."[62]

Of Canton itself, Shaw could say little: "The limits of the Europeans are extremely confined; there being, besides the quay, only a few streets in the suburbs, occupied by the trading people, which they are allowed to frequent. Europeans, after a dozen years' residence, have not seen more than the first month presented to view."[63]

Social life for the Europeans was also extremely limited. To Shaw's surprise, "The Europeans at Canton do not associate together so freely as might be expected; the gentlemen of the respective factories keeping much to themselves, and, excepting in a few instances, observing a very ceremonious and reserved behaviour."[64] The foreign traders did occasionally host each other at dinners, and the Danish factory held a concert each Sunday evening, performed by gentlemen of several nations, which was open to all.

Shaw's journal provides a few more insights to life and developments in China. He found the Chinese hardworking, with no Sabbath and carrying on business every day of the week. He described Chinese New Year as a celebration lasting five days, with festivities and no work. He commented on the common practice of polygamy in China. He was struck by Chinese "idolatry and superstition. . . . In passing the Joss-houses [as Europeans called Chinese places of worship] . . . there is an image of a fat, laughing old man, sitting in a chair at the upper end of the room. . . . As soon as a worshipper enters, he prostrates himself before the idol, and knocks his head three times upon the ground. . . . Besides these Joss-houses, which are always open and much frequented, there are large pagodas or temples, where are . . . various idols, in the form of men and women, but many times larger than life, and of most terrific appearance. There is one of a woman, with many pairs of extended arms. . . . Every house and sampan has its domestic deity, before whom a piece of sandal-wood is kept burning, which serves at the same time to perfume Joss and to light the worshipper's pipe."[65]

Shaw noticed that opium, although officially prohibited, was already widely in use. Much was smuggled in from Macao, where it was permitted by the Portuguese. The Portuguese governor, in fact, was much involved in the trade. Opium was taken ashore at isolated spots along the Pearl River and its many islands. Shaw noted that it "can always be smuggled with the utmost security" to Canton through bribes to the mandarins, or officials. He estimated that more than two thousand chests were smuggled in each year, with the active connivance of Chinese officials.[66] Opium had long been known as a medicinal plant in China, but smoking opium was a relatively recent development, starting after early Portuguese and Spanish traders introduced tobacco smoking into China.[67] Within a few decades, the opium trade would spike and would contribute to foreign intervention and the eventual downfall of the Chinese Empire.

After a few months in Canton, Shaw took issue with the idealized Western view of China's government: "Notwithstanding the encomiums which are generally bestowed on the excellence of the Chinese government, it may, perhaps be questioned, whether there is a more oppressive one to be found in any civilized nation upon earth."[68] The emperor's subjects undergo "every species of oppression," from corruption to arbitrary arrest to cruel punishments. In fact, the once powerful dynasty was already in serious decline by the 1780s.

One issue that persuaded Shaw that China was poorly governed was the extent of poverty and food shortages. "The humanity of a foreigner is constantly shocked by the number of beggars, men, women and children, that frequent the quay in front of the factories,—some of whom have the most loathsome appearance imaginable." Because of a drought, rice prices had more than doubled, causing a calamity for much of the population. Chinese officials tried to alleviate suffering in Canton by distributing rice, but this caused a stampede in July 1786 in which twenty-two people were killed. As a result, charitable food distribution was stopped, and large numbers were dying. "During the last six weeks, since the cold nights have set in, it has been no uncommon thing in the morning to find one or more persons dead on the quay."[69] Shaw was certain this could have been avoided by more effective government action. Shaw also reported that there were disturbances in many parts of the empire, in particular an insurrection on the island of Formosa that had been raging for a full year.

An interesting aside in Shaw's journal notes that four English ships were expected from "Botany Bay, on the southeast coast of New Holland, where they had carried out convicts, of both sexes, from Great Britain, to form a new settlement. . . . There is reason to expect that in time this may become an important settlement."[70] Shaw was recording the establishment of the first English outpost in Australia.

Shaw's second trading expedition to China was much longer than his first. While the *Hope* returned to the United States in early 1787, he stayed on in China to explore other trading opportunities in the Far East. Thomas Randall returned with the *Hope* and arranged for the construction of a larger ship for their growing China trade. Shaw would not return to the United States until mid-1789, more than three years after his departure. During this period he continued to send reports to John Jay on trade and conditions in China.

In the fall of 1788, still more American ships arrived in China, including the first to make the hazardous southern passage around Cape Horn, at the tip of South America, then west across the Pacific. Shaw reported that so much tea was available that the prices were beginning to drop. Ginseng prices had also plummeted, posing a serious threat to American trading prospects.

The threat was abated, however, by another development: John Ledyard's dream of opening a fur trade between the American

Northwest and China was starting to come true, albeit too late to benefit Ledyard. The ship that had rounded South America en route to China was the *Columbia*, accompanied by the sloop *Lady Washington*, which had sailed together from Boston in September 1787, more than a year earlier. The *Columbia* made for the American Northwest, where it traded for furs with Native Americans and gave its name to the Columbia River. The furs found a ready market in Canton. After completing its business, the *Columbia* continued west around the Cape of Good Hope, returning home to Boston after a voyage of three years, the first American ship to sail around the world.[71] The *Lady Washington* went on to Japan, in the first of many failed American attempts to open contact with that country. Shaw and Randall's mercantile company handled the *Columbia*'s cargo, receiving a commission of 7.5 percent on its outbound cargo.[72]

Although the *Columbia*'s long voyage did not produce a profit for her shareholders, it established that the Northwest fur trade was feasible. Many ships followed in the *Columbia*'s wake, and within a few years the trade was well established.[73] The Chinese particularly valued the luxurious soft pelts of the sea otter. The *Columbia* landed 1,050 sea otter pelts, a number that was dwarfed in subsequent years. In the 1806–7 trading season, for instance, American ships landed 17,445 sea otter pelts at Canton, as well as more than 34,000 beaver skins and 140,000 sealskins.[74]

Shaw returned home in 1789, landing in Newport in January. While at sea, he crossed paths with Thomas Randall, who was making his way back to China as part of their continuing partnership. Shaw turned immediately to his next China venture. The new ship he and Randall had commissioned for the China trade, the *Massachusetts*, was launched a few months after Shaw's return. At 820 tons, it was the largest merchant ship built up to that time in the United States, almost three times the size of the *Empress of China*. The ship's launch caused a sensation in Boston, with six thousand people turning out to witness the event. A Boston newspaper called it "as fine a ship of her dimensions as ever went to sea."[75] Still, recruiting a crew was difficult, in no small part because a local fortune-teller, Moll Pitcher, predicted disaster for the *Massachusetts*.[76]

By this time the U.S. Constitution had been ratified and George Washington had taken office as the first president. The Constitution specifically gave the president the power to appoint consuls. Washington reappointed Samuel Shaw as consul at Canton, the first appointment of a consul under the Constitution.[77] Randall was not reappointed as vice consul; that office remained vacant for the next decade. Many years later, Randall would be given another official assignment abroad, albeit much closer to home; he served in 1823–24 as special diplomatic agent in Havana. The new Congress gave a boost to the China trade with the adoption of the first U.S. tariff act in 1789, which gave significant tariff preferences to imports from China carried in American ships.[78]

The *Massachusetts* sailed for Canton by way of Batavia, where Shaw discovered to his distress that the Dutch had issued an order prohibiting trade with the United States. Shaw used his accreditation as consul in Canton to file a formal appeal to the governor-general on behalf of the United States, but to no avail. Shaw duly reported his unsuccessful efforts in a letter to President Washington.[79] Turned away from Batavia, the *Massachusetts* continued its voyage to Canton with a cargo of goods not suitable for trade in China. On arrival, the crew opened the hatches and found the holds were covered in thick mold and that the timbers were warped. The shipbuilders had not properly seasoned the white oak planks used to build the ship. Shaw and Randall could not afford repairs, so they sold the ship at a loss to the Dutch East India Company. The crew dispersed. One of the ship's officers who tried to trace his former shipmates a few years later compiled a list of their fates that included such entries as "died off Cape Horn . . . lost overboard off Japan . . . murdered by the Chinese near Macao . . . died on board an English Indiaman . . . drowned at Whampoa . . . died with the small-pox at Whampoa . . . shot and died at Whampoa . . . murdered by the Chinese . . . died with the leprosy at Macao . . . killed by Chinese pirates."[80] True to the predictions of Moll Pitcher, the *Massachusetts* and many of her crew met tragic ends.

With no ship of his own, Shaw purchased a cargo for sale in Europe, chartered a ship, and returned to the United States by way of Bombay and Ostend (in modern Belgium, but at the time controlled by Austria). His brother Nathaniel, who had sailed with him, fell sick and died on the return trip.

On August 21, 1792, Shaw married Hannah Phillips, the daughter of a prominent Boston merchant. It was Shaw's first and only marriage. He was thirty-eight, and his bride was thirty-five. The wedding did not change his plans to leave again for China.

Shaw sailed for Canton for the fourth time in February 1793 on his last and most harrowing voyage. He stopped in Bombay, where he had made trading contacts on his way home a few months earlier, not reaching Canton until November. Shortly after leaving Bombay, Shaw fell ill. His condition didn't improve in Canton, where he was confined to his house with what local European doctors diagnosed as a liver ailment.

Shortly after Shaw's latest departure for China, Thomas Jefferson, who was now secretary of state, sent him a letter warning of a likely general war in Europe, arising out of the disruptions of the French Revolution. Jefferson instructed Shaw to alert U.S. ships of the danger this might entail and take whatever steps he could to secure them the protections of neutrality. Jefferson also raised an administrative matter: "The law requiring Consuls of the United States to give bond with two or more good sureties for the faithful performance of their duties, I enclose you a blank bond for that purpose. . . . You will be pleased to . . . send the bond when executed, by a safe conveyance, to the Secretary of State . . . with all the expedition the case will admit."[81] Bureaucracy was already beginning to make its way into consular affairs; the Congress had passed the first law regulating the duties of consuls and vice consuls.[82]

On March 17, 1794, Shaw, still ailing, departed Canton for the United States aboard the ship *Washington*. As the weeks at sea dragged on, his condition worsened, despite the best efforts of the ship's surgeon. Thomas Randall was at his side aboard the *Washington*. Randall wrote to Shaw's wife, "Alas! His disease was too inveterate for medical aid. My friend died with a calm strength of mind, and expressed his solicitude for the happiness of his remaining friends to the last."[83] Shaw died at sea on May 30, 1794, not far from the Cape of Good Hope.

Another shipmate wrote, "He was a man of fine talents and considerable cultivation; he placed so high a value upon sentiments of honor that some of his friends thought it was carried to excess. He was candid, just and generous, faithful in his friendships, an agreeable companion, and manly in all his intercourse."[84] Shaw was just thirty-nine. It had been almost exactly ten years since he first sailed from New York aboard the *Empress of China*.

Samuel Snow of Providence, another veteran of the Continental army, eventually replaced Shaw as U.S. consul. Like Shaw, Snow had initially visited China as a supercargo and returned to the United States to begin his own trading ventures. Snow returned to China as consul in 1799 and remained there for six years. By this time the duties of U.S. consuls were more clearly established. Snow, like consuls in other ports, prepared semiannual reports on shipping and was charged with looking after American seamen in distress. In contrast to Shaw, he was a "resident" consul, remaining in Canton until 1805, without seasonal trading trips back to the United States.[85]

By this time, U.S. commerce with China was well established. The long-distance trade was common enough that it was easy for Americans of the day to overlook the continuing uncertainties and dangers that faced the China traders. Voyages to China were no longer front-page news, but they were still adventures that took tiny vessels across thousands of miles of little known and sometimes uncharted waters. American China traders helped map the Pacific. Capt. Robert Gray of the *Columbia* was the first to sail up the Columbia River. Capt. Thomas Read of the *Alliance* discovered two islands off the eastern coast of Australia on his way to China. Capt. Joseph Ingraham of the *Hope* discovered a group of previously uncharted islands in the Marquesas, two of which he named Washington and Adams, in honor of the president and vice president. Both Gray and Ingraham stopped in the Sandwich Islands (now Hawaii), which had been discovered by Captain Cook just a decade earlier. Their visits began a trade in Hawaiian sandalwood to China and established an American toehold that would eventually lead to the annexation of the islands. Meanwhile, the trade route between the American Northwest and China helped establish American claims to the Oregon Territory and to build public support for its annexation. The trade also led to the first American contacts with California.

By the time of Shaw's death, ginseng had given way to furs as America's principal export to China. Today the wild American ginseng that was so abundant in the days of Daniel Boone and Samuel Shaw is a threatened plant species, protected by international conventions.[86] The sea otter, once plentiful along the Pacific coast of the United States, was so overhunted that it is now listed as threatened under the Endangered Species Act.[87]

By the early 1800s, a new product had eclipsed furs. Americans were actively competing with the British in shipping opium to China. In the Opium War of the early 1840s, the British forced the Chinese to open trade at ports other than Canton. Americans traders followed in their wake. In 1843–almost fifty years after Samuel Shaw was appointed as consul—President John Tyler dispatched Caleb Cushing, a member of the House of Representatives, as the first American diplomatic envoy to China. Cushing negotiated the Treaty of Wanghia, giving the United States trading rights similar to those won by the British. U.S. policy over the next several decades was bent on maintaining this "Open Door" to China.

While American exports to China evolved, imports from China continued to be dominated by tea. Ironically, it was the tea trade with China of the late 1790s that finally brought the port of Boston out of the economic doldrums it had suffered ever since the Boston Tea Party a quarter century earlier.[88]

# TWO

# To the Shores of Tripoli

*James Cathcart, William Eaton, and the First Barbary War*

S amuel Shaw was fortunate enough to elude the Barbary cruisers that pursued his ships en route to China. Many other
American mariners were not so lucky. For decades following
the American Revolution, North African pirates posed one of the
most persistent dangers to American shipping.

The Barbary states of Morocco, Algiers, Tunis, and Tripoli were
still part of the Ottoman Empire, owing nominal allegiance to
the sultan in Constantinople, although in practice they operated
largely as independent entities. For centuries they had enriched
themselves by preying on commercial shipping and exacting tribute from maritime nations. Barbary corsairs plied the Mediterranean and eastern Atlantic in search of prizes. Captured ships and
their cargoes were plundered and sold, while crews and passengers were held for ransom and pressed into slavery. The captives
were subject to forced labor, beatings, torture, and even execution.
Many languished in dungeons or toiled in slavery for the remainder of their lives.

Contemporary accounts estimate that Tunis alone held 12,000
Christian slaves. Tripoli, one noted, has some regular trade, but
"they make more of the Christian slaves they take at sea; for they
either set high ransoms upon them, or make them perform all sorts
of work."[1] Algiers, the largest and most powerful of the Barbary
states, was reputed to treat its many Christian slaves with particular cruelty.[2]

The European powers generally safeguarded their shipping by
making huge annual payments to the Barbary rulers for protection

and bestowing lavish "presents" on them. The coerced gifts included gold, jewels, naval supplies, armaments, and even warships, which would be used to seize more captives. These costly and humiliating arrangements were considered preferable to the expense and uncertainty of going to war with the pirates. Before the revolution, American shipping was protected through British payments to the Barbary rulers. After independence, however, the pirates saw American ships as fair game. The small Continental navy created during the revolution ceased to exist in June 1785, when the Continental Congress decommissioned its last remaining ship, the *Alliance*, rather than raise taxes for repairs. The *Alliance* became a privately owned China trader.[3]

Within a month, the *Maria*, a Boston-based schooner, became the first American vessel seized by a Barbary corsair. Five days later, the *Dauphin*, out of Philadelphia, was captured off the coast of Portugal.[4] Both were taken to Algiers, where their wretched crews were to remain in slavery for more than a decade.

The captures of the *Maria* and the *Dauphin* were the first acts of a drama that was to unfold painfully over the next twenty years. As many more ships were taken, American relations with the Barbary states moved from negotiation, to tribute, to America's first foreign war. At times, relations with the Barbary states were a huge domestic political issue. At other times, the captured Americans appeared to be forgotten for years on end. Many died from harsh conditions, poor food, and disease.

The unfolding drama of American relations with the Barbary states featured a diverse and colorful group of American consuls in Algiers, Tunis, and Tripoli. Two of them spent years as slaves in Algiers. Another was best known as a poet. A fourth was a swashbuckling frontier Indian fighter turned diplomat, who eventually led the first U.S. Marines to the shores of Tripoli. Yet another had spent years as George Washington's private secretary and is best remembered for recording Washington's final words. Although each contributed to ending the Barbary threat, they were far from a cooperative group.

Their saga began in the seas off southern Portugal, just outside the Straits of Gibraltar, on July 25, 1785. The *Maria* had crossed the Atlantic and was approaching the port of Cadiz, Spain, when it was sighted and pursued by a small Algerian corsair. The *Maria*, a tiny unarmed vessel with a crew of just six, had no way to resist. Among those captured was James Leander Cathcart, who would come to play a central role in American relations with the Barbary states over the next twenty years, eventually serving as the first U.S. consul in Tripoli.

Although Cathcart was only eighteen, he already had long and harrowing experience at sea. At age nine, at the outset of the American Revolution, he sailed as a cabin boy on an American privateer. Within three years he was aboard the U.S. frigate *Confederacy* as the youngest midshipman in the American navy.[5] His career with the navy was cut short when the British captured the *Confederacy* in 1781. Cathcart, just fourteen years old, was held with the rest of the crew in New York Harbor aboard the dreaded British prison hulks. By the time of his capture off the coast of Spain, Cathcart was an experienced sailor and navigator, he could read and write well, and he spoke French, Spanish, and Portuguese. He kept a journal and a letter book, which provide valuable records of his years in captivity.

Cathcart described the *Maria*'s capture by Algerians, who were unaware of the existence of the United States: "On being boarded the Mahometans asked us for our flag and papers. Of the first they had no knowledge and the papers they could not read." The prisoners were transferred to the Algerian ship. Their shoes and hats were taken from them, leaving them tormented by a scorching summer sun. At night they were shut in a small sail room with captives from other ships: "Let imagination conceive what must have been the sufferings of forty-two men, shut up in a dark room in the hold of a Barbary Cruiser full of men and filthy in extreme, destitute of every nourishment, and nearly suffocated with heat, yet here we were obliged to remain every night until our arrival at Algiers" ten days later.[6] This was just the start of Cathcart's troubles and of his almost eleven years as a slave in Algiers.

A few days after landing, the captives were paraded before the dey, the ruler of Algiers, who purchased all of the *Maria*'s crew except the captain. Captains were usually treated better than their crews and were often left in the care of resident foreign consuls, working as servants or gardeners, although captains, too, were sometimes pressed into hard labor on public works. Cathcart was initially assigned to work in the garden of the dey's palace where, he wrote, "we had not a great deal to do, there being fourteen of us, and, the taking care of two lions, two tigers and two antelopes excepted, the work might have very well been done by four."[7] Nonetheless, the lack of freedom grated on all the captives, who were constantly belittled as infidels and often arbitrarily punished for small transgressions. At the dey's whim, his slaves could be clapped in chains and sent to hard labor or death.

The most common punishment was the "bastinado," beating the soles of a victim's feet with a stick. Slaves were commonly dealt one hundred blows or more for such offenses as being out of their rooms after a certain hour, appearing too lax in their duties, or even speaking too loudly. Cathcart was among the many subjected to this torture. One evening he was among fourteen men bastinadoed as a diversion for the guards. Cathcart was beaten to "the tune of twenty-eight hard blows, which produced the most excruciating pain and left me with four toe nails less than I had before this game commenced."[8] He was bastinadoed twice more during his time in the palace, once for writing and once for speaking to American captives working in other parts of the palace.

For more serious offenses, Christian slaves might be impaled on a stake, roasted alive, or beheaded. An American enslaved in Algiers at the same time as Cathcart described the fate of fourteen slaves captured as they attempted to escape in a small boat: "When they were landed, the dey ordered the steersman and the bowman to be beheaded, and the rest to receive 500 bastinadoes each, and to have a chain of 50 lb. weight fastened to their leg for life, and a block of about 70 lbs. to the end of that, which they were obliged to carry upon their shoulder when they walked about to do their work."[9]

Cathcart's months in the palace garden were light duty as Algerian slavery went. Food and clothing were adequate, and palace slaves received a small amount of money for their personal use through tips left by visitors to the dey. It was customary for visitors to drop small coins into their coffee cups following their audience with the dey; these were distributed each week to the slaves. Throughout his stay at the palace, Cathcart was convinced that the United States would soon pay his ransom and he would be freed. This hope proved vain. After about a year, the dey replaced the Americans working in his garden with more recent captives who Cathcart described as "younger, more handsome youths."[10] Cathcart was sent to a slave prison called the Bagnio Belique to begin hard labor.

For all its cruelties, North African slavery differed in many ways from American slavery. Although the slaves might be held forever, they were generally regarded as temporary captives who might be ransomed and sent home at any time. They were allowed to earn money by working extra hours at the end of their long days, for example, as a shoemaker or blacksmith. Cathcart mentions receiving seven and a half cents a day from the U.S. government to help him subsist during the first years of his captivity, but the subsidy ended in 1789.[11] A few years later, payments resumed at the rate of twelve cents a day for ordinary seamen and slightly more for captains.[12] These small stipends enabled the captives to supplement a diet that otherwise consisted entirely of black bread and olive oil. Captives might be allowed books, and sometimes they could correspond with the outside world. Prisoners with sufficient funds could pay to sleep in private cells rather than communally on the prison floor. There was even a prison tavern where captives could drink away what small funds they had, a surprising privilege in a Muslim country. Prisoners were occasionally allowed freedom to visit town on their way to and from their daily work details, although they could expect to be insulted and spat on by the townspeople. And slaves could gain their freedom by "turning Turk," that is, renouncing their Christian faith, being circumcised, and becoming Muslim. Given their difficult conditions of captivity and uncertain prospects of ever being freed, many did turn Turk. It was not unusual for Barbary corsairs to be manned—or even captained—by former slaves who had converted. At one point, the chief admiral of Tripoli's fleet was a Scotsman who had converted to Islam.

Most of the prisoners of Bagnio Belique were condemned to hard labor on public works, moving huge rocks from the hills to reinforce the harbor. Cathcart's papers do not describe why he was spared this fate. Perhaps he had accumulated enough funds to bribe his way to better duties, or perhaps he managed to impress the prison warden during their first meeting. Instead of joining the work gangs, Cathcart was apprenticed to a carpenter. Still, he had a large iron shackle bolted to his ankle. Unable to afford a cell, he slept on the ground with rats and fleas. A particular horror of the Bagnio Belique was the plague, which frequently ravaged Algiers and especially the prisons. Eventually Cathcart managed to scrape together two dollars, which he used to bribe his way to another prison where conditions were marginally better.

After two years of slavery, Cathcart had an unexpected stroke of luck. In 1787 the king of Naples paid a ransom to free his many captive subjects. This created vacancies in important households in Algiers. Cathcart was selected as a servant for the *vikilharche*, or head of the navy, one of the most powerful people in Algiers. In his new position he was well fed, free from brutal prison guards, and once again had a modest income from the tips visitors left in the vikilharche's coffee cups. Eventually, Cathcart was made chief servant and coffee server. When the vikilharche's assistant, the clerk of the navy, died of the plague, the vikilharche chose Cathcart as his replacement. Impressed with his work, the vikilharche offered him freedom and command of his largest cruiser if he would "turn Turk." Cathcart refused.[13] As the plague claimed further victims, Cathcart took on additional duties, including an appointment as clerk of the Bagnio Gallera prison, after the three previous clerks all died of plague within a single month.

Cathcart's growing prominence substantially changed his situation. As clerk of the navy and of Bagnio Gallera, he enjoyed substantially more freedom and came into contact with prominent personalities, including ships' captains and foreign consuls. An additional perk as clerk of Bagnio Gallera was that he could keep a tavern within the prison. With a loan from the Swedish consul, Cathcart took over the "Mad House Tavern" and purchased a large stock of wine from a captured ship. The investment was apparently a good one; by 1793 Cathcart owned three prison taverns, "kept by Christian slaves who paid me so much per pipe for wine and brandy. This gave me enough for all my needs, plus enough to help others."[14] With part of his proceeds, Cathcart paid hospital expenses for his fellow American prisoners and purchased coffins for those who died.

Cathcart's fortunes continued to rise. He became clerk to the prime minister in 1791. When the dey of Algiers died, Cathcart's former master, the vikilharche, became the new dey. The dey's clerk was ransomed and released, and Cathcart was selected to become the new chief secretary to the dey of Algiers, the highest position in the country open to a Christian. He was just twenty-four years old.

In 1784, before the first American ship was captured, Congress had already recognized the Barbary threat and authorized negotiations for treaties; it had even appropriated money for payments to the Barbary rulers. Morocco was selected as the first target, because there had already been friendly exchanges between the two governments during the revolution and Morocco had pledged not to attack American shipping. The negotiation was delegated to Thomas Barclay, the American consul in Paris. Barclay had remarkable success, signing a treaty with Morocco the following year, which required a onetime payment of ten thousand dollars, and no annual tribute, an astoundingly good deal. Even this amount, however, put a serious strain on the small American budget.[15]

Not long after the Algerians captured the first American ships, the first of many appeals on behalf of the captives was read in the U.S. Congress.[16] Among them was a petition from Richard O'Brien, captain of the *Dauphin*, who remained a prisoner in Algiers. As a captain, O'Brien was put up in a house with other prominent captives, an arrangement engineered by the U.S. minister in Madrid. O'Brien sometimes worked as a servant and gardener to the British consul in Algiers. Cathcart came to know O'Brien well, recording that he "had spent his entire captivity at one or another consul's house, except when called on to make sails for the cruisers, except for one stint at hard labor during which I sent him a meal and a bottle of wine each day."[17] O'Brien, like Cathcart, had served in the Continental navy during the Revolutionary War.

The American minister in Paris at the time was Thomas Jefferson, who soon took up the issue of the prisoners in Algiers, delegating John Lamb to negotiate their release. Without authority from Congress, Jefferson authorized Lamb to pay up to two hundred dollars for the release of each captive, but this proved to be far less than the dey would accept. Separately, Jefferson held secret discussions in Paris with the Mathurins, a religious order established centuries earlier to redeem Christian slaves from the infidels, but the talks were brought to an abrupt end by the onset of the French Revolution. These were just the first of many abortive attempts to ransom the hostages.

The next envoy selected for the job was the American naval hero John Paul Jones, but he died in France before even receiving his commission. Jefferson then turned to Thomas Barclay, who had had such success in Morocco, but he died before he could set out. In 1793 David Humphreys, the U.S. minister in Portugal, undertook a mission to Algiers, but the dey demanded double the amount Congress had authorized.[18] By this time eight years had dragged by.

After Humphreys reported on his failed mission, President Washington and the Congress decided they would have to raise their offer if they wanted to free the captives and end the Algerian threat to U.S. shipping. This was becoming more urgent, since the number of captured Americans had mushroomed to 119 by the end of 1794, with the capture of ten more American ships.[19] As the number of captives grew, the price of peace was going up. Cathcart, who was by this time the dey's secretary, forwarded a message through O'Brien to Humphreys, stating that the dey's price for a treaty and release of the prisoners was now a whopping $2,435,000.[20] This was an exorbitant sum, almost half the federal government's income for an entire year.[21] Still, American captives were dying at an alarming rate—fourteen in the first seven months of 1794—so Humphreys was authorized to offer up to $800,000, a huge amount, but still far short of the demand. At the same time, losing patience with the constant capture of American ships, the Congress acted on President Washington's request to authorize the construction of six frigates of thirty-two guns each to form the basis of a permanent navy. The idea of using federal funds to build naval vessels was not popular, however. Washington's request was approved only after he stipulated that construction would cease in the event of an agreement with Algiers.[22] Even then, the vote in the House of Representatives was just 50–39.

Joseph Donaldson was appointed to assist Humphreys as treaty negotiator with Algiers, then go to Tunis to serve as consul. Joel Barlow, a close friend of Humphreys living in Paris, was named as the first U.S. consul general to Algiers. Humphreys and Donaldson sailed together from Philadelphia to Europe in April 1795. They parted at Gibraltar, with Donaldson traveling to Algiers while Humphreys headed for Paris to find Barlow and to assemble the funds for payment.

Joel Barlow was another remarkable individual. He served as an army chaplain during the American Revolution, becoming friends with George Washington. He later founded a newspaper and worked as a lawyer. He is best known, however, as a poet. He was one of the "Connecticut Wits," a small group of young poets including David Humphreys, known for satirical verse that ridiculed the inefficiencies of the young United States before the adoption of the Constitution.[23] Humphreys had once even written a verse about Barlow, calling him nature's "loftiest poet." Barlow was America's first epic poet, although his masterwork, *The Columbiad*, drew mixed reviews. After the revolution, Barlow went to France to launch a trading business. He published political poems supportive of the French Revolution, which brought him fame and popularity in France. By the time his old friend Humphreys called on him for help, Barlow was one of the best known Americans in Europe and one of the richest Americans on either side of the Atlantic. Barlow began to scour Europe for fantastic presents to win the favor of the dey—jeweled snuffboxes, diamond rings, pistols inlaid with precious stones, brocaded robes, fine linens, damask, and carpets.[24]

Joseph Donaldson, meanwhile, arrived in Algiers on September 3 and began immediately negotiating through the good offices of the dey's chief Christian secretary, James Cathcart. The dey's opening gambit was a demand for $2,247,000 in gold, two 35-gun frigates, a large annuity to be paid in naval supplies, and biennial "presents." Donaldson countered with an offer of $543,000. A deal was eventually struck for $642,500, plus an annual tribute of about $21,600 in naval supplies and the inevitable "presents." Cathcart claims to have convinced the dey to accept the offer by pointing out that almost half the money would go directly to the dey himself and that the total amount was much greater than had recently been paid by the Dutch.[25]

When news of the treaty reached Philadelphia some months later, President Washington informed Congress, which promptly cancelled the construction of three of the six frigates it had authorized. The other three—the *United States*, the *Constitution*, and the *Constellation*—were allowed to continue only because they were already under construction.[26]

Although the treaty was signed, the captives would not be released until the payment was actually made. Despite the congressional authorization, raising the funds proved to be a daunting task, since the U.S. envoys would have to secure credits in Europe. The dey agreed to let Cathcart carry the treaty to Europe and return with the payment. Cathcart was delighted but reluctantly yielded to pressure from Donaldson and O'Brien to let O'Brien have the privilege of carrying the treaty. Although O'Brien had played no part in the negotiations, he was older and was the most senior officer among the captives. Cathcart, after all, was still only twenty-eight years old. Cathcart later complained that after O'Brien sailed away, he never had the courtesy to write and update Cathcart and the other Americans still in slavery about his progress in raising funds. It would be eight more months before their release.

As the months passed, Humphreys, O'Brien, and Barlow sought the necessary cash. One problem was a shortage of gold and silver in Europe due to the unsettled situation caused by the wars of the French Revolution. Six months after the treaty was signed, the dey threatened to resume attacks on American shipping if the payment was not forthcoming immediately. Barlow hurried to Algiers to stall for time, arriving just after the dey had ordered Donaldson to leave. Barlow's arrival brought some cheer to American captives, who were once again starting to despair. One of them, John Foss, wrote in his journal, "This worthy gentleman, whose compassionate services for his distressed countrymen, can never be estimated too highly, nor praised too much, gave us all the encouragement he could, assuring us he would never quit Algiers and leave us in slavery."[27]

Barlow, however, faced the serious problem of placating the angry dey, while knowing that the money promised him was not yet available. From Algiers, Barlow reported that "the Dey is excessively annoyed" and initially refused even to see him. The dey announced that unless he was paid within eight days, he would declare war on the United States. Barlow took a new tack, going beyond his instructions and offering to procure an American-built frigate as an inducement and distributing eighteen thousand dollars in bribes to senior officials.[28] These efforts won the dey's approval for a further three-month delay. The U.S. government eventually approved the total additional cost of fifty-three thousand dollars.

Donaldson sailed to Europe with news of Barlow's agreement. He never returned to North Africa to take up his post as consul in Tunis. Barlow settled in to wait unhappily for the funds. He despised Algiers, which he described in a letter to his wife in Paris:

> With the exception of the climate, the fruit, and the natural beauty of the vicinity, it is doubtless, in all respects, the most detestable place one can imagine. It is a city of about 100,000 inhabitants, built on the ridge of a mountain that commands the harbor. It is impossible to conceive of so much physical and moral discomfort accumulated in a single place. Properly speaking, there are no streets, but little dark alleys, which run crosswise and zig-zag among an enormous heap of houses, thrown together without order and without number. It needs a long residence before being able to walk a hundred

steps in this labyrinth without losing one's self. It needs not only a guide to lead you from one house to another, but also a Turkish guide, to guarantee you from insults and from being crushed by the crowd of peasants. . . . One sees neither women nor girls; it is forbidden a Mohammedan woman, under penalty of a severe beating, to show her face to any man excepting her husband. . . .

The number of mosques . . . is infinite in Algiers . . . but it is forbidden for an Infidel to enter. The penalty for this crime is to become Mohammedan, or to be hanged, or burned alive, according as one is a Christian or Jew. If it happens to me, through intoxication or some other accident, to fall into this death, I shall become a Mohammedan immediately, for I have not enough religion of any kind to make me a martyr.[29]

Within a few weeks, the plague was once again raging in Algiers. Barlow reported the deaths of several more American captives. The dey refused his request to move the Americans to the countryside, where Barlow had offered to care for them, saying they remained his slaves until payment was received.

By June, with time running down on Barlow's ninety-day extension of the treaty, Humphreys sent word that he had at last secured credits for $600,000. Barlow seized the moment and used this news to negotiate a loan with local Jewish bankers to pay for the immediate release of the slaves. The American prisoners were finally freed and loaded aboard a ship bound for Marseilles. After more than a decade in captivity, just half of the original captives from the *Maria* and *Dauphin* remained alive.[30]

Cathcart had grown wealthy enough that he purchased his own ship, the *Independent*, to sail to Philadelphia. He was elated to be free and that he had made such a success of himself, but bitter at his long captivity and that others reaped credit he thought should be his. O'Brien had carried the peace treaty to Europe and basked in its reflected glory, leaving his erstwhile companions to wallow in slavery in Algiers for months. Barlow was credited for negotiating breakthroughs that Cathcart believed he had engineered. As Cathcart headed home, he wrote in his journal that he "made sail after having endured every indignity that a fertile brained Mahomedan could invent to render the existence of a Christian captive unsupportable and having gone through every scene of slavery from a brick-layer's laborer and carrying heavy stones from the mountains, to being the first Christian secretary to the Dey and Regency, during the trying period of ten years, nine months and fourteen days, the remembrance of which makes me tremble with horror."[31]

With the captives finally free, Barlow settled in again to wait for the arrival of the funds. O'Brien, meanwhile, finally sailed for Algiers with most of the promised money. More than three months later, however, Barlow was still waiting. In a letter to his wife he lamented, "It is nine months to-day since my unhappy departure for this cursed country."[32] In fact, a corsair from Tripoli had captured O'Brien's ship. The ship and the money were in the hands of the bashaw, or ruler of Tripoli. O'Brien was once again a captive. Weeks passed before the bashaw thought twice about seizing an envoy with money destined for his more powerful neighbor and released the ship. O'Brien finally arrived in Algiers on October 1, more than a year after the peace treaty was signed, bearing just two-thirds of the money promised at that time.

Barlow was overjoyed, as was the dey. In a sudden effusion of goodwill, the dey asked Barlow if there was anything he could do for him. Yes, Barlow replied, assist in forcing peace treaties on Tunis and Tripoli. The dey agreed immediately and in an uncharacteristic display of generosity offered to lend Barlow the money to pay for the two treaties.

O'Brien was dispatched to Tripoli and then to Tunis to conclude the treaties. After some hard haggling, the bashaw of Tripoli accepted "a firm and perpetual peace" with the United States in exchange for 40,000 Spanish dollars, thirteen watches of gold and silver, five rings including three diamonds, one sapphire and one with a watch in it, 140 piques of cloth, and four caftans of brocade.[33] There were to be no annual payments, although a new consul was to deliver a specific list of "presents" when he arrived in Tripoli. In Tunis the deal was tougher, but O'Brien ultimately agreed to a treaty for $107,000. Barlow had hoped these treaties could be concluded within weeks, but instead it took months. As time dragged by, he felt alone and abandoned in Algiers, writing to his wife that he had not heard from Humphreys for four months or from the U.S. government in Philadelphia for eight months. He could barely wait, he wrote, to leave the affairs of Barbary to the devil. It was July 18, 1797, before the treaty with Tunis was concluded and Barlow blissfully sailed for France. In just over a year, he had overseen the negotiation of treaties with Algiers, Tripoli, and Tunis. The Senate gave its advice and consent to the three treaties late in 1798.

Peace was finally at hand with all the Barbary states. It would not last.

When President John Adams appointed new consuls to Algiers, Tunis, and Tripoli, he turned to familiar names to fill two of the posts: Richard O'Brien was named consul general to Algiers, the most senior position, while James Leander Cathcart was appointed consul to Tripoli. The new consul to Tunis was William Eaton, the most controversial of the many extraordinary Americans involved in the next phase of the Barbary saga.

Eaton was born in Woodstock, Connecticut, on February 23, 1764, the second of thirteen children. Adventurous even as a youngster, he ran away from home at age sixteen and enlisted in the Continental army. He was soon discharged with frostbitten toes, but reenlisted and rose to the rank of sergeant. After the war, Eaton worked his way through Dartmouth College and won a commission as a captain in the army in 1792. He was assigned to what was then the far west, the Ohio River valley. Eaton made time before his departure to marry Eliza Sykes Danielson, a well-to-do widow eleven years his senior with two children. By most accounts it was not a happy marriage; he would see his wife only intermittently over the next twenty years.

Eaton saw action as an Indian fighter, first in Ohio against the Miami nation, then against the Creeks in Georgia. While in Georgia, he successfully speculated in land deals but quarreled with his commanding officer, which led to the end of his army career. Before his resignation took effect, however, he was reassigned to Philadelphia, where he undertook a secret counterespionage mission for the State Department. Secretary of State Timothy Pickering was sufficiently impressed that he recommended Eaton to fill the still-vacant position of consul in Tunis.

Eaton sailed for North Africa on December 22, 1798, on the *Sophia*, almost eighteen months after his appointment as consul. His wife, Eliza, remained in Vermont, but her son Eli Danielson accompanied him as his secretary. Eaton's fellow passengers included James Cathcart and his wife, Jane Bancker Woodside, a Philadelphia belle whom he had married a few months earlier, as well as Betsy Robeson, a "servant girl" employed by the Cathcarts. Jane Cathcart would travel with her husband throughout his diplomatic career; they would have twelve children.

As consuls, Eaton and Cathcart would receive respectable annual salaries of $2,000 to supplement their personal wealth. Richard O'Brien, as consul general in Algiers and their immediate superior, would receive $2,500. Consuls to the Barbary states were the only American consuls at the time to receive a salary, in recognition that their role was more diplomatic than consular.

The *Sophia* made the Atlantic crossing in a relatively quick winter passage of forty-seven days, accompanied by several other ships. One of them, the *Crescent*, constructed in Portsmouth, New Hampshire, was the frigate Barlow had promised the dey of Algiers in exchange for accepting the delay in American payments. On board was Richard O'Brien, with $180,000 to pay the remaining U.S. debt to the dey. Two other ships in the convoy were cruisers the dey had commissioned the United States to build at his own expense. Official records do not comment on the irony of the United States agreeing to build warships for the dey.

The peace treaties with Algiers, Tunis, and Tripoli were tenuous and uneasy; all got off to bad starts. O'Brien, Eaton, and Cathcart would spend much of the next several years trying to stave off the constantly increasing demands of avaricious Barbary rulers.

William Eaton arrived in early 1799 to find the Tunisian ruler, the bey, angry because the naval supplies promised to him had not arrived on time. Although Eaton's credentials were addressed to "the most illustrious and most magnificent prince," he found the bey to be "a huge, shaggy beast sitting on his rump."[34] The bey demanded additional presents, including a warship, threatening war unless his demands were met. Eaton successfully negotiated for time, while he asked the U.S. minister in London to procure further presents, including firearms mounted with gold and diamonds, gold brocade, satin, and diamond watches.[35] Over the coming months, the intermittent arrival of supplies and presents was barely enough to mollify the bey. Eaton, meanwhile, engaged in unsuccessful personal commercial ventures that left him heavily in debt.

In Algiers, the arrival in September 1800 of the U.S. frigate *George Washington*, bearing the annual tribute to the dey, began one of the most humiliating episodes in U.S. naval history. The dey demanded that Capt. William Bainbridge and the ship carry presents from Algiers to the sultan in Constantinople. Bainbridge at first refused, but with the *George Washington* in the sights of Algiers's harbor guns, and with O'Brien urging accommodation, Bainbridge ultimately agreed.[36] The *George Washington* sailed for Constantinople carrying Algerian envoys and nearly $1 million in presents and cash for the sultan, including 100 slave women and children, 150 sheep, 25 head of cattle, 4 horses, 12 parrots, 4 antelopes, 4 lions, and 4 tigers.[37] On his return to Algiers, Bainbridge prudently refused to bring his ship within range of the harbor guns.

In Tripoli James Cathcart arrived to find a furious bashaw, who asserted that at the time of the peace treaty O'Brien had promised him a ship and other presents that had not yet been delivered. Cathcart had, in fact, been authorized to offer the bashaw an armed vessel of ten guns. Unlike his colleagues, Cathcart was well experienced in handling Barbary potentates. Within a few days of negotiations, he denied any knowledge that a ship had been promised, then promised one himself, then negotiated a payment of $18,000 in lieu of both the missing supplies and the armed vessel. Cathcart boasted in a letter to Eaton that the supplies alone would have cost $16,000 and the ship another $25,000, but he was able to settle for less than half that by virtue of "$1,500 in bribes."[38] The bribes were entered into his official accounts as "contingent expenses." After the deal was closed, the bashaw asked for two more gold watches, which Cathcart was able to provide, since he had held some items back from the original consular presents. Next, an aide to the bashaw arrived demanding $100 to "declare the peace." Finally, the bashaw sent his compliments and requested a few bottles of rum; Cathcart sent him eight. Thus ended Cathcart's first negotiation with the bashaw.

Peace with Tripoli reigned, for the moment, and Cathcart settled in to his consular duties. His dispatches from Tripoli touched on the big events of the region: Bonaparte blockaded in Cairo; Tripolitan troops joining Lord Nelson in a campaign against the French; British warships blockading Tripoli demanding that all French citizens be turned over to them; reports on the capture by Tripoli of ships belonging to the Danes, Swedes, and Portuguese. The demand for presents continued. On the occasion of the circumcision of the bashaw's son, Cathcart presented

> one gold repeating watch and chain, a diamond ring, one piece of brocade and one piece of Holland, one dozen of silk handkerchiefs, which I saved out of the consular presents, besides twenty five pieces of striped satin, one piece of striped nankeen and four pair of patent English silk stocking of my own. . . . I am on very good terms with his excellency, and shall endeavor to remain so . . . as I am convinced there is no other way to keep peace with a tyrant than by bribing and soothing his passions, or by the eloquent and all persuasive language of cannon balls.[39]

Cathcart also described a visit to his house by "the Bashaw, his three sons and all the grandees . . . accompanied by seven stands of colors, his music and guards, besides a number of his friends and all the principal men of the city. This put me to some expense but not anything considerable considering the occasion."[40] Another letter announced the birth of his daughter Eliza on May 1, 1799, not long after his arrival in Tripoli.

Faced with mounting demands and pressures, Cathcart, Eaton, and O'Brien all urged a more forceful U.S. policy toward their Barbary hosts. They were increasingly convinced that only a strong show of naval power would free the United States from never-ending demands and that a relatively modest American naval force would be sufficient to bring the Barbary powers to heel.

Meanwhile, Cathcart's relations with O'Brien had grown icy. On June 9, 1799, Cathcart addressed a remarkable letter to Secretary of State Timothy Pickering:

> I've written to O'Brien six times since the departure of the *Sophia* on April 19, but have not received a line in return, although I have heard from several others in Tunis, in one of which, to my astonishment, I am informed that on the 25th of March Consul General O'Brien was married by the Swedish Consul Skjoldebrand to Betsy Robeson, the servant girl I brought out with me to attend on Mrs. Cathcart. She is a native of England and came to me at the call of an advertisement in Brown's paper. I never could learn how she got to America, as she never told a direct story. I had seen enough of her on the passage to cause me to form no very favorable opinion of her, and when Mr. O'Brien wished to take her to the table I objected, as I did not consider her a fit person to be on intimate terms with my wife; especially in a place where there is no other female society. Betsy wished to be discharged—which I did freely.[41]

Months later he bemoaned in a letter to Eaton that he remained on poor terms with O'Brien and still had not received a single letter from him. "I view Mr. O'Brien as one of the most ungrateful of men, and shall never be on terms of intimacy with him again until he gives me suitable satisfaction for his conduct towards me." Cathcart asserted that he had treated O'Brien as a brother for ten years in captivity, had introduced him to the dey in 1795, and had acquiesced to remaining in slavery while O'Brien carried the Algerian peace treaty to Europe. He also ranted again about O'Brien's marriage to Betsy Robeson.[42] It is not hard to imagine that Cathcart's attitude toward Betsy is what offended O'Brien.

Relations with Algiers, Tunis, and Tripoli continued to deteriorate to the point that by early 1801 a declaration of war was expected imminently from any or all of them. The United States, recognizing that the treaties of 1795–97 did not solve their problems, decided it was time to send a small naval squadron to the Mediterranean. The hope was that a demonstration of American power might help keep the peace; if war were declared, then it would be essential to have a naval force in the Mediterranean.

On May 20, 1801, the secretary of the navy ordered Cdre. Richard Dale, who had served as first mate to John Paul Jones during the revolution, to "proceed, with all possible expedition, with the squadron under your command, to the Mediterranean." With his squadron of four ships, Dale was to visit all three ports, to consult with O'Brien, Eaton, and Cathcart, and, if they agreed, to deliver presents to the leaders of the three regencies. "But," the orders continued, "should you find, on your arrival at Gibraltar, that all the Barbary Powers have declared war against the United States, you will then distribute your force in such a manner as your judgment shall direct, so as best to protect our commerce and chastise their insolence." In a statement that was to prove overly optimistic, Dale was informed: "The force of Tunis and Tripoli is contemptible, and might be crushed with any one of the frigates under your command."[43]

The crisis bubbled over even before Dale's orders were written. Bashaw Yusuf of Tripoli was increasingly unhappy as he realized that his treaty with the United States was far less advantageous than those of his fellow rulers. In February 1801 he warned Cathcart that he would declare war unless the United States paid $250,000 plus an annual tribute. Cathcart once again played for time but wrote his fellow consuls around the Mediterranean to warn that war was likely and to recommend that American ships remain in port unless they could travel in a protected convoy.[44]

The ax fell, literally, on May 14, 1801. At one o'clock, the prime minister informed Cathcart that the consulate's flag staff would be taken down, the traditional method of declaring war. Cathcart reported to Secretary of State James Madison: "At quarter past two they effected the grand achievement, and our flag-staff was chopped down six feet from the ground, and left reclining on the terrace. Thus ends the first act of this tragedy. I hope the catastrophe may be happy."[45]

With Tripoli's declaration of war, Cathcart packed up his family and sailed for the Italian port of Leghorn to wait out the coming hostilities. He realized that a conflict with the canny bashaw was not likely to be resolved with a single frigate or even a small squadron. From Leghorn, Cathcart wrote Madison advising that if the United States should find itself at war with all three Barbary powers—as seemed likely–"we must have considerably greater force in the Mediterranean." He proposed "chastising" the rulers one at a time and simultaneously pursuing negotiations with the Ottoman court in Constantinople, which still had nominal sovereignty over the Barbary states.

Most notably, in light of future events, Cathcart proposed that the United States seek to depose the bashaw of Tripoli, Yusuf, in favor of his elder brother, Hamet Karamanli. Yusuf, in fact, was a usurper who had ousted Hamet many years earlier. If the United States could put Hamet back in power, Cathcart reasoned, he would be forever grateful, and peace would be established on a strong basis. Even if the United States failed to reinstate Hamet, having him aboard a U.S. warship was certain to unnerve Yusuf, "striking him with such a panic as could not fail to promote our interests." Since Hamet was living in exile in Tunis, Cathcart took the initiative to ask Eaton to meet with Hamet to see if he would cooperate.[46]

Eaton was enthusiastic. Without awaiting Madison's response, he made contact with Hamet, whom he called "the rightful Bashaw of Tripoli," and sketched out the beginnings of a plan for Hamet to attack "the usurper" by land while the U.S. Navy attacked by sea.[47] This went well beyond Cathcart's concept, which was for the United States to convey Hamet to Constantinople to win the sultan's recognition as the rightful bashaw.[48] Madison's reaction, once he eventually received the letters, was equivocal, demonstrating what would become an ongoing difference of opinion between the U.S. government and Eaton over his support for Hamet and his proposed policy of "regime change" in Tripoli. Madison wrote:

> Although it does not accord with the general sentiments or views of
> the United States to intermeddle with the domestic controversies

of other countries, it cannot be unfair, in the prosecution of a just war, or the accomplishment of a reasonable peace, to take advantage of the hostile co-operation of others. As far, therefore, as the views of the brother may contribute to our success the aid of them may be used for the purpose. . . . In case of a peace treaty with the current Bashaw of Tripoli, perhaps it may be possible to make some stipulation, formal or informal, in favor of the brother, which may be a desirable alleviation of his misfortune.[49]

As these exchanges went forward, Commodore Dale had an early victory with the capture of a Tripolitan warship. After dumping her equipment and armaments overboard, the Americans allowed the ship to limp back to Tripoli, where the unfortunate captain was paraded through the streets on a jackass and then bastinadoed.[50]

Dale then sailed to Tripoli, where the squadron briefly blockaded the port but soon departed due to a lack of supplies and the outbreak of disease on the ships. Dale's squadron spent the rest of 1801 providing convoy protection for American merchantmen. At year's end, Dale returned to the United States, leaving the *Philadelphia* in Sicily to watch over the Tripolitans from a distance. The first year's campaign had inconvenienced Tripoli, but it had not come close to forcing it to terms.

In the spring of the following year, Cathcart was named to replace O'Brien as consul general in Algiers.[51] He was also given a mandate to negotiate peace with Tripoli, but the negotiations came to nothing. Cdre. Richard Morris was dispatched to the Mediterranean in command of a new and stronger naval squadron but lingered in Gibraltar until late summer. His warships stood off Tripoli only briefly, one or two at a time, engaging in inconclusive skirmishes with Tripolitan gunboats. For most of the year, the port of Tripoli remained open. One American merchantman was captured and its crew taken to Tripoli, giving the bashaw a victory. The year 1802 ended with no progress. William Eaton, disgusted with the navy's lack of action, wrote to Madison that the government might as well "send out Quaker meeting houses to float about this sea."[52]

Eaton's insults to the navy were to earn him enemies, who soon enough would take their revenge.

The Americans fared even worse in 1803. The year began with Commodore Morris, accompanied by Cathcart, sailing to attack Tripoli in February. High winds kept him away. In need of supplies and apparently in no hurry to resume the attack, Morris headed for Gibraltar, with stops in Tunis and Algiers. In Tunis Morris stepped ashore and was promptly arrested. The bey said he would not be freed until Eaton paid debts he had accumulated, but relented when Morris promised the loan would be repaid. The bey also announced that Eaton was no longer welcome; he sailed away with Morris and Cathcart. When the ship reached Algiers, the dey refused to accept Cathcart as consul general, nor would he let O'Brien, the departing consul general, remove $30,000 in U.S. funds he was holding there. Eventually, a very frustrated O'Brien also sailed away with Morris, Cathcart, and Eaton, leaving his funds behind. At this point, there were no U.S. consuls in Algiers, Tunis, or Tripoli, highlighting the dangerous state of American relations with all of the Barbary powers. Morris and his squadron did not return to Tripoli until late May.

By this time, more than two years after Tripoli's declaration of war, the U.S. government was despairing over a military victory. Madison authorized Cathcart to offer the bashaw an immediate payment of $20,000, plus up to $10,000 a year to secure peace.[53] Since Cathcart had not been accepted as consul general at Algiers, Madison named him consul to Tunis, replacing Eaton. The bey of Tunis, however, like the dey of Algiers, refused to receive Cathcart, claiming he was a malcontent who had provoked the U.S. war with Tripoli.[54]

Meanwhile, Commodore Morris was recalled to the United States, where a court of inquiry ruled that he was too lax in pursuing the enemy and cashiered him from the navy. His replacement, Cdre. Edward Preble, sailed for the Mediterranean in late August aboard the *Constitution*, accompanied by Tobias Lear, who was named to replace O'Brien as consul general in Algiers following the dey's rejection of Cathcart.

But the military disasters of 1803 were not yet over. On October 31, the *Philadelphia*, captained by William Bainbridge—who three years earlier was forced by the dey of Algiers to sail the *George Washington* to Constantinople—struck a reef outside the port of Tripoli. With its guns at bad angles, the *Philadelphia* was defenseless. As Tripolitan gunboats moved in, Bainbridge and his crew tried desperately to free the ship, dumping anchors, cannon, supplies, and even masts into the sea, to no avail. Bainbridge was forced to surrender, and 315 American officers and men were taken captive to Tripoli. The first mate of the *Philadelphia* was Lt. David Porter, who many years later would have his own diplomatic career in the Near East. The seamen were put to hard labor, while the officers were housed in Cathcart's former residence. To make matters worse, the Tripolitans were eventually able to free the *Philadelphia* from the reef and to raise the jettisoned cannon. The bashaw had won a major naval prize and had hundreds of new American captives to strengthen his bargaining position. He now demanded an astronomical $3 million for peace and the release of the captives.

The conflict—together with intermittent, unsuccessful negotiations—dragged on through 1804. The Americans scored a morale-boosting victory in February, when Lt. Cdr. Stephen Decatur and a small group of sailors rowed into Tripoli Harbor in the dead of night and set fire to the *Philadelphia*, destroying the ship. Lord Nelson called Decatur's exploit "the most bold and daring act of the age."[55] Later in the year, Preble's squadron bombarded Tripoli repeatedly, but was unable to elicit a more reasonable offer from the bashaw.

William Eaton, meanwhile, returned to the United States, where he undertook a vigorous campaign to revive the three-year-old plan to enlist Bashaw Yusuf's deposed brother, Hamet Karamanli, as an ally against Yusuf. Eaton tirelessly presented the idea to congressmen, to President Jefferson, and to the State and Navy Departments. He eventually won enough backing to be appointed as "navy agent for the several Barbary regencies," to accompany Cdre. Samuel Barron, who sailed in the summer of 1804 to replace Preble as commander of the American squadron.

Eaton's relationship with Barron—as with many others—would become stormy and controversial. Eaton's appointment was unambiguous in making him Barron's direct subordinate: "You will receive instructions from and obey the orders of Commodore Barron."[56] Eaton would receive compensation at the rate of $1,200 per annum— well under his consular salary of $2,000–plus the rations of a lieutenant of the U.S. Navy. Barron was given full authority to decide whether and when to support Eaton's plan to enlist Hamet as an ally in the war against Tripoli and was authorized to grant subsidies of up to $20,000 to Hamet.[57]

Barron was also instructed to assist Tobias Lear, who had replaced O'Brien as consul general in Algiers and who had been given full powers to negotiate peace with Tripoli. Secretary of State Madison instructed Lear to place less reliance on Hamet than on the navy. Lear, in any event, was not enthusiastic about cooperation with Hamet, whom he regarded as a man of little conviction or power.[58] If the navy could not force the bashaw into a peace treaty, Lear was authorized to pay $20,000 for peace, $8,000–10,000 a year in presents, plus up to $500 a man for the captured Americans.[59] U.S. policy was thus still very much open to a negotiated peace treaty with the bashaw, albeit with the support of naval power.

The man chosen as chief negotiator, Tobias Lear, would become a central character of the war with Tripoli and a principal nemesis to Eaton. Unlike the other lead players in the Tripoli saga, Lear was not a veteran of the revolution. He was, however, very well known in American political circles, having served as private secretary to George Washington at Mount Vernon after the revolution. In hiring Lear, Washington set out that "Mr. Lear . . . will sit at my table, will live as I live, will mix with the company who resort to the house, will be treated in every respect with civility and proper attention. He will have his washing done in the family, and may have his stockings darned by the maids."[60] Lear served Washington for more than a decade, including during his presidency, coming to know virtually all of the most powerful men in the United States. In 1791 he was made a colonel and military aide to Washington when the general was briefly recalled to military duty in the face of a French threat. Although peace prevailed and Lear never saw action, he chose to be addressed as Colonel Lear for the rest of his life. Lear was at Washington's deathbed in Mount Vernon and recorded his final words and wishes. It was Thomas Jefferson, now president, who appointed Lear to serve concurrently as treaty negotiator and consul general to Algiers. Lear married Washington's niece Frances "Fanny" Dandridge Henley shortly before his departure for North Africa. He and Fanny honeymooned aboard the *Constitution* en route to the Mediterranean.

By the late summer of 1804, Lear, Eaton, and Commodore Barron were together in Sicily, where the American squadron was basing its operations. The three agreed on a general course of action. Eaton would go to Egypt to find Hamet, who had moved there. Hamet would then be conveyed in an American vessel to Derne (now Derna), the capital of the easternmost province of Tripoli. Hamet's landing in Derne, supported by the U.S. Navy, was supposed to lead to a general uprising in that province—Tripoli's richest—in favor of Hamet and against his brother, Yusuf. At the same time, the navy would launch a renewed attack on Tripoli. It was hoped that the combined actions would bring about the defeat of Yusuf or at least force him to sue for peace.[61] The plan would be put into action in the early spring of 1805, since it was already too late to plan a winter military operation.

Eaton's mission was to be secret. Barron ordered one of his ships, the brig *Argus*, to take Eaton to Alexandria to find Hamet and to convey him and his suite to Derne or any other location where he could cooperate with the navy. Eaton landed in Alexandria in late November and discovered that Hamet was in the south of Egypt, where he had joined a group of Mamelukes in rebellion against the Egyptian leadership. Undaunted, Eaton took off for the south, accompanied by several marines and midshipmen from the *Argus*. Not surprisingly, he was met with suspicion by government officials and was arrested twice. Eventually, however, he won the cooperation of the Egyptian authorities, who were apparently happy to be rid of Hamet.

When Eaton and Hamet finally assembled their forces on the edge of the desert outside Alexandria in February 1805, Eaton took it on himself to draft and sign—on behalf of the United States—a formal convention with Hamet. In this extraordinary document Eaton pledged, "The Government of the United States shall use their utmost exertions, so far as comports with their own honor and interest . . . to re-establish the said Hamet Bashaw in the possession of his sovereignty of Tripoli." Eaton, who had never held an army rank above captain and currently held a rank equivalent to a navy lieutenant, also included a clause that read: "William Eaton, a citizen of the United States, now in Egypt, shall be recognised as general and commander-in-chief of the land forces which are or may be called into service against the common enemy." And finally, "The said commander-in-chief of the American forces in the Mediterranean engages to leave said Hamet Bashaw in the peaceable possession of the city and regency of Tripoli."[62]

In one fell swoop, Eaton had committed the United States to install Hamet in power—rather than merely to cooperate with him against his brother, as stipulated in Barron's instructions. Moreover, Eaton himself was to lead a land force across the desert, another very significant departure from his orders, which were to board Hamet and his followers on a ship and deposit them at Derne.

Eaton's concept for victory was for Hamet and his followers to attack Derne by land while the U.S. Navy attacked by sea. Although Eaton had boasted that Hamet could raise a force of 20,000–30,000 supporters in Egypt alone, he appeared in Alexandria with fewer than 100 fighting men.[63] Eaton's own escort consisted of just eight marines, led by Lt. Presley O'Bannon. Together, the group fell far short of what was needed to launch an expedition, even if the people of the eastern provinces of Tripoli were expected to rise up to join them. The lack of manpower threatened Eaton's entire concept and might have caused a different man to think twice about the operation.

Eaton, however, was never one to be put off by obstacles, large or small. He headed back to Alexandria, where within two weeks he assembled a ragtag army of cutthroats, adventurers, and mercenaries. The "army" was roughly divided between 100 Christians of various nationalities and about 400 Arab fighters, including Hamet's force, plus the families of many of the Arabs. Eaton procured the use of some 200 camels and pack animals, at eleven dollars apiece. He estimated that the entire cost of his expedition would be $20,000, the exact amount Commodore Barron had been authorized to spend on subsidies to Hamet.[64] The actual cost would be far higher, causing trouble for Eaton.

Before setting off, Eaton sent news of his exploits to Commodore Barron. He proposed that American ships meet him at the Bay of Bomba, just east of Derne, with supplies, arms, two brass cannons, and 100 Marines for the assault on Derne. The *Argus*, which had been waiting at anchor in Alexandria for three months while Eaton completed his plans, sailed to convey the plan to Barron and then to meet Eaton in the Bay of Bomba to participate in a joint land-sea attack on Derne.

In retrospect, Eaton's plan was audacious and even fantastic. He proposed to march a rabble army across nearly five hundred miles of often barren wasteland, through the deserts of western Egypt and eastern Libya. He had no reliable maps. Finding food and water would be constant problems. His followers were undisciplined. Tensions between his Christian and Muslim troops ran high. His funds were exhausted, so he would have to count on credit or his own wiles to procure supplies along the way. And if he did finally succeed in reaching Derne, he would face a superior force of Tripolitans in a well-fortified town.

Undaunted, Eaton proudly donned his new general's uniform and led his army into the desert on March 8, 1805. Problems began almost immediately.

First, Eaton found that one of his British recruits, in charge of supplies, had embezzled more than a thousand dollars; he was immediately dismissed. Then, after just two days of marching, the camel drivers demanded their pay in advance, threatening to strand the caravan in the desert without supplies. Eaton refused and called their bluff; they backed down and continued the trek. A few days later, the Arab sheikhs accompanying Hamet demanded more cash. With no funds available and perceiving their threat to be real, Eaton passed the hat among the Christian members of the expedition and came up with $673, which proved to be enough to renew their loyalty.[65] These were just the beginnings of Eaton's troubles.

Progress on the march was much slower than Eaton had hoped, as he dealt repeatedly with extortion, desertions, and mutinies. There were constant disputes over the distribution of supplies and horses. Various Arab clan leaders deserted, only to return days later. On March 28, Hamet himself deserted with his followers, but appeared again two hours later. Eaton bemoaned in his journal: "We have experienced continual altercations, contentions, and delays among the Arabs. They have no sense of patriotism, truth, honor; and no attachment where they have no prospect of gain."[66]

There was occasional good news. The army's ranks were swollen by Arab tribesmen and their families who joined along the march; Eaton was never sure of the exact number, but he believed his fighting force had doubled. The new recruits, while purporting to join the expedition out of loyalty to Hamet, demanded to be paid. Eaton, now penniless, promised to pay them from assets to be seized at Derne.

Eaton happily found that the Arabs were much impressed with his uniform. In one village, he wrote proudly, "Curiosity brought every Arab to me who belonged to the tribe. They examined the lace of my hat, epaulettes, buttons, spurs, and mounting of my arms. These they took to be all gold and silver. They were astonished, that *God should permit people to possess such riches, who followed the religion of the Devil!*"[67]

By April 8, after more than a month on the march and with food running dangerously short, the situation reached a crisis. Hamet ordered the caravan to stop and make camp while he dispatched scouts to see if the American ships were really waiting in Bomba. Eaton was frantic. By this time, he wrote, "We had only six days' rations of rice; no bread nor meat."[68] Any further delay could mean a slow death in the desert. Eaton took a desperate step, cutting off food to the Arabs until they agreed to resume the march. The two sides faced each other across the desert, weapons drawn, for an hour. Eaton finally pulled Hamet aside and reached an agreement: rice would be distributed immediately and the march would resume.

The last rations of rice were exhausted on April 12. They were still days away from Bomba. On the thirteenth, they had to slaughter pack animals, which they ate with no bread or salt. On the fifteenth, there was no food and the famished army foraged for edible plants as it marched. Late that evening the expedition staggered to the coast. There were no American ships to be seen.

Eaton had reached the coast more than twenty miles short of Bomba, but in the absence of good maps, he was not sure exactly where he was. The situation was desperate. The Arabs made preparations to desert in the morning. Eaton's men built signal fires on a bluff and kept them burning all night. At 8:00 a.m., the sails of the *Argus* pulled into view. The expedition was saved.

The *Argus* landed critical supplies and arms as well as a brass cannon. Equally welcome for Eaton was seven thousand dollars in cash. His Arab companions had been insisting on another payment before launching an attack on Derne. Eaton distributed two thousand dollars to the Arab leaders to cement their participation.

The *Argus* also brought with it news that could only have been disturbing to Eaton. A letter from Commodore Barron dated almost a month earlier applauded "the energy and perseverance that has characterized your progress through a series of perplexing and discouraging difficulties." He also assured Eaton of the continued support of the squadron. But, Barron continued, "there are certain things in your dispatches, which, when brought to the test of my instructions from home, give birth to feelings of doubt and uneasiness." Barron made clear that he did not approve of Eaton's pledge to return Hamet to power in Tripoli and stressed that the United States might still decide to conclude a peace treaty with the current bashaw, Yusuf, "should he offer terms honorable and advantageous to our country."[69] As for Hamet, if Eaton helped him take possession of Derne, then Hamet should be able to use his own energy, courage, and talents to regain power in Tripoli. Eaton was distressed, but there was little he could do from his desert camp. There would be time to remonstrate later. For now, Derne still lay ahead.

The attack on Derne began at 2:00 p.m. on April 27. Three American warships—the *Argus*, *Hornet*, and *Nautilus*—bombarded the town's fortifications for an hour. When Derne's defensive cannons fell silent, Eaton personally led the land charge against heavy musket fire from the town's defenders. Within an hour Marine Lieutenant O'Bannon led an assault on the main rampart, hauled down the Tripolitan flag, and raised the Stars and Stripes. The event is commemorated every time the Marine Hymn is sung, "From the Halls of Montezuma, to the shores of Tripoli." Casualties among Eaton's forces were relatively light, although Eaton himself was among the wounded. He took a musket ball in the wrist while leading the charge.

Eaton happily reported the victory to Barron: "We are in possession of the most valuable province of Tripoli."[70] While he did not dispute the points in Barron's letter to him, he did comment that "it would seem incumbent on the honor of our government, in the event of peace, at least to place Hamet Bashaw in a situation as eligible as that from which he has been drawn. . . . He may perhaps be made satisfied with such an accommodation."[71] In light of later events it is noteworthy that at this stage—even after the victory at Derne—Eaton did not argue against a negotiated peace with Tripoli.

Eaton remained convinced that a land attack on the city of Tripoli was viable, but only with substantial levels of U.S. support. Derne lay eight hundred miles from Tripoli, far longer than the grueling march from Alexandria to Derne, and this time through hostile territory. Eaton pleaded for more money, claiming that the secretary of the navy had promised him fifty thousand dollars and saying that Hamet would have to purchase the loyalty of an army. He appealed also for help in Derne, saying, "If it is determined either to proceed or hold a position here, further supplies of cash and provisions must immediately be sent to the coast."[72] With regard to his convention with Hamet, he wrote that it included an escape clause, since the undertaking was to reestablish Hamet "so far as comports with their [the United States'] own honor and interest."

Having sent his reports to Barron, Eaton settled in to await an expected counterattack by Yusuf's forces. The first attack came on May 13; there were several more thereafter. The attacks were beaten off, thanks in large part to the continued presence of the *Argus* and its guns.

About the time of Eaton's arrival in Egypt the previous November, the bashaw of Tripoli began seriously to explore peace overtures to the United States. In December the Spanish consul in Tripoli wrote to Tobias Lear that the bashaw appeared ready to treat for peace. In March, as Eaton set out across the desert toward Derne, the bashaw's peace feelers were renewed through both the Spanish and Danish consuls. Capt. William Bainbridge of the *Philadelphia*, still captive in Tripoli with his three hundred crewmen, wrote to Commodore Barron that the peace overtures were serious.[73] By April 21, a few days before the attack on Derne, Lear received a specific offer from the dey: for two hundred thousand dollars he would declare peace and return the American captives. This was just a tenth of what he demanded sixteen months earlier, a clear indication that the blockade and other American military action were having an effect. By the time of this proposal, the bashaw may or may not have been aware of the existence of Eaton's expedition, which was still slogging through the Egyptian desert with uncertain prospects. Lear was authorized to pay substantially more than the bashaw was now demanding. Still, Lear thought he could do better. He did not even reply to the offer.[74]

Within a month, however, Lear and Barron agreed the time had come to close a deal. In a letter to Lear dated May 18, 1805, Barron wrote that "the present [is] auspicious beyond any former occasion" for negotiations. One reason for this was the capture of Derne, which should make the bashaw rethink his intransigence. Another was that Barron had no faith in Hamet's ability to advance from Derne. In light of Hamet's "want of energy and military talents . . . he must be considered no longer a fit subject for our support or co-operation."[75]

There were other considerations. Barron's squadron was in dire need of repairs and could not sustain another winter's blockade. He also feared for the lives of the American captives in the event of an assault on Tripoli. Even if an attack were successful, the bashaw might retreat inland, taking the prisoners with him. Under these circumstances, "no reasonable and honorable occasion should be neglected, which affords a prospect of releasing them from the bondage of a bigoted and unfeeling tyrant."[76] Finally, although unstated in the letter, Barron was seriously ill. After months of trying to recuperate in Sicily and Malta, he was finally ready to relinquish command of the squadron.

Lear agreed with Barron's reasoning: "I have maturely considered the several points mentioned in your letter . . . and, upon a view of my instructions from the Government of the United States on that subject, I conceive it my duty to endeavor to open and bring to a happy issue a negotiation for peace . . . whenever the commander of our naval force in this sea shall judge that the occasion is proper and favorable." Lear did not believe that American cooperation with Hamet had any positive effect on Yusuf's mind-set, although he conceded that the "undaunted bravery and perseverance" of the Americans in Derne would provide "a further proof of what we can do alone against him."[77] In his formal report to the secretary of state, Lear wrote, "I have always been opposed to the Egyptian and Derne expedition."[78]

Lear arrived off Tripoli on May 26. He refused to go ashore, but conducted the negotiations from the *Constitution*, through the Spanish and Danish consuls. The bashaw was now willing to offer a peace treaty at no cost but demanded a ransom of $130,000 for the American captives and the return of all Tripolitans captured by the U.S. Navy. Lear refused, insisting there be an exchange of prisoners man for man. Since the bashaw held about three hundred Americans, while the navy held about one hundred Tripolitans, Lear agreed to $60,000 as the difference, or about $300 a man (his instructions allowed him to offer up to $500 a man). This formed the basis for a deal. Beyond the ransom, there would be no annual payments, but the inevitable "presents" would be offered with the arrival of a new consul.

There was some further haggling over Hamet. The bashaw wanted assurances that the United States would withdraw from Derne and endeavor to convince Hamet to withdraw as well. Lear agreed. A final point involved the fate of Hamet's wife and children, who had been held hostage for years in Tripoli. Lear asked that they be restored to Hamet. The bashaw initially refused, but ultimately relented, provided that the release was not immediate. Lear didn't want to risk the peace agreement for the sake of Hamet's family and ultimately agreed to a secret clause allowing for a delay of four years for their release.[79] Lear never reported the secret clause to his own government, which would contribute to a later controversy.

With that, the negotiations were concluded. The war was finally at an end, more than four years after Cathcart's flagpole was chopped down. Lear entered Tripoli on June 2, to a 21-gun salute. Captain Bainbridge, Lt. David Porter, and the rest of the *Philadelphia*'s officers, who had been in captivity for twenty months, met him at the dock "with a sensibility more easily to be conceived than described." Lear met with the bashaw and "was received with every mark of respect and attention." The *Constitution* left for Malta and Sicily to pick up the Tripolitan prisoners and the $60,000. The *Constellation* sailed for Derne to take the news to Eaton.

In Derne, meanwhile, Eaton continued to face intermittent counterattacks from the bashaw's troops. Neither side had heard news of the peace. On June 11, the bashaw's troops launched another vicious assault; the fighting was heavy, and casualties were high. Without the guns of the *Argus*, the town might have been lost. That evening, as Eaton's army regrouped and tended to the wounded, the *Constellation* arrived at Derne, with orders for the Americans to withdraw.[80]

After his tribulations of the past eight months, Eaton was devastated by the news. He cannot have been entirely surprised following his exchanges with Barron, but that hardly softened the blow.

He was dismayed to take the news to Hamet, who asked to leave with him rather than take his chances in Derne. Hamet, Eaton, and the remaining Christian members of the expedition slipped away in the night, leaving Hamet's Arab followers to fend for themselves, a humiliating end to the adventure. As the *Argus* pulled out of Derne's harbor, a melancholy Eaton wrote, "In a few minutes more we shall lose sight of the devoted city, which has experienced as strange a reverse in as short a time as ever was recorded in the disasters of war; thrown from proud success and elevated prospects into an abyss of helpless wretchedness." Hamet, meanwhile, had fallen "from the most flattering prospects of a kingdom to beggary." [81] Eaton conceded that despite his disappointment, the treaty was an honorable one. As time passed, however, he would grow increasingly bitter and vituperative about the treaty and what he considered Lear's and Barron's treachery.

With the signing of the peace treaty, Eaton considered his work to be at an end; he asked to return to the United States on the first naval ship going home. In Sicily he performed one more duty, serving as judge advocate of a court of inquiry aboard the *Constitution*, which exonerated Captain Bainbridge of blame for the loss of the *Philadelphia*. Also in Sicily, he received a touching letter from Hamet, thanking him, "at this moment of our final separation, for your generous and manly exertions in my behalf. . . . I am satisfied with all your nation has done concerning me. I submit to the will of God; and thank the King of America, and all his servants, for their kind dispositions towards me."[82]

The 1805 treaty with Tripoli became—and remains—an issue of great controversy. Eaton, bitter at having his campaign cut short and at the American abandonment of Hamet, launched a personal campaign to vilify the treaty and, in particular, Tobias Lear and Richard Barron. On August 6, the day he left Sicily for the United States, he wrote to the secretary of the navy that the treaty "reflects a wound on our national dignity." He even penned a verse that belittled Lear as a "provisional" colonel,

Who never set a squadron in the field,
Nor the division of a battle knows,
More than a spinster.[83]

Eaton demanded a congressional investigation of the circumstances surrounding the treaty. He stirred up a huge political storm,
fanning the sharp political party divisions of the day and winning
support from the Federalists, who opposed President Jefferson.

History has not been kind to the treaty. The preponderance of
historians, with the advantage of hindsight, have argued that the
peace was too precipitous and that the much-strengthened U.S.
squadron in the Mediterranean should have been able to force Tripoli to make peace with no payment at all. Eaton's swashbuckling
exploits in the desert have captured the imaginations of authors,
poets and filmmakers. His many biographers have recounted his
adventures and lauded his daring. Lear, in contrast, is often por-
trayed as a weakling or villain.

The balance, however, is not quite so simple. Virtually all of
the American leaders on the spot—most of them navy captains—
supported the treaty. Commodore Barron was a strong backer and
doubted that a further land campaign was possible or would be
of much military value. Commodore Rodgers, his replacement in
the final days of the war, also supported the peace treaty. Rodgers,
in fact, was willing to pay $200,000 for the release of the prison-
ers rather than the $60,000 ultimately paid.[84] Captain Bainbridge
of the *Philadelphia* also urged agreement to the terms, although,
as a captive in Tripoli, perhaps his views should not be given equal
weight. And of course Lear, who was actually given the commission to negotiate peace on behalf of the United States, considered
the treaty a great success. Even Eaton at first conceded that the
treaty "is certainly more favorable, and considered separately, more
honorable than any peace obtained by any Christian nation with a
Barbary regency, at any period within a hundred years."[85]

One can only speculate what the result of further military action
might have been. Much evidence suggests the military balance had
shifted clearly to the Americans, that the bashaw was weakening,

and that the navy might finally have been able to pound him into submission. But the navy had already been pounding the bashaw intermittently for years, and he had not yet submitted. And in wartime there was always the danger of another mishap, such as the wreck of the *Philadelphia*. The bashaw's threat to move inland with the prisoners might also have aborted a clear victory. As for Eaton's proposed land campaign, he was still facing vigorous counterattacks in Derne. It is far from clear that he could have marched his ragtag army successfully across another eight hundred miles of desert in midsummer or that he could have taken the city of Tripoli even if he did complete the march. Doing so would certainly have cost more lives and money than the $60,000 paid for the peaceful release of the captives, although opponents of the treaty might argue that honor, not money, should have driven the decision.

Eaton returned home to a hero's welcome. He was feted in cities up and down the East Coast. The Massachusetts state legislature voted him ten thousand acres of land in Maine, which at the time was still part of Massachusetts. He was elected to the Massachusetts legislature. President Jefferson mentioned Eaton's exploits in his annual message. Not everything went Eaton's way, however. His increasingly vicious attacks on Lear, Barron, and the treaty earned him political enemies, particularly since Jefferson supported the treaty. Eaton's supporters in Congress moved to award him a gold medal but fell short of the votes needed.

In the Senate, the Tripoli treaty was hotly debated for weeks. One issue repeatedly raised was that Hamet's family had not been restored to him; no one in Washington was aware of Lear's secret clause providing for a four-year delay. Finally, however, on April 12, 1806, the Senate ratified the treaty by a vote of 21–8, just two votes beyond the required two-thirds majority.[86] Congress also voted $2,400 for Hamet.

Despite the peace with Tripoli and subsequent accommodations with Tunis and Algiers, the Barbary powers continued to cause sporadic problems for the United States for another decade. In 1815

President James Madison—who was secretary of state through the earlier crises with the Barbary states—asked Congress to declare war on Algiers, which had once again begun seizing U.S. ships. Stephen Decatur, who had led the daring raid to burn the *Philadelphia* in Tripoli's harbor twelve years before, commanded a squadron that forced a new peace treaty on Algiers. Decatur's squadron then visited Tunis and Tripoli, where he exacted payments from the bey and the bashaw for captured American ships, a stark reversal of previous practice.

William Eaton remained bitter and turned to drink. As the Tripoli debate in the Senate was unfurling, Eaton was approached by Aaron Burr, the former vice president, to join in Burr's traitorous scheme to create an empire in the American West. Burr offered to make Eaton his third in command. Eaton, always the patriot, revealed the plot to President Jefferson, who at the time did not take it seriously. Eaton later testified against Burr at his trial in Richmond in 1807. By this time, however, Eaton's stature as a hero had been diminished by his growing reputation as an eccentric, a braggart, and a drunk. One observer in Richmond commented that "the once redoubted Eaton has dwindled down in the eyes of this sarcastic town into a ridiculous mountebank, strutting about the streets . . . when he is not tippling in the taverns."[87] Gambling losses—including wagers on the outcome of the Burr trial—left him in debt. He was not reelected to a second term in the Massachusetts legislature. He retired to his wife's home in Brimfield, Massachusetts, where he unhappily spent his final years. He continued to exchange occasional letters with Hamet and Cathcart. Eaton began to suffer from rheumatism and gout. The hero of Derne died in the summer of 1811 at age forty-seven and was buried with military honors. He is still commonly referred to as "General Eaton."

Tobias Lear remained in Algiers as consul general until 1812. He and his wife, Fanny, returned to the United States at the outset of the War of 1812, the year after Eaton's death. Lear became an accountant to the War Department. He suffered from depression and headaches, perhaps brought on by the damage to his reputation that Eaton had wreaked. Nonetheless, Lear was still a prominent, wealthy, and respectable citizen when he took his own life with a pistol on October 11, 1816. He did not leave a suicide note.

James Leander Cathcart returned to Leghorn after his abortive attempts to take up office as consul general in Algiers and consul in Tunis. He returned to the United States with his wife, Eliza, and four children in 1805. Two years later, he was appointed consul in Madeira, where he spent seven years, followed by three years as consul in Cadiz. He later served as a U.S. agent in Louisiana, then spent many years in Washington as a government comptroller. He lived until 1843. His descendants treasure a note from Thomas Jefferson to the Senate that reads in part, "Cathcart . . . is personally known to me; he is the honestest and ablest consul we have with the Barbary powers; a man of sound judgment and fearless."[88]

Joel Barlow, the poet who concluded the first treaty with Tripoli in 1795, served later as U.S. minister to France during the waning days of Napoleon's empire. In 1812, as Tobias Lear was returning to the United States, Barlow undertook a dangerous mission to meet with Emperor Napoleon during his invasion of Russia. Barlow found himself caught up in the horrors of Napoleon's retreat from Moscow. He died in the tiny Polish village of Zarnowiec from the effects of exposure.

Hamet Karmanli remained for some time in Sicily, where he had been put ashore by the U.S. squadron. In 1807 the new American consul in Tripoli, George Davis, discovered and reported to the State Department the secret clause negotiated by Tobias Lear that permitted a four-year delay in the release of Hamet's family. Under pressure from Davis, the bashaw restored Hamet's wife and children to him the same year. By 1809 Hamet managed to mend fences with Yusuf. In a final irony, Yusuf appointed Hamet as governor of Derne.

# THREE

# Diplomacy in New Orleans
## *The Intriguing Career of Daniel Clark*

While the United States struggled with pirates in the Mediterranean, it was also involved in other momentous international events that would shape the country. The most important of these was the Louisiana Purchase. The international diplomacy surrounding the purchase is well known: in 1803 President Thomas Jefferson instructed envoys Robert Livingston and James Monroe to buy the city of New Orleans from France. Instead, they ended up purchasing the entire Louisiana Territory and doubling the size of the United States. Almost unknown, however, is the story of intrigue and suspense that unfolded simultaneously in New Orleans.

A central character in this drama was the U.S. consul in New Orleans, Daniel Clark. His largely forgotten role was so critical to the territorial transfer that Joseph Belchasse, the last commander of the Spanish and French garrisons at New Orleans, once commented that "the United States owe the acquisition of Louisiana to Daniel Clark."[1] In fact, the transfer of Louisiana was far too complex an event to credit to a single individual. It involved the leading statesmen of the day and was intertwined with developments in distant parts of the globe. Of the many characters involved, however, perhaps none was more remarkable than Daniel Clark. As consul in the turbulent years leading to the Louisiana Purchase, Clark was the only official American representative in the territory. He protected U.S. citizens, won trade concessions that turned New Orleans into a boomtown, ferreted out information on settler plots and frontier Indian problems, and collected astonishingly detailed intelligence on French and Spanish military activities and maneuvering. All the while, Clark vociferously advocated U.S. acquisition of Louisiana, by force if necessary, helping to build national sentiment in favor of the purchase. His role was pivotal in advancing U.S. interests on the ground during the critical and confused months of 1803 when Louisiana hovered in the balance between Spanish, French, and U.S. ownership.

Nor does Clark's story end with the arrival of U.S. forces in New Orleans. He went on to serve in Congress, to duel with a governor, and to leave a tangled legacy that became one of the most celebrated court cases of nineteenth-century America.

Daniel Clark's name first appears in U.S. diplomatic records in March 1798, styled as "acting vice consul" in what was then the Spanish city of New Orleans. At the time, there was not and never had been an officially appointed American consul in the city. Although Clark had not received an official appointment, he was asked to take on the duties of vice consul by two of the most prominent U.S. officials in what was then the American far west, Border Commissioner Andrew Ellicott and Isaac Guion, captain of the U.S. garrison at Natchez. Neither Ellicott nor Guion had the authority to make consular appointments. Clark, however, was never one to shy away from self-promotion; he promptly took on the title as well as the functions. Surprisingly, the State Department tacitly accepted the irregular appointment and routinely marked his earliest letters "from the American Vice Consul at New Orleans."[2] At the time, Clark was not even a U.S. citizen; he had immigrated to New Orleans from Ireland as a boy and had never taken out either Spanish or American citizenship.

Formalities aside, there was a burning need for an official American presence in New Orleans in the final years of the eighteenth century. Andrew Ellicott's journal singled out the most pressing problem as French privateers, which were gathering in alarming numbers in the Gulf of Mexico with the onset of the Napoleonic Wars in Europe. Although French privateers were ostensibly preying only on British shipping, they frequently captured American ships as prizes, claiming that either the vessels or their cargoes were

British. Worse still, outright pirates were taking advantage of the unsettled situation, indiscriminately attacking American ships. Spanish New Orleans, with its lax law enforcement and easily corruptible officials, became a favorite stopping point for the marauders.

Typically, a privateer or pirate would escort his prize to New Orleans, present its papers—often forged—and have the ship and cargo condemned and sold for his benefit. The captain and crew of the captured ships, if they survived, would be put ashore, often without means of subsistence, while their personal belongings were plundered. With no American representative in New Orleans to assist them, they found themselves destitute in an unfamiliar foreign port and often landed in jail.

As a merchant and shipowner, Daniel Clark was acutely aware of the dangers posed by privateering. He lost no time in making the most of his new powers, however tenuous they may have been. He represented himself to the Spanish governor, Manuel Gayoso, as the American vice consul and won the governor's recognition. After the fact, Clark wrote to Secretary of State Timothy Pickering acknowledging that he was "deeply conscious of the irregularity" in his appointment but hoped that Pickering would acknowledge the documents he had already begun to issue to American vessels to prove their nationality.[3]

With the power of the American government seemingly behind him, Clark leaned heavily on Governor Gayoso to crack down on the privateers. He intimated, without authority, that the U.S. minister in Madrid might protest to the Spanish court about the governor's behavior. Clark complained of the "most shameful partiality in favor of the French" and of transgressions by the pirates being "winked at for reasons best known to the Officers of Government."[4] Through Clark's intervention, at least three American ships were restored to their owners and a pirate posing as a privateer had his ship seized and sold to defray damages. Pirates began to avoid New Orleans.

As vice consul, Clark also took on the task of tending to the needs of American seamen in New Orleans who were sick, injured, or destitute and arranging for their passage home. Oppressed or unhappy sailors often deserted in New Orleans, while brutal captains some-times had sailors imprisoned and then sailed without them. Clark complained that seamen were often jailed "on very light and frivo-lous pretenses." Unruly Americans were yet another problem; flat-boat and keel boat operators bringing goods down the Mississippi were legendary ruffians and brawlers who caused endless prob-lems. According to one contemporary account, New Orleans was "exposed to the riots of untractable sailors, drunken Indians, and Kentucky boatmen more vicious and savage than either."[5]

While Clark had notable success in dealing with pirates and des-peradoes, his most significant achievement of 1798 lay elsewhere. Working quietly with Spanish colonial officials, Clark scored a tre-mendous commercial success for the United States by winning trade concessions that opened New Orleans and the entire Mississippi River valley to profitable U.S. commerce. Although Americans had the right of free navigation on the Mississippi beginning in 1795, the viability of trade on the river depended entirely on access to New Orleans, where high duties still stymied all but Spanish ship-ping. In June 1798 Clark reported matter-of-factly to Secretary of State Pickering that he had negotiated an agreement for American ships to enjoy the same rates of duty as Spanish vessels.[6] Duties on American imports and exports through New Orleans were sud-denly slashed from 21 percent to just 6 percent. Leading American statesmen including Pickering, John Jay, and Robert Morris had tried and failed for years to open Spanish colonial ports to Ameri-can shipping. Now, suddenly, the virtually unknown vice consul in New Orleans succeeded in the most important port of all. Trade along the Mississippi, which to that point had grown slowly and sporadically, was poised to boom.

   Clark's trade coup was carefully contrived. The ongoing wars in Europe led to a downturn in Atlantic shipping that dried up the customs duties on which the local Spanish authorities depended. The drop in shipping also left Louisiana without enough supplies and consumer goods. Recognizing an opportunity, Clark privately persuaded the Spanish official in charge of revenues and then the governor of the benefits of allowing American shipping to take up the slack. The arrangement proved so profitable for both the traders and the local government that it was kept in place even after the Spanish crown later ordered its revocation.

Within the next two years, imports to U.S. territories through New Orleans doubled, while exports from the United States to Spanish Louisiana tripled. By 1802, almost two hundred American ships a year arrived in New Orleans from the Gulf of Mexico, far exceeding those of any other nation. Aside from the financial benefits to American merchants—including Clark himself—the opening of Mississippi trade had a profound impact in Americanizing the lower Mississippi valley and creating pressures for annexation.

Despite his successes, Clark did not win an official appointment for some time. The first American officially appointed as consul at New Orleans was Procopio Pollock, but Pollock did not accept the post. Clark continued to act until late in 1798, when President Adams named William Hulings, a retired doctor living in New Orleans, as vice consul. Some months later Adams appointed Evan Jones, a New Yorker long residing in New Orleans, as consul, with Hulings remaining as vice consul.

Jones and Hulings ran into problems almost from the start. Jones had once been a Spanish citizen and an officer in the Spanish territorial militia; he had apparently never resigned. The Spanish regarded his acceptance of a U.S. appointment as a criminal offense, and Jones only narrowly avoided being sent to Havana in chains. He remained in New Orleans, but under the circumstances his effectiveness as consul was minimal. Hulings, meanwhile, performed in a satisfactory but unspectacular manner.

In late 1799 a new governor, the Marquis de Casa Calvo, informed Jones and Hulings that the Spanish court did not permit foreign consuls to operate in Spain's colonial ports; he told them to desist immediately. Lower-level officials, however, quietly let them know they could continue to minister to the needs of Americans if they adopted such a low profile that Spanish officials could plead ignorance of their activities. Jones declined, but Hulings agreed. This prompted an outraged Jones to write the secretary of state asking whether a vice consul has "the authority to act without orders and contrary to the approbation of the consul?"[7]

Daniel Clark, meanwhile, continued to amass a fortune through trading ventures, both along the Mississippi and to ports around the Gulf of Mexico and the East Coast of the United States. Late in 1798 Clark traveled upriver to Natchez, where he became an American citizen, taking an oath of allegiance to the United States. Back in New Orleans, he steadily increased his influence and strengthened his relationships with local officials. Perhaps recognizing the limitations of Jones and Hulings, Clark continued to file occasional reports to the State Department on conditions in Louisiana. American merchants in New Orleans, recognizing that Spanish officials would never accept Jones, petitioned the department to appoint a new consul. President Jefferson chose Clark, naming him in a recess appointment on July 16, 1801. Local officials appear to have acquiesced at least tacitly in the appointment despite the prohibition on consuls, perhaps because of Clark's stature in the city and good relations with them.

As an individual, Clark was an enigma, with a character and motives often shrouded in mystery. Comments on Clark by his contemporaries are contradictory and often colored by the writers' personal relationship with him. A business partner recorded that "he possesses handsome talents, a considerable acquired fortune, of his own in Louisiana. . . . He is the only proper character in Louisiana for the office of Consul."[8] Andrew Ellicott and Isaac Guion, who also recommended him as consul, wrote that he "rendered essential services to our country . . . which cannot fail to be acceptable to the President and Senate of the U.S. and the citizens at large."[9] Joseph Belchasse, another admirer, recalled that "few men were equal to Clark in talents and intelligence."[10] On the other hand, James Wilkinson, an American military commander who would later clash bitterly with Clark, commented that he "is rather an Englishman at heart. . . . He is unpopular here, . . . cunning and overbearing."[11] Another acquaintance called him "deficient in dignity of character and sterling veracity," adding that he "is liked by few Americans here. . . . His talents fit him for public office but he is not popular enough to get it."[12] The last French prefect of New Orleans, who was often at odds with Clark, wrote that his "talents for intrigue are carried to a rare degree of excellence. . . . No one . . . could make a more convincing parade of indignation at the devious ways of others."[13] Even his rivals, however, conceded his influence; Wilkinson concluded that Clark had the capacity "to do more good or harm than any other individual in the province."[14]

Clark was impulsive, action-oriented, decisive, and sometimes even conspiratorial or rash. He had an ability to work with or around his enemies and an enormous capacity for getting things done even under the most difficult circumstances. Pragmatism rather than principle seems to have been his guide. Still, he took great risks for the United States, and whatever his methods, he achieved remarkable success.

Clark was born in Sligo, Ireland, in 1766 and attended some of the finest English schools, including Eton. At age twenty, he traveled to New Orleans to join an uncle who was already a prosperous merchant and landowner. Young Daniel Clark became fluent in French and Spanish and served for a time as a clerk in the office of the Spanish governor, making contacts and gaining knowledge that contributed to his effectiveness. By 1801 he may have been the wealthiest and most influential American in New Orleans, building a fortune through trading ventures, including slave trading, land speculation, and a variety of other business activities. In that year he began what has been termed "an irregular connection" with a married woman, Zulime Des Granges, who has been described as a "voluptuous beauty."[15] Zulime was just eighteen but had already been married for five years to Jerome Des Granges, a minor French nobleman—or by some accounts a pretended nobleman who was actually a poor confectioner—who took refuge in New Orleans during the French Revolution. Zulime's affair with Clark began when Jerome returned to France in 1801; she eventually bore Clark a daughter. The details of Clark's tangled private life were to emerge only long after his death.

New Orleans at the time was a bustling Spanish colonial city, the capital of Louisiana, and the key port on the lower Mississippi.[16] With almost ten thousand inhabitants, it was already one of the major cities of North America, about twice the size of Richmond, Providence, or Quebec. New Orleans was neatly laid out, extending almost a mile along the east bank of the river and surrounded by a decaying rampart. The streets, very narrow and generally unpaved, were spaced at even intervals and intersected at right angles. The buildings were new following a major fire that had destroyed the town a decade earlier. The rebuilt houses were mainly brick, plastered over and painted; many were two stories. At the center of the city along the river was the Place des Armes (now Jackson Square), a dusty parade ground surrounded by the principal government buildings and the unfinished St. Louis Cathedral. New Orleans in 1800 also boasted extensive barracks and warehouses, a crumbling customs house, a small but well-supplied market, a convent, two hospitals, and an insane asylum. The city was partially surrounded by swamps, making it unhealthy in the summer, with yellow fever endemic.

Most residents were still of French descent, but since Spain's acquisition of the Louisiana Territory from France in 1769, a sizable proportion of the population had become Spanish, and an increasing number of Americans were settling in New Orleans. Catholicism was still the official religion. Public drunkenness was a serious problem. There was only one school in all of Louisiana, with a rudimentary curriculum in Spanish. By one estimate, no more than two hundred residents of the entire territory could read and write. Clark, with his British public school background, was a rarity indeed; his education alone was enough to give him some prominence in the city.

As Clark took up his consular duties in 1801, he was again faced with the problems of privateers, trade, Americans in need of assistance, and other issues familiar to consuls around the world. Unlike American consuls in any other port, however, Clark was also confronted by the unique problems of America's western frontier, which then comprised all the territories from the Appalachian Mountains to the Mississippi River.

A multiplicity of plots and political schemes were afoot in the Mississippi valley, many of them so secretive and complex that they have still not been fully unraveled. Some Spanish officials were conspiring to take over America's western territories. Others had vague plans for Spanish Louisiana to become an independent country that would spearhead the liberation of the rest of Spanish America. At the same time, some settlers were making plans to expel Spain from both Florida and Louisiana and to have those territories annexed to either the United States or Great Britain. War between the United States and Spain repeatedly threatened to erupt. Americans as prominent as Alexander Hamilton planned for an invasion of the Spanish territories. Others, notably Vice President Aaron Burr, continued to plot as late as 1806, well after the Louisiana Purchase. Influential British and French leaders also had designs on territories on both sides of the Mississippi River. As rumors began to circulate in 1801 of French plans to reacquire and occupy Louisiana, the western plots became still more intense.[17]

As early as 1798 a letter from Clark warned the U.S. government that Gen. James Wilkinson, commander of U.S. forces in the west and the highest-ranking officer of the U.S. Army, was up to no good in the lower Mississippi valley. "He is no friend of the U.S.," Clark reported in a letter that reached the secretary of state.[18] As it turned out, Wilkinson was on the Spanish payroll, a fact not proven until the Spanish archives were opened many years later. Wilkinson would play a major role in coming events.

The following year, Clark reported a Spanish effort "to detach the Chactaws from the interests of the U.S. and to form a connection with the Spaniards." Although Spanish officials denied the plot, Clark claimed to have solid information on Spanish meddling with Native Americans inside U.S. borders. Spanish gunboats on the river and visits to New Orleans by Creek and Choctaw leaders suggested a plan to inflame those tribes against the United States.[19] Foreign intrigues with Native Americans continued virtually to the moment the United States acquired Louisiana. The French at one point assembled an arsenal of thousands of muskets and other arms to distribute to the Mississippi tribes to win their allegiance.[20] Clark reported "many endeavors . . . to attract the Indians from all quarters and I respectfully advise the necessity of counteracting the effect of their presents."[21]

At President Jefferson's request, Clark reported as much information as he could gather on the Indian nations. He came to be regarded in Washington as an expert on the subject. A few months before Louisiana was transferred to the United States, Secretary of State Madison instructed Clark to "prepare the Indians for the change which is to take place."[22] A bewildered Clark replied that only agents who speak Indian languages could prepare them for cession. The Indians rarely came to New Orleans, he continued, and those who did were likely to be involved in Spanish plots. He advised that "some presents will be needed to win their loyalty."[23]

As the years passed, Clark warned the State Department with increasing urgency about western plotting. The Spanish, he wrote in early 1803, were trying to buy the loyalties of Americans in New Orleans and had already purchased some of them.[24] A week later Clark reported that a shady Kentucky adventurer was conspiring with France to bring in hundreds of French settlers, in a "dangerous" scheme that could "affect the integrity of the union."[25]

All of Clark's struggles with pirates and Indians and intrigues, however valuable, were to some extent a sideshow to the other critical international events unfolding around Louisiana. Shortly before Jefferson appointed Clark as consul in 1801, and unknown to the United States, Spain agreed to end its thirty-year ownership of Louisiana and signed a secret treaty retroceding the territory to France. In return for Louisiana, the Spanish king's brother-in-law was made king of Tuscany. The trade didn't seem as lopsided at the time as it does today; Louisiana was still costing Spain more to administer than it made in revenue. Rumors of the transfer appeared in French newspapers but were denied. It was more than a year before the U.S. minister in Paris obtained proof of the deal. Still, both French and Spanish officials denied its existence.

By this time, the outlines of a grand French colonial scheme in America were beginning to take shape. Late in 1801, following the short-lived British-French Peace of Amiens, twenty thousand French troops under Gen. Charles Victor-Emmanuel Leclerc, Napoleon's brother-in-law, embarked for Santo Domingo, the island that today encompasses the Dominican Republic and Haiti. This rich sugar-producing island was to be the centerpiece of new French dominions in America. Within three months of their arrival, the French forces captured rebel leader Toussaint L'Ouverture and secured control of the island. Under the French plan, Louisiana would provide a base of supply and food for Santo Domingo, ensuring its viability. The success of the plan required both territories to remain in French hands.

Napoleon thus planned to follow up the conquest of Santo Domingo by dispatching French forces to Louisiana. By mid-1802 troops were assembled in Europe under Gen. Claude Victor-Perrin. Napoleon instructed Victor-Perrin to fortify Louisiana sufficiently to defend itself even if it became completely isolated from France in a war. As a second priority, Victor-Perrin was to win the support of the Native Americans against the United States but to avoid provoking a direct conflict.

Efforts to embark the French troops became a comedy of errors uncharacteristic of Napoleon's usually effective military machine. Victor-Perrin and his men were in Holland, but the supplies needed for the voyage were in Dunkirk. By the time troops and supplies were assembled together in December, their ships were diverted to carry reinforcements to Santo Domingo. Through the rest of the winter, the Dutch ports were iced shut. It was not until April 1803 that the troops were finally boarded and ready to sail. All this time New Orleans waited apprehensively for their arrival.

While the French forces assembled, the Paris press noted that if France closed New Orleans to American commerce, the territories along the Ohio and Mississippi Rivers would be strangled economically and would find it in their self-interest to separate from the United States and join France. The French threat and the military activity surrounding it did not escape the attention of the American government. Jefferson saw Spain as a weak neighbor that could be controlled if necessary. French control of New Orleans would be a very different matter. Unlike Spain, France was a first-rate military power, and its intentions did not appear friendly.

The threat to New Orleans and to commerce on the Mississippi River was a top priority for Jefferson and his advisors. Secretary of State Madison wrote as early as 1801 to his minister in Madrid, David Humphreys—the same David Humphreys who worked for years to free the Americans held captive in Algiers—that for the American West the Mississippi River "is everything. It is the Hudson, the Delaware, the Potomac . . . formed into one stream."[26] Jefferson, acutely aware of the dangers of French occupation, wrote to Robert Livingston, his minister in Paris: "There is on the globe one spot, the possessor of which is our natural enemy. It is New Orleans, through which the produce of three-eighths of our territory must pass. . . . Perhaps nothing since the revolutionary war has produced more uneasy sensations through the body of the nation."[27]

When Clark learned of the French plan to occupy Louisiana, he immediately embarked for Paris. His aim, it seems, was to assess the likely impact of French administration on commerce and American interests in New Orleans. He doubtless also hoped to establish the same kind of close personal relationships with the new French administrators that had served him so well with top Spanish officials. In Paris, Minister Livingston introduced him to both General Victor-Perrin and Pierre-Clément Laussat, soon to be French prefect in Louisiana. The discussions were unsatisfactory. Victor-Perrin denied the United States had trading rights on the Mississippi and suggested that the French force in Louisiana would be financed through new duties on New Orleans trade. Laussat struck Clark as officious and likely to make trouble for the United States. Clark returned to New Orleans early in 1803 implacably opposed to French occupation. He began a steady drumbeat of agitation for the United States to take action.

Clark's preferred solution for the problem of impending French occupation was simple: the United States should seize New Orleans from Spain before France could land its troops. He wrote to Madison: "There is nothing to oppose us should we think proper to take possession of the Country either by way of indemnification for past injuries or security for the future. There is no energy in the Government, no money in the Treasury, no troops, no fortifications that could withstand us for a moment."[28] Clark argued the United States would have no choice but to occupy New Orleans sooner or later; delay would only raise the cost in blood and treasure.

Without waiting for Madison's answer, Clark traveled north to Fort Adams, in the Mississippi Territory, to meet the governor, William C. C. Claiborne, and James Wilkinson, still commander of U.S. forces in the West. Both men would figure prominently in Clark's later life as political adversaries. Clark urged Claiborne and Wilkinson to march their troops downstream immediately and seize New Orleans. With war fever on the rise in America's western territories, Clark's proposal was not regarded as unreasonable at the time. Claiborne, however, was as cautious as Clark was impulsive; he declined to act. Wilkinson, who was still secretly on the Spanish payroll, was not about to involve himself.

Undaunted, Clark returned to New Orleans, where he continued to file reports on the problems facing Americans, the deviousness of Spanish and French officials, and the need for U.S. action. Although his more inflammatory proposals were not taken up, his reports certainly contributed to the sense of unease in Washington and to the atmosphere of crisis surrounding the Louisiana issue. Reading Clark's reports solidified Jefferson's conviction that a French takeover would be disastrous for the United States.

French prefect Laussat arrived in New Orleans in March 1803 with a small contingent of officials. His first task was to prepare for the arrival of General Victor-Perrin and the troops, now expected in less than a month. Clark, always blunt, reported that Laussat was off to a bad start: the prefect's "tone of authority . . . disgusts the rich and frightens the poor. . . . Vanity and presumption are, I believe, leading traits in the Prefect's character."[29] According to Clark, Laussat's haughty manner and his refusal to pay adequate compensation for requisitioned goods and labor quickly made him unpopular, even with the French Creoles. Clark concluded that Laussat was "a violent and bad man" with "projects of plunder and monopoly."[30]

Clark's reports made clear that France would not allow a U.S. consul to operate in New Orleans. This would have a sharply negative impact both on traders and on other Americans in the territory, who counted on the consul for documents, advice, protection, and intervention with local authorities. Jefferson instructed his minister in Paris that a key American objective was to gain French acceptance of a consul in New Orleans. Meanwhile Clark, always on the lookout for practical solutions, suggested to Madison that a consul might conduct his business on an American ship on the Mississippi River, "which is common to both nations."[31]

Tension in New Orleans mounted as 1803 wore on, with the arrival of French troops always expected imminently. Although Jefferson rejected calls by Clark and others for annexation, he was sufficiently concerned for American interests that in March he dispatched James Monroe to join Robert Livingston in Paris with instructions to try to purchase New Orleans and west Florida. Although Florida still belonged to Spain, there was sufficient confusion surrounding the details of the retrocession of Louisiana to France that American officials were uncertain at that point, and for many months to follow, exactly who controlled Louisiana and Florida.

The rest of the story in Paris is well known. Jefferson's timing was auspicious. Just weeks earlier, news arrived in Paris that the French army in Santo Domingo had been decimated by disease, with General Leclerc himself one of the victims. Meanwhile, French relations with Great Britain again reached the breaking point. With war brewing in Europe, Napoleon lost his taste for grand colonial schemes. The day before Monroe's arrival in Paris, Foreign Minister Talleyrand offered Robert Livingston the opportunity to purchase not only New Orleans but all of Louisiana. Monroe and Livingston exceeded their instructions and accepted. Within three weeks the deal was closed. For $12 million that the United States did not have and agreement to assume another $3 million in claims against France, the United States acquired a huge expanse of unknown western territory. Curiously, a British company provided the loan that financed the purchase, putting money into Napoleon's coffers to wage war on Britain.

In New Orleans, however, the drama was far from over. For another six months rumors would continue to fly, intrigues to unfold, and tensions to mount.

The Louisiana Purchase was anything but neat. When France reacquired Louisiana, Napoleon promised Spain he would never relinquish it to a third party. The Spanish, already unhappy to lose the vast Louisiana territory to France, were livid at Napoleon's betrayal. And Spain, of course, was still in control on the ground in Louisiana; General Victor-Perrin had never arrived to take possession for France. The Spanish garrisons in New Orleans and the frontier outposts were small, but there were well-trained reinforcements available in Havana. Spain might try to hold on to its territory or to delay the transfer pending the outcome of the European war, when its claims and fortunes might have improved. In any event, Spain vigorously protested the legality of the sale in both Washington and Paris. Spanish authorities intimated they would not comply with a U.S.-French agreement that they strongly opposed. Spanish officials in New Orleans were left with no instructions on what to do, thus introducing yet another wild card into the already muddled situation.

French prefect Laussat, meanwhile, was anxious to carry through with the transfer of Louisiana from Spain to France. Although his motives are not entirely clear, Laussat seemed driven to head a French empire in Louisiana, even if only for a short transitional period. Perhaps he also had the European war on his mind and hoped a quick French victory would lead to second thoughts about the sale. French forces in Santo Domingo fought on, despite their setbacks. As far as anyone in New Orleans knew, General Victor-Perrin was still poised to sail for Louisiana or might already be on the high seas. Anything might happen.

Throughout the year, New Orleans remained awash in rumors concerning the timing and nature of the French occupation. In

July, three months after Monroe and Livingston completed the purchase, residents of New Orleans were still expecting the arrival of French troops. Late that month rumors of the U.S. acquisition began to circulate in New Orleans, but it was early August before Clark received a personal letter from President Jefferson confirming the purchase.[32] Clark was elated. He wrote Madison that he felt "the sincerest joy on the accomplishment of an object so dear to the heart of every American."[33]

Clark, however, still considered the danger of Spanish or French treachery to be very real. Even if Laussat had every intention of handing over the territory to the United States—and it was not clear that he did—a temporary French acquisition, with no French troops and without sufficient power to control events on the ground, invited lawlessness, civil disturbances, and even insurrection. French-Spanish relations in New Orleans nosedived as the transfer approached, with tensions between the Spanish governor and the French prefect reaching a feverish pitch. Settler intrigues continued, Indian problems festered, and the renewed war in Europe led to a resurgence of privateering in the Gulf of Mexico. Clark would have his hands full for the remainder of 1803.

President Jefferson planned to call Congress into session early to ratify the purchase of Louisiana. Realizing how little he knew about America's new lands, Jefferson turned to his consul in New Orleans for information. He gave Clark six weeks to file a comprehensive report on the largely unknown territory. Clark proceeded with astonishing insight, vigor, and access to inside information. Jefferson was deeply impressed with the result and commended Clark's report to his cabinet secretaries.[34]

Clark's ability to procure state secrets from both Spanish and French officials suggests either that he was on the most intimate terms with both or that he was a master spy. The evidence points to a bit of each. Clark's 1803 reports are laced with hints of intrigue. As early as March, fearing for his personal safety, Clark warned Secretary of State Madison to hold his dispatches in the closest confidence. "Should it be necessary to make any part of them public, be pleased to give me timely information that I may depart from hence and if possible withdraw my own property."[35] In April, Clark provided Madison with a detailed list of all French officers on the way to New Orleans, with their ranks and intended duties, commenting that it was procured with "a great deal of trouble and expense." "To prevent accident," he continued, "perhaps it would be well to furnish me with a cypher."[36] In May Clark reported Spain's intention to keep Florida, adding, "The Prefect has not the least idea of this." He continued, "I am promised a sight of the (Spanish) Royal Orders and secret instructions to the Commissioners, the contents of which I shall advise you of."[37] When the French prefect sent an envoy to the Native American tribes, Clark reported that he had sources close to the mission and would keep Madison informed.[38] Other reports provided detailed information on the organization of the Spanish militia—5,440 men—and of the strength of Spanish garrisons at ten outposts around Louisiana.[39] Later Clark commented that if dispatches arrive from the Spanish court, "I shall endeavor to learn their contents before they are delivered" and to suppress them if necessary.[40] If Clark was buying information, which seems likely, he was doing so with his own funds. There is no record in the diplomatic archives suggesting he was authorized or compensated for bribes to local officials. Still, Jefferson and Madison, who both read Clark's dispatches with the greatest interest, could not have been unaware of what was going on.

The president and the secretary of state remained deeply concerned over problems that could still arise with cession. Madison instructed Clark that "the President wishes you to watch every symptom which may shew itself" of French plans to obstruct the transfer.[41] Just weeks before the cession, uncertainty over Spanish and French intentions still ran so high that Madison asked Clark to be ready to put together an armed force of local inhabitants to assist with a U.S. invasion of Louisiana.[42]

As 1803 wore on, Clark reported more and more indications of Spain's intention to delay the transfer. As late as November, Spanish officials in New Orleans were still vacillating. Casa Calvo, who had been replaced as governor but was back in New Orleans as

Spanish commissioner, told Clark he did not have the authority to deliver Louisiana to France.[43] French prefect Laussat, meanwhile, was agitating with Casa Calvo and the new governor to complete the transfer as quickly as possible.

In the face of these conflicting signals, Clark continued to appeal for the dispatch of U.S. troops.[44] Even a modest show of force, he argued, would bring the Spanish around before they handed over power to the French. The idea of Laussat taking over power in New Orleans appalled Clark. He found Laussat "violent, meddling, troublesome, . . . a man who has on all occasions shewn himself the implacable Enemy of the Americans."[45] What bothered Clark most was that the prefect's dreams of grandeur posed a very real danger on the ground. Laussat planned to take over the government of Louisiana and modify its administration in the face of hostile Spaniards, unruly American settlers, and restive Creoles, all on the eve of transferring the territory to the United States and while the French had no means to enforce order or laws. This seemed to be a recipe for disaster. "I wish this experiment of his were not to be attempted," Clark wrote mournfully to Madison. It is "not without danger," and I "dread the consequences that may ensue."[46]

Further complicating an already troubled situation, French-Spanish tensions in New Orleans were moving from bad to worse. In addition to hard feelings between the two governments, personal relations between French prefect Laussat and Spanish commissioner Casa Calvo were so bad that the two no longer spoke with each other. Their relations were peppered by insults and incidents. Shortly after Laussat's arrival in New Orleans, his wife was arrested by the Spanish constabulary for driving to Mass in a carriage on Holy Thursday. The Spanish apologized, explaining that even the king walked to Mass on that holy day, and they punished the patrol involved. Laussat, however, would not be placated. He contrived a personal insult to Casa Calvo, storming out of the latter's home on the pretext of not liking one of the other guests. Casa Calvo was barely restrained from challenging him to a duel.[47] Later, a group of Spanish officers and their wives retaliated by failing to appear at a dinner at Laussat's residence. Clark, who attended the dinner, gleefully reported the affair to Washington, writing that Mrs. Laussat raged before the assembled guests that the Spanish were "souls of filth and mean slaves. . . . The scene was carried to the highest pitch, to the astonishment of all present."[48] Clark quietly did what he could to encourage French-Spanish feuding, believing their mutual hostility would strengthen the U.S. position.[49]

Jefferson grew concerned enough about the uneasy situation that he finally heeded Clark's appeal for action. He warned the Spanish minister in Washington that if Spain continued to oppose the American purchase, the United States might use force to occupy Louisiana and might occupy Florida as well. At the same time, he ordered the mobilization of U.S. troops and volunteers in the west and instructed General Wilkinson and Governor Claiborne to move south with sufficient force to overwhelm any possible resistance. Wilkinson and Claiborne were designated as U.S. commissioners to receive Louisiana. Clark urged that U.S. troops arrive promptly, with a view to seeing Louisiana transferred from Spain to France to the United States, all in a single day. Wilkinson, however, still secretly on the Spanish payroll, found repeated excuses to delay the march south. Clark was left as the man on the spot, to manage as well as he might.

By November, Clark was pleading with Claiborne to make haste: "for God's sake lose no time in marching this way to put an End to the horrid situation we are in—We are placed over a Mine that may explode from one moment to another and the effect may be dreadful beyond our conception."[50] On November 24, Clark reported he had made arrangements with the mayor on where to lodge U.S. troops once they arrived. This was quite a coup, since the Spanish had not yet agreed to vacate.

In late November, with tensions in the city continuing to escalate, Casa Calvo still had no instructions from Madrid. Laussat, meanwhile, was also acting without instructions from Paris in pressing for a quick handover to France. The French government, for its part, was somehow under the impression that Laussat had died and made plans to send out another official to act in his place.[51] Finally, on November 25, Casa Calvo—who still had not heard that his government was protesting the French sale of Louisiana to the United States—bowed to the mounting local pressures. He informed Clark he would cede Louisiana to France on November 30, just five days hence. News of the Spanish diplomatic protests of the sale reached Casa Calvo less than two weeks later, on December 7, but by that time Louisiana was back in French hands.

Casa Calvo's decision to move ahead with cession removed one of the major concerns that had plagued Clark for months. For the first time Clark could assure U.S. commissioners Wilkinson and Claiborne—who were still fumbling to assemble troops in Mississippi—that there was no likelihood of hostilities with Spain. But with cession to France only five days away, it was clear that despite Clark's months of urging, U.S. forces would not arrive in time to avoid the prospect of a French interim administration in Louisiana, with all the dangers that might entail. The Spanish governor offered Laussat use of his troops to maintain order in the interim, but the haughty prefect declined.

Left alone to fend for U.S. interests, Clark took matters into his own hands. As Laussat and Casa Calvo met the morning of November 30 to discuss the final arrangements for the transfer ceremony that afternoon, Clark assembled a large group of his friends and sympathizers at George King's Coffee House, a favorite haunt of the American community in New Orleans. The Americans agreed to form a volunteer military company to protect U.S. interests and maintain order until the forces under Wilkinson and Claiborne arrived. Not surprisingly, they elected Consul Clark as their captain. Within days, almost three hundred men had joined the force. Clark offered the unit's services to Laussat to help maintain order in the city under the French administration. Laussat, faced with a fait accompli and a choice of having the force either under his nominal direction or in opposition to him, accepted the offer. Clark's force outnumbered a small contingent of French volunteers that Laussat had assembled to keep order in New Orleans. For the next three weeks the American volunteer force patrolled the city night and day, each man with a black cockade in his hat as the unit's symbol. One member later wrote, "We . . . served faithfully twenty days and nights, keeping the City in better order than I had ever known it to be before, and no doubt prevented the dreaded outbreak."[52]

The French administration in Louisiana was ushered in during a torrential rain at a city hall ceremony on November 30. Casa Calvo handed Laussat the keys to New Orleans on a silver platter; he then released the people of Louisiana from obedience to Spain. According to Clark's account, as the French flag rose over New Orleans for the first time since 1769, "the most gloomy silence prevailed and nothing could induce the numerous spectators to express the least joy or give any sign of satisfaction on the occasion."[53]

As Clark had feared, Laussat promptly introduced profound changes in the organization and administration of the territory. A new city council was appointed for New Orleans. Adoption of the French legal system was proclaimed. New officials were named to all important government posts. Laussat, however, sought Clark's advice, changing several of his initial appointments at Clark's recommendation. As a measure of insurance for a smooth transfer, Clark arranged for a Creole friend to accept the command of the militia, which was still constituted as it had been under the Spanish regime. Clark continued to implore Wilkinson and Claiborne to hurry south with the troops.

The much-feared civil disturbances did not materialize. Curiously, the twenty days of the French interregnum were largely given over to festivities. Laussat arranged major fetes, with fireworks, feasting, dancing, gambling, and other amusements to celebrate France's short-lived reacquisition of Louisiana. Casa Calvo, relieved of his burdens of office, also organized a huge fiesta in honor of the French. Laussat, setting aside past animosity, reciprocated with a ball in Casa Calvo's honor.

Wilkinson and Claiborne were still slowly gathering troops in Natchez when Clark informed them of the peaceful transfer of Louisiana to France. Only then did they finally move south, fulfilling orders they had received months before. With Spain no longer in control of Louisiana, Wilkinson had no further incentive for delay. American troops did not arrive in New Orleans until December 17.

Still, the transfer to the United States was not without last-minute threats. Two incidents in particular caused concerns. Three days after the transfer to France, word reached New Orleans of the imminent arrival of twelve hundred French soldiers, now British prisoners of war captured in Santo Domingo. The British, wanting to avoid the expense of maintaining them, decided to send them to New Orleans, where they could be landed without fear they would reinforce the French war effort against Britain. Clark feared that the arrival of so many French troops could derail the transfer and entreated Laussat to put a stop to it. Laussat, however, had no power to prevent the arrival of a British man-of-war, even if he had wished to. In the end, the prisoners did not arrive until after the United States took possession, and they were so weakened by captivity, hunger, and disease that they posed no danger to the new administration.

The second threat was potentially still more ominous: a rumor circulated that malcontents planned to set New Orleans ablaze the night the United States took over. The threat was viewed with the greatest seriousness; just fifteen years earlier, a major fire had devastated New Orleans, destroying 90 percent of the city. General Wilkinson posted a heavy guard; the threatened arson did not take place.

On December 20, much of the populace of New Orleans assembled in the Place des Armes to witness the transfer of Louisiana to the United States. According to Laussat, "The beautiful women and fashionable men of the city adorned all the balconies of the square. The Spanish officers were distinguishable in the crowd by their plumes. At none of the preceding ceremonies was there an equal number of spectators. The eleven galleries of the city hall were filled with beauties."[54] Americans cheered enthusiastically as the American flag was raised and the French standard lowered. French and Spanish citizens looked on in silence. Laussat noted that the American flag did not unfurl as it was raised. Then, overtaken by emotion, Laussat left the square. Wilkinson reported, "The operation was hurried in my judgment with improper vivacity and impatience on the part of the Prefect."[55] Clark left no record of his impressions of the ceremony. That evening saw another major fete, with dancing and carousing until dawn in the streets of New Orleans. Louisiana was American.

Word of the peaceful transfer from Spain to France did not reach Washington until Christmas Day; news of the U.S. takeover followed in mid-January 1804 by special courier. The lingering suspense was finally over. News of the successful transfer set off a tremendous wave of celebrations around the United States.

In many ways, the career of Daniel Clark climaxed with the U.S. acquisition of New Orleans. It was the culmination of years of effort and of intrigues, handled masterfully. Before making his exit, however, Clark had a few more marks to etch on the history of Louisiana.

President Jefferson had hoped to persuade the Marquis de Lafayette to become the first governor of America's new territories. It was a brilliant choice that might have united the Creoles and Americans. But Lafayette did not accept, and Jefferson's second choice, James Monroe, likewise declined. Daniel Clark, who was politically ambitious, apparently thought he would be a good choice for governor. Ultimately, however, Jefferson appointed William Claiborne, who was to serve for many years and would become one of the most distinguished names in Louisiana history.

Claiborne and Clark were already off to a bad start. Clark regarded Claiborne as plodding and indecisive, the man who had refused Clark's request to invade Louisiana prior to the U.S. purchase and who had delayed interminably in getting his troops to New Orleans after the purchase. As governor, Claiborne earned Clark's further resentment for championing the cause of the new American immigrants flooding into New Orleans at the expense of the established interests Clark represented. Claiborne, for his part, considered Clark impetuous, conspiratorial, and power-hungry. Worse, he perceived Clark's popularity and influence in New Orleans as a threat to his new administration. Claiborne came to regard Clark as his principal political enemy and developed a deep hatred for him. Claiborne's letters are replete with poisonous personal attacks on Clark. The records show no indication that Clark harbored the same sort of animosity for Claiborne.

The two men clashed almost immediately. Claiborne was not initially popular in New Orleans; Clark led the opposition to a number of measures he introduced. In addition, Clark organized a campaign for statehood, which would lead to the election of a governor and bring Claiborne's appointment to an end. The ambitious Clark may have harbored designs on the office.[56]

Claiborne was trying with difficulty at this stage to establish an appointed legislative council. Jefferson overrode Claiborne's recommendations and instructed him to name Clark and several of Clark's supporters to the council.[57] Claiborne, chagrined, grudgingly offered Clark the post, but he declined, as did most other nominees. Claiborne blamed Clark for sabotaging the council. Later that year, Clark was chosen as director of the Bank of Louisiana.

In 1806 Clark was elected as the first delegate to Congress from the U.S. Territory of Orleans, overwhelming a candidate backed by Claiborne. Clark wrote to General Wilkinson, with whom he would not be on good terms much longer, gloating that "my nomination has been a severe shock to W.C.C.C. [Claiborne] and his gang, they are much chop-fallen, and all the first character and best men here have united against them."[58]

Clark served two terms in Congress, from 1807 to 1810. He was a strong Federalist, joining the opposition to Jefferson. He actively supported the introduction of postal services into America's new territories and the building of canals to improve access to the Mississippi River. Even Claiborne admitted Clark's popularity as a congressman.[59] Clark's term in office, however, was colored by the old problem of settler intrigues and by a clash with General Wilkinson, all brought to a head by the Burr conspiracy.

The story is a muddled one. Vice President Aaron Burr was clearly planning some sort of western adventure, perhaps to lead an unauthorized military expedition against Spanish Mexico but more likely to split off the western portion of the United States into a new country. Wilkinson was a confidant of Burr's and seems to have been deeply involved in the plot. Wilkinson introduced Burr to a range of prominent westerners, including Daniel Clark. In 1806 one of Wilkinson's political enemies began to expose his plotting with Burr and his earlier Spanish connection. In an effort to save himself, Wilkinson turned on Burr and warned Jefferson of a plot to destroy the Union. Wilkinson moved his troops to New Orleans, where, with Claiborne's hesitant support, he instituted martial law, suspended civil rights, and took draconian measures against a large number of supposed Burr supporters. At the same time, Wilkinson secretly contacted Spanish officials to seek a cash reward for his treachery against Burr. Wilkinson became the chief witness against Burr at the much-celebrated trial at which William Eaton, the hero of Derne, also testified against Burr. Burr was eventually acquitted. Evidence that emerged at Burr's trial led to a separate investigation of Wilkinson, who was also acquitted.

The extent of Daniel Clark's involvement in these events, if any, is unclear. We know that Clark turned against the devious Wilkinson and provided much of the hard evidence against him. Congress seemed to back Clark, voting 52–30 to publish his accusations against Wilkinson. President Jefferson backed Wilkinson, belittling Clark's charges and in the process tarnishing Clark's image. Perhaps seeing an opportunity or perhaps at Wilkinson's urging, Claiborne charged that Clark was in league with Burr. Two trading voyages Clark made to Mexico in 1805 and 1806 were alleged to have been connected with the Burr plot. A much more damning piece of evidence has since emerged. The British archives contain a report from Sir Anthony Merry, British ambassador in Washington, referring to Burr's plans and suggesting that the Admiralty send a fleet to lie off the mouth of the Mississippi and wait until "Daniel Clark of New Orleans" should send word that "the revolution has taken place."[60] The British chose not to act on Sir Anthony's recommendation.

Burr was certainly capable of implicating others without their agreement. But Clark, for his part, was no novice in intrigue. What is uncertain is whether Clark, a sitting member of Congress and still among the wealthiest and most influential citizens of New

Orleans, was sufficiently angered with Claiborne, Jefferson, and the course of American rule in Louisiana after less than three years that he was willing to undo the U.S. administration he had worked so hard to achieve. As with so much that surrounds the period, the records are inconclusive. Clark was never formally charged with any part in the conspiracy. In May 1807 he planned to travel from New Orleans to Richmond to testify in the Burr trial. His appearance might have shed light on some of the mysteries. But another remarkable event intervened.

On the morning of May 23, Governor Claiborne dispatched a letter by special messenger to Clark. The letter referred to statements Clark was reported to have made in Congress that were critical of Claiborne's handling of the territorial militia. When Clark refused to retract his criticism, Claiborne demanded satisfaction, challenging him to a duel.

Clark, an officer in the militia (appointed by Claiborne), was in a reasonable position to comment on its effectiveness. His criticism seems rather mild to have provoked Claiborne to risk death to avenge the insult. Certainly Clark's comments did not compare to the personal criticisms of Clark that Claiborne continued to send to Washington on an almost weekly basis. One can only imagine that Claiborne's frustrations with Clark had become more than he could stand. At the time of the challenge, Clark had just returned from Washington to New Orleans, where even by Claiborne's account he was greeted enthusiastically. Claiborne's popularity, meanwhile, was at low ebb in the wake of his agreement to Wilkinson's draconian martial law regime in New Orleans. Claiborne may have judged that a challenge could both boost his sagging fortunes and rid him of his chief political rival.

Clark accepted the challenge. He and Claiborne each appointed seconds, and after an exchange of several letters, the arrangements were made. Dueling was illegal in the Orleans Territory, and it would have been unseemly for the governor to participate in an illegal duel in his own domain. With this in mind, Claiborne slipped quietly out of town on June 3, followed shortly thereafter by Clark, and crossed the border into Spanish West Florida. On Monday,

June 8, the two men met on a field of honor near the river Ibreville. At precisely one o'clock, with the sweltering summer sun overhead, they drew pistols, strode ten paces, and turned to face each other. The languid tropical silence of what is now the Bayou Manchac was shattered by two simultaneous shots. The duel was over in an instant; Claiborne lay bleeding in the grass.

The wound was serious but not fatal. Clark's bullet traveled clear through Claiborne's thigh and lodged in his other leg. Claiborne was confined to his bed for more than a month. At the end of June he wrote Jefferson that his wound was still "infinitely more painful than anticipated. . . . I have been sufficiently punished for my imprudence."[61] Clark, meanwhile, wrote a friend shortly after the duel, "I look upon this business as settled, and will return to Orleans in three or four days. I keep away from it merely to avoid the congratulations and exultation of the public on the occasion."[62] Wherever he appeared after the duel, Clark said, he was greeted with warmth and affection.

By the time Clark returned to Washington and Congress in 1808, Burr had been acquitted. Attention was focused on Clark's charges against General Wilkinson. When Jefferson came to Wilkinson's defense, Clark found himself embroiled in a political battle against a powerful president, and he faced renewed allegations that he was an ally of Burr, an odious charge despite Burr's acquittal. The president admitted in a report to Congress that Clark had been providing him since 1801 with information on plots to dismember the Union, but the documents Clark had provided, Jefferson said, were somehow "missing" from the government archives.[63] Wilkinson was ultimately acquitted, albeit wrongly, handing Clark his first major political defeat. The next year Clark published a book, *Proofs of the Corruption of Gen. James Wilkinson, and His Connexion with Aaron Burr*, detailing his charges against Wilkinson. The publication led to another investigation and court-martial of the general, who was again acquitted (this time to the chagrin of President Madison), as he was in a third investigation of wrongdoing some years later.

By mid-1808 Claiborne reported from New Orleans, "Parties for and against Mr. Clark in this City are becoming violent—A newspaper war is raging."[64] Clark continued to be an important political force in New Orleans and a thorn in Claiborne's side for some years to come. But New Orleans was changing. Clark had ridden into office on the support of the city's established interests: the businessmen, the wealthy planters, the Creoles, and the Americans residing in New Orleans at the time of transfer. So many new settlers had flooded into the city since then that its demography had changed. The newcomers tended to support Claiborne. Clark, sensing that he could not win, chose not to run for a third term in Congress.

Clark's personal life had also grown more complicated. His long relationship with the beautiful young Zulime Des Granges came to a stormy end in 1807. The level of intrigue surrounding this affair is characteristic of Clark; its complexity rivals the Burr and Wilkinson plots. According to some accounts, Clark and Zulime were secretly married in Philadelphia in 1802, after her first husband, Jerome Des Granges, had returned to France. It seems that Jerome was a bigamist, with at least one other wife, but there is no record of his marriage to Zulime being dissolved. In any event, Clark set up a residence for Zulime in New Orleans and spent much of his time there for several years, while also maintaining his own residence and reportedly becoming involved in other romances including a short-lived marriage. Clark's marriage to Des Granges, if it ever happened, was never publicly acknowledged, purportedly because there was no documentary evidence of her former husband's bigamy. Without such proof, Clark and Des Granges themselves could have been charged with bigamy, a crime that could have drawn the death penalty under the Spanish law in force in 1802. If the wedding did take place, it is not clear why it was not announced after the U.S. takeover.

Zulime Des Granges married again following her stormy parting from Clark, without leaving any record of a divorce from Clark, just as there was no record of a divorce or annulment from her first husband. At least one daughter, Myra, was born to Clark and Des Granges and raised by close friends of Clark's. He never publicly acknowledged parenthood, but he provided for Myra and spent a great deal of time with her. This tangled legacy led to fifty years of litigation over Clark's sizable estate, largely sparked by the efforts of daughter Myra Clark Gaines to claim her inheritance. The case became one of the most publicized court battles of nineteenth-century America. The U.S. Supreme Court considered aspects of the case half a dozen times over several decades, ultimately ruling that Clark had legally wed Zulime Des Granges, thus providing Myra with legal legitimacy. She died, however, before the final ruling.

Daniel Clark fell ill in New Orleans in the summer of 1813. He was not to recover. Aged just forty-seven, he was laid to rest in a vault in the old St. Louis cemetery, at what was then the edge of his beloved New Orleans. He died, his epitaph tells us, "wept of all good men."

# FOUR

# Inventing Interventionism

*Joel Poinsett in Argentina, Chile, and Mexico*

Daniel Clark's adventures in New Orleans were part of a much larger political transformation that reshaped the world during the tumultuous first decade of the 1800s. As the United States doubled in size with the Louisiana Purchase, Napoleon's armies swept through Europe, creating the largest European empire since the Romans. Great Britain ruled the seas, extending its domains to distant outposts from the Caribbean to the Cape of Good Hope to India. The Spanish Empire, still the largest in the world, began to crumble.

Spain was once the world's superpower. At the opening of the nineteenth century, its empire still stretched from northern California to the tip of South America and included far-flung colonies in Africa and Asia. Although the cession of Louisiana to France was the largest loss of Spanish territory, it was not the first and would not be the last. The British had already captured Trinidad and were threatening other Caribbean islands. It was clear that Spain could not defend its colonies. At the same time, revolutionary ideals imported from the United States and France were starting to inspire South Americans, who were chafing under Spain's heavy taxes, restrictions, and monopolies.

In 1806 Spain formed an alliance with Napoleon. Two years later, however, the accession of Ferdinand VII to the Spanish throne led to a popular uprising against the French. Napoleon responded by invading Spain, installing his brother Joseph Bonaparte as king and arresting Ferdinand. Spain fell into civil war, with Joseph on the throne and an opposition junta leading an insurgency to expel the French. Spain's American colonies were thrown into disarray as rival agents of King Ferdinand, King Joseph, and the junta sought their loyalty.

Turmoil ran deep all over Spanish America. Some leaders pressed the idea of independence. Others saw an opportunity to end the excesses of colonial rule, without severing ties with Spain. Others—in particular a strong aristocratic class and a powerful Catholic Church hierarchy—continued to support the old order. The mix was explosive. Political confusion reigned, with viceroys deposed and juntas established throughout Spanish America. Most purported loyalty to Ferdinand.

The unfolding developments in Spanish America were watched with great interest but little understanding in the United States. The region was becoming increasingly important to U.S. traders. Although most commerce was prohibited by colonial monopolies, smugglers and legitimate traders alike were beginning to carry goods from the United States to Spanish America, while New England whalers and China traders stopped in its ports on their long journeys to the Pacific. Several of the new juntas eased trade restrictions and opened their ports to U.S. merchants. Commercial interests aside, Americans were naturally sympathetic to revolts against colonialism.

With Europe at war, Americans became increasingly concerned about British intentions in Spanish America. Great Britain was still by far the world's predominant naval and trading power. At best, the British would be a formidable commercial competitor; at worst, they might try to replace Spain as colonial master. Throughout the first decade of the nineteenth century, tensions between the United States and Great Britain threatened to break into open conflict; in 1812, war would erupt.

In 1810, President James Madison decided it was time to dispatch the first official American envoys to establish contact with the new juntas. The envoys were instructed to look into the situation in Spanish America, report home on conditions, seek friendly relations, and promote commercial ties. This promised to be a difficult and possibly perilous mission. The envoys would face political unrest, civil war, unfriendly colonial officials, and hostile British interests, in addition to the hardships and dangers of any long-distance travel at the time. They could expect to be away from their homes and families for many years. As the first of these envoys, Madison chose a young South Carolinian named Joel Roberts Poinsett.

Poinsett was part of a new generation of Americans. Unlike Shaw, Cathcart, and others who had been named to represent the United States abroad, Poinsett was too young to have fought in the American Revolution. The son of a well-to-do Charleston physician, Joel Poinsett was just thirty-one years old at the time of his appointment, but he had already lived a life of adventure that made him one of America's most traveled men and earned him a favorable reputation in Washington. Poinsett's family was wealthy enough to ensure him a first-class education, with private tutors and then elite schools in South Carolina, Connecticut, London, and Edinburgh. He proved particularly adept at languages, learning French, German, Spanish, and Italian, as well as classical Greek and Latin. Following his father's wish, young Poinsett enrolled in medical school in Edinburgh, but soon decided that medicine was not his calling. He favored a career in the army and began to study military science. His father disapproved and called him home. Poinsett then tried law school but, again, found it not to his liking.

At age twenty-two and with no career yet in sight, Poinsett, with his family's blessing, took off for an extended tour of Europe, despite the unsettled political conditions there. Young Americans in Europe were still a curiosity, which helped open doors for Poinsett and won him introductions to many of the most prominent men of the day, including Napoleon and Austrian foreign minister Klemens von Metternich. Poinsett's tour turned into a three-year marathon, taking him to France, Switzerland, Italy, Sicily, Malta, Austria, and the Netherlands. In Switzerland, Poinsett found a war under way and joined the army of Swiss patriot Aloys Reding, fighting against pro-French forces. He participated in a short military campaign before Reding's defeat.

In 1806, after returning briefly to the United States, Poinsett set sail again for Europe, this time determined to visit Russia. He reached St. Petersburg, the capital, by way of Sweden and Finland. There was no American diplomatic representative in Russia, but there was a consul, Levett Harris, who arranged for him to meet Czar Alexander I. Poinsett made a strong impression on the czar and became a favorite at the court. Alexander offered him a position in Russia's army or civil service, but Poinsett declined, writing that "the prospect is a brilliant one but somehow I cannot reconcile it to my sense of duty to abandon my country."[1] Alexander then asked Poinsett if he would visit distant parts of the Russian Empire and bring back an account of the conditions he found. Poinsett readily agreed.

Poinsett departed St. Petersburg for Moscow in early 1807, then traveled down the Volga and overland to the Caucasus, escorted by several Russian officials and three hundred Cossack soldiers, who inspired terror wherever they went. He visited Baku, "a gloomy desert" regarded with superstition as the "land of eternal fire," because of its large petroleum deposits.[2] In Armenia, he witnessed an unsuccessful Russian siege of the city of Yerevan. None of the local leaders Poinsett met had ever heard of the United States; one asked after the health of the "King of America." The return journey overland to St. Petersburg was so arduous that only three of the nine officials who originally set off survived the trip.

Throughout these early travels, as well as in later years, Poinsett was a keen observer of politics, society, and nature. He was a prolific correspondent who left detailed descriptions of the conditions he met and the countryside through which he traveled. Poinsett's experiences in Europe, and particularly in Russia, convinced him of the benefits of American democracy and solidified him as an ardent nationalist.

Poinsett returned to Paris in 1808, where he found that tensions between the United States and Great Britain were running high. He expected war and headed home in hope of being appointed as an officer in the army.

Poinsett's reputation preceded him to Washington. The Russian minister to the United States—presumably at the czar's request—had suggested that the State Department name Poinsett as its minister to Russia. That assignment, however, went to John Quincy Adams. Instead, as President Madison cast about for possible envoys to Spanish America, the well-traveled and well-spoken Poinsett appeared to be a good candidate. Madison offered him the position of agent to Buenos Aires, Chile, and Peru. Poinsett accepted but with some reluctance; he would have preferred an army post and still hoped to return and join the army if war broke out.

Since Spanish America was not yet independent, and since Spanish authorities would not accept the appointment of U.S. consuls in their colonies, Poinsett would use the title "agent for seamen and commerce." State Department records, however, list him as "special diplomatic agent," a title more in keeping with his real duties and responsibilities, which included negotiating treaties of friendship and commerce with the new juntas.[3] His instructions from Secretary of State Robert Smith said:

> You have been selected to proceed, without delay, to Buenos Ayres. You will make it your object, wherever it may be proper, to diffuse the impression that the United States cherish the sincerest good will towards the people of Spanish America . . . whatever may be their internal system or European relation, with respect to which no interference of any sort is pretended: and that, in the event of a political separation from the parent country, and of the establishment of an independent system of National Government, it will coincide with the sentiments and policy of the United States to promote the most friendly relations.[4]

In addition, Poinsett was instructed to report on conditions in each area, including their population, wealth, military resources, and finances. A separate letter from Smith reminded him of the "neutral character" of the United States. Finally Smith noted that "secrecy as far as possible is desirable," since the Spanish authorities might not approve of his appointment and the British might also cause trouble if they learned of his planned arrival.[5] As a practical matter, Poinsett was given all the duties of both a minister and a consul—representing the United States, negotiating, reporting, and protecting American citizens and interests.

After Buenos Aires, Poinsett was to go on to Santiago and, if possible, to Lima. His instructions made clear that he was commissioned to serve not only in Buenos Aires but also in "such other ports as shall be nearer to it than to any other agent of the United States."[6] Thus a single American was to represent the United States in a territory that covered half of South America and that today includes seven countries. And this in an era when a journey between South American cities could take weeks or months.

On October 15, 1810, four months after his instruction to "proceed without delay," Poinsett sailed from New York, bound for Rio de Janeiro. Four months would not have been regarded as an unreasonable period to make arrangements for so long and difficult an assignment, especially since he could not expect to see the United States again for years. The journey to Rio took seventy days. Poinsett recorded in his journal that since "there was neither sextant, nor chronometer on board, to ascertain correctly the longitude," the captain often didn't know where they were and had trouble finding the port. When they did arrive, Poinsett was awed by the beauty of the setting, describing it as "one of the finest basins in the world."[7] The city itself, however, was less impressive. He was particularly distressed by the condition of the slaves, which must have been bad indeed to shock a South Carolinian. Poinsett wrote:

> The streets swarm with blacks, who from neglect are a prey to all the diseases of a tropical climate, leprosy, saran and elephantiasis are common disorders among them, and the miserable wretches, when they first come out of the depot where they are kept and sold . . . present a most revolting spectacle of itch, smallpox and swelled limbs. The treatment of these unfortunate people, throughout the Brazils, is inconceivably barbarous, and constantly intrudes itself upon the stranger, whose compassion and indignation are alternately excited at every step.[8]

In Rio, Poinsett met Thomas Sumter, a fellow South Carolinian serving as U.S. minister to the Portuguese court, which was then living in exile in Brazil, to escape Napoleon. He learned from Sumter that Buenos Aires was under blockade by the junta in Montevideo, with only British ships allowed through. He therefore took passage on a British ship, planning to pass as an Englishman if he encountered difficulties with the blockade.[9]

It took twenty-five days to sail to the Rio de la Plata, the river of Buenos Aires. To help future travelers, Poinsett recorded detailed instructions on how to navigate the river's strong and dangerous currents. To his relief, the blockading squadron was not on duty, and his ship sailed freely into port. His first view of Buenos Aires, however, was depressing: "On approaching the shore the town presents a melancholy appearance. I saw only a long line of low irregular built houses, and in the centre, an old fort of four bastions."[10]

The political situation in Buenos Aires was in turmoil when Poinsett arrived, rocked by instability, internal dissention, fighting, and changing viceroys and juntas. The various provinces of Rio de la Plata were intermittently at war with each other, hence Montevideo's blockade of Buenos Aires. The current Buenos Aires junta under Manuel Belgrano was also under attack from royalist forces from Peru, as well as under threat from the Portuguese in Brazil, who saw the instability as an opportunity for expansion. The confusion was hardly promising for a successful American mission.

Poinsett's prospects were further complicated by the British, whose stature was on the rise in Spanish America because they were supporting the Spanish juntas fighting Napoleon. Buenos Aires had become attached to the cheap British consumer goods available since colonial trade barriers had come down. The British, for their part, wanted to ensure that the colonies remained hostile to Joseph Bonaparte. The British were deeply suspicious of American intentions and regarded all American agents in South America as tools of the French.[11] They soon came to regard Poinsett as the "most suspicious character" in Spanish America.[12]

In contrast to the British, the United States was officially neutral in the European war and had not recognized either the Spanish insurgents or Joseph Bonaparte. This neutrality led many of the South American juntas to mistrust the Americans. Worse, while Poinsett was en route to Buenos Aires, the United States seized west Florida from Spain, heightening suspicions about American intentions.

On Poinsett's first day in Buenos Aires, February 13, 1811, he called on the junta, unannounced, and pressed its members immediately to negotiate a treaty of amity and commerce. They were pleased to receive an American envoy but disappointed that he was only an "agent," rather than a minister or a consul, which would have signified a greater level of recognition.[13] The first meeting apparently went well, for the same day the junta addressed a letter to President Madison acknowledging that "Don Josef R Poinsetts" had been accepted as an agent and that the junta looked forward to a treaty.[14]

Poinsett achieved another success when the junta agreed—over the objections of British merchants—that U.S. traders would henceforth receive the same treatment as the British. This agreement alone fulfilled a major element of Poinsett's instructions, although its immediate effect was limited by the intermittent blockade of Buenos Aires by Montevideo.

The people of Buenos Aires also welcomed Poinsett: "As soon as it was generally known that a stranger had arrived from the United States, with an intention to reside in Buenos Ayres, all the Creoles [people of Spanish descent but born in the colonies] of distinction called upon me, invited me to their houses and treated me with great politeness and attention."[15] He found lodging at the home of a prominent Creole.

Poinsett reported in great detail on the structure of the junta, its history, and its personalities. He assessed that the common people were not much involved in politics; very few had ever voted, and no more than two hundred or so attended the town meetings that often installed new governments. He provided candid assessments of government luminaries (e.g., "a useful and good friend of the Americans" or "a pompous, ignorant man obsequious to all parties and useful to none").[16] He found the administration of justice to be "very relaxed in Buenos Ayres, and crimes of the blackest dye were committed with impunity. Assassination was common, and bodies were exposed every morning before the Cabildo in order to be recognized by their friends."[17]

A subject of particular interest to Poinsett was whether the junta would declare its independence from Spain, which he favored and regarded as inevitable, reporting early in his stay: "All South America will be separated from the Parent country. They have passed the Rubicon."[18] He asked the State Department for urgent instructions on what position to take if Buenos Aires should declare independence and suggested that the United States encourage the formation of a union of independent Spanish American provinces to balance the power of Brazil. The new secretary of state, James Monroe, responded that "the disposition shewn by most of the Spanish provinces to separate from Europe and to erect themselves into independent States excites great interest here," but "the destiny of those provinces must depend on themselves. Should such a revolution however take place, it cannot be doubted that our relation with them will be more intimate, and our friendship stronger than it can be while they are colonies of any European power."[19]

Monroe expressed deep appreciation for Poinsett's reporting. President Madison, he said, had decided to upgrade Poinsett from "agent" to consul general for Buenos Aires, Chile, and Peru. His increased stature pleased the junta but stoked British suspicions of American intentions. The British naval commander for Rio de la Plata reported that some U.S. citizens "have been very busy in the politics of these people. . . . Many of these gentlemen, and particularly a Mr. Poinsett, who is styled Consul-General of the United States . . . are particularly diligent and active in propagating doctrines and opinions prejudicial to the British government and subjects."[20]

Beyond his official duties, Poinsett took an interest in every aspect of life in Buenos Aires and the surrounding provinces. His reports and journals provide the most extensive American account of conditions there at the time. He described the climate as healthy and temperate. The people, he wrote, are divided into three castes—

the Creoles, the Indians, and the Negroes, with very few people of mixed blood. The Indians were darker and heavier than those in the United States. All slaves had recently been freed "without any serious injury to society."[21] The Creoles were generally well informed and industrious. Conditions for the common people were generally good. The population was much given to dice, cards, and dancing. The women were animated and intelligent. The higher-class women wore French fashions, while ordinary folk wore the "gayest colours. . . . The cloak worn universally by the common people is called Poncho and consists of a piece of cloth two yards long and one and three-quarters wide with a hole in the centre large enough to admit the head," providing good protection from the weather.[22]

Agriculture, Poinsett found, was in a sad state, despite the rich soil. Farmers still used crude wooden ploughs and primitive oxcarts. The region was teeming with wildlife: "Tigers and Leopards abound in the jungles on the banks of the River. They are caught in traps, or shot, and their skins form a considerable article of commerce."[23] He described the sloth, a profusion of monkeys and birds, and ostriches that could outrun a horse. He was much interested in the local flora, describing the abundance of peach orchards and wild artichokes.

At carnival time Poinsett found himself as the guest of honor at a bullfight. He was fascinated with the spectacle but disgusted by the extended torment of the bulls. The matador "gave me to understand, that he would kill the bull in my honor, a custom which gives the Spaniards an opportunity of displaying their ostentation by throwing a handful of money to the matador. . . . I conformed to the custom." Poinsett assessed that "the frequent exhibition of this sanguinary spectacle familiarizes the people to scenes of blood and tends to augment the ferocious character of the lower orders."[24]

Buenos Aires was a bustling city of forty thousand, about the size of Baltimore, the third largest U.S. city at the time (after New York and Philadelphia). The city extended for three miles along the banks of the Rio de la Plata. "The houses are generally two stories high, and are built with terrace roofs. The city is defended by a fort, and is ornamented by convents, nunneries, [and] churches."[25] In front of the fort was a large and handsome square. The streets were generally unpaved, developing huge potholes in winter that made them almost impassable. Because of the scarcity of stone and wood, Poinsett wrote, they use bones and the carcasses of animals to fill up the holes, "the effect of which may easily be imagined."[26]

By late 1811 Poinsett felt that he had accomplished most of what he could in Buenos Aires. The commercial agreement was in place. He had made American views well known to the junta and reported extensively on local conditions. Buenos Aires and Montevideo had worked out their differences and, at least for the moment, were again at peace. The likelihood of independence, he judged, had receded. He was correct; it would be five more years before Buenos Aires declared its independence.

In October Poinsett got word that a revolution was brewing in neighboring Chile. Since this was also in his area of responsibility, he decided it was time to visit Santiago.

To reach Chile from Buenos Aires required either a dangerous sea voyage around Cape Horn or an arduous trek over the plains and the high Andes. Poinsett's friends in Buenos Aires advised him to go by sea, but he chose the land route so he could see more of the country. As testimony of the good relations he had established in Buenos Aires, the junta sent a team of dragoons to accompany him as far as the border, hundreds of miles away. Since supplies would be scarce along the way, he carried enough bread, salt, and wine for a month long journey. To transport this, he purchased a large and awkward Spanish coach and hired four drivers.

He set out in November, springtime in the Southern Hemisphere, traveling west across the vast pampas, which reminded him of the steppes of Russia. Within just twenty-five miles of Buenos Aires, he wrote, "The eye looks in vain for an object to rest on. Level and unbroken, the plains form, like the sea, a perfect horizon, and when the grass is parched by the excessive heat of the summer, presents a most gloomy and desolate appearance."[27]

Still, he found much to interest him. There were enormous herds of cattle, tended by skilled horsemen. Poinsett described with admiration the lasso, "which every Peasant carries fastened to his saddle girth," and the bolo, "which they whirl and throw so as to entangle the legs of the animal as it runs."[28] The cattle were raised for hides and tallow; most of the beef was left in the fields to rot or be eaten by scavengers. Because wood was so scarce, hides were used to build houses, furniture, and even boats; leather thongs were used in construction instead of nails. The rest houses along his route were huts made of hides with earthen floors and were crawling with "an insect called the *benchuca*, very little larger than a bed bug but much more troublesome."[29] Because of these tiny terrors and the appalling condition of the huts, Poinsett slept most nights in his carriage.

After five weeks of bumping across the empty pampas—some 750 miles—Poinsett reached Mendoza, at the foot of the Andes. Here he had to abandon his carriage and hire muleteers and ten mules to carry him across the treacherous high passes. The landscape changed dramatically with the passes covered in snow even in midsummer. After weeks in the blazing heat of the pampas, he now suffered from the icy cold. He was fascinated by the wild llamas; he shot one, "which yielded us all a sumptuous repast."[30] The paths were so narrow and precipitous that it seemed almost impossible for men or mules to keep from tumbling off the sheer cliffs. As Poinsett made his way along the precarious ledges, one of the muleteers happily regaled him with countless stories of unlucky travelers and mules who lost their footing and plunged to their deaths far below.

On December 29, 1811, Poinsett finally rode into Santiago.

Chile, like Buenos Aires, was in a state of political upheaval with repeated changes of government. Although each new junta proclaimed its allegiance to Ferdinand VII, there was also growing sentiment for independence. The current leader was José Miguel Carrera, a young Chilean recently returned from the Spanish wars against Napoleon, who favored independence. His stern rule, however, prompted a split with another prominent leader, Bernardo O'Higgins. The rift among the Chilean republicans opened the way for an invasion of Chile by royalist armies based in Peru.

Poinsett soon met with Carrera, and the two men established an instant bond. The Chilean leader, just twenty-six, was six years younger than Poinsett, whom he soon came to regard as a mentor and a valued advisor. Poinsett was the first foreign official of any country accredited to Chile. Carrera made a grand occasion of the official accreditation, hosting an elaborate ceremony on February 24.

Through his close ties with Carrera, Poinsett found himself at the center of fast breaking developments. He actively encouraged the idea of independence. At the junta's request, he provided introductions to arms dealers in the United States. He advised the junta on organizing a police force and establishing a bank. Always interested in agriculture, he suggested introducing the cultivation of cotton and tobacco, which he thought would thrive in Chile's climate. When the junta designed a new Chilean flag—three horizontal stripes of blue, white and yellow—he arranged with Carrera for it to be flown for the first time at his residence during a Fourth of July party he hosted for three hundred of Santiago's leading citizens.

Soon afterwards, the junta named Poinsett to a small commission charged with drafting a constitution for Chile. The meetings were held at Poinsett's house, and a draft was completed by October. During the same months, Poinsett negotiated a reconciliation between Carrera and his brother, solidifying the stability of the junta.

These activities were making Poinsett a significant figure in the Chilean revolution. He reported regularly to Washington on political events in Chile—an assassination attempt against Carrera, developments within the junta, the struggle between the junta and the pro-royalist Catholic Church—but he did not make clear the extent of his own involvement in politics.[31] At the same time, he was increasingly distressed that he had no further guidance from Washington. In August 1812 he wrote to a friend in Charleston that he had not received instructions from the State Department in more than a year.[32] And, for all his influence with the Chileans, he was frustrated that they had not yet declared independence: "Their timidity vexes me."[33]

Although Washington was silent, Poinsett's role did not go unnoticed by other governments. The viceroy of Peru, who was still a strong royalist, complained to the Chilean junta that Poinsett was really "a French spy under the specious title of Consul General from the United States."[34] British naval captain Peter Heywood, who had previously complained of Poinsett's behavior in Buenos Aires, grumbled that "again Mr. Poinsett is busy in contaminating the whole population on that side of the continent."[35]

In June 1812 the United States declared war on Great Britain. Many months passed, however, before the news reached Chile. Definitive word came only in March 1813, when the USS *Essex* arrived at the Chilean port of Valparaíso on a mission to harass British ships in the Pacific. The ship's captain was David Porter, who had been first lieutenant aboard the USS *Philadelphia* ten years earlier when the ship ran aground in Tripoli Harbor and who was among the captives freed by Tobias Lear's peace treaty of 1805.

Porter immediately sent word of his arrival to the American consul general. Poinsett hurried from Santiago to Valparaíso. He boarded the *Essex* to a salute of eleven guns, joined by a party of Valparaíso's leading citizens. At that point, a sail appeared in the distance. Assuming it was British, the guests were rushed ashore. Poinsett, however, was determined to participate in the battle and stayed aboard. The decks were cleared for action, but when the approaching ship pulled into full view, it turned out to be a friendly Portuguese merchantman. Some days later the *Essex* departed to continue its mission; it would not return for almost a year. On its departure, Captain Porter wrote that Poinsett was going with Carrera to Concepción, Chile's second largest city, "with the view of fortifying and making the place more secure against foreign invasion."[36] Porter, for one, did not think it strange that an American consul general would be involved in Chile's war preparations.

The invasion was not long in coming. The royalist viceroy of Peru landed troops in southern Chile, occupying Talcahuano, the port of Concepción. The viceroy also commissioned privateers to capture any ships calling at ports controlled by the junta. At least half a dozen American whalers were among the many ships seized and taken to Talcahuano. The invasion prompted the squabbling Chilean factions to put their differences aside, at least temporarily. Carrera's rival, Bernardo O'Higgins, joined the effort to repulse the royalists.

Carrera marched south to meet the enemy. With him went Joel

Poinsett. At first Poinsett served as an adviser, working to improve discipline and logistics among the Chilean forces. Soon, however, Carrera appointed him a general in the Chilean army and put him in command of a division. Poinsett led a cavalry charge in the battle of San Carlos, winning a victory for the Chileans.[37]

Shortly thereafter, Poinsett learned through an intercepted letter about the captured American ships held in Talcahuano. The letter ominously reported to the viceroy that the crews would be sent to Peru as prisoners as soon as a "set of irons could be completed for the purpose of securing the men."[38] Poinsett immediately set out for Talcahuano at the head of a battery of artillery. Arriving after dark, he placed his guns in a commanding position on the hills overlooking the port. The town capitulated to him the following day. The grateful American seamen were astonished to learn that none other than the American consul general had liberated them.

Although the documentary record is not entirely clear, it seems that Poinsett served actively with the Chilean army from May through September of 1813. At the time, the United States was officially neutral in the conflicts between Spain and its colonies. Poinsett rationalized that the viceroy became an enemy of the United States when he seized American ships. Since Poinsett had been without any word at all from the State Department for eighteen months, and it was impossible to seek guidance, he was forced to rely on his own judgment in difficult and fast-moving circumstances. Still, he must have known that his actions went far beyond the proper role of a diplomat. During the period of Poinsett's military service, the fortunes of the republicans generally ran high, and the province of Concepción was retaken from the Peruvian royalists. Within months, the tide would turn.

Back in Santiago, Poinsett resumed his normal routine, to the extent that his activities can be considered either normal or routine. As always during his travels, he compiled detailed descriptions of places, people, customs, history, government, agriculture, and wildlife. Poinsett found the Chileans generally less sophisticated than the people of the Rio de la Plata, which he attributed to their isolation and lack of contact with foreigners. They are, he wrote, "more under the influence of the clergy and more ignorant and superstitious" than the people of Buenos Aires.[39] The Creoles of Santiago rose very early, dined at one, then retired for siestas until five. Supper was at midnight, after which the people retired immediately to bed. Shops closed between noon and six. Dinners usually consisted of several courses of "very good cookery." It was the custom for people to meet at each other's homes in the evenings to play cards and dance. At these functions, "the ladies dress with a great deal of taste and vie with each other in magnificence and in expensive dresses, which they never appear in a second time." "They dance to the music of the guitar" in a manner that is "indefatigable and sometimes indecent." On summer evenings, people promenaded in the streets in fine clothes.[40]

Chile was a beautiful country of high mountains and lush valleys. "The abundance of water and peculiarity of climate enable them to raise all the fruits of the earth in great perfection," Poinsett wrote. The fields produced wheat, corn, hemp, flax, and olives. Unlike Buenos Aires, wood was abundant. The mineral wealth was astounding. Although the gold mines had been abandoned, copper was still produced, and the silver mines were "the richest ever known."[41]

Santiago, unlike Buenos Aires, had well paved streets and sidewalks made of flagstones. Because of frequent earthquakes, the houses were generally just one story but were nicely laid out around courtyards. Small canals brought fresh water to every house, while sewers along every street carried off the filth. The principal square was flanked by the cathedral, "a large heavy building," and the Government House. The nicest building in the city, to Poinsett's eye, was the mint.[42] From the main square a wide street led to an impressive bridge over the river Mapocho, "which is built of stone and brick, and stands on nine lofty arches. The view from it along the banks of the Mapocho, and toward the Andes is very picturesque, and the inhabitants resort to this bridge in the summer afternoons, to enjoy the refreshing air from the mountains."[43]

Santiago also boasted a university "with ten professorships," two colleges, a gaudily painted College of Jesuits, a customs house, courthouses, several handsome churches, and "seven nunneries and seven convents of monks." A large road, "like the boulevards in Paris," extended around the south side of the city, separating it from the extensive and well-built suburbs. Tropical diseases were still endemic; during Poinsett's residence, a sickness "similar to typhus" carried off hundreds.[44]

By late 1813 the junta's fortunes had changed for the worse. Royalist forces were again advancing. As the military tide turned against the junta, Carrera was imprisoned and his rival, Bernardo O'Higgins, took charge of Chilean forces. Since Poinsett was so closely associated with Carrera, his stature also fell. These events, together with Poinsett's longing to join in the U.S. war against Great Britain, led him to decide to return home. This was easier said than done, since there was no regular shipping between Chile and the United States, and the British fleet patrolled both Pacific and Atlantic shipping lanes.

Poinsett's opportunity to return to the United States came in January 1814 with the return of the uss Essex to Chile. Before the Essex could depart Valparaíso, however, two British warships appeared outside the port, blocking its departure. Captain Porter chose to stay in the neutral port rather than confront the more powerful British force. Weeks passed as the warships warily watched each other. Poinsett won a promise from Chileans to turn the guns of the fort on the British if they should attack Essex while it remained in the neutral port.[45] Finally, in late March, the Essex, with Poinsett aboard, tried to slip out of the harbor. Although it had a good start on its British pursuers, the winds suddenly changed and a squall broke the Essex's mainmast. As the British closed in, Poinsett rowed ashore to try to persuade the fort's commander to fire on the British if they attacked, since although the Essex had left port, it was still within Chilean neutral waters. The Chileans refused. Valparaíso's citizens gathered on shore to watch the bloody attack on the disabled American frigate. After two and a half hours and more than fifty broadsides, almost one hundred American crewmen were dead or wounded. With the Essex about to sink, Captain Porter struck his flag and surrendered.

The British allowed Porter and his remaining crew to return to the United States aboard a small unarmed ship but refused to let Poinsett accompany them. The victory over the *Essex* greatly strengthened British stature in Chile. In April, under strong British pressure, the new Chilean junta asked Poinsett to leave the country, as he was in any case trying to do. With the sea-lanes blocked, on April 28 he began the long overland journey back to Buenos Aires. Before his departure, he received assurances from the junta that Chilean ports would remain open to American commerce.[46]

The revolution in Chile took more twists and turns after his departure. In May, after continuing military reverses, the republicans reluctantly signed a treaty acknowledging their allegiance to Spain. In return, the royalist forces declared an amnesty and agreed to leave Chile. Carrera, who had been excluded from the amnesty, escaped from prison and capitalized on public discontent with the treaty to seize power once again in Santiago. O'Higgins, who supported the treaty, marched against him. Their armies met at Maipy, where Carrera's forces were victorious. Carrera dispatched a letter to Poinsett, who by this time was back in Buenos Aries, thanking him for his services to Chile and concluding, "It will be a happy day for us, when your excellency shall decide to return to the country, which will never blot from its memory the obligations that it owes to you."[47]

Poinsett's last official dispatches on developments in Chile, written from Buenos Aires, were discouraging. The viceroy had invaded again, and the royalists were back in power. Both Carrera and O'Higgins had escaped over the Andes. The revolution, Poinsett reported, had been undermined by the sharp divisions and infighting among the republicans. Eventually, he believed, the revolution would lead to independence from Spain, but it might also result in military despotism. He was right on both counts.

As for developments in Buenos Aires, Poinsett reported that the government was now in the hands of a "Supreme Director" who was trying to win control over all the provinces of the Rio de la Plata. The government had sent envoys to assure Spain of its allegiance, but insisted on the right to choose its own leaders and to maintain its own army. A declaration of independence appeared unlikely. British influence had grown even stronger during his years in Chile. Poinsett did find time in Buenos Aires to conclude a new commercial agreement with the government, which allowed most U.S. goods to enter entirely free of duty. He ended his dispatch to Secretary of State Monroe with the comment that he was planning to return to the United States because he had received no instructions for two years![48]

Since the war between the United States and Great Britain was still disrupting shipping, Poinsett slipped out of Buenos Aries on a small boat under cover of darkness and took passage on a Portuguese ship to Brazil. It was May 1815 by the time he reached Charleston. He had been away for four and a half years. While he was en route home, the United States and Great Britain concluded the Treaty of Ghent, ending the War of 1812. Secretary of State Monroe—unaware of the extent to which Poinsett had become involved in local politics—wrote to thank him for his ability and zeal in discharging his duty, telling him that his work had "obtained the approbation" of President Madison.[49]

Back in the United States, Poinsett retained his interest, and to some extent his involvement, in South American affairs. He was now regarded as an expert on the subject, and the State Department continued to seek his advice. He warned that many republican leaders in South America had their own interests at heart rather than those of their countries. Because of endemic instability, he advised against U.S. recognition of any government that wasn't fully in control of its territory or of any government that didn't treat the United States on equal terms with Great Britain.

On July 9, 1816, the Congress in Buenos Aires finally declared its independence as the "United Provinces of South America" (more often called the United Provinces of Rio de la Plata). The same year, José Miguel Carrera, still exiled from Chile, came to the United States seeking arms and support for an expedition against the royalists who were in power in Santiago. Poinsett gave him introductions to President Madison and to Capt. David Porter, who was then stationed at naval headquarters in Washington. He also introduced Carrera to John Jacob Astor, who he hoped might provide financial backing. By late in the year, Carrera had gathered a band of supporters and sailed for South America. Their efforts ended in failure. He and Poinsett never saw each other again. In 1817 José de San Martin and Bernardo O'Higgins—without Carrera—led an army over the Andes and defeated the royalists. Chile finally declared its independence a year later. Carrera continued his quest to return to power. In 1821 he planned another invasion of Chile but was captured and executed on the orders of O'Higgins.

U.S. recognition of the South American republics was delayed for several more years, largely because it was still negotiating with Spain over the acquisition of Florida and thought recognition might scuttle the negotiations. Once the Florida treaty was signed in 1819, recognition of the republics soon followed. One stipulation of the Florida treaty is particularly important at a later stage in this story: an agreement that the new boundary between the United States and the Spanish territories in North America would be the Sabine River. The United States agreed that all the land west of the Sabine—that is, Texas—would belong to Spain.

Poinsett's life began to focus for the first time on domestic affairs. He served two terms in South Carolina's state legislature. In 1821 he was elected to Congress, winning by just forty-two votes in a nasty election campaign in which he was accused of deserting his post in South America. Because of his foreign experience, he was named to the House Foreign Affairs Committee.

Poinsett also joined the Masonic Lodge, an organization that would play an important part in his future foreign undertakings. By 1821 he was already Grand High Priest of the Grand Chapter of South Carolina.[50]

In 1822, while Poinsett was still a congressman, President Monroe offered him another diplomatic assignment, an exploratory mission to Mexico. Monroe, reporting to Congress in the spring of 1822 on the situation in Latin America, noted that in regard to "Mexico our information is less authentic, but it is, nevertheless, distinctly understood that the new Government has declared its independence, and that there is now no opposition to it there."[51] On this basis, the Congress adopted an act recognizing Mexican independence. Conditions there were still in turmoil, however, and little was known in Washington about the leadership or the political situation. This lack of information was the reason for Poinsett's mission, an early version of today's fact-finding mission. It was to be what was then considered a quick trip—four or five months— with transportation provided by the navy.

In some ways, political developments in Mexico paralleled those in the rest of Spanish America. When Napoleon occupied Madrid and put his brother Joseph Bonaparte on the throne of Spain, Mexico's loyalties remained firmly with Ferdinand VII and the old regime. A pro-Ferdinand junta was established under the viceroy in Mexico City. Secret political societies were formed, and revolutionary fervor began to spread.

In 1810 politics took a different turn when Miguel Hidalgo, a previously unknown Creole priest from the countryside, began a revolutionary movement aimed at independence and social reform. Hidalgo, who is now widely regarded as the father of Mexican independence, inspired tens of thousands of followers who formed a popular army and marched toward Mexico City. This movement contrasted starkly with those in other parts of South America, where the revolutions were in the hands of the leading families and the upper class. Hidalgo's army won several victories before being crushed by the viceroy's far smaller but more disciplined troops. Hidalgo and his key followers were executed, and their heads were hung in a city square, where they remained for years as a gruesome warning to others who might seek to upset the established social order.

Although the Hidalgo revolution was short-lived, it spawned a number of successor movements that kept Mexico in tumult for decades. A series of viceroys and revolutionary leaders were established and overthrown. It was not until 1820 that the divided factions in Mexico—still generally known at the time as "New Spain"— united behind independence. The impetus was a new government in Spain that began to take anticlerical measures. The Catholic

Church was still one of the strongest institutions in Mexico; when its leaders threw their backing to independence, the stage was set. Prominent royalist and rebel leaders set aside their differences and effected a bloodless change of power. A royalist military commander, Augustín de Iturbide, took the reins of power in a newly independent Mexico in September 1821.

This was the situation in Mexico City when Poinsett was enlisted for his mission. A few months later on July 21, 1822, Iturbide was proclaimed Emperor Augustín I, but this was not yet known in Washington when Poinsett departed.

On August 28, 1822, to the sound of pipes playing and drums beating, Poinsett set sail from Charleston aboard the *John Adams*, a U.S. Navy frigate that twenty years earlier had participated in the blockade of Tripoli. The moment brought home to Poinsett his love of travel and adventure: "To me this has ever been a moment of delightful excitement. I have frequently stood on the deck of a gallant ship, when the anchor was weighing and the topsails sheeting home, and always with strong feelings of hopes and exultation, whether as at present, bound on a voyage to visit and explore new countries, or returning to my native land."[52]

A few weeks later he arrived at the port of Vera Cruz where he found a strange situation and his first indication of how unsettled the political situation remained. The city was in the hands of the new government, but the castle overlooking the town and its harbor was still occupied by royalists. There was an uneasy truce between the two forces, each of which separately collected customs duties from all ships arriving in port. As a result, trade was in shambles.

Poinsett called on the governor, a young military officer named Antonio de Padua María Severino López de Santa Anna y Pérez de Lebrón. Santa Anna, as he was known, would dominate Mexican politics over the next three decades, serving as president eleven times. Poinsett described him as "a young man, who at the head of the desultory forces of the country, succeeded in driving the Royalists out of the city [Vera Cruz]. . . . About 30 years of age, of middle stature, slightly yet well made, and possessing a very intelligent and expressive countenance." Santa Anna gave Poinsett a cordial reception and invited him to dinner. He accepted, but halfheartedly, since "a ceremonious Spanish dinner is of all things the most odious to me."[53]

Poinsett didn't linger in Vera Cruz. Santa Anna insisted on providing a military escort of half a dozen cavalrymen, who rode ahead of Poinsett's carriage with scarlet banners flying from their lances. "I was forced to submit . . . to the annoyance of being escorted," Poinsett wrote, "against which I remonstrated in vain. All parties unite in presenting the roads to be insecure. . . . I confess, however, that I am much more afraid of the climate: not only are black vomit and bilious fevers undignified dangers, but I would rather fall into the hands of banditti than into those of a Mexican physician."[54]

Poinsett, always the strong republican, was suspicious from the start of Emperor Agustín. Everyone he met in Vera Cruz tried to convince him that Iturbide's coronation as emperor was a truly popular movement. Poinsett couldn't believe it. His initial impression, he wrote, was that "from his actions he must be an extraordinary man; but . . . from his sudden elevation to the throne, I fear he is extraordinarily bad."[55]

The overland journey from Vera Cruz to Mexico City was one that few Americans had attempted. For most Americans, Mexico was still a mysterious place. Poinsett found it a country of contrasts: natural beauty and desolation, great wealth and desperate poverty, revolutionary pretensions and imperialist government.

Even for a seasoned traveler like Poinsett, the journey was a difficult one. "It is impossible, without experience," he wrote, "to form an idea of the torments of the crawling, skipping and flying insects of this country."[56] The heat was so intense that he often had to travel by night. The roads were bad. The accommodations were worse. His traveling party was slow and lazy. One of his muleteers mishandled the guns in his baggage and wounded both a bystander and a horse; the muleteer swore that the gun was discharged by the devil.

On the other hand, Poinsett was impressed with the infrastructure, particularly the bridges across every river and stream, in contrast to the United States, where it was still common to ford rivers.

The food was plentiful and good. There was chocolate to drink each morning. The fields were fertile and planted with corn that grew as high as in Indiana or Kentucky. The exotic flora was magnificent. The scenery varied from barren plains ("nothing can be more ruinous and gloomy") to rich fields ("nothing can exceed the beauty and fertility of the country") to high mountains and snow-capped volcanoes.[57]

He was struck by what he called "an unnecessary number of churches and convents" in every city, but he praised "the equality on which all people worship the Deity in a catholic church. There are no pews nor seats for the rich." All people prayed and worshiped together.[58] He found a striking contrast between the splendor of some cathedrals and the poverty of the people inside, particularly the Indians. Another contrast was between the huge haciendas of the rich and the squalor of the poor. Of one village, he wrote, "I certainly never saw a negro house in Carolina so comfortless. Any master, who, in our country, should lodge his slaves in this manner, would be considered barbarous and inhuman."[59] Everywhere he saw destroyed buildings from the civil wars of the past decade, not yet rebuilt.

Mexico City was also a study in contrasts. The first view, from the hills above the town, was inspiring: "It was a magnificent sight. . . . At a distance, Mexico surpasses in appearance any other city in North America," due in part to "the size and magnificence of the churches, and the number of towers and spires that adorn them."[60] The public squares were spacious and surrounded by attractive buildings. The city had an air of grandeur and solidity "which are wanting in the cities of the United States. With us, however, a stranger does not see that striking and disgusting contrast between the magnificence of the wealthy and the squalid penury of the poor, which constantly meets his view in Mexico."[61] Mexico City's population at the time approached 150,000, larger than any U.S. city.

Poinsett took advantage of his short stay to explore many of the city's wonders, regretting that he did not have more time. He visited the cathedral, the mint, the university, churches, a cigar factory, the academy of fine arts, and the botanic garden. He found the markets well stocked with fruit and vegetables. Water was distributed to the houses by men who carried it in jars on their back, supported by a band across the forehead. The shops resembled the bazaars of the Middle East. The streets were crowded with homeless people and beggars. He was advised not to go out in the evenings unless armed with a saber because of the danger of robbery, although Mexico's streets were better lighted than those of U.S. cities.

An informal caste system continued to operate, with Indians at the bottom, although all Mexicans were now officially equal. Even the poorest people appeared to be literate. When the clock struck noon each day, everyone on the streets would stop whatever they were doing and say a short silent prayer. People were never in a hurry and seemed surprised if an American should complain about delays. Cockfighting was the favorite pastime of the rich and poor alike, although bullfighting was also popular. Even well-heeled women would attend the bullfights and "manifest rather more interest in the torment and death of a bull, than you . . . would think becoming."[62] He was scandalized that most Mexican ladies smoked in public, which he found to be a detestable habit. The women married very young: thirteen was not unusual. It was common for married women to take a lover, he wrote, "and a *liaison* of that nature does not affect the lady's reputation."[63]

Poinsett reported on the production of tobacco, cotton, vanilla, and other crops ("the quantity of red pepper raised in all parts of the country is almost incredible"), as well as gold and manufactured goods.[64] The production of silver was remarkable, with private individuals using silver plates and serving pieces far more commonly than in the United States. He recorded details on trade and tariffs, commenting that Mexico would not be a good market for manufactured goods for many years, due to poverty, transportation difficulties, and trade restrictions. He concluded that the overall economic situation was poor, largely because of the disruptions caused by the revolution. He wrote extensive descriptions of local flora and collected seeds to take home with him.

Poinsett's top priority, however, was to collect political information. He called on senior officials and prominent personalities. He found that many were reluctant to talk about politics, and others could not be trusted to offer an honest opinion. As he learned about developments, he was increasingly dismayed that Mexico had broken its bonds with Spain only to seat its own emperor. Poinsett met with several republicans who were "exceedingly alarmed" that the United States might "send a mission to the imperial court, and by our recognition of an usurper, add moral strength to his cause."[65]

Poinsett had an extremely cordial meeting with Iturbide, Emperor Augustín I, on November 3:

> The emperor was in his cabinet and received us with great politeness. Two of his favourites were with him. We were all seated, and he conversed with us for half an hour in an easy, unembarrassed manner, taking occasion to compliment the United States and our institutions, and to lament that they were not suited to the circumstances of his country. He modestly insinuated that he had yielded very reluctantly to the wishes of the people, but had been compelled to suffer them to place the crown upon his head to prevent misrule and anarchy.[66]

Poinsett was not impressed. The emperor, he discovered, had started his career as a royalist soldier, distinguishing himself as a cruel and bloodthirsty persecutor of republicans, routinely executing prisoners. Although this was not an unusual practice in Mexico's civil wars, Poinsett found it repugnant. Moreover, Poinsett wrote, "In a society not remarkable for strict morals, he was distinguished for his immorality. His usurpation of the chief authority has been the most glaring, and unjustifiable; and his exercise of power arbitrary and tyrannical." His official proclamations and speeches were "absurd." Poinsett predicted that Iturbide would be able to hold on to the throne only as long as he could continue to pay his army.[67]

Iturbide did, however, assist Poinsett on two matters. He agreed to release about twenty Americans who were imprisoned in Mexico on charges of conspiring against the governor of Texas. He also promised to restore funds that had been seized from several U.S. merchants.

With this accomplished, Poinsett hurried to the coast to rendezvous with the *John Adams*. He arrived at Tampico to find a yellow fever epidemic ravaging the city. The *John Adams* had arrived but could not make port because of adverse winds. For two weeks Poinsett waited for the winds to shift, twice having to change lodgings when people died of fever in the houses where he was staying. On December 22 he finally "escaped from a land of pestilence," boarded the ship, and started the journey home.

Back in the United States, Poinsett recommended against sending a permanent envoy to Mexico. He predicted that Iturbide would not remain long on the throne. "By recognizing the Emperor during the present contest we [would] give him an advantage over the republican party. We [would] take part against the majority of the nation."[68]

Soon after Poinsett's departure from Mexico, in fact, Iturbide was forced to abdicate after a reign of just eight months and flee to exile in Italy. But exile could not hold Iturbide. He returned to Mexico in July 1824, hoping to reclaim power. Within days of his arrival, he was captured by government forces and executed by a firing squad.

Poinsett happily reclaimed his seat in the House of Representatives and, once again, put diplomacy aside. His account of his journey, published soon after his return as *Notes on Mexico*, was the most thorough description of the country in English up to that time. The author was listed simply as "a citizen of the United States," perhaps in deference to the official nature of his mission.

Despite the fall of Iturbide and his replacement by a republican regime, it was more than two years before the United States sent its first regular diplomatic envoy to Mexico. The day after John Quincy Adams was inaugurated as president in 1825, he offered Poinsett the position of minister plenipotentiary to Mexico. In many ways Poinsett appeared to be the perfect candidate. He already had extensive diplomatic experience in Latin America, he had recently completed a diplomatic mission to Mexico, his book on Mexico was the most authoritative account of the country available, and he spoke excellent Spanish. At the same time, there were already danger signals about how Poinsett might perform. He was clearly partisan in his views of Mexican politics, and his service in Chile had shown that he could be actively interventionist. Adams apparently did not regard these as drawbacks. At the time, any respectable American envoy would have had strong antiroyalist leanings.

The new secretary of state, Henry Clay, stressed to Poinsett that his appointment was a particularly important one, the first time an American would officially represent the United States in a neighboring independent country. Poinsett was to lay the groundwork for a treaty of friendship and commerce and to win navigation and trading privileges. He was to encourage a peaceful resolution of Mexico's remaining problems with Spain and to discourage any Mexican attempts to seize Spanish Cuba, as it was rumored to want to do. Finally, Poinsett was to bring to the attention of the Mexican government the new U.S. policy opposing any future European colonization of the Americas.[69] This policy, now commonly called the Monroe Doctrine, was included as part of President Monroe's annual message to Congress a year earlier.

Poinsett's appointment as "minister plenipotentiary" gave him the authority to act on behalf of the United States without receiving further specific instructions. He had the power to conclude treaties and agreements, although any treaties would have to be ratified by the Senate before they took effect. Since it took at least five weeks for a letter from Mexico City to reach Washington and another five for the response, Poinsett could not count on guidance from Washington. Moreover, as he had experienced in Chile, his dispatches might never be answered at all. At the time Poinsett left for Mexico, the State Department's domestic personnel totaled just fifteen people, who were responsible not only for communicating with more than one hundred diplomatic and consular posts around the world but also for major domestic duties such as the census. Poinsett knew he would be left largely to his own devices in dealing with the Mexicans.

While Poinsett was the first U.S. diplomatic representative to Mexico, the United States had previously appointed a number of consuls to Mexico to assist Americans and promote trade; some of these were Mexican citizens. Although American consuls in some countries became involved in politics—as was the case with Daniel Clark in New Orleans, William Eaton and James Cathcart in

North Africa, and even Poinsett himself in Chile—this was the exception. The American consuls in Mexico did not take on a political role. The same would not be true of the American minister.

By May 5, 1825, Poinsett was back in Vera Cruz. In the two years since his special mission, the political situation in Mexico had changed. The president was now Guadalupe Victoria, a former antiroyalist rebel leader, who had been elected six months earlier. Much of his government, however, was deeply conservative, including Vice President Nicolás Bravo. Both were suspicious of U.S. intentions. Victoria once commented that Americans were always ready to encroach on Mexican territory. Moreover, although Victoria was once an antiroyalist leader, he now envisaged becoming a monarch himself. Poinsett was soon writing to Clay, "I ought to inform you that President Victoria is not and never will be a friend of the United States."[70]

To Poinsett's great distress, Victoria was also currying favor with the British. British banks and businessmen had begun to make sizable loans to the Mexican government. The British minister, Henry Ward, was well connected and well entrenched in Mexico City. Poinsett bemoaned to Clay that "I have been sent here at least one year too late. . . . I will do my best to recover the lost ground."[71]

Rivalry with the British would become a major theme of Poinsett's tenure, as it was in Buenos Aires and Chile, touching almost every issue he dealt with. Ward proved to be a formidable adversary who was extremely influential with President Victoria and who used every occasion to stoke growing Mexican fears that the United States was an expansionist neighbor and not to be trusted. Poinsett reported that Ward was bribing officials and plotting with "the Countess of Regla, a pretty creole possessed of great shrewdness and exercising great influence over Victoria," to stack his cabinet with pro-British ministers. Ward's strategy worked, and by October 1825 the British had secured overwhelming influence in the cabinet.[72] Poinsett became so irritated with Ward's activities that he wrote the American minister in London asking him to take up the issue with the British foreign minister.

Beyond the rivalry with Henry Ward, Poinsett would deal with three major foreign policy issues during his four and a half years in Mexico: Mexican designs on Cuba, negotiating a commercial treaty, and the question of the U.S.-Mexico border. The first to arise was Cuba. The United States considered a neutral Cuba as vital to its Caribbean trade. Under Spain's weak rule, Cuban ports were open to the United States, and Cuba posed no military threat. The United States feared that Great Britain or France might seize Cuba and was concerned to a lesser extent that Mexico or Colombia might do so. Thus one of Clay's original instructions to Poinsett was to discourage a Mexican invasion.

One of Poinsett's first dispatches to Washington reported that Colombia had asked Mexico to join it in an attack on Cuba. The Mexicans replied that the timing was not good for them. Poinsett judged, however, that Mexico declined because it wanted to seize Cuba for itself, not jointly with Colombia. A few weeks later he reported a warning from the Mexican government that France was assembling a force in Martinique to attack Cuba. In October he wrote that the Mexicans were preparing their own expedition. In February 1826, with the Mexican preparations still moving forward, he raised the issue with President Victoria, who explained that Mexico just wanted to help Cuba win its independence, after which Mexican forces would withdraw. In April Poinsett reported that the Mexicans believed—on the basis of intelligence from their minister in Washington—that the United States had its own territorial designs on Cuba. The Mexicans eventually abandoned the planned expedition, but the issue continued to arise intermittently for the next several years. One of Poinsett's last dispatches from Mexico in 1829 reported renewed Mexican plotting to acquire Cuba.[73]

Poinsett's second issue, a commercial agreement, was important because American traders in Mexico faced constantly changing tariffs and capricious behavior by customs officials. When Poinsett filed complaints, they were met with what he called the Mexican "national love of procrastination."[74] Poinsett began the treaty negotiations soon after his arrival. He had been instructed to obtain most favored nation status for the United States, that is, U.S. trade would be treated no less favorably than that of any of Mexico's other trading partners. This initially proved difficult because Mexico's policy was to grant preferred status to the other Latin American republics. Henry Ward had accepted this and agreed to forego most favored nation status for Great Britain. Only when London repudiated Ward's treaty did the Mexicans back down and agree to most favored nation treatment for both Great Britain and the United States.

The commercial treaty was signed in July 1826. The Mexican Senate, to its credit, refused to ratify, objecting to a clause that required Mexico to return fugitive slaves to the United States. Poinsett negotiated a new treaty in 1828, which was again ratified by the U.S. Senate but turned down by the Mexican Senate. Trade between the United States and Mexico continued, but with constant complications. The absence of a treaty led to capricious treatment and increased smuggling.

The most difficult—indeed, hopeless—of the three key issues facing Poinsett was the question of the boundary between the United States and Mexico. The border problem first arose with the Louisiana Purchase and its vague definitions of exactly how much territory the United States had acquired. This was finally resolved by the Florida treaty of 1819, which set the western border of the United States at the Sabine River, the modern-day boundary between Louisiana and Texas. John Quincy Adams, who was now president, had negotiated that borderline only six years earlier while he was secretary of state. Nonetheless, Poinsett was given instructions to "rectify" the line westward, hopefully all the way to the Rio Grande, which would make the entire Mexican province of Texas part of the United States. When Poinsett raised the issue not long after his arrival, it confirmed to the Mexican government that the United States did indeed have expansionist designs. Mexican foreign minister Alamán replied he would be pleased to discuss rectifying the border and suggested moving it eastward to the Mississippi River. Poinsett realized that continuing to press the issue would only sour relations with Mexico. He quietly let the matter drop.

The Texas question, however, would not go away so easily. Late in 1826 a small group of American settlers in Texas took up arms against Mexico in the short-lived "Fredonian Revolt." The revolt did not win the backing of most American settlers—even Stephen Austin opposed it—and it was quickly quashed. The Mexican authorities, however, believed that the U.S. government might have been behind the uprising. President Adams and Secretary of State Clay chose this unfortunate moment to instruct Poinsett to attempt to purchase Texas. He was to offer $1 million for all of Texas or half that amount for the land between the Sabine and the Colorado River of Texas. This stingy proposal only reinforced Mexican suspicions. Poinsett made the offer but did not press it. He advised Clay that as more American settlers moved into Texas, the Mexicans would find them "difficult to govern, and perhaps after a short period they may not be so averse to part with that portion of their territory as they are at present."[75]

At Mexican insistence, the commercial treaty signed by Poinsett in 1828 included a clause confirming the Sabine as the boundary. The U.S. Senate duly ratified the treaty, although Mexico did not. Still, when Andrew Jackson became president the next year, Poinsett was again instructed to try to purchase Texas, this time for $5 million.[76] Poinsett advised the new secretary of state, Martin Van Buren, that "I am still convinced that we can never expect to extend our boundary south of the river Sabine, without quarreling with these people and driving them to court a more strict alliance with some European power."[77] Poinsett, who by then was close to the end of his tenure, chose to leave the instruction for his successor to pursue.

Poinsett's tenure in Mexico is better remembered for his influence on Mexican domestic politics than for foreign policy issues. At the time of his arrival, power was largely in the hands of the "centralists," the conservative successor group of the royalists. Poinsett was more favorably disposed toward the opposition, the successors of the republicans, now known as "federalists." As Poinsett encountered hostility from the centralists at the top levels of government, he became increasingly involved in supporting the opposition.

The initial support took a curious form. Opposition members who had founded local Masonic Lodges asked Poinsett, who was still a prominent Mason, to obtain charters for them from the United States. Poinsett was happy to oblige, although the request had political overtones. Many centralist leaders were already Masons, belonging to the Scottish Rite of Masonry, known in Mexico as the Escosses, or Scottish. Poinsett was a member of the York Rite and obtained York charters for the oppositionists, who became known as Yorkinos. Poinsett helped the Yorkinos establish their own grand lodge, installing it at his home. The Yorkino movement mushroomed, becoming a magnet for opposition sympathizers; soon there were more than eighty Yorkino lodges. Prominent army officers, including Santa Anna, became members.

The Yorkino lodges became a thin cover for opposition activity. Yorkino political influence soon became so strong that it forced a reorganization of the cabinet. President Victoria was sufficiently concerned with Poinsett's growing influence that he visited Poinsett at his home to assure him of the Mexican government's friendship for the United States. The opposition won a decisive victory in the 1826 legislative elections, although Victoria retained executive power.

Poinsett later claimed that he never attended a Masonic meeting in Mexico where politics were discussed, and he stopped attending meetings entirely as soon as the Yorkino movement began to take on political overtones. He admitted in a dispatch to Secretary of State Clay, however, that he helped form an opposition political party, arguing that the alternative would have been to leave British sympathizers in control of Mexico. Moreover, he explained, some of the Yorkinos had planned to launch a new revolution, and he persuaded them to take democratic political action instead.[78] In regard to the British, Poinsett gloated, they "are now as much alarmed as they were formerly confident of their ascendancy. They cannot conceal either their mortification or fears, and Mr. Ward has dispatched a messenger to Mr. Canning [the British foreign minister] with the most exaggerated accounts of my influence. I only wish one half of what he believes were true."[79]

As the power of the Yorkinos increased, the centralists began to issue public criticisms of Poinsett's role. By 1827 the two state legislatures controlled by the centralists—Puebla and Vera Cruz—demanded his recall. They claimed that Poinsett's establishment of the York Rite was "more dangerous and destructive than . . . the landing of twenty battalions of Spanish troops in the country."[80] The term "poinsettismo" was coined, meaning an intrusive style.

Poinsett was clear-headed enough to realize that his usefulness as American representative was coming to an end. He reported home forthrightly on the growing public uproar against him, which he attributed in large part to the efforts of the British and other European agents. He even discussed the problem with President Victoria, who offered to write and assure President Adams that Poinsett had done nothing wrong.[81] Nonetheless, Poinsett informed Washington of his desire to resign. Adams refused to accept the resignation. He either still had faith in Poinsett or, with an American election in the offing, preferred to leave Poinsett in Mexico, where he could not effectively support Adams's rival, Andrew Jackson.

The internal turmoil in Mexico had not yet reached its peak. At the end of 1827, a group of prominent centralists, led by Vice President Bravo, took up arms against the government. Among their demands was the expulsion of Poinsett. Bravo was the head of the Escosses Masons, as well as a political leader of the centralists. The government forces were commanded by Gen. Vicente Guerrero, a former antiroyalist revolutionary, who happened also to be the head of the Yorkino Masons. The two armies met on a battlefield outside Mexico City. Bravo was defeated and fled into exile. Poinsett belittled the Bravo revolt as a "ridiculous attempt to effect a Revolution against the constituted authorities of the Country, and against the will of the people."[82]

A new crisis erupted with the presidential elections of 1828. The centralist candidate was the war minister, Gen. Gómez Pedraza, while the federalists ran the popular Guerrero. Under Mexico's election system, each state cast one vote for president, decided by its legislature. Pedraza, according to Poinsett, used his wealth and the military power at his disposal to bribe and intimidate state legislatures.[83] Pedraza was elected, but before he took office, the federalists revolted. Santa Anna and others marshaled their troops and marched on Mexico City. As federalist forces approached the capital, rioting broke out, with mobs targeting centralists and their supporters. A group of prominent centralists sought refuge in Poinsett's home. As the mob attacked the house, a bullet whizzed through the window and lodged in Poinsett's cloak. He grabbed an American flag and strode onto his balcony to face the mob. When the crowd saw who he was, it moved on to other targets.

Pedraza fled and the Mexican Congress declared Guerrero president. He was inaugurated early in 1829. His administration has been called "perhaps the only Mexican government of the nineteenth century which attempted to benefit the common people and to establish what would be called later a democracy."[84]

The victory of Poinsett's federalist friends, however, did little to improve his standing in Mexico. The press continued to rail against him, as did some state legislatures. Newspapers carried assassination threats. Poinsett duly reported to Washington the personal attacks on him while protesting his innocence: "I should be sensibly mortified in communicating to you the violent attacks which have been made upon me of late by the Aristocratic faction of the Country and especially that by the Legislature of the State of Mexico, if I could attribute them to any misconduct or even to any want of prudence on my part. But these attacks have been entirely unprovoked, and . . . utterly unfounded."[85] President Guerrero, he said, had expressed regret over the attacks and assured Poinsett that he was satisfied with his conduct. Poinsett again asked to resign.

By this time Poinsett had become a political liability even to his closest Mexican friends. In July 1829 Guerrero, despite his private assurances to Poinsett, wrote to the new American president, Andrew Jackson, avoiding direct criticism of Poinsett but saying that the time had come for him to go home.[86] In October Secretary of State Van Buren wrote to Poinsett accepting his resignation, adding that President Jackson was confident the public clamor against him was unjustified. Van Buren added that it was Jackson's "anxious wish that your return should not be attended by any circumstances which might wear the appearance of censure or afford countenance to the imputations of your enemies."[87] It was December before Poinsett finally received his letter of recall. He left Mexico City for the last time on Christmas Day 1829. His diplomatic career was at an end.

The next U.S. minister to Mexico was Col. Anthony Butler of Massachusetts, who was warned in his instructions "to avoid giving any pretext for a repetition against yourself of the imputations which have been cast upon Mr. Poinsett, of having interfered in the domestic politics of the country."[88] Butler, however, proved to be "a vain and ignorant swindler who thought that if he greased the right palms in Mexico City he could buy anything."[89] Jackson eventually heard of his shady dealings and recalled him.

Poinsett arrived home to find himself regarded as a hero. He was feted in Baltimore and Philadelphia. His friends urged him to reenter politics. His name was mentioned for a position in Jackson's cabinet. He was almost immediately installed as General Grand High Priest, Royal Arch Masons.[90] Poinsett, however, was tired. His health had suffered in Mexico, and he wanted nothing more than to retire from public life.

But retirement was not yet on the agenda for Poinsett. Within the United States, tensions were already starting to build between north and south. Soon after his return to South Carolina, he became enmeshed in the "nullification" controversy. Southern advocates of states' rights claimed that any state could nullify acts of the U.S. Congress. Poinsett believed nullification could destroy the viability of the United States, and he became a champion of the South Carolina unionists. When the "nullifiers" won a majority in the state legislature and threatened to secede from the Union, Poinsett began a private correspondence with Jackson, urging military action if the nullifiers followed through on their threats. The crisis was postponed through a compromise worked out by Henry Clay in 1833. Poinsett's opposition to nullification ended any hopes he might have had of running for office in South Carolina.

On October 24, 1833, at age fifty-four, Poinsett was married, for the first time, to Mary Izard Pringle, the widow of a friend. He retired to a plantation near Georgetown, South Carolina, where he cultivated rice and flowers and enjoyed a quieter life.

He continued to correspond with friends and colleagues from his diplomatic days. In 1836, when Santa Anna was captured by the Texans while trying to stamp out their independence movement, Poinsett sent him a gruff message: "Tell General Santa Anna that when I remember how ardent an advocate he was of liberty ten years ago, I have no sympathy for him now; he has what he deserves." Santa Anna replied: "Tell Mr. Poinsett that it is very true that I threw up my hat for liberty with great ardor and perfect sincerity, but very soon found the folly of it. A hundred years from now my people will not be fit for freedom."[91]

Poinsett's retirement was a short one. In 1837 Martin Van Buren, newly elected as president, named him to the cabinet as secretary of war. Poinsett energetically reorganized the army and improved the artillery. On Van Buren's orders, he appointed Gen. Winfield Scott to remove the Cherokee Nation to lands west of the Mississippi, in accordance with a treaty dating from the Jackson administration. This forced relocation, the "trail of tears," was one of the darkest episodes in the grim history of U.S. relations with Native Americans.

As secretary of war he also took a keen interest in exploration. Most notably, he launched the U.S. Exploring Expedition of 1838–42, a naval mission that would send half a dozen U.S. ships around the world to chart unmapped waters and collect scientific information. This was properly the task of the Navy Department, but when naval officers blocked progress, Van Buren turned to Poinsett to rescue the expedition. Poinsett chose a little known officer, Lt. Charles Wilkes, as its head and organized the necessary support. The expedition is still regarded as one of the most important scientific missions ever undertaken by the United States.[92]

Poinsett was equally supportive of exploring the American west, much of which was still unknown wilderness. In 1838 he appointed an eager young colleague, John Frémont, to the U.S. Army's topographical corps and sent him on his first expedition, to explore the upper Mississippi and the Wisconsin Territory. Young Frémont gushed with excitement at his first appointment and sent Mrs. Poinsett a gift of buffalo tongues on his return from the expedition.[93] Frémont would go on to become one of the great explorers of the American west and a towering figure in the history of California.

Following his tenure as secretary of war, Poinsett became a founder and the first president of the National Institute for the Promotion of Science. He advocated the creation of a national museum to house the specimens collected by the Wilkes expedition. The timing coincided with James Smithson's bequest to create an institute for the increase and diffusion of knowledge, together with Smithson's own scientific collection. Poinsett arranged for the collections to be housed together in the Patent Office in Washington under the auspices of his Institute, along with patent models and other collected treasures such as George Washington's mess kit and Benjamin Franklin's printing press. These were put on display in a huge hall and became the first national museum of the United States. In 1862 the Institute's collections and library were incorporated into the Smithsonian Institution, which by that time was up and running.

In his final years, Poinsett continued to take an active interest in domestic and international politics. He opposed the U.S.-Mexican War, writing: "Let us not by an unnecessary act of hostility convert into deadly animosity that kind of friendly feeling which was once entertained toward us by the federal republican party in that country."[94] He supported the Compromise of 1850, intended to keep the United States whole, although most South Carolinians were already secessionists.

In late 1851 Poinsett's health failed. An attack of influenza turned into pneumonia and carried him away on December 12. His wife survived him by six years.

History's verdict on Joel Poinsett has been mixed. His experiences were extraordinary and his achievements significant. At the same time, he was always surrounded by controversies, often of his own creation. He can be regarded as the first official American to intervene actively in Latin American political affairs, beginning a long tradition of U.S. policy. Considering the breadth of his adventures and the importance of the issues in which he was involved both at home and abroad, it is surprising that he is so little remembered as a diplomat, congressman, cabinet secretary, or museum founder.

Instead, he is remembered for a flower. A deep red bloom he brought back from Mexico was once named *cuetlaxochitl* by the Aztecs and later called the "fire plant," "painted leaf," and the *Noche Buena*, the flower of Christmas Eve. Poinsett cultivated the flowers in his greenhouse in South Carolina and sent specimens to his friends and to botanical gardens. Today it bears his name and has become the most popular flowering plant grown and sold in the United States, *Euphorbia pulcherrima*, the poinsettia.

# FIVE

## Cochin China, Siam, and Muscat
*The Remarkable Travels of Edmund Roberts*

C harles Endicott was one of the many mariners who by the early 1800s were transforming the United States into one of the world's leading commercial nations. Captain of the *Friendship*, out of Salem, Massachusetts, Endicott had spent fifteen years cruising the East Indies, carrying home pepper and other spices for the growing American market. It was a profitable but sometimes perilous vocation; many of the rocky shores were still uncharted, and the waters around the islands teemed with pirates.

On Monday morning, February 7, 1831, the *Friendship* was anchored off Qualah Battoo (now Kuala Batu), a small, fortified town on the island of Sumatra. The local residents, some of whom Endicott knew well from previous journeys, invited him ashore with a promise to supply one hundred bags of pepper in return for Endicott's cargo of opium and silver dollars. Endicott went ashore with five seamen from the *Friendship*'s crew of seventeen to close the deal. In Qualah Battoo, however, he began to feel uneasy. The usually friendly residents seemed jumpy and even threatening. A local trading partner took him aside and warned him that a plan was afoot to seize his ship and its cargo. Endicott and his men rushed back to their launch. They had no sooner cast off than an angry crowd appeared on the shore waving spears menacingly. As they approached the *Friendship*, they saw it was already in the hands of armed locals. Outnumbered and unarmed, they beat a hasty retreat.

The pirates who seized the *Friendship* murdered most of the crew. A few saved themselves by jumping overboard and swimming to shore, where they hid in the jungle. Endicott and his remaining men rowed north through the night to seek safety with two other

American trading vessels he knew were in the area. With their help, he sailed back to Qualah Battoo and retook the *Friendship*, which had been stripped of its cargo, armaments, fittings, and supplies. Endicott managed to repurchase his sextant and chronometer at the local market and to obtain some supplies. He then sailed for home in his empty ship.[1]

The Qualah Battoo affair created a sensation in the United States. It was not the first time American ships had fallen victim to pirates in the Indies. The attack on the *Friendship*, however, was particularly inflammatory, since it seemed to have been carried out with the connivance of local authorities and since some of the crew survived to tell the story. The Congress demanded action. President Andrew Jackson was quick to oblige. The level of public interest was so high that Jackson even mentioned the incident in his State of the Union address:

> A daring outrage having been committed . . . by the plunder of one of our merchant-men engaged in the pepper trade at a port in Sumatra, and the piratical perpetrators belonging to tribes in such a state of society that the usual course of proceedings between civilized nations could not be pursued, I forthwith dispatched a frigate with orders to require immediate satisfaction for the injury and indemnity to the sufferers.[2]

The frigate chosen for the task was the USS *Potomac*. Secretary of the Navy Levi Woodbury sent instructions to Cdre. John Downes to proceed with the *Potomac* to Qualah Battoo, enter the port, conduct an inquiry, and demand reparations. Woodbury, formerly a senator from New Hampshire, was an enthusiast of expanding American trade in the East. If the attack on the *Friendship* were not avenged, he believed, it could embolden other local potentates to attack American shipping and undercut American trade throughout the Indies. In case the *Potomac* should encounter any mishap, Woodbury sent the same orders to another naval vessel, the sloop of war USS *Peacock*.

The *Peacock* was selected for this mission because it was already scheduled for a voyage to the Far East, an extremely rare visit to the area by an American warship. The original purpose of the visit was friendly. The *Peacock* would be carrying an American envoy, Edmund Roberts, on a secret mission to negotiate the first U.S. treaties of commerce and friendship with the far-flung empires of Cochin China, Siam, and Muscat.

The *Peacock* sailed from Boston in March 1832, more than forty years after Samuel Shaw and the *Empress of China* launched American trade with the Far East. During those decades, American merchantmen had become frequent visitors to China, the Indies, and other parts of the Pacific and Indian Oceans, while American whalers dominated the Pacific fisheries.

American commerce, however, was not on a strong footing in Asia. According to contemporary accounts, American trade was "precarious . . . subject to every species of imposition which avarice might think proper to inflict, as the price of an uncertain protection."[3] Unlike the British, Dutch, Portuguese, and others, the United States had no colonies in the region from which to stage its trade. As relative newcomers to the East, American traders were often subject to higher duties than other foreigners. There were no American diplomats anywhere in Asia, although there were a few consuls. In the forty years since Shaw was appointed as the first consul in Canton, American consuls had been appointed to more than seventy foreign ports, but only a handful of these were in the East—Canton, Calcutta, Batavia (Jakarta), and Manila.

The Jackson administration was sympathetic to calls for a stronger official American presence in the Far East. By 1831 it decided that the time had come to try to open formal relations with countries in Asia. To carry out the task, it turned to Roberts, an American merchant who was among those advocating commercial treaties. Roberts was related by marriage to Secretary of the Navy Woodbury, who used his influence to have Roberts appointed. Although it was not the first time an envoy was appointed as a result of personal connections, this practice would reach a new high under President Jackson.

Edmund Quincy Roberts was born in Portsmouth, New Hampshire, on June 29, 1784. His parents died when he was a child, and he was left in the care of a bachelor uncle, a sea captain and merchant whose trading house was based in Buenos Aires. Young Roberts learned his uncle's business, spending years living in South America and in London. He returned to Portsmouth at age twenty-four and married Catherine Langdon, the daughter of a prominent local family. They would have eight daughters.

In 1827 Roberts chartered the brig *Mary Ann* and sailed for the first time to the Indian Ocean, visiting Zanzibar and India and sparking an interest in the East that would continue for the rest of his life. In Zanzibar, Roberts met the sultan of Muscat, who controlled much of the coast of East Africa and Arabia. During his meeting with the sultan, Roberts broached the idea of a commercial treaty that would guarantee American traders the same rights as those of other countries. Although the sultan was receptive, Roberts had no authority to negotiate, so the matter ended. When he returned home, however, Roberts pressed the idea with Woodbury, who at the time was a senator from his home state of New Hampshire but would soon be named secretary of the navy.

Roberts made several more visits to the Indian Ocean, but his ventures did not meet with much commercial success, leaving him in strained financial circumstances. At home he continued to agitate for commercial treaties, lobbying with Woodbury and others to be named as envoy to negotiate the treaties. In January 1832 his wish was granted; he was appointed as special diplomatic agent to negotiate treaties with Cochin China (now Vietnam), Siam (now Thailand), and Muscat (now Oman). In addition, he was given separate instructions that if he found "the prospect favorable," he should also visit Japan and seek to establish official relations there.[4] This odd combination of countries was largely the result of lobbying by Roberts and other merchants with special commercial interests. The combination of countries was not the only odd aspect of Roberts's appointment.

Roberts's mission was to be secret, in order to prevent other powers from trying to thwart his objectives. In particular, the British, who dominated the Far East trade, might be expected to create obstacles for competitor countries. Roberts, in fact, was instructed to investigate the operations of the British East India Company.[5]

As his "cover" to ensure the secrecy of the mission, Roberts was to join the *Peacock* as the captain's clerk. While the captain would know his real status, he was not to reveal it to others on board unless it became necessary for the success of his mission.[6] This deception proved impractical, since it soon became apparent to everyone on the ship that Roberts, not the captain, was in charge of negotiations and relations with local officials at each port. The subterfuge also caused Roberts some personal problems. The captain only begrudgingly shared his cabin with Roberts, telling him "frequently & in the most insulting manner [that] he is admitted there by sufferance."[7] Roberts's pay was six dollars a day, plus upkeep and expenses, a quite reasonable package in the 1830s and one of the reasons he sought the position.

Secretary of State Edward Livingston sent Roberts a lengthy letter of instructions, telling him to go first to Cochin China, where he should "proceed to the capital of the country Hué, sometimes called Huefoo, or such other of the royal cities as the king may reside at." Once there, the letter continued,

> You will present yourself to the King with your power and the letter addressed to him. You will state that the President having heard of his fame for justice and desire to improve the advantages of commerce for the good of his people has sent you to inquire whether he is willing to admit our ships into his harbors with such articles of merchandise as will be useful to him and his people, and to receive in return the products of their industry or of their soil. That we manufacture and can bring arms, ammunition, cloths of cotton and wool, glass, &c (enumerating all the articles that you find they usually import), that we can furnish them cheaper than any other nation because it is against the principles of our nation to build forts or make expensive establishments in foreign countries, that we never make conquests, or ask any nations to let us establish ourselves in their countries as the English, the French, and the Dutch have done in the East Indies. All we ask is free liberty to come and go for the purpose of buying and selling.[8]

Roberts's instructions for Siam and for "the powers of Arabia on the Red Sea" were identical. In each country, Roberts was empowered to negotiate a treaty and to promise "verbally or in writing, that the usual presents shall be made on the exchange of the ratification of which you may settle a list of such things as may be most agreeable, not exceeding ten thousand dollars in value for each power."[9] In addition to concluding treaties, Roberts was told to gather detailed information on each country's trade with other nations, the duties and other fees imposed, the country's manufactured and agricultural products, its military strength, and its imports or desired imports.

The *Peacock*, on which Roberts embarked, was a small sloop of war, just 118 feet long and 31 feet at the beam. With a crew of two hundred officers and seamen, this made for extremely tight quarters. For a small ship, the *Peacock* packed a sizable wallop: twenty 32-pound carronades and two long 12-pounders.[10] The ship was designed and built to take part in the U.S. Exploring Expedition, which was already in the planning stages, although it would be six more years before Joel Poinsett, as Van Buren's secretary of war, finally broke the bureaucratic logjam and got the expedition on its way in 1838.

According to one member of the ship's company, the *Peacock* "has no commendable quality. She is an indifferent sailer, very wet, and both for officers and crew, the accommodations are very limited."[11] Another wrote that "a sloop-of-war is totally unfit to be employed on a long cruise in hot climates, like that for which the *Peacock* was destined; because it is impossible that a ship of that class can possess those accommodations for the officers & men, which are indispensably necessary for their health & comfort, & at the same time, carry a sufficient supply of water & provisions. No vessel of a smaller rate than a frigate, should ever be employed on such a cruise." The ship's surgeon, Dr. Benajah Ticknor, described his tiny berth as "so entirely destitute of those accommodations which an officer's state-room ought to possess, that it was scarcely fit to be used as a dog kennel."[12]

The commander of the *Peacock* was David Geisinger, a forty-four-year-old naval officer from Maryland who had distinguished himself in the War of 1812. By some accounts Geisinger was a capable and affable officer—when he was sober. Dr. Ticknor, however, described him as weak and incompetent, recounting several instances of his drunkenness and abusive behavior. Ticknor also decried Geisinger's constant use of profanity, even ashore and in front of ladies! While this was hardly unusual in sailors, it was strictly contrary to naval regulations. Roberts, for his part, wrote to the secretary of state following the mission that the next captain selected "must be a gentleman in the strictest sense of the word—a sober—discreet & moral man . . . nor a Drunkard nor a quarrelsome man."[13]

Under these grim conditions, the *Peacock* set sail in February 1832 on a voyage that would last more than two years. The *Peacock* was to be accompanied by the *Boxer*, a small supply schooner. The *Boxer*, however, started the voyage later and traveled by a different route, not reaching the East until months after the *Peacock*. This would cause some embarrassment for Roberts.

The *Peacock* initially carried two diplomatic envoys. In addition to Roberts, it was transporting Francis Baylies, a Massachusetts politician and Jackson supporter, who had just been appointed as chargé d'affaires to Argentina. The ship therefore sailed first to Buenos Aires.

After ensuring that Baylies was safely established, Commander Geisinger's orders were to sail to Qualah Battoo to seek reparations for the outrage on the *Friendship* before proceeding on Roberts's diplomatic mission. It took three months to reach the Indies from Argentina, by way of the Cape of Good Hope. When the *Peacock* reached Sumatra, Roberts learned, to his great relief, that the *Potomac* had already "chastised" the inhabitants of Qualah Battoo, which "rendered a visit from the *Peacock* to that place unnecessary."[14]

The "chastisement" of Qualah Battoo was not an event that reflects great credit on the U.S. Navy. Commodore Downes, despite his orders to visit Qualah Battoo and demand reparations, decided instead to try to capture the rajah and hold him hostage until reparations were paid. He disguised the *Potomac* as a merchant ship in order to approach the port undetected. At dawn on February 6, 1832, he landed a force of 250 marines and seamen who attacked and set fire to the town's principal fort, killing most of the defenders. The fires in the fort spread, destroying much of the town. The troops then reassembled and, to the tune of "Yankee Doodle," returned to the ship. The following morning, for good measure, the *Potomac* bombarded and destroyed the town's last remaining fort.[15] According to one account, 170 inhabitants were killed, and the town was completely destroyed.[16] Two Americans died in the fighting.

Roberts's reaction to "the entire destruction of Qualah Battoo, by the *Potomac*," was that it "happily precluded the necessity of an unpleasant visit and saved the officers and crew the painful duty which would otherwise have devolved on the *Peacock*. The demolition of this place struck terror into the inhabitants of all the ports on the coast and will doubtless produce a salutary effect."[17]

Washington's reaction to the attack was far less favorable. Secretary of the Navy Woodbury wrote to Commodore Downes expressing "the President's regrets" that the attack took place before Downes obtained more information about the *Friendship* incident or before he demanded compensation, as he had been ordered.[18] Nonetheless, Jackson made the best of the incident in his next State of the Union address, reporting that an American frigate inflicted "chastisement" on "a band of lawless pirates" on the coast of Sumatra, the effect of which "has been an increased respect for our flag in those distant seas and additional security for our commerce."[19]

With the Qualah Battoo affair set to rest, Roberts and the *Peacock* were free to begin their diplomatic mission. They appeared to be in no hurry to reach Cochin China, however, sailing first to Manila in the Spanish Philippines, then to Canton. Their stop in Manila was cut short by an outbreak of cholera. After two sailors died of the disease, Dr. Ticknor insisted that the ship depart, over Commander Geisinger's vigorous and salty objections. Thirty-six members of the crew came down with cholera, but recovered once the ship was at sea.

In Canton, Roberts found conditions to be strikingly similar to those that had faced Samuel Shaw forty years earlier. Foreign traders were still confined to "factories" and not allowed into other parts of China. One difference was that there were now seven American mercantile houses in Canton, second only to Great Britain's nine. There was even an American-owned hotel. Several American ships were in port, including one trading illegally in opium. Foreigners in Canton still led a luxurious but strictly confined life. Western women were not allowed to reside there. The American consul, John Grosvenor, was free to operate informally, but was not recognized by the government. Roberts lingered for several weeks in Canton, gathering information that might be useful to American merchants and trying to learn what he could about Cochin China, Siam, and Japan, as well as about the operations of the British East India Company.

Before leaving Canton, Roberts hired a young man named John Morrison to serve as his secretary and interpreter. Morrison, who was just eighteen, was the son of the first British Protestant missionary in China. Born in Macao and tutored by his father, "this young gentleman appeared as familiar with the Chinese written language, as the mandarins themselves."[20] He also spoke fluent Portuguese. Since these were the two languages most commonly spoken by foreigners in Cochin China and Siam, his services would be invaluable. Morrison would go on to a distinguished career as a scholar, colonial official, and supporter of missionary efforts in China. Roberts's mission was Morrison's first foray into diplomacy; he would make important contributions in the months ahead.

Roberts and the *Peacock* finally left Canton for Cochin China in late December 1832, nine months after leaving Boston. This would prove to be the most difficult and exasperating leg of their mission. Cochin China was still a largely closed country. Some Catholic missionaries had made modest inroads there, but repeated French, British, and other European efforts to open trade had always failed. The first American attempt to trade with Cochin China, in 1803 by the Salem trader *Fame*, was unsuccessful. In 1819, John White sailed up the Mekong River to Saigon in another American attempt to open trade. White left with the most negative impression: "the rapacious, faithless, despotic, and anti-commercial character of the government, will, as long as these causes exist, render Cochin China the least desirable country for mercantile adventures."[21] The situation became even worse after 1820, when Emperor Minh Mang ascended the throne and adopted a closed-door policy.

Because of adverse currents and winds, the *Peacock* could not make port near the capital of Hué. It eventually dropped anchor in Phuyen Bay, "the fine harbour of Vung-lam . . . truly one of the finest harbours in the world. . . . It is beautifully picturesque and bold."[22] This was, however, some three hundred miles from the capital, which greatly hampered efforts to open negotiations. Roberts did not realize that he was so far from Hué and that Vung-lam was not a major city; this colored his impressions of the country.

Their first contact was with the village headman, "an old man with a long white beard descending to his breast, and clad in a most miserable garb," who came aboard the ship.[23]

John Morrison was able to communicate with him by writing in Chinese. They learned from the headman that the name of the king was "Ming-meng," highlighting how little they knew about Cochin China; Minh Mang had already been emperor for over a decade. They informed the headman of the purpose of their visit and asked him to pass word to the capital. As a sign of respect, the *Peacock* fired a salute of thirteen guns. The old man returned later with some other officials who happily got drunk on the ship's brandy. The old man, Roberts later learned, was subsequently put in jail for not being sufficiently prompt in reporting the ship's arrival.

The encounters with the headman were the first in a long series of visits and exchanges. On January 6 the ship was visited by two officials of the ninth rank—the lowest class of government official—to verify where it came from and its purpose. The following day, two higher-level officials arrived with a retinue including umbrella-bearers, trumpeters, sword-bearers, a party of soldiers with pikes, and three elephants. Roberts was unimpressed: "The two deputies appeared anxious to make as much as possible of themselves. . . . They then entered upon a number of impertinent queries, such as, whether there were any presents for the king; what were the contents of the letter to him; asking to see a copy of the envoy's dispatch to the capital, and the envoy and captain's commissions. In all these inquiries they were immediately checked."[24] After much discussion, the officials agreed to carry a letter from Roberts to the king asking for a meeting. Roberts's lack of candor led to further delays and complications.

Some days later, a large galley appeared, rowed by thirty-two soldiers wearing red-lacquered peaked caps. It carried two officials from Hué (officials of the fifth rank), together with the governor (of the third rank), all dressed in ceremonial robes of blue with satin trousers of red and yellow, black turbans, and Chinese shoes. They brought interpreters who spoke Portuguese and some English, but the conversation was again interpreted mainly by Morrison, writing in Chinese. The officials made the same inquiries about the nationality of the ship and the nature of Roberts's mission. They "produced a large sheet, containing representations of every known national flag, with the names of the countries attached, in French and in Chinese characters. The flag of the United States was pointed out to them."[25] Cochin China, they told Roberts, was now called "Wietnam" and was ruled by an emperor, not a king. They had not delivered Roberts's letter, since it was not properly addressed and did not use appropriate language.

The officials proposed a revised text for Roberts's letter to the emperor. Roberts rejected the draft immediately, finding "the tone . . . extremely objectionable, for, besides the servileness of particular expressions, the general language is that of an inferior." This began an extended and frustrating negotiation over the form of letter that Roberts wanted to send to the emperor announcing his arrival and asking for a meeting to present a letter from President Jackson. Much of the discussion was carried out on shore because the governor became seasick every time he visited the ship. The two sides failed to agree on an appropriate text for the emperor, but eventually compromised instead on a letter from Roberts to the prime minister, which Roberts accepted as "respectful, but not mean or servile."[26] The officials pressed Roberts to know whether he had any presents for the emperor. He refused to answer, reasoning that if he said yes, he would appear to be bearing tribute, and if he said no, it might undermine the prospects of a meeting. After days of haggling, the letter was finally dispatched to Hué, leaving Roberts with an unhappy first taste of diplomacy in the Far East.

While awaiting the response, Roberts took the opportunity to learn what he could about Cochin China. He did not much like what he found. His initial impression of a beautiful, well-kept country was not borne out: "on a more close examination this beautiful vision is not realized. The inhabitants are without exception the most filthy people in the world . . . all having a mangy appearance; being covered with some scorbutic disease, the itch or small-pox, and frequently with white leprous spots. The teeth . . . even of the children . . . are of a coal black . . . stained with chewing areca &c., their faces are nasty, their hands unwashed, and their whole persons most offensive to the sight and smell. . . . In the course of a whole month . . . I have not seen a single person bathe."[27] The ship's surgeon, Dr. Ticknor, shared this impression, writing about the people's "total unconcern about every thing that regards personal cleanliness" and noting that even the officials were infested with vermin. He was particularly struck by the abject poverty. On one outing a poor mother tried to get him to take her baby, leading him to conclude that the "condition of life must certainly be wretched in the extreme."[28] The children, Roberts wrote, are brought up in idleness and do not attend school. Although the soil seemed rich, most of the population was engaged in fishing. There appeared to be little commerce, but there was some interest in obtaining American ginseng. The soldiers, he noted, were armed only with spears. Roberts saw no temples or houses of worship, but observed that the people took great care over the remains of the dead. Men and women generally dressed the same, with a wide long shirt and a pair of short trousers. Elephants abounded, some tame and used for domestic purposes, while others roamed wild. Tigers were a constant threat, sometimes stealing pigs from the villages.

Ten days after Roberts dispatched his letter to the prime minister, two still higher-level officials arrived from Hué with long white beards that "gave them quite a venerable aspect." On behalf of the emperor, they sent a feast on board the ship, consisting of fifty-one dishes, including beef, four dogs, an entire tortoise, fresh boiled pork, roasted ducks, stewed pigeons, stewed eel, mullet, rice, eggs, and fruit, plus five jars of native liquor "made from rice, which is a very tolerable substitute for wine."[29] The feast, Roberts wrote, "was brought on board in handsomely varnished and gilded cases; to all outward appearance, it was very neat and cleanly; but we could not divest ourselves of the idea, that it was cooked in the uncleanly vessels we had seen on shore."[30] They could not bring themselves to eat it.

Roberts was invited ashore for discussions but refused to go, considering that the officials should first call on him in light of his rank as a presidential envoy. Instead, he sent John Morrison ashore to open discussions. It must certainly have offended the senior officials to be asked to deal with an eighteen-year-old. They insisted on seeing the letter from President Jackson to the emperor; Roberts refused. They had difficulty understanding the concept of an elected president and questioned whether he could really hold the same rank as an emperor. Roberts found this deeply insulting. By the third day of stalemate, the exchanges had deteriorated to the point of name-calling.[31]

After several more days, Roberts finally yielded and provided a copy of both his cover letter and Jackson's letter to the emperor, with a Chinese translation. Jackson's letter was, in fact, a single paragraph introducing Roberts as an envoy and asking the emperor, "my great and good friend," to work with him in full confidence.[32] It contained nothing that Roberts had not already told the officials, leading one to wonder about his reluctance to reveal its contents.

More aggravation lay ahead. The officials carefully reviewed the letters and insisted they must be "corrected" before they could be forwarded. Roberts objected vigorously to this "unheard of and arrogant" request.[33] Nonetheless, the officials proceeded to criticize every sentence of the cover letter. In the long ensuing discussion, Roberts did agree to a number of small changes that he considered unobjectionable.

The officials then turned to the president's letter, again raising Roberts's ire that they should even suggest changes. There was much discussion of the phrase "great and good friend," which the officials considered too familiar for an emperor. They questioned what was meant by "the fifty-sixth year of independence" of the United States. They asked to change the words "I pray God to . . . have you under his safe and holy keeping" to a prayer to "imperial heaven, for the continual peace of your majesty's sacred person." Roberts indignantly refused because it would "present the President in the light of an idolater." Finally, the officials insisted the letter should be transmitted either "with silent awe" or "with uplifted hands." Roberts rejected both formulations as unworthy of a president. Ultimately he refused to alter the president's letter itself, but did agree to some "trivial" alterations to the Chinese translation.[34] He chose to have the word "president" translated into Chinese as "king" in order not to yield to the idea that a president held a lower rank than a king.

With the dispute over the letter seemingly resolved, the officials next asked Roberts if he would submit to the etiquette of the court at an audience with the emperor, saying they had doubts considering his resistance to writing an appropriate letter. The normal court ceremony included a kowtow, with visitors expected to make five prostrations, touching the ground with their foreheads. Roberts replied that "nothing beyond a bow, as to the President, would be performed."[35] Asked if he would make five bows, he replied that he would make as many as they wished, but not on his knees.

To Roberts's utter dismay, the officials then returned to the question of transmitting the letter with "uplifted hands," saying it could not be delivered without this phrase. For Roberts, this was the end. He preferred failure of his mission to dishonorable concessions. He refused to make the change. He told the officials he would wait seven days for a response from the capital, then he would sail away.

Eight days later, having received no further response, the *Peacock* made preparations to depart. The next day they set sail. Although they spent the entire day making their way slowly out of the harbor, "nothing more was seen of the Cochin-Chinese."[36]

The first leg of Roberts's mission had collapsed. He regretted that "the insulting formalities required as preliminaries to the treaty by the ministers from the capital of Cochin-China, left me no alternative, save that of terminating a protracted correspondence, singularly marked from its commencement to its termination by duplicity and prevarication in the official servants of the emperor." The government of Cochin-China, he concluded bitterly, "is thoroughly despotic, being framed in close imitation of that of China. . . . the present emperor of Cochin-China is an ignorant, blood-thirsty savage."[37]

Vietnamese official documents of the period mention the Roberts mission. Highlighting the clash of cultures, they express puzzlement at the strange attitudes of the American visitors. The documents record that the foreigners were polite, but that "the translation of the credential letter appeared to be rather erroneous, absurd, ambiguous."[38] Two officials were dispatched to tell Roberts that trade might be possible but that no foreigners would be allowed to reside permanently on shore. The *Peacock* was gone by the time these officials reached Vung-lam.

From Cochin China the *Peacock* plied its way south then west through the South China Sea toward its next destination: Siam. Traveling without accurate maps, the ship passed a group of uncharted islands, three of which they named Roberts, Geisinger, and Peacock.

After ten days at sea, the *Peacock* arrived off the coast of Siam. It was February 18, 1833.

Although Siam was better known to westerners than Cochin China, it was still a mysterious and exotic place. The Portuguese were the first Europeans to make contact, more than three hundred years earlier. Siam was not much visited, however, as it lay well north of the principal trade routes. Still, it was a major regional power; in 1832, just the year before Roberts arrived, Siam brought most of the Malay Peninsula under its control. The British had tried and failed to open relations with Siam in 1822. They had more success after their victory in the First Anglo-Burmese War (1824–26). A British mission under Henry Burney signed a treaty in 1826 that regularized trade on somewhat better terms than previously. The Siamese, however, refused Burney's request to station a representative in Bangkok. Of the European nations, only Portugal had official representation in Siam by virtue of its long presence there; a Portuguese consul functioned largely as a trade representative.

Roberts's timing was auspicious, following a few years behind the British. The Siamese were inclined to give equal treatment to other Western states, in part from a desire to balance growing British power in the region.

Once off the coast, Roberts and Geisinger dispatched John Morrison and one of the ship's officers ashore to announce their arrival and begin arrangements for Roberts to visit the capital. Morrison returned saying they had been asked "with a good deal of interest respecting the Siamese Twins, who were natives of a place not far from Bangkok."[39] The twins in question were Chang and Eng, born in 1811 and joined by a flap of skin at the bottom of their ribs. At age eighteen, just four years earlier, they had been recruited by an American sea captain and taken to Europe and the United States. They traveled widely in America, where they created such a sensation that conjoined twins are still referred to as Siamese twins. Chang and Eng eventually settled in North Carolina, where they married two sisters and together had twenty-one children. The brothers died within hours of each other at the age of sixty-one. The crew of the *Peacock* would certainly have been familiar with Chang and Eng; for most of them it may have been their only knowledge of Siam.

The following day an official came on board asking questions about the purpose of the visit and, of course, whether they had brought any presents for the king. Roberts, annoyed at this impertinence, refused to respond.

A better omen arrived two days later, through the captain of the port, who sent word that his majesty the king is "very desirous of having a friendly commercial intercourse with the United States." They were informed that preparations were under way for their reception and a feast was planned in their honor. On February 24, less than a week after their arrival, large boats arrived to convey them ashore, each one eighty feet long—nearly the length of the *Peacock*—with forty Burmese slaves at the oars, dressed in the king's uniforms. Roberts, Morrison, Geisinger, and several of the ship's officers were rowed up a river with banks "as flat as the Arkansas or Mississippi." At the dock they were received by the captain of the port and a company of gentlemen, as well as hundreds of curious onlookers who maintained "the utmost decorum, made no small show, and produced upon the whole, rather an imposing effect, for this was the first envoy ever sent to the 'magnificent king of Siam,' from the United States."[40]

They were taken to the best house in the village to meet the governor, who was attended by a sword-bearer, silver-stick bearers, and a man fanning him with a fan of feathers "to keep him cool and to drive off the myriads of moschetoes." Here Roberts and his companions had their first horrified view of Siamese hierarchy: "His menials were all prostrate, resting on their knees and elbows, coming in and going out in the same attitude, always keeping their faces turned towards him." The Americans were shocked by the groveling; they would become increasingly disgusted as their sojourn continued. For now, Roberts's reaction was that the servants kneel down "in a more humble manner than suits our republican notions." Later he would comment that "subordination of rank is carried to a most degrading and revolting point." Nonetheless, the people are "all seemingly happy, although living under one of the most despotic governments in the world."[41]

The governor served them food "well cooked in the Portuguese fashion" together with a Dutch bottle of gin. It was immediately clear that Siam—though still largely isolated from the West—was familiar with Western customs. The Americans came prepared with their own utensils: "knives & forks being articles of luxury that were not known there, . . . we had brought them with us."[42]

The Americans were conveyed by boat to Bangkok, a day's travel upriver, with Burmese slaves pulling at the oars. This was their first chance for a view of the countryside, the people, and their strikingly different way of life. They marveled at the amount of activity on the river, including hundreds of huge junks, far larger than the *Peacock*, thousands of smaller boats, and "floating houses" that lined the shores, sometimes four to five deep. As far as the Americans could tell, there were no bridges and no roads; all transportation was by water. Along the river they got their first view of banyan trees, "one of the most curious of nature's productions."[43]

Roberts was struck also by the poverty: "The ground everywhere was very low and swampy, and the houses mean; the people appeared to be wretchedly poor, diseased and dirty, but still cleaner than the Cochin-Chinese." He noted extensive fortifications on both sides of the river, but Bangkok itself appeared poorly defended, with its walls unmanned and broken up by canals. The Siamese military appeared weak; its soldiers did not even carry muskets, while its war boats "would be altogether useless in a sea-fight."[44]

The Americans were well received and housed in Bangkok as guests of Chao Phaya P'hra-klang, generally referred to by Roberts as "the *praklang*," an official who functioned as prime minister and foreign minister. Each day they were brought food by servants, who knelt to present it.

Bangkok was an immense metropolis, with a population estimated by Roberts at 460,000, more than twice the size of the largest American cities at the time. The real capital of Siam, Roberts commented, was "Si-a-Yuthia," across the river from Bangkok, on the left bank. The Siamese, he noted, would correct foreigners who referred to Bangkok as the capital.

In happy contrast to his experience in Cochin China, Roberts was received promptly by the praklang, whom he described as "a very heavy unwieldy man, weighing, probably, nearly three hundred pounds, and about fifty-five years of age; his only dress was a waist-cloth of silk; he was resting on a new crimson velvet cushion." His attendants, including interpreters, secretaries, sword-bearer, and others, "were all crouching, in a brute-like attitude, on their knees and elbows. . . . in the court-yard, were a great number of people, all in this humiliating posture. His sons, when called, crawled as well as the others, and went backward in the same attitude, always facing their lord and master." Roberts and his companions greeted the minister with a "bow in the usual style of our country, on entering and retiring."[45]

The Siamese treated the Americans to an evening's entertainment, with an exhibition of dancing and singing that Roberts found "not altogether unmusical." Dr. Ticknor concurred, reporting that the music "did not strike my ear more unpleasantly than that of an Italian opera." By Roberts's description, "the principal singer . . . the prima donna, squalled to the very top of her voice, various ditties in a melancholy strain, until I thought she would have swooned from exhaustion: but I was mistaken; for she was made of tougher materials, than ever fell to the lot of any other female." The show also included "a most excellent company of vaulters and tumblers . . . which surpassed every thing of the kind that I ever witnessed."[46]

The following day, Roberts met the praklang to begin treaty negotiations. The minister's initial position was that there was no need for a commercial treaty, since Americans were already free to trade in Siam. He asked Roberts what more he wanted. Roberts, surprisingly, replied that if the minister would give him a copy of the treaty negotiated with the British a few years earlier, he would propose specific terms.[47] The minister agreed, and as a result the U.S. treaty is quite similar to the Burney treaty of 1826.

The principal issues of negotiation were duties, debtors, protection of Americans, and the appointment of an American consul. With respect to duties, Roberts's goal was a single rate of duty based on the size of the ship, to replace the myriad charges on different items of import and export, as well as other port fees and expenses. The Siamese agreed, but declined his request for duties lower than those imposed on the British. They agreed also that American merchants could buy and sell freely to anyone, not being limited by royal monopolies; the only exceptions were firearms and rice. The exception of rice, it turned out, significantly limited the benefits of the treaty, since rice was the only Siamese export that American traders might have carried profitably from Siam to China.

The issue of debtors was more unusual. The practice in Siam at the time was that a debtor who defaulted was entirely at the mercy of his creditor and might even be sold into slavery, either permanently or for a set period of time, to repay the debt. Alternatively, the creditor could have the debtor flogged or otherwise tortured. The Siamese ultimately agreed that an American debtor could be required to surrender all his possessions, but that would be the limit of his liability. Roberts also won agreement that the Siamese would care for shipwrecked Americans and return any American vessels captured by pirates in Siamese waters.

Roberts's request to station an American consul in Siam was denied, just as the British had been. The treaty did, however, stipulate that if any country other than Portugal—the only country that already had a consul—were granted the right to appoint a consul, then the United States could also do so.

Roberts found the discussions exasperatingly tedious and slow. The Siamese, he bemoaned, "attach a ridiculous importance to mere form and ceremony." Moreover, "there was always a disposition evinced to hint obscurely at things, like the Chinese, rather than express their full meaning." When the minister did agree to a clause, he often reneged at the next session, giving Roberts the impression that the Siamese "are extremely disingenuous and fickle-minded."[48]

Dr. Ticknor was once called on to treat the praklang, then stayed on to observe the evening's negotiations. The minister, he wrote, appeared "to make no effort to fix his attention upon the business before him, or to impose the least restraint upon his actions, which were frequently very ludicrous for one in his situation negotiating an important treaty with a foreign Envoy, lying sometimes on his back with his hand hold of his feet, & sometimes on his face extended at full length; then perhaps, kneeling & leaning forward on his cushions, & thus by turns assuming almost every variety of uncouth posture. In the course of the evening he drank a good deal of tea, & smoked, first a cigar & then a long pipe, & chewed the arica-nut masticatory with but little intermission."[49] Throughout the discussions, the minister's retainers remained prostrate or on their knees and elbows.

A parallel negotiation took place on the question of presents. This was raised with Roberts at his very first meeting with the minister. Roberts replied that the American presents were sent out to Canton (on the *Boxer*, which had still not caught up with the *Peacock*), but they did not arrive and were presumed lost at sea. As a consequence, he purchased replacement presents in Canton. The Siamese were not pleased and did not believe this story. They much preferred gifts made in Europe or the United States, since Chinese products were readily available in Siam.

Roberts had gifts both for the minister and for the king, which he intended to deliver once the negotiations were concluded. To his surprise, however, the minister, "having obtained information by some means, that I had a present for him, sent . . . to inquire of what it consisted, *and the cost*," and then sent officials to examine the gifts and take an inventory. The officials hinted that delivering the presents immediately would facilitate the negotiations. Although this seemed highly improper to Roberts, he yielded and sent the minister his gifts, which consisted of "an elegant gold watch, set in pearls, two cases of silks, and four elegant filigreed silver baskets, edged with gold, and ornamented with enameled figures."[50]

The minister also managed to extort another gift from Roberts. On the occasion of the shaving of the heads of his two sons, an important ceremony, Roberts received a message that the U.S. envoy would, of course, make a present. Roberts regarded this approach as outrageously impolite. The negotiations, however, were at a delicate juncture, so he complied with a gift of one hundred silver dollars. To his shock, these were counted in front of him and then reported to the minister to be acceptable.

For the king's presents, Roberts had purchased in Canton "silks, elegant watches set in pearls, and very superior silver filigreed baskets, with gold rims, and enameled with birds and flowers." Again, he was asked how much the gifts cost, and inspectors were sent to ensure that they were suitable for the king. Roberts seethed with indignation and more so when the inspectors commented that a different color of silk might have better suited the king. Nonetheless, the gifts were accepted.

In general, the Siamese were not much impressed with the American presents. By the same token, Roberts placed little value on gifts the Siamese gave him, dismissing them as "some presents of the productions of the country . . . of very mean quality, and of inconsiderable value."[51] The Siamese gifts were samples of products from

Siam's rainforests, including elephant's teeth (tusks), sugar-candy, pepper, spices and exotic woods.[52] Roberts did not bother to bring the gifts back to the United States.

During breaks in the negotiations, Roberts and his companions had the chance to explore Bangkok. They were amazed at the proliferation of Buddhist temples, which Roberts estimated at more than four hundred. Although most were very small, all were neat and colorful. The larger temples were covered with colored tiles, highly ornamented, and blazing in gold, having a "very splendid appearance." Of one temple in particular, Roberts wrote, "any description I can give . . . will fall short of reality. . . . [The] glittering gold and flowers, recalls . . . the brilliant and splendid castles of fairy-land."[53] The many priests and monks, identifiable by their yellow waistcloths and shaven heads and eyebrows, lived on charity, leading Roberts to conclude that the Siamese were a very generous people.

In contrast to other Asian countries, the government of Siam admitted foreign missionaries. The Catholics were long established but had made little headway. Roberts estimated that there were only four hundred Catholics in the country, most of them descendants of the Portuguese. There were four Catholic churches in Bangkok, but three of them were no more than sheds. Roberts observed that the Catholic missionaries were unfriendly to the more recently arrived Protestants, including a few American missionaries.

Roberts recorded that "women are allowed more freedom here, than in any other country where polygamy is tolerated." They wore no veils and "apparently, do most of the labours of the field, and are employed in the boats on the river in great numbers. They are the principal traders, and are said to be very shrewd and cunning." Divorces were easily obtained, and each partner got back what they brought into the marriage. Most women wore only a sarong, with no clothing above the waist, leading Dr. Ticknor to comment on their "shameless nudity," adding that their habit of chewing areca nut left them with disgustingly blackened teeth.[54] Roberts found the Siamese "excessively lascivious and immoral," recounting that "temporary marriages are so notorious, that to sell a daughter wholly to a stranger, or for a stipulated term of time, is as common among the middling and lower classes of people, as to sell any common commodity."[55]

To the Americans' surprise, bread was largely unknown, and there was not a single baker in Bangkok. Dr. Ticknor noticed that there was no apothecary in the city. For amusement, the population sang and played instruments and flew kites. They were entertained by dancing girls, tumblers, ropedancers, actors, and snake charmers. There was much gambling. Siam abounded with tigers, leopards, bats, snakes, alligators, and elephants. A constant torment was the "moschetoes," which Roberts found to be worse than those in "the swamps of Louisiana and Texas."[56]

As for trade, Roberts wrote that Americans could make money exporting textiles to Siam, with red by far the favored color. Major export items from Siam included pepper, sugar, tin, ivory, animal skins, "dragon's blood" (a tree resin used for medicinal purposes and dyes), shark fins, peacock tails, and rattans. Siam also exported entire carcasses of tiger and rhinoceros to China, where they were used for medicinal purposes. The Chinese, he found, were illegally importing opium into Siam.

As Roberts neared the conclusion of his negotiations, he was granted an audience with the king. The formalities were carefully prepared. Roberts told court officials that he would show proper respect to the king, but would do nothing servile. He was asked to make three bows in the European style, then sit down in Asiatic style with his feet behind him and make three more bows. Roberts agreed, "seeing nothing unreasonable or degrading in this formality." He was pleasantly surprised to find that he was not asked to enter in a stooping position or to remove his shoes, "which could not have been complied with."[57] Roberts recalled that during British envoy Henry Burney's visit, Burney had been asked to remove his shoes before being admitted to see the king. Burney was insulted by the request and said he would agree only on condition that he could keep his hat on. The Siamese decided they preferred for him to keep his shoes on and remove his hat, which he did. This anecdote highlights the levels of silliness that sometimes accompanied diplomatic protocol. In the Far East, however, Western envoys had become extremely sensitive to anything that might suggest they were "kowtowing" to local rulers, which Roberts described as "that debasing and disgusting ceremony of the Ko-tou or Knock-head."[58] He commented with pride that during his negotiations in the East he sometimes endured personal slights in the interest of American diplomacy, but he never let American honor be jeopardized by "humiliating and degrading concessions to eastern etiquette."[59]

By prior arrangement, Roberts was carried to the palace on a palanquin with eight bearers, led by officials wearing elaborate silk dresses and turbans, while the rest of the Americans in his entourage rode horses. They proceeded past a lineup of royal elephants and then past several hundred musicians in red coats and caps, whose drums and horns made "a most deafening noise." Next was an "immense number of military with a vast many officers richly clad and splendidly dressed. . . . The spectacle . . . was quite imposing." Finally they were ushered into the presence of his majesty, Rama III, the magnificent king of Siam. "There lay prostrate, or rather on all fours resting on their knees and elbows, with hands united and head bowed low, all the princes and nobility of the land: it was an impressive but abasing sight, such as no freeman could look on, with any other feelings than those of indignation and disgust. . . . When the courtiers enter, they crawl in on all fours, and, when dismissed, crawl out again backward, 'à la crab,' or 'à la lobster,' and when the numbers are great, their appearance is most ludicrous."[60]

Roberts recorded that "his majesty is a very stout fleshy man, apparently about 45 years of age, of a pleasing countenance. He was dressed in a cloth of gold tissue around the waist, while a mantle was thrown gracefully over the left shoulder." He was said to have eight hundred wives. The king asked a few questions about the health of President Jackson and the other great men of the United States, and he inquired how long Roberts's trip had been, what countries he had visited, and where he was bound after Siam. Each question was repeated in a low voice by a senior advisor, then whispered by another official to the interpreter, who then translated it in a similar low voice. Roberts's answers were returned through the same chain. This lengthy procedure did not allow much of an exchange, since the meeting lasted only about thirty minutes. At that point, the king ordered that his guests be shown the palace grounds and the royal white elephants. Then "the curtain was drawn and his majesty disappeared; the court made three solemn kotows, and we our three salams, and then retired. . . . The thermometer being at nearly a hundred, we remained but a short time. We returned . . . much gratified with our reception, and rejoiced that it was at an end."[61] This was Roberts's only encounter with the king.

A few days later, on April 1, the treaty was signed and sealed. The negotiations that seemed endless to Roberts had taken twenty-two days, a very short time for an international negotiation, even in the 1830s. The final document was nine feet, seven inches long, and was written in English, Portuguese, Chinese, and Siamese. Although it did not include everything Roberts had hoped for, he was quite pleased with the result. The first clause stipulated, "There shall be a perpetual peace between the United States of America and the Magnificent King of Siam." The remaining provisions covered duties, debtors, and protection for shipwrecked Americans. Roberts estimated that with the new flat-rate duties based on a ship's tonnage, a typical American ship of 250 tons would pay a total of about $4,000, compared with more than $30,000 previously. Roberts thus considered that the treaty "brought my mission to a close in a very satisfactory manner."[62]

Historians have debated the extent to which the treaty of 1833 really served to open up commerce between the United States and Siam. One prominent history calls it an "ineffectual commercial treaty."[63] Another, however, notes that it succeeded in opening the door to U.S. commerce in Siam on a most favored nation basis.[64] The number of U.S. ships calling in Siam did increase appreciably, although it is hard to judge how much of this was a direct result of the treaty. Real change would not come until the 1850s and the accession of Prince Mongkut as king.

The Roberts treaty was the first ever signed by the United States with an Asian country. Its conclusion was symbolic of a change in the direction of American foreign policy toward a more activist approach for the United States in oceans and countries far from home and the increasing emergence of the United States as a world power.

On the evening before Roberts's departure from Siam, he was invited to make a farewell call on the praklang. The minister wanted to offer his final assurances that every facility would be granted to American commerce. But there was one other important matter the minister wanted to bring to Roberts's attention: presents. The minister told Roberts that when he returned with the ratified treaty (the treaty would still have to be ratified by the Senate to become official), he should be sure to bring along gifts. The king's desire was for "five pairs of stone statues of men and women; some of the natural and some of the larger size, *clothed in various costumes of the United States.* Ten pair of vase lamps, of the largest size, plain glass. One pair of swords, with gold hilt and scabbards; the latter of gold, not *gilt*—shape of the blade, a little curved." The minister himself desired "one mirror, (or pair of mirrors,) three cubits long by two broad, fixed in a stand, so as to form a screen; frame, carved and gilt; back, painted green. Soft, hairy carpeting, of certain dimensions; and some flower and fruit trees, planted, or in seed, with flower-pots."[65] With that, and with many reassurances of goodwill, Roberts took his leave of the minister and of Siam.

From Siam the *Peacock* sailed to Singapore, arriving on May 1, 1833. This British outpost had been founded just a dozen years earlier, but it was already a bustling free port. The population was about twenty thousand, with men outnumbering women by three to one. In Singapore, young Robert Morrison was discharged and paid six hundred dollars for his services. Morrison immediately returned to China, where he would have an increasingly distinguished career. The *Peacock* pressed on to Batavia, where it finally rendezvoused with its supply schooner, the *Boxer.* The two ships then set out west together, across the Indian Ocean.

Recounting routes and stops does not give an adequate picture to today's reader of the tedium of sea travel in the 1830s. Although ships continually improved in construction, they still depended on wind, weather, and currents to make their slow passage. By the 1830s, steam paddle wheelers were already common on coastal and river routes, but effective transoceanic steamships were still decades away. The *Peacock* took twenty-five days to cover the thousand miles from Siam to Singapore, then another twenty-six days to sail nine hundred miles to Batavia. From there, crossing the Indian Ocean to reach their next destination, Muscat, would take another fifty days.

On leaving Siam, therefore, Roberts and his shipmates had to look forward to endless weeks at sea with very few stops or diversions. More than two hundred men were crowded onto a ship hardly more than one hundred feet long. Food was monotonous. Disease was common. And on the *Peacock*, Commander Geisinger was abusive and often drunk, while the first mate was strict and overbearing. Roberts and Geisinger fought frequently, and in the ship's confined quarters their disputes were common knowledge. Roberts put the best face on conditions in letters home to his daughters, assuring them that all was well, "and every Sabbath all the crew have been mustered on the quarter-deck, dressed neat & clean, and prayers and the Scriptures have been read by our excellent Surgeon, Dr. Ticknor."[66] U.S. Navy regulations at the time required divine services every Sunday.

The *Peacock* sailed past the island of "Crockatoa" off the coast of Java, which Ticknor described as "of small extent. . . . Its height seemed to be disproportioned to its size."[67] Fifty years later, the island would explode in one of the most violent volcanic eruptions in recorded history.

The *Peacock* sighted the coast of East Africa on August 20, then sailed northeast, following the coast of Arabia, along a "mountainous, barren, rocky and sandy" shoreline, punctuated by occasional villages and groves of date palms.[68] As they approached Muscat, they began to pass large numbers of fishing boats. To their astonishment, these included shark fishermen, who dove into the water with harpoons to pursue their prey.

It was September 18 when the *Peacock* and the *Boxer* finally anchored in the cove of Muscat. The small harbor was bounded by precipitous black cliffs over three hundred feet high. On some of the promontories were old, round Portuguese towers, showing again—as in Macao and Siam—that the Americans were following trade routes pioneered by the Portuguese three centuries earlier. Roberts was awed by the eerie desolation: "no place . . . presents a more forbidding aspect than this; not a green thing is to be seen, whether tree, shrub, or plant, from the roadstead."[69]

This bleak port was the home of Syed Syeed bin Sultan (Said bin Sultan), one of the most powerful rulers of the Indian Ocean littoral. The sultan's domains included the entire east coast of Arabia, much of the Persian Gulf, and more than two thousand miles of the coast of East Africa, from modern-day Somalia to Mozambique, with important bases on the islands of Zanzibar and Pemba. He was, in fact, planning to relocate his capital from Muscat to Zanzibar. The sultan had developed a modern navy, which Roberts assessed as "a more efficient naval force than all the native princes combined from the Cape of Good Hope to Japan."[70]

Muscat lay at the mouth of the Persian Gulf, where it developed into a commercial hub between the Middle East, the Far East, and Africa. The sultan derived his wealth from duties, tribute, presents, taxes, and clove plantations in Zanzibar. Much of his revenue came from the extensive East African slave trade. To his credit, the sultan protected Christians and Jews within his territories.

On reaching the harbor, the *Peacock* exchanged salutes with the shore batteries and sent a boat to inform the sultan of the ship's arrival and its purpose. The sultan's reply was encouraging: he was "highly flattered, that, at length, United States' ships-of-war should, for the first time, visit his ports, and more especially for the object of the mission." The sultan received Roberts and members of the ship's company on the very afternoon of their arrival. The reception was gracious. In contrast with Siam, in Muscat there was no crawling or "knocking heads" on the ground, "but all was manly, and every one stood on his feet."[71] The sultan shook the hand of each American and served them coffee in tiny cups. He also served sherbet, a treat that was entirely new to some of the Americans.[72]

Roberts was full of praise for the sultan, who he described as being "of a mild and peaceable demeanour, of unquestionable bravery, as was evinced during the Wahabee war, where he was severely wounded in endeavouring to save an English artilleryman. He is a strict lover of justice, possessing a humane disposition, and greatly beloved by his subjects. He possesses just and liberal views in regard to commerce, . . . encouraging foreigners as well as his own subjects."[73] Dr. Ticknor, who accompanied Roberts on the initial call, recorded that the sultan had about thirty wives, and "consequently there must have been employment for a considerable number of eunuchs, . . . those wretched beings, who have undergone a denaturalizing mutilation, for the purpose of being employed in the Sultan's harem."[74]

This was the same Sultan Syed whom Roberts had met on a private trading visit five years earlier and who had discussed with him then the possibility of a commercial treaty with the United States. In the intervening years, American commerce with Muscat had increased; thirty-two American ships had visited Muscat in the eighteen months before Roberts's arrival, far more than those of any European nation.[75] This created a growing American incentive for a commercial treaty. From the sultan's perspective, the United States might prove to be a source of modern arms for Muscat and might help balance the growing British influence in the region.

To Roberts's great satisfaction, the sultan was ready to get right down to business. He quickly agreed to grant American traders the same most favored status as the British, "to wit: by paying a duty of five per cent on the cargo *landed*, and free from every other charge whatever, either on imports or exports, or even the charge of pilotage."[76] The sultan was amenable also to all the other points Roberts proposed, with a single exception: he refused a proposed article under which the United States would reimburse him for caring for any shipwrecked American seamen, insisting that Arab hospitality required him personally to bear any such expense. By the end of Roberts's first meeting with the sultan, all the basic elements of the treaty were in place.

During this and subsequent meetings, one of the sultan's naval captains, Sayed Ben Calfoun, served as interpreter between English and Arabic. The Americans were so impressed with Ben Calfoun that years later he was appointed as U.S. consul to Muscat, serving from 1843 to 1847.[77]

The town of Muscat held few attractions for the Americans. It was a small place for a powerful seat of government, with fewer than ten thousand inhabitants. The heat was suffocating. With the exception of the sultan's palace and a few other decent-looking houses, Roberts wrote, the other habitations are "small, dark, and filthy, made of palm-branches only."[78] Ticknor commented after his first walk through the town that "the more we saw of it the more were we disgusted with it. The streets rarely exceeded four feet in width, & were unpaved, & extremely crooked, & filled with a variety of rubbish." Industry was limited to a few weavers, blacksmiths, coppersmiths, rope makers, carpenters, and sandal-makers, all using what the Americans considered to be crude equipment. The women were all veiled. Poverty was the rule, with beggars everywhere and many inhabitants owning little more than a mat to sleep on and an earthen cooking pot. Roberts and Ticknor both remarked on the large number of blind people, "seen in groups at the corners of the streets, crying out in the most piteous manner."[79]

Although the population lived in poverty, there was no difficulty finding fresh meat, vegetables, and nuts to provision the ships. Water was drawn from a deep well outside the town's walls, hauled up by a buffalo, then carried in skins on men's backs to the dock. Commander Geisinger was able to hire divers to clean the *Peacock*'s hull, which had become infested with barnacles and other debris. Ticknor marveled at the divers' capacity; he clocked one who remained under water for more than two minutes.

The Americans also visited Muscat's slave bazaar, held near the dock every evening at sunset. Slave markets were still common in the southern United States at the time, so the market might not have been entirely unusual to the Americans, although it had its exotic qualities. In Muscat, the slaves were paraded through the streets of town before the auction. At the auction site, "the slaves are well oiled, to show a smooth skin, and they are decently dressed. . . . The slave-bazar is a great resort for Arab dandies; decorated with fine sabres and silver-hilted crooked daggers . . . their long beards well perfumed, and their turbans arranged according to the prevailing fashion, they examine females as well as males, with little regard to delicacy, or even to common decency."[80]

On September 30, 1833, less than two weeks after arriving in Muscat, Roberts and the sultan signed the treaty of amity and commerce, which was entitled in Arabic "the Treaty made between His Highness the heaven-protected, the Seid Sa'id son of the Seid Sultan, Defender of Maskat and its Dependencies, and the United States, i.e., the Territory of America, for the Sake of Intercourse, and Amity, and Promotion of Trade."[81] The first clause, as in the Siam treaty, provided for perpetual peace between the two countries. The second stipulated that American citizens were free to enter and trade in any products at all of the sultan's ports, with prices set entirely by market conditions; the only exception was a prohibition on the sale of firearms in the port of Zanzibar. The provisions on duties and protection of Americans were favorable. Finally, the treaty allowed for the appointment of American consuls, with legal immunity, in any of the sultan's ports. Roberts was extremely pleased.

In the final days before the *Peacock*'s departure, the sultan asked to visit the ship. This led to a burst of activity aboard, as all hands were pressed to put the vessel into top shape to receive the visitor. The crew prepared for a full week, painting the entire ship inside and out, and applying coal tar to all the guns and ironwork, a particularly nasty job in the torrid temperatures. With the *Peacock* in shipshape, the day of the visit arrived. The sultan stayed just thirty minutes, leaving some to wonder if their long, hard labor in the heat had been worth the effort.

Following his visit, the sultan sent aboard gifts, including "a valuable sword as a present to Capt. Geisinger, or as was pretended, in order to evade the law which forbids any officer to receive a present from any foreign prince or potentate, for the Captain's son; and a cashmere shawl for the wife of Capt. Shields [of the *Boxer*]."[82] He also sent presents for the wives or sisters of the junior officers who had escorted him around the *Peacock*. The sultan proposed to send two pairs of fine Arabian horses to President Jackson, but Roberts declined, since the ship was not equipped to carry them. The sultan did, however, send a letter addressed "to the high and mighty Andrew Jackson, President of the United States, whose name shines with so much splendor throughout the world." It pledged friendship until "time is no more" and assured the president that the treaty "shall be faithfully observed by myself and my successors, as long as the world endures."[83] A few years later, the sultan made good on his desire to send a gift of horses to the president, conveying them in his ship, the *Sultany*, the first Arab vessel to cross the Atlantic.[84]

The *Peacock* departed on the afternoon of October 7, 1833. It fired eighteen guns "as a parting salute to the hospitable sultan," which were returned by twenty-one guns from the shore batteries. Not wanting to be outdone in an act of courtesy, the *Peacock* fired three more guns. "The effect produced by the echo, among the serrated and cavernous rocks and mountains about the cove of Muscat, and the neighbouring hill, was surpassingly fine; loud, distinct, and repeated charges were heard, apparently, for the space of several minutes, until the reverberations died away, in faint echoes, among the distant hills."[85]

Thus ended one of the longest, most far-flung, and unusual missions in the annals of early American diplomacy. Roberts was returning with two treaties, the first ever negotiated by the United States with Asian powers, both of which promised to put American relations and commerce on a greatly improved footing. He had failed in Cochin China, and he decided not to attempt a trip to Japan, since conditions for opening relations there did not appear promising. In addition to the treaties, Roberts gathered enough information on the Far East to fill a volume exceeding four hundred pages, much of it practical information that could assist American merchants.

It took almost six months for Roberts to return home, sailing by way of the Cape of Good Hope and Rio de Janeiro. In Rio, Roberts and his companions received mail from home for the first time in twenty months. The *Peacock* remained off the coast of South America for some time longer, but Roberts transferred to another navy sloop, the USS *Lexington*, to hurry the treaties back to the United States. Faced with adverse winds, it was eight more weeks before the *Lexington* put into Boston Harbor. Roberts's mission had taken him more than 45,000 miles in 434 days at sea, plus many more weeks in foreign ports. As Roberts disembarked the next morning, "the music played 'Home, Sweet Home,' which I was upon the eve of visiting, after a painful absence of twenty-six months."[86]

Roberts's travels, however, were not yet over. He was asked to return to the East to deliver the ratified treaties, which were quickly approved by the Senate and were touted by President Jackson in his next State of the Union address.[87] Roberts was first to deliver the treaties to Muscat and Siam, then to make another attempt at a treaty with Cochin China, and then finally to continue on to Japan to pursue a treaty there. He was furnished with presents for the king of Siam and the sultan of Muscat, as well as with an array of presents for the Japanese emperor, including a gold watch with a heavy gold chain eight feet long, a saber, a rifle, a shotgun, and a pair of pistols, an assortment of broadcloth, cut glass, a music box, maps, a set of U.S. coins, prints of American naval victories, and ten Merino sheep.

On April 23, 1835, almost a year to the day after his return from his first mission, Roberts sailed from New York, once again upon the *Peacock*, although under a different captain and accompanied this time by the schooner *Enterprise*.

During his year back in the United States, Roberts worked on a book recounting his mission. He didn't have time to complete the manuscript but left what he had written and piles of additional papers with his son-in-law, who hired a prominent writer to finish the job. The book was published in 1837 as *Embassy to the Eastern Courts of Cochin-China, Siam and Muscat in the U.S. Sloop-of-War* Peacock, *David Geisinger, Commander, during the Years 1832-3-4*. Like many travel books of the day, it used, without acknowledgment, passages from other books containing general descriptions of countries and peoples.[88] Roberts also spent much of his year in the United States trying to get the State Department to reimburse him for $7,297 in personal expenses. He succeeded only when a member of Congress intervened on his behalf.[89]

The second voyage saw new difficulties and hazards, which can be described only briefly here. They sailed first to Muscat, but the *Peacock* ran aground and stuck tight on a coral reef off the coast of Arabia four hundred miles away. As small pirate vessels began to gather in hopes of plunder, Roberts and seven crewmembers took one of the *Peacock*'s small boats and slipped away to Muscat for help—taking with him the ratified treaty. The perilous trip took five days in the tiny open boat, under the blistering Arabian sun, chased part of the way by a pirate dhow. The boat was nearly swamped by heavy seas, but finally reached Muscat, where Roberts was warmly received by the sultan, who immediately dispatched his own ships on a rescue mission. The *Peacock*, however, managed to free itself from the reef a few days later, after the crew threw half the cannons and supplies overboard to lighten her.[90] The sultan later dispatched a team to raise the cannons, which he had delivered to the *Peacock* a few weeks later in Bombay. Roberts exchanged ratified treaties with the sultan and presented him with a number of gifts.

In Bombay, the *Peacock* underwent extensive repairs to the damage sustained on the reef. While there, the crew was treated to the sight of Halley's Comet in the evening sky. The ship then sailed on to Siam by way of Colombo and Batavia, arriving on March 26, eleven months after leaving New York. Based on his previous experience in Siam, Roberts believed he would be received with more respect if he put on a show of pomp and circumstance. He and the officers, therefore, made all their public appearances in full dress, preceded by the ship's band. Not surprisingly, they drew a crowd everywhere they went.[91] Roberts handed over the ratified treaty with great ceremony. According to one account:

> The officers were formed into a procession headed by Mr. Roberts, two of them bearing a box, containing the American copy of the treaty, and marched to the river, distant about a hundred yards, pre-

ceded by our band. At the place of embarkation, a canoe eighty feet long, rowed by thirty-four oars, both ends curving upwards, awaited to receive it. A bright crimson silk canopy, embroidered in gold, overhung the centre of the canoe, with which all the ornaments of the vessel were in keeping. The rowers wore the red livery of the king.

On reaching the margin of the river, Mr. Roberts took the treaty in his hand, and, after holding it up above his head in token of respect, delivered it to a Siamese officer, the secretary of the P'hra Klang. He also held it above his head, and then, shaded by a royal chat, a large white silk umbrella, borne by a slave, passed it into the boat, where it was received upon an ornamented stand, and after covering it with a cone of gilt paper, it was placed beneath the canopy. At this moment our band ceased, and that of the Siamese began to play. The canoe shoved off, and we turned our steps homeward to the merry tune of yankee doodle.[92]

The king of Siam's seal was affixed to the treaty "on the fourteenth day of the fifth month of the year, called the Monkey, eleven hundred and ninety-eight," or April 14, 1836. Roberts distributed gifts to the king and senior nobles, including "lamps, Nankins, carpeting, male and female costumes of the United States, two very large and elegant mirrors, an American flag, shawls, a set of United States' coins, and two splendid swords in gold scabbards."[93] He thus delivered some but not all of the items requested by the praklang on his previous visit.

The set of American coins Roberts presented to the king have become some of the most famous and valuable coins in the world, now known as the "King of Siam" set. Four sets of the coins were specially minted in 1834 at the request of the State Department for Roberts to present in Muscat, Siam, Cochin China, and Japan. Although minted in 1834, they bore the date 1804, the last year that U.S. ten-dollar gold pieces were minted. Of the four sets, only the "King of Siam" set remains. Legend has it that the set passed down in the royal family and was eventually given to Anna Leonowens (of *Anna and the King of Siam*, later popularized in adaptations such as *The King and I*), who arrived in Siam twenty-five years later. The set of coins appeared in London in the 1950s and was sold by two women believed to be her descendants. In 1979 the set was sold again, for $1 million.[94]

All of the *Peacock*'s officers who went upriver to Bangkok fell ill, some of them seriously, including Roberts. By the time they put to sea for Cochin China, so many of the crew were sick that the ship resembled a hospital. The ship's doctor for this voyage, William Ruschenberger, wrote: "It would be difficult to present, to those who did not witness it, an adequate idea of the distressing state of things existing on board of the ship. One-fourth of the crew were confined, by sickness, to their hammocks, and those who were not under medical treatment, enfeebled by previous disease."[95]

There were no adverse winds as they approached Cochin China, so the *Peacock* was able this time to sail into Turan Bay, near Da Nang. Roberts sent a letter ashore addressed to the prime minister in Hué. As on the previous visit, a series of officials of increasingly high rank visited the *Peacock* to inquire about the purpose of the visit. The officials initially refused to believe that Roberts was the envoy, since, unlike the ship's officers, he did not wear a uniform and epaulettes. By the time the third official visited the ship, Roberts was too ill to receive him; the refusal caused great offense.

Communications were difficult because Roberts did not have a Chinese interpreter. He had assumed the negotiations could be conducted in French, since there had long been a French presence in Hué. The Cochin Chinese, however, insisted that there was no one in Hué who knew French well enough to serve as interpreter. The Americans concluded that they were not serious about negotiations. With the talks apparently going nowhere and Roberts now dangerously ill, the *Peacock* sailed for Macao to rest while Roberts and the many sick crewmen recovered.

The failure of Roberts's second mission to Cochin China was not surprising, although Roberts could not have been fully aware of the reasons. Since his visit two years earlier, Emperor Minh Mang had put down a rebellion in which Christians were involved, had increased his repression of Christians, and had adopted a policy of refusing foreign trade and diplomatic contacts.[96]

So many crewmembers of the *Peacock* and the *Enterprise* had fallen ill that in Macao the ship's doctor secured a large house to use as a hospital. The first to die ashore was the commander of the *Enterprise*, Archibald Campbell. A few days later, on June 12, 1836, Edmund Roberts passed away. The *Peacock's* doctor recorded that "a long exposure in the climates of the East, actively engaged in the service of his country, proved too much for his age and constitution. He had been long out of health, and, at Bangkok, was attacked with the prevailing disease, which he at first neglected, through his desire to lose no time in discharging the duties which had brought him to Siam." The deaths "cast a shade of melancholy over us all." Roberts was buried in Macao's British Protestant cemetery, with a tombstone recalling that as "Special Diplomatic Agent to Several Asiatic Courts . . . He devised and executed . . . Treaties of Amity and Commerce, between the United States and the Courts of Muscat and Siam."[97] A memorial window to Roberts was later erected at St. John's Church in his hometown of Portsmouth, New Hampshire.

With Roberts's death, the mission to Japan was abandoned. The effort to conclude a treaty with Japan would stretch over two more decades. The *Peacock*, for its part, continued home, by way of Hawaii and Rio de Janeiro, circumnavigating the globe. Two years later the *Peacock* joined the famous U.S. Exploring Expedition of 1838–42. She ran aground in heavy seas at the mouth of the Columbia River. The crew was saved, but the *Peacock* was abandoned and dashed to pieces by the surf.

Trading in the East Indies remained a dangerous business for both American merchants and the local population. Seven years after pirates seized the *Friendship* off Qualah Battoo, pirates in nearby Muckie attacked another American merchantman, the *Eclipse*, killing her captain and some of the crew. This led to a reprise of the Qualah Battoo incident. Cdre. George Read, aboard the frigate USS *Columbia*, heard of the attack on the *Eclipse* and sailed immediately, on his own initiative, to Sumatra. When the local Rajahs could not or would not turn over the pirates and make restitution for the *Eclipse*, the *Columbia* bombarded Qualah Battoo, even though the attack had not taken place there. Read then sailed on to Muckie, where he first bombarded the town, then put two hundred men ashore to set fire to what remained. The *Columbia*'s chaplain recorded, without regret, that "the destruction was complete."[98] It seems that little had changed in the seven years since the *Potomac* "chastised" Qualah Battoo. Despite such retaliatory vengeance, piracy remained a problem in the region for the rest of the nineteenth century.

With the ratification of the Roberts treaties, American commerce in the Far East continued to grow. A decade after Roberts's missions, trade with China was substantially opened in the wake of the first Opium War. A decade after that, in 1856, another American envoy, Townsend Harris, negotiated a new treaty with Siam, which further expanded trade. Harris's adventures, which form the last chapter of this volume, center on his role in opening Japan. Cochin China, meanwhile, remained largely closed to outsiders until the French military occupation in the 1860s. American relations with Said bin Sultan of Muscat, who moved his capital to Zanzibar in 1840, remained friendly until his death in 1856. The sultan continued to send gifts to American leaders, including lions for the Washington Zoo and more fine Arabian horses for the presidents.

# SIX

# The Commodore as Diplomat
*David Porter at the Sublime Porte*

Edmund Roberts was not the only American of the 1830s to launch a diplomatic career based on his connections to political leaders. Andrew Jackson's administration, which took office in 1829, became notorious for ushering in the "spoils system," a form of political cronyism under which government jobs were doled out freely to friends and political supporters. Diplomatic posts were high on the list of patronage positions that Jackson handed out to backers, irrespective of their qualifications for office. Shamefully, the same system of politically motivated appointments remains in place today for many senior diplomatic positions.

When Jackson decided to appoint America's first resident envoy to the Ottoman Empire, it may have had less to do with his interest in building a relationship with the great power of the eastern Mediterranean than his desire to find a respectable position for a friend and supporter. The man in question was David Porter, the feisty naval hero of the War of 1812, who had fallen on hard times. Jackson was determined to find a government position for him, and after several false starts he appointed Porter as the first resident envoy of the United States to the Ottoman Empire.

Constantinople, today's Istanbul, was the Ottoman capital. For more than 1,500 years it had been the seat of great empires and one of the most resplendent and powerful cities on earth. Founded on the crossroads of Europe and Asia by the Roman emperor Constantine in the year 330, it served successively as the capital city of the Romans, the Byzantines, and the Ottomans. In the early years of the nineteenth century, the Ottoman sultans still held sway over a vast realm that stretched from Morocco to the Black Sea and from the Balkans to Arabia. Constantinople remained the center of the Islamic world, a city of glittering palaces and monumental mosques. The Ottoman government came to be known in the West as the Sublime Porte, after the impressive gate through which diplomats were received.

The United States first came into direct contact with the empire during the Barbary Wars, when Capt. William Bainbridge was forced to sail the U.S. frigate *George Washington* from Algiers to Constantinople, carrying presents to the sultan from the dey of Algiers. It was not until thirty years later that the United States and the Ottoman Empire concluded a treaty of amity, commerce, and navigation. At the time, the United States did not even have a consul in Constantinople, although consuls were assigned to a few of the empire's other ports, notably in the Barbary states and in the bustling trading city of Smyrna (now Izmir).

David Porter was one of the best-known and most successful naval captains of his generation. His exploits took him to far-flung corners of the globe and included victories at sea over Britain, Tripoli, and Caribbean pirates. During a long and generally distinguished naval career, Porter won a reputation for being hotheaded and impulsive, traits that may have served him well in battle, but which occasionally landed him in trouble. In his later life as a diplomat, he followed the pattern he had established in the navy, isolating himself from his subordinates and demanding their unquestioning obedience. He was prickly, easily offended, and unforgiving to those who crossed him, often carrying grudges for years. Under the patronage of the president, however, he was secure in his position, whatever trouble his personality might cause.

Porter's action-packed career and audacious naval exploits have inspired biographers and filled volumes. His diplomatic service, in contrast, is seldom mentioned or remembered, even though he represented the United States for more than a dozen tumultuous years in one of the most important capitals of Europe and the Middle East.

Born in Boston in 1780, Porter seemed destined from birth for a life at sea. His grandfather captained a merchantman, and his father commanded a small ship in the Continental navy during the American Revolution. David went to sea at age sixteen, working first aboard merchant ships trading with the West Indies. He was twice impressed into the British navy—that is, taken off American ships at gunpoint and forcibly conscripted into the British naval service—but each time he escaped. In 1798 he was appointed as a midshipman in the U.S. Navy. At age eighteen, he was rather old for a midshipman in those days. At the time, the United States was involved in what was called the "Quasi-War" with France, an undeclared conflict that pitted the two countries' navies against each other. Porter saw his first naval combat during this period.

After action against the French and against pirates in the West Indies, Porter was assigned to duty in the Mediterranean during the Barbary Wars, where he was twice wounded in action and rose steadily through the ranks. By 1803, he was first mate aboard the ill-fated USS *Philadelphia*, which ran aground on a reef outside the harbor of Tripoli in 1803. Porter was among the 315 Americans held captive in Tripoli for nineteen long months until Tobias Lear negotiated the crew's release as part of the peace agreement of 1805. Porter's health suffered greatly during this period and would continue to be a problem for the rest of his life. On his release, Porter resumed active duty and was awarded command of his own ship.

In 1808, back in the United States, Porter was smitten with Evelina Anderson, the daughter of a Pennsylvania congressman. Porter was twenty-eight; Evelina was just fifteen. The Anderson family opposed the match, considering that a naval officer was below Evelina's station. According to family lore, Porter threatened to throw Evelina's brother out the window when he objected to the courtship, showing off his "impulsive manner of doing everything."[1] The marriage went forward despite the family's initial objections. Although David and Evelina lived apart for most of their marriage, they had six sons and two daughters. During one of Porter's many long absences at sea, Evelina wrote a curious letter congratulating Andrew Jackson on his election as president and denouncing rumors of her infidelity.[2] Evelina did not join Porter on his diplomatic assignment to Turkey, although some other members of his family did.

The year he was married, Porter was placed in charge of the U.S. naval station in New Orleans, where he led a squadron operating against pirates in the Gulf of Mexico. This position made Porter one of the city's prominent personalities. He would certainly have known Daniel Clark, the onetime U.S. consul, who was then the U.S. congressman for the Orleans Territory. While in New Orleans, Porter adopted a boy, James Farragut, from a large family of modest means, taking him as a foster son and agreeing to raise him in the navy. James was renamed David, after his new foster father. Just nine years old when Porter took him to sea as a midshipman, David Farragut was destined to become America's most celebrated admiral.

Porter reached the pinnacle of his naval career during the War of 1812 as commander of the 32-gun frigate *Essex*. He won America's first naval victory of the war and went on to prey successfully on British shipping and troop transports, capturing more than two dozen ships and virtually destroying the British whaling industry in the South Pacific.

Among Porter's other exploits during the war was the conquest of one of the Marquesa Islands, an episode that tarnished what is otherwise regarded as one of the great wartime cruises of American naval history. In 1813 the *Essex* anchored in Nookaheeva Bay (now Nuku Hiva), to seek supplies and make repairs. This was in the group of islands discovered in 1791 by Capt. Joseph Igraham of the *Hope*, one of America's first China traders in the days of Samuel Shaw. The *Essex* was greeted by the islanders in the traditional warm style of the South Pacific. The American sailors were captivated by the easy life on the island and by the beautiful Polynesian women, who wore little clothing and were free with their favors.

Not all of the islanders welcomed the Americans, however. One tribe, the Typees, refused to join in providing supplies. Porter found this lack of cooperation intolerable and sent his troops against them, leaving their villages in ruins. Porter's son and biographer described the aftermath of the fighting as "a scene of desolation he had left behind him—where in the morning all was abundance and happiness—now a line of smoking ruins marked the path of the invader, from one end of the valley to the other. The opposite hills were covered with the unhappy fugitives, and horror and destruction were on every hand."[3]

With the islanders subdued, Porter raised the Stars and Stripes, claiming Nookaheeva for the United States and renaming it "Madison's Island" in honor of the president. The United States never ratified or supported his claim. He sailed away to continue his cruise, promising to return, but his travels never took him back to the Marquesas.

It was a few months later, in early 1814, that Porter and the *Essex* arrived at Valparaíso, Chile, where U.S. consul general Joel Poinsett warmly welcomed him and where he was defeated by British ships that had been tracking him. The British allowed Porter and the other survivors of the engagement to sail home in a small, unarmed ship. Porter was welcomed back to the United States with great honors. He was given one more wartime assignment, to help with the defense of Washington DC, but he arrived too late; the British had already burned the town.

When the war ended a few months later, Porter's reputation and his fortunes were at their height. He was appointed as one of three members of the newly created Navy Board of Commissioners. He had amassed a small fortune in prize money during the war, as American captains were entitled to keep a percentage when a captured ship was sold. Porter used his earnings to purchase 157 acres of what was then farmland, just a mile or two north of the White House. He erected a mansion, which he dubbed "Meridian Hill," since his property stood directly on the line of longitude that Thomas Jefferson had unsuccessfully championed as the prime meridian. Today the site is Washington DC's Meridian Park, with its Italian-inspired gardens lying on the same north-south axis as the White House, the Washington Monument, and the Jefferson Memorial. Porter invested most of his fortune in the farm and mansion. It turned out to be a disastrous mistake. He could not turn a profit from the farm. Other investments also went bad, including a new "horse boat" service across the Potomac between Washington and Alexandria, Virginia.

During this period, Porter suggested that the United States undertake an exploring expedition to chart the Pacific Ocean and the west coast of North America and also visit Japan, to open that closed empire to American trade. Porter was ready to lead the expedition. Although initial preparations were begun, the voyage never took place. The idea would not see fruition for another twenty years, until Joel Poinsett launched the U.S. Exploring Expedition. The opening of Japan would take still longer, as chronicled in the final chapter of this volume.

With his financial situation rapidly declining, Porter went back to sea in 1823. He took command of what became known as the "Mosquito Fleet," a squadron established to fight the continuing problem of pirates in the Caribbean. Porter was appointed commodore, which at the time was not actually an American naval rank but a temporary title given to officers commanding squadrons. Porter would proudly use the title "commodore" for the rest of his life. As his flagship, Porter selected the frigate *John Adams*, which just a year earlier had carried Joel Poinsett on his first mission to Mexico.

One incident during this command bears special mention. Porter was convinced that the Spanish authorities on Puerto Rico were allowing pirates to use the town of Foxardo (actually Fojardo) as a safe haven. One of his officers who went to investigate was arrested. Porter sailed for Foxardo, landed two hundred men, destroyed the shore batteries, and demanded an apology, which he received. The United States and Spain were at peace, however, so the outraged Spanish authorities filed an official protest with the U.S. government. Porter was hauled before a court-martial.

The case created a furor in the United States, with prominent politicians lining up for and against Porter. The court found Porter guilty of exceeding his authority. Taking into account his distinguished record, he was given a light sentence, six months suspension from duty. For the rest of his life, Porter held a deep grudge against everyone even loosely connected with the court-martial, up to President John Quincy Adams, who he believed should have come to his defense.

Porter's estrangement from the navy left him in uncomfortable circumstances, both personally and financially. His investments had gone bad, and he now had eight children to educate and support. While the court's verdict was just a slap on the wrist, he feared that he might never get another command at sea, which meant no prize money to supplement his naval salary. On top of this, he was too proud to consider returning to serve with the men who had condemned his actions at Foxardo.

Porter was rescued from his dilemma from an unlikely quarter. His old friend from Valparaíso, Joel Poinsett, who was now the American minister in Mexico, recommended Porter to the Mexican government, which offered him the position of commander in chief of the newly formed Mexican navy. Mexico was still in a prolonged war with Spain, which had not yet recognized its independence. Porter accepted the offer and resigned from the U.S. Navy.

Over the next three years, Porter revamped Mexico's small fleet and launched successful attacks against Spanish shipping around the Gulf of Mexico and the Caribbean, capturing many prizes. Problems soon began to emerge, however. The handsome salary he was promised was usually late and often not paid at all. Prize money proved difficult to collect. His personal finances continued to decline, and he was forced to sell Meridian Hill to cover debts. The Mexican government did not appropriate enough to keep his ships outfitted, forcing him to downsize the small fleet. His success at sea sparked jealousy among some Mexican army officers who plotted against him. There were two failed attempts on his life, for which he came to suspect Santa Anna. By 1828 Porter had had enough. In December he wrote to his wife, who had remained in the United States, that "the wretched state of this country is such that I cannot reconcile it to myself to remain any longer than I can leave it with decency; it is split into fragments by the most horrid and bloody revolution."[4]

He was cheered by the news that Andrew Jackson had defeated John Quincy Adams in the presidential election of 1828. On learning of the election results Porter wrote to his wife: "John Q. Adams has been thus far my ruin and the ruin of my family. I shall still have my satisfaction, I hope, on the 4th of March next, about 10 o'clock in the morning, to be on the steps of the North door of the White House to make another bow to him as he leaves it."[5] Ironically, however, it was Adams who had the last laugh. After leaving the White House, Adams went to live in Porter's old mansion on Meridian Hill.

Early in 1829, Porter got word that Jackson wanted him to come home and take a government position. With great relief, he resigned from the Mexican service and headed back to Washington. Jackson initially planned to reinstate Porter into the navy, even though this might mean a fight with the Senate, since Porter was still a controversial figure. Porter refused, however; he still could not stand the idea of serving with—or worse, under—men who had been involved in his court-martial. Still, Jackson was determined to find a position for his friend. Porter declined several offers that would have put him in close contact with or under the command of the navy, including heading the naval hospital in Philadelphia or serving as naval agent in Gibraltar. He also turned down the position of marshal of the District of Columbia. Jackson then offered to appoint him as consul general in Algiers, the same position once held by Joel Barlow, Tobias Lear, and James Leander Cathcart. This time Porter agreed.

When Porter arrived in the Mediterranean in the summer of 1830, however, an unhappy surprise awaited him. In July France had invaded and conquered Algiers. The dey of Algiers, to whom Porter was accredited, had fled into exile in Italy, taking much of his treasure with him. Porter's diplomatic career appeared to be over even before it began.

Jackson, however, was still resolved to take care of his friend. As it happened, in that same summer of 1830, the United States finally completed its decade-long treaty negotiations with Turkey. Jackson offered to make Porter the first U.S. chargé d'affaires in Constantinople. Porter gratefully accepted.

Turkey—the Ottoman Empire—was still one of the great empires of the world in 1830, but its glory days were long past. The empire was in a sad state of decline, threatened from every direction. The Barbary dominions in North Africa had long been effectively independent, and France had just occupied the most powerful of them. In Egypt, Muhammad Ali, another vassal of the sultan, was amassing so much independent power that he threatened the regime. In the Balkans, the empire was beginning to crumble under assault from a variety of nationalist movements, notably the Greek struggle for independence. Just a few years earlier, in 1826, the Ottoman fleet was annihilated by a combined British, French, and Russian force in the Battle of Navarino, highlighting Turkey's military inferiority. In 1828 Russia declared war on Turkey, and the czar's armies swept across the Danube into Ottoman territories in Europe. The Russians might well have occupied Constantinople but for British and French intervention.

The Ottoman sultan in 1830 was Mahmud II, who took power in 1808 after his predecessor—his brother—failed in an attempt to murder him. Mahmud spent much of his life attempting to solidify his power and to quash rebellions, but with little success. He realized that wide-reaching changes were needed if the empire was to survive and cautiously began to reform its legal, administrative, tax, and military systems. He even decreed a change of dress at the court to a somewhat more European style. Among other changes, the fez replaced the turban.

Throughout this period, the United States had little contact with the Porte. George Washington had commissioned a minister to Constantinople as early as 1799, but he never made the trip. It was 1820 before the first envoys were sent to explore the idea of a treaty of commerce and friendship. The attempt failed, but the envoys left their local interpreter, Nicolas Navoni, to continue the effort. Over the next decade several more envoys were entrusted by the State Department with the same mission, but none succeeded, perhaps because many prominent Americans—notably Daniel Webster and Henry Clay—were speaking out forcefully for American assistance to the Greek rebels.

It was not until 1830 that the on-and-off negotiations began to make progress under new American envoys led by Charles Rhind. He arranged with the Turks to conduct the negotiations during Ramadan—a highly unusual concession—and at night in order to keep the talks secret from the European powers, "our enemies," as Rhind called them.[6] The terms of the draft treaty he worked out were auspicious: the United States would get most favored nation status; American ships would be allowed to pass freely through the Dardanelles and the Bosporus; and a resident American minister would have jurisdiction over Americans charged with crimes. The draft treaty included a secret clause that gave the sultan the right to contract for the construction of naval vessels in the United States. When the negotiators left for Washington with the draft treaty, Rhind left Nicolas Navoni in charge, as his predecessors had done a decade earlier.

The U.S. Senate ratified the treaty in early 1831 but rejected the secret clause. The State Department then commissioned Navoni to serve as "dragoman," a title exclusive to the Ottoman Empire, which was roughly equivalent to diplomatic secretary and interpreter. At the same time, the Department sent a message to David Porter, who was still in the Mediterranean wondering what to do with himself following the French conquest of Algiers, with an offer to serve as chargé d'affaires to Turkey.

Porter's new commission and instructions were carried to him by William Hodgson, a young man who would play an important role in Porter's early years in Turkey. Hodgson, who was not yet thirty, was largely self-educated and had a flair for languages. Despite a lack of formal schooling, he was a brilliant scholar; Princeton awarded him an honorary degree at age twenty-three, even though he never studied there. Hodgson had secured a junior position at the State Department during the presidency of John Quincy Adams. He was then sent to Algiers to assist the American consul and to hone his skill in oriental languages. Most recently, he had gone to Constantinople as an assistant to Rhind.

Porter's instructions, signed by Secretary of State Martin Van Buren, were to ensure that Turkey ratified the treaty despite the Senate's rejection of the secret article. In addition, he was to expand American commerce, protect American citizens, and report on important developments. He was authorized to draw $25,000 for "incidental expenses"—principally presents for the sultan and his officials—and given an annual contingency fund of $3,000 for office and other expenses. Porter's annual salary as chargé would be $4,500. Van Buren also sent Porter a cipher to use for confidential communications.

The frigate *John Adams*, Porter's onetime flagship, was assigned to carry him to Constantinople. Porter stopped first in Smyrna, on the Aegean Sea, where he sent word to the dragoman, Nicolas Navoni, to seek permission for the *John Adams* to pass through the Dardanelles—the narrow straits separating Europe and Asia—and to make other preparations for his arrival, then to come to Smyrna to accompany him to Constantinople. Then, without waiting to hear back from Navoni, Porter changed his mind and decided to travel on to Constantinople, stopping en route to visit a site that he believed to be ancient Troy. This was more than thirty years before Heinrich Schliemann began his famous excavations of Troy, at a time when most people believed Homer's tales of the Trojan War were fantasy. Porter knew enough of the classics to be awestruck to stand on the site where Achilles and Hector were said to have battled millennia before. He found the plain of Troy to be "little more than a dreary waste," but, he wrote to a friend, there were still enough ruins visible that "I can testify that there is abundance of proof to corroborate the description given by Homer."[7]

The *John Adams* then proceeded to Constantinople without awaiting word from Navoni on the key issue of whether the warship would have to dismount its guns to pass through the straits. Porter, harking back to his seafaring days, insisted that it would be an affront to U.S. dignity for an American naval vessel to dismount its guns, although this was the required practice for European and other warships in the straits. The Turks allowed exceptions only for newly appointed ambassadors arriving in warships. Porter, however, was not an ambassador, a title the United States would not confer on its highest envoys for another sixty years. He was not even a minister, the next highest rank of envoy, but just a chargé d'affaires, and as such he was not entitled to a waiver of the rules. Fortunately, Navoni had managed, with considerable difficulty, to secure a special exception for the *John Adams*, despite complaints from other envoys who had not been given the same privilege. This was Porter's first unhappy experience with diplomatic protocol; his rank as chargé would become an increasing irritant and embarrassment to him.

Arriving off Constantinople in early August 1831, Porter was struck with the majesty of the city, with its seemingly endless lines of castles, domes, and spires and its commotion. The harbor bustled with countless ships of all kinds. "To say the scene is magnificent is to say nothing," he wrote. "Imagination cannot depict and words cannot express what it is; to conceive it, it must be seen."[8]

Porter sent immediately for Navoni, demanding that he come aboard the *John Adams* at once, although Navoni had sent word he was bedridden with a fever. Once aboard, Navoni tried to advise Porter on the intricate procedures of the Ottoman court and how he should go about requesting meetings to present his credentials. Porter would have none of it. He ordered Navoni to set up an immediate interview with the Reis Effendi (the foreign minister) to present his credentials and to arrange for the *John Adams* to be saluted by the shore batteries, a courtesy never before accorded to a chargé. When Navoni remonstrated, Porter flew into a rage and told Hodgson to put the instruction into writing. As Porter was about to sign the letter, however, "he was assailed by a nervous attack which prevented him from placing his signature to it. He rose up, and took several turns in the cabin . . . but not being yet recovered he withdrew into a state room."[9]

Navoni made his way back to shore and carried out his instructions but met a cold reception from the Reis Effendi. The minister, he reported, laughed out loud and complained that he had never known such rudeness from a friendly nation. The Reis reiterated that there could be no salute for a chargé. As for an appointment, Porter should first politely announce his arrival and then wait to be summoned.

Porter was not off to an auspicious start, although he didn't seem to recognize this. On August 11 he wrote the secretary of state extolling how well he had been received by the Pasha of the Dardanelles during his transit and the special honor conferred on the

*John Adams* in not having to dismount its guns to pass the straits. He mentioned his concern that being a chargé could prove to be a disadvantage but expressed confidence he could overcome the problem.

Three weeks later, he was still waiting for his interview with the Reis Effendi and the *John Adams* had not yet been allowed to dock. To try to speed things along, Porter ordered Hodgson and Navoni to deliver a letter he was carrying from President Jackson to the sultan. The Turks refused to receive it, saying that any business would have to wait until Porter had formally presented his credentials and been acknowledged by the minister. Porter was getting his first taste of Eastern bureaucracy. He started to blame the problems on Navoni, who thrived on court niceties and continued to try to advise Porter on proper protocol.

The Reis Effendi let Porter cool his heels for almost six weeks. When they did finally meet, much of the conversation centered on the Reis's anger that the United States had rejected the secret article of the treaty. Porter tried to explain the division of powers between the president and the Senate, but, he reported, "It was utterly impossible to make them understand the nature of our government." Still, Porter found the meeting to be satisfactory and predicted that the Turks would ratify the treaty within two or three days. The Turks, he said, were sending an officer to the United States to purchase naval supplies; if the mission succeeded, this would allay their concerns about the rejection of the secret clause. In general, he wrote after this first meeting, he found the Turks to be "a reasonable people, ready to fulfill their own engagements."[10]

Navoni's description of the interview contrasts sharply with Porter's official report, portraying the meeting as a fiasco. Porter began, Navoni said, by telling the Reis Effendi he should be received as minister rather than a chargé and trying to persuade the Reis that he had actually been appointed minister. The Reis thought this was extraordinary because on his arrival he had announced himself as chargé. When Porter persisted, the incredulous minister could barely stifle a laugh. Soon it became clear even to Porter that the scene was becoming ridiculous, and he finally conceded, saying, "Well, we will drop this, and I will be only chargé d'affaires." Hodgson acted as interpreter and did well as long as the conversation was in French, but there was much confusion when he tried to translate directly into Turkish. Porter wouldn't permit Navoni to speak or to translate, and Hodgson wouldn't admit that he couldn't translate all that Porter said. The meeting degenerated until the Reis brought it to an end, saying that since they couldn't understand each other, Porter should put whatever he wanted to say into writing, so his staff could translate it.[11]

As the weeks passed, Porter began to realize that he was facing serious problems. He blamed his difficulties on Rhind for agreeing to the secret clause and on Navoni for insisting on adherence to court procedures. He railed against both in his dispatches to Washington. Soon he became so angry with Navoni that he suspended him from his duties as dragoman and withheld his pay. He sent a series of letters to the State Department complaining about Navoni's character and conduct and requesting his dismissal. He recommended that Hodgson be appointed as dragoman in his place and be given the additional title of secretary of legation.

The Turks finally approved the treaty a few weeks later. The exchange of ratifications took place without ceremony at the Reis Effendi's home, which, to Porter's surprise, was a "very ordinary old red wooden house." The minister served coffee and sherbet, as well as water pipes. When Porter received the Turkish version of the treaty, he was amused to find it inscribed, "This is the Imperial ratification of the treaty between the noble and glorious possessor of the world, and the noble chief of the United States of America."[12] In addition to exchanging treaties, Porter handed over the expected gifts. For the sultan, he had purchased a diamond-studded snuffbox for $9,000—"of such beauty as no description can convey"—and an agate fan inlaid with diamonds for $5,000. He distributed eighteen other jewel-encrusted snuffboxes to lower-level officials, with values corresponding to their ranks. Porter spent substantially more on the gifts than he had been authorized.

Shortly after the exchange of ratifications, Hodgson left for the United States to deliver the signed and sealed treaty. By December, he had still not arrived back in Washington. President Jackson reported to Congress in his State of the Union address that there had been some difficulties on the arrival of the new American chargé at the Porte, "but at the date of his last official dispatch he supposed they had been obviated and that there was every prospect of the exchange [of treaty ratifications] being speedily effected."[13]

Porter's private life in Constantinople got off to an even rockier start. He leased a large house in a suburb near the city and employed a number of servants including two guards who wore rich and exotic costumes. The guards sat outside his door all day long, Porter said, "without any earthly thing to do that I know of, but to smoke their pipes and drink their coffee. But . . . they are absolutely necessary to support the dignity of the establishment, as are also a porter at the entrance of the house, and a valet," whose principal tasks were to strike a bell when a visitor arrived and to run ahead to give notice when Porter planned to visit someone.[14]

Under Porter's house was a stable, which was leased separately by the building's owner to a neighbor, a prominent banker named Elias Hava. Porter asked Hava to remove his horses from the stable, which Hava refused to do, referring Porter to his lease. The following day Porter went to the stable with a pair of pistols in hand, forced the stable attendants to turn out Hava's horses, took the key, and threatened to shoot anyone who dared to enter the stable. The escapade drew a large crowd and was even reported in the local press. Hava complained to the authorities; the Reis Effendi ordered Porter to return the key. Thus began the American chargé's daily life at the refined court of Constantinople.

Over the next few months, Porter settled slowly into his new life as a diplomat. He made the required round of meetings with Turkish officials and with his diplomatic counterparts. He greatly enjoyed "the splendid parties given by the different legations here, and for magnificence, it would be difficult anywhere to excel them. The foreign legations are also distinguished for the elegance of their manners, intelligence, and strict propriety of conduct," a somewhat odd comment, in light of his own behavior. Balls with dancing and high-stakes gambling at cards often followed the dinners.

A special irritant for Porter was the amount of emphasis accorded to the rank of each person attending a social gathering. His status as chargé put him near the bottom of the diplomatic ladder, so he always found himself seated at one of the least prestigious places at the table or near the end of the reception line. He chafed at the better treatment given to ambassadors and ministers from countries much smaller and less powerful than the United States. In consequence, perhaps, Porter always used the title "commodore" rather than his diplomatic title. He was particularly irked that his rank of chargé d'affaires did not entitle him to call on the sultan, a restriction that he found unreasonable. He began agitating almost immediately for an audience.

Porter remained at odds with Navoni, who might have been able to ease his way through the maze of local protocol. Porter at first thought he could do without a dragoman, writing to the secretary of state: "The dragomans of this place are in no way to be relied on nor are they absolutely necessary to carry on negotiations with the Sublime Porte. They are all . . . worse than useless—mischievous and dangerous."[15] Porter fired Navoni and assured Washington that American relations at the Porte were on a sound footing without him.

With Hodgson's departure for Washington to deliver the treaty, however, Porter's estrangement from Navoni began to take a greater toll. As a naval officer used to having a large staff to jump at his command, Porter now found himself entirely on his own in an unfamiliar environment. He spoke no Turkish and considered himself too old to learn. He regarded his French—the language of the diplomatic community—as passable, but in fact he was not fluent enough to carry on a business conversation. Since he no longer had a secretary, he was forced to write his own dispatches and keep his own books. He felt very much alone, in a strange land, without a single friend.[16]

His disdain for bureaucratic procedures apparently extended to his own government as well as the Porte; he annoyed the State

Department by repeatedly neglecting to number his dispatches or submit them in the required form. His dispatches during this period are in his personal, sometimes indecipherable scrawl, a sharp contrast with Navoni's flowery script or Hodgson's handsome cursive. Porter's solution to his problem was to badger the State Department to appoint Hodgson as dragoman and return him promptly to Constantinople. He wrote effusively about Hodgson's fine performance and incalculable services. Porter also sent for two of his nephews to come serve as his assistants. He explained to the secretary of state: "With them I shall be satisfied. I hope however, that a suitable allowance will be made to relieve me from the expense of their maintenance and their tuition in the Oriental languages."[17] Nepotism was not considered a vice at the time, but his request did raise some eyebrows at the State Department. While Porter had the insight to realize that his staff, at least, should speak the local language, the Department informed him that Congress had refused to authorize any funding for language training. Finally admitting he could not operate on his own, he broke down and hired an "assistant dragoman." Navoni described the man as unfamiliar with the court and so terrified of dealing with high-level officials that he visibly trembled in their presence. The State Department later reprimanded Porter for hiring an assistant dragoman without authorization, commenting dryly that there did not seem to be enough work at the legation to justify the expense.

Porter had been in Constantinople less than two months when he made the first of many requests to Washington for increased funding. He explained that his presents to the sultan and other officials cost more than his allotment for the year, and to make matters worse, the Turks were already agitating for more presents. Porter was finding life to be far more expensive than he expected, and he was still supporting a large family back home that was often short of money. By springtime Porter asked the State Department to increase the proportion of his pay being sent directly to his wife. To cut costs, he moved to a less expensive house. After eighteen months, he was pleading to the State Department that "it is utterly impossible for me with all my efforts at economy, bordering on meanness, to live on my pay."[18] His hope that a diplomatic assignment would solve his financial problems was proving to be a chimera.

Contrary to Porter's expectations, moreover, relations with the Porte did not improve after Navoni's dismissal. The treaty had been ratified, but it was not being implemented. The United States was supposed to have most favored nation status, but American ships were still facing charges higher than those of some other nations and permission for passage into the Black Sea was not always easy to obtain. In fact, very few American ships were visiting Constantinople. In the first eight months of 1831, only nine American ships docked there, a miniscule proportion of the port's huge volume of international shipping. To try to increase trade with the empire, Porter appointed a U.S. commercial agent at Salonica and consular agents at Alexandria and Beirut. He asked the Department to appoint consuls in half a dozen other cities and islands, and when it did not respond quickly enough, he appointed acting consuls himself. He pressed for the U.S. Navy to visit Constantinople more often, believing this would put pressure on the Turks to comply with the treaty, with the extra benefit of giving more prestige and respect to the U.S. chargé.

For his first six months in Constantinople, Porter's dispatches to Washington barely touched on political matters, focusing instead on his administrative concerns. He urged Washington to authorize more presents, even suggesting that the United States send a steamboat as a gift for the sultan, who he still had not met. A new Reis Effendi took office, and Porter wanted to present him with a gift valued at about $8,000. He complained repeatedly about his need for more funding. And he kept up a lengthy and tiresome litany of complaints against Navoni, who he believed was intriguing against him both politically and personally. In one dispatch, he apologized for providing so much detail on Navoni, but explained that he wanted to protect himself "from the charge of rashness, which has too frequently been supposed to be a strong trait in my character."[19] One proof of Navoni's supposed treachery, which prompted a seventeen-page letter to the State Department, was his failure to obtain a certificate that would give Porter the right to go hunting in any part of the empire. Porter wrote that he had taken this issue up three times with the foreign minister. One can only imagine the minister's reaction to being repeatedly pestered with this sort of issue. The State Department, for its part, did not bother to respond.

It is remarkable that Porter's dispatches during this period included almost no reporting of the major political events that were under way in the empire. In late October 1831, Mohammed Ali of Egypt, who was still technically a vassal of the sultan, sent an army to invade Syria, another of the sultan's dominions. This was the start of the first Turko-Egyptian war. The Egyptian forces, led by Mohammed Ali's eldest son, Ibrahim Pasha, quickly routed the sultan's army, captured most of the Levant, and laid siege to the great fortress of Acre, the sultan's last stronghold in the region. The empire was being dismembered and was in danger of collapse. Not until March 1832, with Acre on the verge of surrender, did Porter finally report that a war was under way.

Another series of major events that largely escaped Porter's diplomatic reporting was the dramatic developments in Greece. Greece had effectively secured its independence several years earlier under the general protection of Great Britain, France, and Russia, but the sultan had not formally acknowledged the loss of this territory. Despite its new status, political turmoil raged in Greece, culminating with the assassination of the governor in 1831. With the threat that Greece might fall into complete chaos, the great powers again intervened. At a conference in London in May 1832, the British, French, and Russians decided, without consulting the Greeks, that Greece should be made a kingdom. The throne, they decided, would be offered to Prince Otto of Bavaria, who was only seventeen at the time. It fell to the European diplomats at the Sublime Porte, led by the British ambassador, to work out the details of this arrangement in the Treaty of Constantinople. Signed on July 21, 1832, the treaty formally established Greece as a monarchy, with the three great powers as guarantors. The sultan was compensated in cash— the equivalent of about $8 million—for his loss of Greece. Porter's dispatches never mentioned the Treaty of Constantinople or offered any further details on Turkey's continuing problems with Greece.

1. Samuel Shaw, the first American to trade with China and the first American consul in China. Frontispiece from *The Journals of Major Samuel Shaw, the First American Consul at Canton*, edited by Josiah Quincy (Boston: Wm. Crosby and H. P. Nichols, 1847).

2. The Boston Tea Party, a seminal event leading to the American Revolution, underscored the extent to which tea had become a staple in America by the late eighteenth century. Demand for tea sparked the opening of U.S. trade with China. Lithograph by Nathaniel Currier, 1846. Library of Congress, LC-USZC4–523.

3. (*opposite top*) American ginseng, *panax quinquefolius*, was in high demand in China and helped launch U.S.-China trade. This is an early nineteenth-century depiction by Jacob Bigelow, from *American medical botany, being a collection of the native medicinal plants of the United States* (Boston: Cummings and Hilliard, 1817–20). Wikimedia Commons.

4. (*opposite bottom*) The foreign "factories," or trading centers, in Canton, about 1800, with the American flag visible in the center. Painting by an unknown Chinese artist, ca. 1800. Wikimedia Commons.

*Panax quinquefolium*

5. James Leander Cathcart was held as a slave in Algiers for eleven years. He later served as the first American consul to Tripoli. Library of Congress, LC-USZ62–40593.

6. William Eaton, the swashbuckling U.S. consul in Tunis and self-styled general, led a ragtag army and a handful of U.S. Marines across the Sahara to attack the Libyan stronghold of Derne. Engraving on paper by Charles Balthazar Julien Févret de Saint-Mémin, 1808. National Portrait Gallery, Smithsonian Institution; gift of Mr. and Mrs. Paul Mellon.

7. Joel Barlow, America's first
epic poet, served as consul
in Algiers and negotiated
the first American treaties
with the Barbary states of
Algiers, Tripoli, and Tunis.
Watercolor on ivory by
William Dunlap, 1806.
National Portrait Gallery,
Smithsonian Institution; gift
of Mr. and Mrs. Joel Barlow.
Conserved with funds from
the Smithsonian Women's
Committee.

8. Tobias Lear, once George
Washington's private secretary,
served as consul general in
Algiers. He negotiated the 1805
treaty with Tripoli that ended
the First Barbary War and won
the release of more than one
hundred American naval officers
and seamen. Naval History
and Heritage Command,
Washington DC, photography
collection, cat.
no. NH 81.

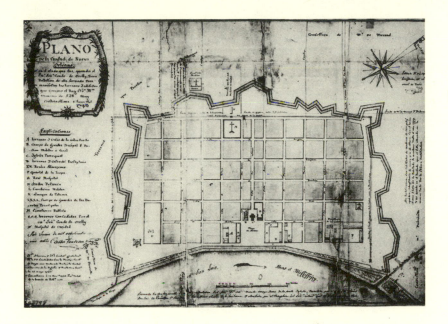

9. (*opposite top*) The U.S. frigate *Philadelphia*, aflame in Tripoli's fortified harbor in 1804. At left, the ketch *Intrepid*, commanded by Lt. Stephen Decatur, is leaving the harbor after setting the ship afire. Engraving by F. Kearney, 1808. Naval History and Heritage Command, Washington DC, photography collection, cat. no. NH 56751.

10. (*opposite bottom*) William Eaton and his Libyan ally, Hamet Karamanli, on their march to Derne in 1805. Woodcut. Naval History and Heritage Command, Washington DC, photography collection, cat. no. NH 56755.

11. (*above*) Although New Orleans was already one of the most important cities in North America by 1801, this contemporary map shows it was still a small town, compressed into about sixty blocks surrounded by a protective wall. Spanish colonial map, 1801. Wikimedia Commons.

12. Gen. James Wilkinson, commander of U.S. forces in the West and the highest-ranking officer of the U.S. Army, was accused by Daniel Clark of treason and corruption. Long after their deaths, documents from the Spanish archives proved that Wilkinson was on the Spanish payroll as he commanded U.S. troops. Oil on canvas by an unidentified artist, ca. 1820. National Portrait Gallery, Smithsonian Institution.

13. William C. C. Claiborne was the first American governor of the "Territory of Orleans" and a bitter political rival of Daniel Clark. Their enmity led to a duel in which Claiborne was shot. Engraving on paper by Charles Balthazar Julien Févret de Saint-Mémin, 1798. National Portrait Gallery, Smithsonian Institution; gift of Mr. and Mrs. Paul Mellon.

14. The American flag was finally raised over New Orleans on December 20, 1803, eight tumultuous months after the Louisiana Purchase agreement was signed in Paris. *Raising of the American Flag: Louisiana Transfer Ceremonies*, oil on canvas by Thure de Thulstrup, ca. 1902. Courtesy of the Louisiana State Museum and Louisiana Historical Society.

15. Joel Poinsett was pivotal in opening American relations with Latin America, serving as the first U.S. diplomatic representative to Argentina, Chile, and Mexico. He adopted an interventionist approach that would come to characterize future American policy in the region. Portrait by Albert Newsam after William James Hubard, lithographer Cephas Grier Childs, ca. 1830. National Portrait Gallery, Smithsonian Institution.

16. A dashing young general, José Miguel de Carrera was a leader of Chile's struggle for independence and ruled the country during most of Joel Poinsett's tenure there. Posthumous portrait, ca. 1858. Wikimedia Commons.

17. Bernardo O'Higgins, another principal leader of Chile's independence struggle, was a rival of Carrera's. Portrait by José Gil de Castro, nineteenth century. Wikimedia Commons.

18. Gen. Augustín de Iturbide took power in newly independent Mexico in 1821, then ruled briefly as Emperor Augustín before being forced into exile. Joel Poinsett considered him "arbitrary and tyrannical." Portrait by an unknown artist, 1821. Wikimedia Commons.

19. Edmund Roberts launched American diplomatic relations with countries of Southeast Asia and the Indian Ocean, undertaking two epic voyages to negotiate and deliver treaties. This is the only known image of Roberts, a wax relief made while he was a young man, which he considered "a very good likeness." Wax relief from life, thought to have been done in London by a French artist, ca. 1804. Courtesy of the Portsmouth Historical Society.

20. Dr. Benajah Ticknor served as ship's surgeon on the uss *Peacock's* voyage of 1832–34, leaving a detailed account of his journey with Edmund Roberts. Courtesy of Cobblestone Farm Association.

21. A view of Bangkok in about 1830, as it would have appeared to Edmund Roberts. From John Crawfurd, *Journal of an Embassy from the Governor-General of India to the Courts of Siam and Cochin China* (London: Henry Colburn and Richard Bentley, 1830). Wikimedia Commons.

22. One of the most powerful rulers of his time, Syed Syeed bin Sultan reigned over domains that included the entire east coast of Arabia, much of the Persian Gulf, and over two thousand miles of the coast of East Africa. The sultan welcomed the establishment of relations with the United States. Painting by an American sailor, possibly Lt. William F. Lynch, ca. 1855. Wikimedia Commons.

23. Cdre. David Porter, a hero of the War of 1812, was appointed by President Andrew Jackson as the first resident American envoy to Turkey. Porter's hotheaded and domineering approach proved more suited to naval combat than to diplomacy. Portrait in oils, possibly by John Trumbull. Naval History and Heritage Command, Washington DC, photography collection, cat. no. NH 80-G-K-17588.

24. William Hodgson, an accomplished scholar and brilliant linguist, served as the first American dragoman at the U.S. legation in Constantinople, where he clashed with David Porter. Miniature, watercolor on ivory by Ernest Joseph Angelon Girard, 1842. Telfair Museum of Art, Savannah, Georgia. Gift of Mr. and Mrs. William K. Wallbridge, 1959.

25. Mahmud II was sultan of the Ottoman Empire from 1808 until 1839, overseeing major reforms aimed at modernizing and opening formal diplomatic relations with the United States. Wikimedia Commons.

26. A view of Constantinople from the harbor, as it appeared in David Porter's day. *Constantinople from the Entrance of the Golden Horn*, watercolor by Thomas Allom, ca. 1834. Wikimedia Commons.

27. The Ottoman government came to be known in the West as the Sublime Porte, after this impressive gate in Constantinople through which diplomats were received. The engraving depicts the gate as it appeared in David Porter's day. Engraving by Thomas Allom, ca. 1840. Wikimedia Commons.

28. Jacques-Antoine
Moerenhout, a Belgian,
served as the first American
consul in Tahiti and, in a
curious twist, then became
the French consul there. He
subsequently served as French
consul in California during the
gold rush. Miniature, oil on
ivory, possibly a self-portrait.
Frontispiece from Jacques-
Antoine Moerenhout, *The
Inside Story of the Gold Rush*
(San Francisco: California
Historical Society, 1935).
Courtesy of the California
Historical Society, 979.404.

29. George Prichard went
to Tahiti as a missionary.
He became head of the
Protestant mission, a
principal advisor to Queen
Pomare, and the first British
consul on the island. This
portrait shows Prichard
in his consular uniform,
with Papeete Harbor in the
background. Print by George
Baxter, 1845. Wikimedia
Commons.

30. Queen Pomare IV clashed frequently with the first American consuls in Tahiti. Her fifty-year reign saw the French military occupation and the declaration of a French protectorate. Portrait by Charles Giraud, 1851. Wikimedia Commons.

31. The harbor of Papeete sketched by Jacques-Antoine Moerenhout. Lithograph from a drawing by Moerenhout, ca. 1835. Courtesy of the Assembly of French Polynesia.

32. Thomas Larkin, the only U.S. consul in Mexican California, was a tireless campaigner for a peaceful approach to making California part of the United States. San Francisco History Center, San Francisco Public Library.

33. William Leidesdorff, appointed by Thomas Larkin as vice consul in Yerba Buena (later San Francisco), was the first American of African descent to serve as a consular officer. Portrait by an unknown artist, ca. 1845. Wikimedia Commons.

34. John Frémont, an explorer and U.S. Army topographer, was a leader of the rebellion that wrested California from Mexico. Portrait by George Healy, date unknown. Wikimedia Commons.

35. Although Monterey was the capital of California, it was still a small town when Larkin served as consul, as seen in this 1845 illustration. *Monterey—Capitol of California*, sketch by J. W. Revere, U.S. Navy, 1845. Courtesy, Special Collections, University of Texas at Arlington Libraries.

36. Sutter's Fort, New Helvetia, in 1849, soon after the U.S. acquisition of California. Sutter welcomed American settlers here and discovered gold nearby, sparking the California gold rush. Sketch by J. W. Revere, U.S. Navy, ca. 1849. Wikimedia Commons.

37. A Japanese depiction of an American "black ship" that landed at Uraga during Commodore Perry's first visit in 1853. Naval History and Heritage Command, Washington DC, photography collection, cat. no. USN 900929.

38. Cdre. Matthew Perry, as
depicted in a Japanese woodcut
about 1854. The print may be
one of the first depictions
of westerners in Japanese
art. Library of Congress,
LC–USZC4–1307.

北亞墨利加人物
ペルり像

39. Townsend Harris was the first
American consul general and
minister resident in Japan. From
his isolated outpost in Shimoda,
Harris managed to persuade
the Japanese to receive him at
the shogun's court and to sign a
meaningful treaty.
Naval History and Heritage
Command, Washington DC,
photography collection,
cat. no. NH 49264.

40. A Japanese depiction of Townsend Harris being carried through the streets of Yedo in a traditional Japanese *norimon*, accompanied by retainers. Harris hated being carried in this fashion, but yielded to Japanese custom because it engendered greater respect for the United States. Print by an unknown Japanese artist, ca. 1857. Courtesy of Archives, City University of New York.

In contrast, one issue that did catch Porter's attention was the danger of Greek pirates in the Aegean Sea. Having spent much of his own career fighting piracy, Porter took a special interest in the problem and reported frequently on it. Although no American shipping was ever disturbed, he complained that the U.S. Mediterranean squadron should be more active in patrolling the Aegean against pirates.

Many months passed before the State Department responded to Porter's initial dispatches. It still took almost three months for a letter to reach Washington from Constantinople and another three months for the reply to make its way back. When the first reply did arrive, written in the spring of 1832, it had a decidedly frosty tone. The Department supported some of Porter's requests but also delivered several sharp rebukes, in a manner unusual for State Department correspondence of the time. In regard to the Navoni saga, Secretary of State Edward Livingston wrote that President Jackson had acceded to Porter's desire to have William Hodgson appointed as dragoman. "But I am, nevertheless, instructed by him to inform you that it would have been more agreeable if you had awaited our directions" before taking action against a man appointed by the president and confirmed by the Senate.[20] Navoni's salary, Livingston added, must continue to be paid to him until the Senate confirmed Hodgson as his successor. Hodgson could not be named secretary in addition to dragoman, as Porter had requested, because only ministers—not chargés—were entitled to have secretaries. Porter's diplomatic rank was becoming increasingly irksome.

Livingston's second response was even sterner. Porter, he wrote, should never exceed his authorized financial allotment. His proposal for more presents for Turkish officials was out of the question. He should give care to numbering all his dispatches, since that was the only way for the Department to ensure it had received them all. Most importantly, the Department judged from Porter's dispatches that the state of American relations with Turkey was "by no means agreeable," despite Porter's assurances that all problems would be resolved by the dismissal of Navoni. Since the Turks were still not complying with the treaty, Porter should insist that they "act in good faith as Mussulmans." Finally, Livingston added, Porter should provide more information on trade opportunities with Turkey.[21] Porter must have felt stung indeed by the tone of the Department's letters.

By this time he had been in Turkey almost a year and was falling into a routine. Hodgson returned from the United States to take up his new duties as dragoman, which greatly relieved the strain Porter had faced during his months alone, though judging from his official reports it does not appear that his position as chargé was too taxing.

Meanwhile, the sultan's war against Egypt was going very badly. Porter reported only briefly and intermittently on military developments. Of far more interest to him, the sultan had hired an American naval architect to build a new fleet to replace the Turkish ships lost in the disaster at Navarino several years earlier. Porter judged the new Turkish navy to be the most impressive he had ever seen, splendidly outfitted and armed. The fleet included the largest warship in the world, sporting an incredible 156 guns, about five times the firepower of Porter's most famous ship, the *Essex*. The ongoing reforms of the army, he believed, had also led to a much more disciplined, impressive force. These appearances, however, did not translate into effectiveness. The fortress of Acre fell to the Egyptians in May 1832, leaving all of Syria in the hands of Ibrahim Pasha. The sultan began to assemble a large force to defend against Ibrahim, who was preparing to march on Constantinople.

When Porter did report war news to Washington, he seemed to do so almost as an afterthought, mentioning developments in passing in dispatches dealing primarily with other topics. For other diplomats in Constantinople, the war was a burning issue that could significantly affect the balance of power in Europe. The British, in particular, feared that a weak Turkey could fall prey to Russia, threatening Britain's increasingly important trade routes to the East. France, for its part, had developed a special relationship with Mohammed Ali and saw Egypt's victories as a boon to French ambitions in the region. The European powers would soon become directly involved in the conflict.

During this period of political crisis, Porter spent much of his time in a touristic exploration of Constantinople. He remained enthralled with the city's monumental architecture, its fifteen centuries of history, its narrow streets and exotic markets. He found the people and their habits to be a never-ending fascination. Sometimes, he wrote, he would spend an entire day just watching people on the street under his window, an endless parade of color, noise, and aromas. He was so excited when the Porte granted him permission to visit Constantinople's principal mosques—which were normally off limits to Christians—that he reported the event to Washington and invited many of the Americans resident in the city to join him. Constantinople's famous bazaars, which covered almost a quarter of the city, provided another allure. They are impossible to conceive, he wrote, without visiting them in person, being "one of the most busy and animated scenes in the world, and I never tire of visiting the bazaar."[22]

Porter described his impressions in lengthy letters to a friend who, with his permission, compiled and published them in 1835 as *Constantinople and Its Environs*. Porter's name did not appear on the book; the author was listed simply as "an American long resident at Constantinople." The two-volume work includes descriptions of a number of Porter's activities as chargé but with the letters edited to make it appear that the writer was accompanying the American "minister" to meetings or events. The descriptions of diplomatic meetings and of Turkish officials contained in the book are far more detailed than those in Porter's official diplomatic dispatches.

Part of *Constantinople and Its Environs* is designed as a tourist guide, giving a detailed, weeklong itinerary of how best to visit the city's many attractions, as well as extensive background on each. Porter paints vivid pictures of people, alleyways, shops, bazaars, and classical ruins. His occasional attempts to draw comparisons with American cities can appear comical to modern-day readers, such as a comment that in Constantinople, dogs "are fully as numerous as the hogs once were in the streets of New-York."[23] In the book's pages, Porter emerges as a man of some wit and warmth, in stark contrast to the cranky and officious portrait that arises from his dispatches.

Porter's general admiration and affection for the Turks, and in particular for Sultan Mahmud, come through repeatedly in the book, albeit tinged with Western condescension about their efforts to catch up with the more "civilized" nations. His descriptions also highlight some of the deep prejudices that he shared with many Americans of his day. Jews, who numbered some fifty thousand residents of Constantinople, were "tricky," "querulous," and of "contemptible dishonesty." Armenians were misers and even trickier than Jews— trickier, in fact, than any other race, including even the Chinese.[24]

The book also shows that Porter would not stand for any slight to his dignity from a Turk. He recounts an incident in which two drunken Turkish soldiers "were insulting to me in their manner."[25] He complained to their barracks commander, who identified the culprits and sentenced them each to three hundred bastinadoes— blows with a stick to the soles of their feet—which Porter seemed to accept as a reasonable punishment for offending him.

Porter had been in Constantinople nearly a year when he finally met the sultan for the first time. The occasion was the delivery of a warship constructed by the American naval architect in the sultan's employ. Porter accompanied the architect and described the sultan as handsome, with a rosy complexion and a short black beard. The sultan wore a red fez with a blue silk tassel, a light blue silk jacket, crimson silk trousers, and European shoes. "The whole dress was simple and very becoming. It resembled, except in the fez, such as gentlemen of the United States put on their sons between the ages of six and eight. . . . In fact, there was a slight air of dandyism about him."[26] Porter discovered that the sultan had a strong interest in naval affairs, which, of course, was Porter's own greatest interest and expertise, so they quickly found a common area for conversation.

In September 1832, Porter finally secured his first private meeting with the sultan. This was something of a coup, since as a chargé, he was still not entitled to an official audience. The sultan, however, was apparently looking forward to another discussion of naval issues and agreed to meet with Porter informally, with none of the ceremonies usually attending diplomatic visits. Porter reported briefly to the State Department that the meeting had taken place and that the sultan was favorably disposed toward the United States, but he provided no further details. He told his family, however, that the meeting was short and that it began with pipes and coffee served in diamond-studded cup holders. Porter's assistant dragoman fell immediately to his knees before the sultan and "bumped his head against the floor with force enough to knock an ordinary man's brains out."[27]

While Porter said very little about the sultan or his policies in his official dispatches, he effusively praised Mahmud II in private letters, calling him "an extraordinary man . . . graceful and dignified. . . . He possesses not only an expanded genius but great courage." Mahmud was making good progress in "the noble yet difficult task of adapting this government and those institutions in some degree to the progress of intelligence in the rest of the civilized world." Although some Europeans saw Mahmud as a barbarian, Porter lauded him as "Mahmud the Great."[28]

As the summer of 1832 wore on, Porter came face to face with a horror that frequently ravaged Constantinople: the plague. One of his servants came down with an unknown illness in August. Porter, who had acquired some medical knowledge during his years at sea, treated the man before it was clear he had the plague. Having been in such close contact with a plague victim, he was presumed to have become infected. A 30-day quarantine was immediately slapped on the entire household. Porter and his guests and servants were confined to tents in the yard. Every item in the house that may have been contaminated was burned. Miraculously, neither Porter nor anyone else in his household came down with the disease.

Elsewhere in Constantinople, however, thousands were dying every week. Dead bodies were piled in the streets. People withdrew into their households. Even close friends avoided each other and would no longer shake hands. Porter, like other residents of the city, built a box outside his door in which everything that entered the house—including people—was thoroughly smoked as a means of purification. In addition, a large tub of water was placed by the door and any article that would not be ruined by getting wet was passed through the tub as an extra precaution.

After the fall of Acre, Ibrahim Pasha led his army north into Anatolia, toward Constantinople. In a bloody battle at Konya in December 1832, where some 40,000 soldiers were killed, the Egyptians routed the sultan's army and captured its commander. Ibrahim Pasha's forces regrouped and resumed their march north. There were no major defensive strongholds left between the Egyptians and Constantinople.

A wave of panic overtook the capital as news of the disaster made its way north. Popular sentiment against the sultan rose sharply. With the empire in upheaval, Porter finally took it upon himself to write a lengthy dispatch describing the dangerous situation. His dispatch, however, was addressed not to the State Department, but to Cdre. Daniel Patterson of the U.S. Navy's Mediterranean squadron. He asked Patterson to send a naval force to Constantinople and to Smyrna to protect Americans in both cities from the outrages he was certain they would face if the "wild and undisciplined Arabs" should gain possession of either city or if the local inhabitants should rise up against the sultan.

The next day Porter sent the secretary of state a copy of his letter to Commodore Patterson, with the additional news that the sultan had accepted an offer of assistance from his erstwhile enemy, Czar Nicolas I of Russia. Porter commented that Mahmud II's terror must be great indeed to invite Russian troops into the empire, in view of the long-term threat they could pose to his sovereignty.

Although the sultan was willing to take the risk of having Russians troops in Turkey, the European powers were not. Great Britain and France began to mediate a peace, sending their fleets to show that they were prepared to use military power to force a settlement if necessary. The settlement gave Mohammed Ali, who was still nominally the sultan's vassal, control of all Syria and the island of Crete, as well as the holy cities of Mecca and Medina. It was a staggering blow for the Ottoman Empire.

Following Porter's appeal for a visit by American warships, he reported very little of subsequent developments, scarcely mentioning the moves toward peace. On January 4, 1833, for example, he noted in a dispatch, with little elaboration, that "the difficulties of the Porte seem to occupy much of the attention of the Great European Powers."[29] His own apparent lack of interest might perhaps be attributed charitably to a disdain for European great power politics. Still, Porter's relative silence on such major events not only stands at odds with his instructions to report on developments but also in sharp contrast to other prominent American diplomats of his era. Porter seemed to care very little about the monumental political developments rocking Turkey, although these certainly had a major impact on American trade and American citizens in the region. It was almost as if he were sulking in exile. The contrast is striking between his lack of action as a diplomat and his previous activism as a naval officer.

Porter's health began to deteriorate not long after his arrival in Constantinople, which added to his misery and may have contributed to his lethargy. He suffered from "bilious fever" and the "blue devils" (intestinal disorders and depression). He complained regularly of these and many other ailments in letters to friends and family and sometimes to the State Department. In early January 1833, he wrote to a friend: "I have crawled from the verge of the grave, where I have been lying for the last twelve days. . . . It was scarcely expected that I could live. . . . In less than two hours, I was bled copiously three times; and besides in the course of the morning, leeched in both temples, in the abdomen, and cupped in the back of my neck. Besides mustard plasters all over, and prescriptions without number. Nothing else could have saved my life; but it has almost destroyed me."[30] His illness left him weak and further depressed. And, in fact, he did get worse. His "inflammatory fever" returned, confining him to bed for months. He fell into a downward spiral, with his illness and depression feeding on each other.

Porter said later that he was saved by the arrival in Constantinople of his brother-in-law, Dr. Heap, two of his sisters, and several other family members. Their presence renewed his spirits, and he began slowly, tenuously, to recover. Porter invited one of his sisters, Mary Brown, a widow, and her son John Porter Brown, to stay in Constantinople with him. She agreed and would remain with him for the rest of his life. His nephew John was educated and groomed to assist Porter with his diplomatic duties.

In addition to health problems, Porter's financial situation was going from bad to worse. The same month he wrote a friend about having "crawled from the verge of the grave," he wrote two dispatches to the secretary of state. The first reported, on a single page, that the sultan's troops were starting to return to Constantinople and that peace talks seemed to be in the offing. The second ran to ten full pages complaining about his salary. He called his pay a "miserable pittance." Although he kept his expenses to an absolute minimum, he wrote, he had had to borrow at a rate of 10 percent just to make ends meet. His rent alone cost $800 a year, since it was "indispensable" to have two residences, one in the city and another in the countryside "to flee to in case of fire, plague or other disaster." He had to keep two horses, one for himself and one for his personal guard, since "walking in comfort after the slightest rain is impracticable" on the city's muddy streets. The cost of food, clothing, and charcoal was higher than in the United States. He had a host of servants to pay. Every Turkish peasant demanded a tip for even the smallest service. On his salary, he continued, "Entertaining is entirely out of the question, therefore to avoid the imputation of meanness I am compelled to decline the acceptance of civilities, which it is out of my power to return."[31] Porter's lengthy plea spurred the State Department to ask Congress to raise his pay. Although a raise was eventually forthcoming, it did not resolve his financial woes.

Porter's life was further complicated by a falling out with his dragoman, William Hodgson, whom he had so lavishly praised in letters to the State Department. The records are not clear on exactly what caused the estrangement, but it seems that Porter was upset with Hodgson's role in managing the legation's official business during his long illness. By early 1833, Porter was considering assigning one of his nephews as dragoman, in Hodgson's place. Hodgson, for his part, asked the Department to transfer him to one of the Barbary consulates on account of unspecified differences with Porter.

Although Porter was bedridden and used this as an excuse for not reporting on political developments, he was not too ill to launch a campaign of letters to the State Department against Hodgson. In March 1833, without specifying a particular offense, Porter wrote that Hodgson had not given him the "respect and obedience due me" and that "the pretensions and assumptions of this young gentleman cannot be much longer borne with."[32] This was the first in what would become a seemingly endless series of increasingly sharp and vindictive attacks on Hodgson, reminiscent of his earlier complaints about Navoni, but even more vitriolic. By May Porter was complaining bitterly that Hodgson had used the legation's seal without his authorization, although Porter himself was too ill to attend to official business. Porter was "outraged" by the insolence and "offenses of this young gentleman" and would henceforth dispense with his services.[33] More long letters of complaint against Hodgson followed throughout May, June, and July, a period during which Porter sent virtually no reports on the dramatic political events unfolding around him. By the end of summer, the two refused even to speak with each other.

Hodgson wrote separately to the Department several times giving his side of the dispute. Among other offenses, he asserted, Porter acted arbitrarily, failed to organize the legation effectively, sent offensive letters to the Reis Effendi, and was paying his nephews out of the legation's contingency fund. Porter's decision to reside in a village far from the capital was having a negative effect on the legation's business. In addition, Hodgson said, Porter had virtually abandoned his responsibility to protect American citizens. Hodgson asked repeatedly for a transfer.

A new and curious phase of Porter's dispute with Hodgson opened in October, with Porter complaining that Hodgson had received and kept a horse, a gift from a Turkish pasha that was actually intended for Porter. Hodgson claimed that the horse was a gift to him and that he had reciprocated with a gift of equal value. For the next year and longer, Porter railed to the Department in letter after letter about how Hodgson had defrauded him over the horse. The U.S. diplomatic archives are overflowing with documents on this dispute, which far outnumber Porter's reports on any other issue. At one point, Porter even asked the Turkish government to arrest Hodgson for theft.

About this time, Porter also fell out with William Churchill, the acting U.S. consul in Constantinople, over how to settle the estate of a wealthy American who died in the city. Porter had apparently expected to receive a commission, and he flew into a rage when Churchill settled the estate, as a consular official would be expected to do. Churchill informed the State Department, "During nearly two years that I have been acting consul here I had been a fortunate exception in preserving the good graces of Commodore Porter, and I should be stung by his vituperation were it not that I am surrounded by fellow sufferers from his violence. Mr. Charles Rhind, Mr. Nicholas Navoni, Mr. Wm B Hodgson, and several other most respectable individuals keep me in countenance; and I may add that his quarrels have extended to some of the Turkish ministers of State."[34] Porter's behavior, Churchill concluded, was detrimental to American relations with Turkey.

The State Department was slow to respond to Porter's dozens of angry letters about Hodgson and others. Washington appeared discomfited about the controversies and perhaps hoped that the disputes, if ignored, might simply go away. By September 1833, however, Porter was insisting that the Department make a decision between him and Hodgson, asserting that Hodgson was mentally unbalanced. The dispute was even brought to the attention of President Jackson.

The Department eventually responded in a letter that did not reach Porter until the following year. The new secretary of state, Louis McLane, wrote Porter that "the President regrets the want of harmony which has so long been permitted to exist between yourself and Mr. Hodgson, the first Dragoman."[35] To end the dispute, the Department withdrew Hodgson and sent him on a confidential mission to Egypt to collect political and commercial information. Hodgson was to continue to receive his salary, and Porter was not to appoint a replacement for him. In addition, McLane asked Porter to explain his quarrel with Churchill and instructed him to refrain from any further involvement in the disputed estate. Finally, McLane reminded Porter that he should be submitting commercial information more regularly.

McLane's long-awaited letter must have come as a heavy blow to Porter. The letter contained nothing that showed the least sympathy for his position, and the tone was far from friendly or approving. Despite Porter's vigorous denunciations, the Department appointed Hodgson to another position of trust. Worse, sending Hodgson on a secret mission to collect information in territories nominally under Porter's jurisdiction could be read as a suggestion that Porter had not been providing the information desired by the Department, which, of course, he had not. In addition, Porter was slapped on the wrist over his dispute with Churchill. The Department was clearly not pleased with Porter's performance. However, President Jackson apparently still did not want to remove his friend from office.

Hodgson, needless to say, was delighted. He left Constantinople in the summer of 1834, after more than a year of unhappy feuding with Porter.

As if his difference with Hodgson were not enough, Porter also began to lodge a series of official complaints against Acting Consul Churchill. In February Porter removed Churchill from office and eventually appointed his nephew, John Porter Brown, to replace him. Porter's quarrels soon expanded to include other subordinates. He fired the American consular agent for the Dardanelles, another of his own appointments, after that gentleman wrote a letter in support of Hodgson about the long-disputed gift horse. Separately, Porter revoked the appointments of the U.S. consular agents for Jerusalem and Tenedos, two more of his appointments who had managed to offend him. Meanwhile, Hogdson's departure did not put a stop to Porter's interminable official complaints against him. Porter's relentless criticisms of Hodgson are so vituperative that they are embarrassing to read, even two centuries later.

By late 1835, after more than two years of Porter's constant complaints against Hodgson, the State Department finally had had enough. Secretary of State Forsyth wrote Porter a stern letter telling him to cease and desist: "As he [Hodgson] was withdrawn from the Legation, and all occasions of future difficulty was thereby removed, it was thought most conducive to the public interest that the matter should be dismissed without further discussion."[36]

Perhaps chastened by the State Department's reprimands, Porter began to report more broadly, if not in detail, on a number of the political events still rocking the empire: the inhabitants of Crete were being viciously persecuted by the sultan's troops; there was an outrage against an American missionary in Beirut; a band of outlaws was threatening Mohammed Ali's hold on Mecca; increasing numbers of Americans were visiting the holy sites in Jerusalem; Greek pirates continued to commit depredations in the Aegean; and the new Greek minister still had not been received by the sultan, and if he ever is, it will be done "with the same grace as a southern planter would receive an ambassador from his rebellious slaves."[37]

Porter's improved political reporting won him a mild pat on the back from Secretary of State Forsyth. Porter's recent messages, Forsyth wrote in 1835, "contain much useful information and indicate a watchfulness over the concerns of the United States committed to your care, which meets the approbation of the Department." The same letter, however, reprimanded Porter for not submitting the required quarterly financial reports, reminding him pointedly that failure to do so was grounds for dismissal and warning that "it is hoped that you will for the future conform in this respect, as in every other, strictly to the tenor of your instructions."[38]

Porter continued to chafe at being a chargé rather than minister. He sent repeated pleas to the Department to upgrade his position, arguing with considerable justification that a higher-ranking American envoy could be more effective in advancing American interests in a country that gave so much weight to rank.

When the plague reappeared in Constantinople in the summer of 1834, Porter moved out of the city, as he and other diplomats did every summer. This time, the move was to San Stephano (now Yesilkoy), a tiny village on the shores of the Sea of Marmara, even further from Constantinople than the previous residence that Hodgson had complained was too remote to conduct business. Porter was so taken with San Stephano that he decided to purchase a house there; it became his residence and office for the remainder of his tenure.

Porter informed the State Department in June that "I have now established the legation in this village," explaining that it provided him with fine air, good water, and a temperate climate. There were good roads for exercising on horseback. He hoped that all these advantages might help restore his health. Moreover, his new residence was "more suited to my limited means." Finally, he explained, the sultan often visited the area to review troops at a nearby military camp, so he might be able to have more contact with Mahmud in San Stephano than he did in the capital.[39]

He provided a somewhat different rationale for the move in a letter to a friend, writing of the beauty of the place, the magnificent view of the sea, the excellent quail hunting, the "charming sea bathing," and the absence of official intrusions. "No person can possibly enjoy solitude in greater perfection than I do within my little kiosk."[40] From this time forward, Porter was largely isolated from events in the capital and the information available there. He did retain a small residence in the diplomatic quarter of Constantinople to use on the increasingly rare occasions that he had to attend ceremonies or make official visits to the city.

The residence in San Stephano was initially a small brick cottage surrounded by a porch, situated on six acres overlooking the sea in one direction and facing the mountains in another. Porter soon began expanding the house. According to one of his sons, he "added so much to the size of his kiosk that the original building was quite lost sight of, and in its place appeared a very handsome residence, in the modern Greek style, containing all the conveniences that could be desired." Porter playfully called his residence "the Palace," echoing a term commonly used by the Turks to describe foreign missions. He manicured the gardens and stocked a stable with fine horses, "among them several Arabians which were not surpassed by any in the sultan's stables. . . . He had also fine carriage horses and good English carriages, which contributed essentially to his enjoyment."[41] This account—in a biography by his son—can only make one wonder at Porter's repeated complaints about his salary. Perhaps, however, the son's description of Porter's lifestyle is exaggerated, as is his account of other aspects of Porter's life.

Life in "the Palace" followed a strict routine, which apparently did not include too taxing a schedule of official duties. According to his son, Porter "had been so long accustomed to the discipline of a ship of war, that he carried out the same system in his household affairs, and no one would have any more dreamed of disobeying his orders, than if they had been serving under his command on shipboard." He had a tall flagpole erected in his yard that could be seen by passing ships, and each morning the Stars and Stripes was hoisted with great ceremony, as if he were still commanding a warship. "It was his habit to have his sister read to him a couple of hours every morning. . . . At the conclusion he would retire to his room for several hours, where no one ventured to disturb him. . . . At an appointed time after dinner, the Commodore's carriage and Hungarian coach horses were at the door . . . and he would drive around the environs of Constantinople."[42] He enjoyed Turkish food and coffee and fell into the habit of smoking water pipes.

Despite his idyllic surroundings, he seems to have been unhappy and largely friendless. The perilous state of his finances continued to preoccupy him. He had not seen his wife or most of his children for six years. His health took another downturn. There is no indication, however, in either the official records or in his personal correspondence that he ever contemplated relinquishing his assignment and returning home. Nor is there any indication that the State Department, despite the complaints against him and its frequent unhappiness with his performance, ever seriously contemplated dismissing such a high-profile friend of the president.

Porter's diplomatic career in Constantinople would limp on for another seven years. Through the end of Andrew Jackson's second administration in early 1837, Porter's position was secure by virtue of Jackson's personal protection. It was Porter's good fortune that Jackson's successor, Martin Van Buren, pledged to continue all of Jackson's policies and to retain his appointments. Van Buren reappointed Jackson's entire cabinet, with the exception of the secretary of war. As war secretary, Van Buren appointed Joel Poinsett, Porter's old friend from Chile and Mexico. Porter's position was secure for at least another four years.

In April 1838 Porter took leave and sailed for the United States, after an absence of eight years, leaving John Porter Brown in charge of the legation. In the United States, Porter was reunited with his family and attended the weddings of two of his sons. He spent considerable time trying to straighten out his accounts with the State Department, acknowledging that he could not adequately account for $7,196 in government funds, a substantial sum at the time.

While he was in the United States, Porter also worked tirelessly to convince the State Department that he should be elevated to the rank of minister. His debts to the government, however, stood in the way. Porter broke the logjam by agreeing to have all his debts repaid through quarterly deductions from his salary. With this accomplished, Porter was finally appointed as "minister resident" to Turkey, fulfilling a goal he had held for eight years.

Porter's visit to the United States kept him away from his post for an entire year. His return was further delayed by a twenty-one-day quarantine in Smyrna on account of the plague and by an accident that almost cost him his life. While in Smyrna, Porter was thrown from his horse, which then stepped on his head. He wrote his wife from Smyrna in mid-July that he was out of danger but somewhat disfigured.

Porter arrived back in Constantinople to find that Sultan Mahmud II had died a few weeks earlier and was succeeded by his son, Abdel Meguid (Abdulmecid), a boy of seventeen. Aside from this, Porter reported that after a year's absence, "Everything is quiet here and our affairs are as I left them to go to the US."[43] In fact, things were not quiet at all; major events had transpired and were still under way. Mohammed Ali's forces had swept across Arabia to the Persian Gulf and the Indian Ocean. A Turkish envoy had gone to London to seek a military alliance with the British. Mahmud II had launched another invasion of Syria, but his forces were crushed by Ibrahim Pasha at the Battle of Nesib. In July 1839 the Turkish fleet—which Porter was so proud of—had deserted to Alexandria and surrendered to Mohammed Ali.

Nor did subsequent political and military developments capture Porter's attention. On November 3, 1839, under the influence of reformist ministers, the young sultan promulgated the Tanzimat Firman, sometimes known as the Edict of the Rose Chamber. This decree launched a revolutionary set of administrative, social, and legal reforms that is generally regarded as among the most important of the early efforts to modernize Turkey. The decree was followed over the next months and years by a wave of reform measures, from tax and military reforms to the establishment of a more modern and representative government. It was not until almost a year later that one of Porter's dispatches even mentioned the reforms, and then only peripherally.

Shortly after his return, Porter received a letter from the State Department complaining, on the basis of reports from American traders, that the Turks were again violating the most favored nation clause of the U.S.-Turkish treaty. Porter replied that the Reis Effendi would need a "present" before the problem could be resolved and that he would attempt to determine the required amount. The State Department's logbook records incredulously that Porter proposed to *bribe* the foreign minister![44]

The remaining years of Porter's long career as the first resident American diplomat in Constantinople are a story of continuing decline. Porter was either too ill or lacked the interest to deal with the many political issues still rocking Turkey. In 1840 there was a major uprising in Syria and throughout the Levant against the Egyptian occupation. Ibrahim Pasha was finally forced out of Syria. The situation spilled over into European politics, with Britain, Austria, Prussia, and Russia backing the sultan, while France supported its old ally,

Mohammed Ali. The British fleet bombarded Beirut and landed troops that captured Beirut and Acre. Tensions flared to the point that there was danger of war erupting in Europe. The crisis abated only when the French government fell. Under intense European pressure, Mohammed Ali was forced to give up northern Syria, Crete, and the holy cities of Mecca and Medina, and to return the sultan's fleet, in exchange for being recognized as hereditary ruler of Egypt. Sultan Abdel Meguid was also forced to accept the agreement, which guaranteed the survival of his empire but at the cost of one of its richest and most powerful possessions.

A year later, the great powers signed the Straits Convention in London, under which the Bosporus and the Dardanelles were closed to all warships. This was one of the major geopolitical events of the era, solidifying British dominance in the Mediterranean and ending Russia's long-held dream for a European warm water port. The events of 1840–41 reshaped the Middle East and had repercussions far beyond, but they drew less than half a dozen desultory reports from the American minister in Constantinople.

Another noteworthy issue of this period was the persecution and torture in 1840 of the Jewish communities in Damascus and on the island of Rhodes, both Ottoman territories. The incidents prompted outrage throughout the West and sparked the first effective effort by Western Jewish communities to bring governmental pressure to bear on regimes that persecuted Jews. Secretary of State Forsyth wrote to Porter on August 17, 1840, expressing the "profound feelings of surprise and pain" felt by the president and the American people over the cruelty, "which has caused a shudder throughout the civilized world." Forsyth instructed Porter to use his "zeal and discretion" to work "against the employment of torture . . . , a subject which appeals so strongly to the universal sentiments of justice and humanity."[45] In addition to its significance to the Jewish community in the Ottoman Empire, this was one of the first instances of the United States' willingness to intervene diplomatically on a human rights issue, a policy that would not become common until the second half of the twentieth century. Porter, however, never made the requested intervention. A month after receiving his instructions, Porter forwarded a newspaper article reporting an official pronouncement from the Porte that Jews were not to be molested, commenting that there was thus no need for him to intervene. His dispatch did not explain why he waited a month without carrying out his instructions or why he never felt it necessary to make U.S. views on the subject known to Ottoman officials.

Porter lingered in Constantinople, now a fixture, an aging, ailing American naval hero who had found a niche far from home. Porter's name had long ceased to spark the kind of political controversy it had when he was appointed a decade earlier. To the extent that anyone in the United States thought of Porter at all, they were more likely to remember his naval victories of the War of 1812 than his subsequent controversies. The American legation in Turkey was apparently his to have and to hold, regardless whether he was the best man for the job or if he did the job at all. Although he had effectively ceased to function as a diplomat, the State Department stopped criticizing his performance.

In his final years, Porter seldom left the seclusion of San Stephano. He was often too ill and weak even to put pen to paper. He was still attended by his sister Mary and by his two nephews, George Porter and John Porter Brown. George wrote his family letters for him, while John prepared his official correspondence. Every letter refers to his failing health.

Porter seems to have lived the last years of his life as a sad and bitter old man, made miserable by his ill health and his never-ending financial woes. Even memories of his naval glories did not console him. When he reflected back on his years in the navy, he wrote, his thoughts "are always unpleasant. During the whole thirty and one years, that I have been in the naval service, I do not recollect having passed one day, I will not say of happiness, but of pleasure."[46] It was a sad end to an eminent life.

On March 6, 1843, John Porter Brown wrote to Secretary of State Daniel Webster:

It is my painful duty to inform the Department of State of the decease of my much lamented chief, Commodore David Porter, Minister Resident of the United States at the Sublime Porte, after a protracted and painful illness. . . .

At the special request of the deceased I have had his body interred in a vault at the foot of the flagstaff of the legation at St. Steffano. It is the desire of his relations here, among whom is his daughter, that his body be removed to the United States, and with this expectation I have had his remains put in spirits in a lead coffin with strong wooden cases for their preservation. . . .

I have taken charge of the legation until the intentions of the government are made known to me.[47]

In the fall of 1843, Porter's remains were carried home aboard the USS *Truxtun*. He was laid to rest with military honors at the Philadelphia Naval Asylum, more appreciated in death than in life.

Sultan Abdel Meguid continued his reign as a reformer, trying with limited success to drag his empire out of the past to claim its place as a modern power. Despite the significant transformations that he brought about, Turkey remained subject to incessant meddling by the European powers. The Ottoman Empire staggered on for another seventy-five years, finally collapsing in the aftermath of World War I.

William Hodgson went on to a successful and varied career. After his secret mission to Egypt, he worked briefly at the U.S. legation in London and then at the State Department. Hodgson was appointed consul to Tunis in 1841, the same position once held by William Eaton, who led the overland attack on Tripoli in 1805. On his way there Hodgson stopped in Paris, where he met and became engaged to a southern belle, the daughter of the governor of Georgia. He resigned his consular commission without proceeding to Tunis and settled with her in Savannah, overseeing the family's plantations from there. Hodgson became one of the state's leading intellectuals. He mastered thirteen languages, published papers on subjects as varied as ethnography and geology, and was elected curator of the Georgia Historical Society.

Porter's son David Dixon Porter and his adopted son, David Farragut, became the greatest American naval heroes of their era, winning renown especially for their exploits in the American Civil War. They were the first two Americans awarded the rank of admiral. Both of them first went to sea as midshipmen under Porter's command. Porter's five other sons, whom he seldom saw, all died in military service, four in the navy.

John Porter Brown served at the American legation in Constantinople for almost forty years, until his death in 1872, as dragoman, secretary of legation, and from time to time as chargé d'affaires. As chargé during the American Civil War, he kept a close watch to ensure that no Confederate envoys were received at the Porte. Brown became fluent in Turkish, Farsi, and Arabic and is sometimes regarded as the State Department's first "regional specialist." As a result of his lifetime of service, he died so poor that his widow could not afford to buy a ticket home. The sultan, out of respect for Brown, paid her passage to the United States.

David Porter's relaxed stewardship over the American legation in Constantinople stands in sharp contrast to the activist roles adopted by many of his contemporaries as American diplomats. Most of the men whose lives are recounted in this book dove headfirst into great power politics and strained to increase American fortunes and influence. Porter, despite his reputation as a naval commander who was energetic to the point of rashness, was an extraordinarily subdued diplomat. Unlike Joel Poinsett, Daniel Clark, or so many others that he certainly knew personally, Porter was strangely detached from the great events unfolding around him. For Porter, Constantinople was a respectable exile rather than an office of trust. At a time when the United States was emerging as one of the world's great powers with growing influence around the globe, its role in the turbulent history of the Ottoman Empire was hardly more than a footnote.

# SEVEN

## Adventures in Paradise

*Jacques–Antoine Moerenhout, Samuel Blackler,*
*and the Occupation of Tahiti*

On the other side of the world, in the South Pacific, diplomacy could hardly have been more different than at the Ottoman court. Not only was there no bureaucracy, but there were no diplomats or consuls from any nation on any island of the South Pacific at the time David Porter took up his duties in Constantinople.

American and European sailing ships had been regular visitors to the South Pacific for half a century by the time the first Western power officially assigned a consul to protect and promote its interests in Oceania. The distinction fell to Jacques-Antoine Moerenhout, a trader who had spent many years in the Pacific islands. Born in 1796 in Ekeren, Belgium (at that time a part of France), Moerenhout served briefly with Napoleon's army. He moved to South America in 1826, where he established a mercantile business and became the Dutch commercial agent in Valparaíso, Chile. Moerenhout would later become a French consul and colonial official. The flag he raised above his consular premises in 1836, however, was not that of France, the Netherlands, or newly independent of Belgium. On Moerenhout's flagstaff fluttered the Stars and Stripes of the United States.

The island that had the dubious honor to host the first foreign consul was Tahiti, then still commonly known as the Kingdom of Otaheite or O-taiti. When Moerenhout raised his flag in the little harbor of Papeete in January, he became the first foreign official formally accredited to any of the Pacific island governments. With the appointment of Moerenhout, the South Pacific was drawn formally into the orbit of Western diplomacy and, ultimately, into the political designs of the great naval powers. Future developments in the Pacific would be driven by a variety of factors, many of them far beyond the control of local consuls. In Tahiti, however, the actions of Moerenhout and his successor, Samuel Blackler, together with the British consul, came to dominate island politics. Operating half a world away from their home governments, usually without instructions or guidance, and often with less than admirable motives, the foreign consuls on Tahiti wielded enormous power over local events and had a profound effect in shaping the island's future.

At the time of his appointment, Moerenhout was a longtime resident trader in Tahiti who had come to the attention of visiting U.S. naval captains as a prominent and respectable foreign resident of the island. Moerenhout controlled what were perhaps the largest foreign business interests in Tahiti. He was a shipowner as well as a merchant. He had traveled widely through much of the South Pacific and was on his way to amassing a fortune, largely through the trade in pearl shell. Passing by way of the United States on a trip home to Europe in 1835, Moerenhout drew on the support of American shipping interests to secure his appointment as consul. Although one of Moerenhout's responsibilities as consul was to promote American trade, when he reached France, he helped organize the first French mercantile expedition to the South Pacific.

The Tahiti of Jacques-Antoine Moerenhout and Samuel Blackler was an exotic and exciting port of call. Early visitors marveled at its beauty. French explorer Louis de Bougainville compared Tahiti to the Garden of Eden. A contemporary geography book called "Otaheiti . . . the brightest gem of the Pacific," the most beautiful, fruitful, and civilized of the islands of the South Seas.[1] Herman Melville, who spent several months in Tahiti while Blackler was consul, called Tahiti "an object unrivalled for its stately beauty." The island was so enchanting, he wrote, "that it seems a fairy world. . . . It is no exaggeration to say, that to a European of any sensibility . . . the . . . beauty of the landscape is such, that every object strikes him like something seen in a dream."[2] For weary travelers who had been at sea for endless months, a stop in Tahiti seemed to rival paradise.

Moerenhout, like other early travelers, found the setting magical. He described his first sight of the island during a trading voyage: "The surprised European, in contemplating the luxury of the tropics in all its splendor, in the bosom of the enchanting island, is astonished to see the most amiable fictions of the poets come to life there. However stately this picture may appear, it is, however, not at all exaggerated."[3] Moerenhout traveled widely around the South Pacific. While serving as U.S. consul, he published *Travels to the Islands of the Pacific Ocean*, one of the best contemporary accounts of the islands, illustrated with his own drawings. Fifty years later Moerenhout's *Travels* was still readily available in its original French; the book inspired the artist Paul Gaugin to leave France for the South Pacific.

Despite initial appearances, Tahiti was not entirely a paradise, but a study in contrasts. The seemingly peaceful people were frequently at war among themselves and with other islands. Although at first glance people appeared to live in full equality, Tahiti was in fact an aristocracy with a privileged nobility. Years of contact with the West had begun to transform island traditions, mingling them in curious ways with European influences. British missionaries worked to cultivate strict Victorian moral standards, while visiting seamen by the hundreds pulled the island in the opposite direction.

At the time of Moerenhout's first visit to Tahiti in 1829, island girls still flocked to visiting ships to offer their favors. A whaling captain who stopped in Tahiti in the early 1830s wrote that the lax laws "permitted the sensuality of a sea port to be carried to a boundless extent [and] caused scenes of riot and debauchery to be nightly exhibited at Papeete."[4] Such conduct, however, was rapidly coming to an end under the influence of Christian missionaries. Charles Darwin, who visited Tahiti in 1835 during his famous voyage aboard the *Beagle*, reported that the free sexual license for which Tahiti was known was already becoming a thing of the past, although women and girls bathed openly, and it was not unusual for them to invite visitors to join them.[5] Moerenhout purported to be scandalized by Tahitian morals, adding that venereal disease ("a detestable disease which we have transmitted to them") infected most inhabitants of Papeete.[6] Whatever Moerenhout's moral sensitivities on arriving in Tahiti, a dozen years later he fathered a child by a Tahitian woman, a son whom he acknowledged and to whom he left an inheritance.

By the time of Moerenhout's arrival, Tahiti had been in intermittent contact with Europeans for centuries and in constant contact for decades.[7] The island had been claimed by early navigators and explorers from England (Samuel Wallis, 1767), France (Louis de Bougainville, 1768), and Spain (Tomás Gayangos, 1774); but the Tahitians were little affected by these early claims, which were not followed up. Tahiti became celebrated in Europe through the writings of these and other early visitors. The accounts of explorer Capt. James Cook's three voyages to Tahiti late in the eighteenth century were especially notable, helping develop the mystique of the "noble savage," man unspoiled by civilization and at peace with nature. The HMS *Bounty*, under Capt. William Bligh, paid its ill-fated visit in 1788. The first missionaries landed in Tahiti in 1797, and by Moerenhout's time they held enormous sway over the population. Tahiti was largely Christian, with a literacy rate far higher than European countries. One amazed visitor reported that almost the entire population could read and write.[8] By the time Moerenhout raised his flag in 1836, the earlier territorial claims of the great powers had been largely forgotten, and Tahiti was recognized by the Western powers as an independent country.

Moerenhout's appointment reflected that Americans as well as Europeans were frequent visitors to the South Seas. American China traders were passing through the islands before the end of the eighteenth century. During the War of 1812, David Porter in the USS *Essex* preyed on British shipping in the area and laid claim to the island of Nookaheeva. In 1826 Capt. Thomas ap Catesby Jones, commanding the USS *Peacock*—the same ship that was later rebuilt and carried Edmund Roberts on his far-flung travels—was dispatched to the South Pacific, where he signed treaties of commerce and amity with the indigenous leaders of Hawaii and Tahiti. This U.S recognition of island governments was in sharp contrast to the usual practices of other naval powers. Three years later, in 1829, Capt. Charles Stewart, commanding the USS *Vincennes*, reached Tahiti and reported meeting there "a Dutch gentleman" named Moerenhout.[9] U.S. naval visits to Tahiti were rare, however, and almost a decade would pass before the U.S. government outfitted its next major South Pacific voyage.

British captain Samuel Wallis was the first to turn the guns of a warship on the Tahitians. In describing his arrival, Wallis recorded nonchalantly that "after a brisk war, in which the simple people sustained a severe loss in life and property, peace was established on a firm basis."[10] The scene was repeated many times on Tahiti and neighboring islands as inhabitants offended their uninvited European guests, most often through their tendency to pilfer items from visiting ships. Even Captain Cook, who reported so enthusiastically on Tahitian hospitality, clashed with the islanders. Cook at times became so exasperated that he resorted to harsh and arbitrary punishments, once cutting off the ears of an offender.

For all the impact of military power, other Western imports had even more devastating effects. European diseases wreaked havoc on the indigenous population. Cook estimated the population of Tahiti at more than two hundred thousand. Later studies judged that the actual number when Cook visited was probably about fifty thousand. In any event, by the time of Moerenhout and Blackler, European diseases had reduced the population to about eight thousand.

The Tahitians who survived came under the sway of European culture largely through the efforts of the London Missionary Society. Tahiti became the first site of organized Protestant missionary activity when Presbyterian missionaries arrived in 1797. After fifteen years of effort they scored a spectacular success with the conversion of King Pomare II. The people followed the king into Christianity, idols were destroyed, and human sacrifice was abandoned. Scores of churches were constructed, including a magnificent structure seven hundred feet long that could seat five thousand worshipers. Strict moral standards were introduced, alcohol was prohibited, and the traditional revealing garb for women was replaced by modest, loose fitting dresses that covered the body from neck to ankle. Herman

Melville complained that the missionaries used their "unbounded influence with the natives" to prohibit even harmless customs and attractive elements of Tahitian culture.[11] Melville chronicled that sports such as wrestling, foot racing, and javelin throwing were prohibited; dancing, flute playing, and kite flying became punishable offenses; and wearing flower necklaces was forbidden.

Because of the prominent role of the London Missionary Society, missionary influence in Tahiti came to be associated with Great Britain. This connection was personified in George Pritchard, who was simultaneously head of the Protestant Mission and a principal advisor to Queen Pomare. Pritchard also carried on private business activities and owned a sugar plantation. He was later accredited as the British consul. Bolstering Pritchard's influence, British warships visited Tahiti regularly, as did British traders and whalers. The settlement of Australia increased British influence throughout the South Pacific; by the 1830s the government in London began to contemplate annexation of other Pacific islands. French warships also visited the Pacific regularly. French activities elsewhere in the world—such as their conquest of Algeria in 1830—suggested a growing tendency toward an annexationist policy, but French presence and influence in Tahiti and the other islands was still minimal.

In contrast to the creeping colonialism of the British and French, U.S. interests in the South Pacific centered on whaling and commerce. The islands were convenient ports of call for American traders to the Far East and for the many American whalers plying the Pacific. Although the extent of trade with the islands was not large in dollar amounts, they did produce some exports, including pearl shell and pearls, sugar, coconut oil, and sandalwood. It was with these interests in mind that the United States became the first country to appoint commercial agents and consuls in many of the islands.

The first U.S. commercial agent was named to the Sandwich Islands (Hawaii) in 1820, but no consul was accredited to that American-dominated group for another twenty years. Hawaii was more frequently visited and more developed than Tahiti. A captain who visited both islands in 1835 wrote that "Tahiti remains at least half a century behind Oahu in civilized improvements."[12] The United

States also appointed representatives in other parts of the South Pacific not long after Moerenhout's appointment: James Clendon was named consul in the Bay of Islands (New Zealand) in 1838, and John Williams became acting consul in the Navigator Islands (Samoa) the following year and later represented the United States in Fiji. While these appointments were enough to make the European powers suspect the United States of expansionist motives, the government in Washington had little interest in either its Pacific representatives or the islands where they resided. Sometimes years would pass with no communications from the State Department to its representatives. Moerenhout actually apologized for troubling the Department with so many letters when he wrote twice within a three-month period.[13]

Despite the limited U.S. government interest, private American vessels were beginning to dominate trade and fisheries in much of the Pacific by the 1830s. Only the British presented any serious rivalry to American traders in the central and eastern Pacific. Preeminent among American ships were the whalers, usually out of Massachusetts. These rugged little ships, with crews of thirty to forty men, would scour the South Seas in search of their prey, generally not returning home until their holds were fully loaded with whale oil, a process that could take as long as three years. Whaling voyages could turn large profits, but the crews' share was small, the work was dangerous, and the living conditions were wretched. Whalers tended to attract only the most desperate seamen or those of the most questionable character. By the time of Moerenhout's appointment, almost one hundred American whalers visited Tahiti every year, often putting ashore crews of desperadoes who caused endless troubles for him and his successors. It was the whaling interests, in fact, that first pressed for consular representatives in the islands, hoping consuls would provide assistance for injured seamen, secure the return of deserters, and provide official support in dealing with mutineers and with local rulers.

American consuls in the 1830s and 1840s were charged to deal with precisely these types of problems, in particular seamen in distress. Seamen, the U.S. consular instructions explained, are "a class of our fellow citizens, whose habits of life require a kind of guardianship of their persons and interests in foreign countries, but, at the same time, a strict vigilance over their conduct." The State Department reminded its consuls that they had no diplomatic powers. While consuls were expected to promote American commerce, they were "particularly cautioned not to enter into any contentions that can be avoided . . . with the authorities of the country in which they reside" and "scrupulously to abstain from all participation whatever, direct or indirect, in the political concerns of the countries to which they are appointed."[14] The first two American consuls in Tahiti, Moerenhout and Samuel Blackler, like their counterparts in other countries, were to stretch these instructions to the breaking point and beyond. They not only became involved in "contentions" but emerged as guiding hands behind some of the great political events that would shape the destiny of the South Pacific.

Moerenhout reported in his first dispatch to Secretary of State John Forsyth that Queen Pomare and her chiefs were "highly gratified" by his appointment.[15] Pomare was about twenty-three at the time. Charles Darwin, who had met Pomare the previous year, described her as "a large, awkward woman without any beauty, grace, or dignity."[16] A watercolor of the queen by Moerenhout, however, depicts a handsome woman with deep, dark eyes, a straight nose, and long, curly black hair. Whatever her physical attributes, Pomare was much respected by foreigners and by Tahitians. She did not assume royal airs, instead mixing unpretentiously with her subjects, living as they did, mingling with them, and usually eating with her fingers, although she was "well versed in forks and knives."[17]

"Everything is quiet and peaceable on Otaheite," Moerenhout wrote to Forsyth.[18] Foreigners could walk about freely without the least fear for their persons or property. Reflecting Tahiti's already established importance as a Pacific transit center, Moerenhout noted that three American vessels were in the harbor when he arrived to begin his service as consul, traders in coconut oil bound for Australia and for the United States. Several other American ships, mainly whalers, had recently visited. Moerenhout found several destitute

American seamen on the island, some of them ill and others survivors of the wreck of a whaler; he set about finding them employment on other ships.

Although Moerenhout would be an odd choice today for a U.S. representative abroad, in the 1830s his selection was not unusual. It was not uncommon at the time for the United States to name foreigners as consuls when no Americans were interested or available. In some instances the individuals named did not even speak English and submitted their dispatches to the State Department in French, which was still the language of international diplomacy. Although Moerenhout's correspondence with Washington was carried on in excellent English, the evidence suggests his command of the language was weak; he probably employed a translator. British acting consul George Pritchard once urged the State Department to send out an American citizen as consul, "or at least someone acquainted with the English language."[19] Whatever his language abilities, Moerenhout's loyalties were certainly divided.

Moerenhout bore a commission signed by President Andrew Jackson. The flag he raised above his consulate had twenty-four stars; the slow communications between the United States and Tahiti meant he would not learn until much later that two more states (Arkansas and Michigan) had joined the Union between the time of his appointment and the time he took up his duties. He paid sixty-two dollars to purchase the flag and his consular seals, for which he duly charged the State Department, but he had to pay out of his own pocket for his elaborate consular uniform, including a jacket with gold braid, shoes with gilt buckles, cocked hat, and sword. Despite the absurdity of this type of garb for a tropical island, foreign consuls and naval officers often strolled the islands fully decked out in their ruffles and braid. Such attire also became fashionable to Tahitian men, many of whom proudly sported cast-off remnants of military uniforms.

Moerenhout's relationship with the government got off on a weak footing almost from the start. After reporting the initial gratification of the Tahitians at his appointment, Moerenhout's next dispatch to Washington recounted his first meeting with the assembly of chiefs, for which George Pritchard acted as the magistrate, translator, and convener. Moerenhout announced his mission as "merely commercial," and was questioned closely about the status of the treaty signed with Capt. Thomas ap Catesby Jones in 1826, about which the Tahitians were having second thoughts. Amazingly, Moerenhout pleaded ignorance of the treaty, and the Tahitians ultimately let the matter drop.[20] That the first U.S. consul was never even informed that a treaty existed between the United States and Tahiti is startling evidence of how poorly the State Department prepared him for his assignment, as well as of the general U.S. lack of interest in the Pacific islands.

Throughout his first year as consul, Moerenhout dealt primarily with the problems of American ships and seamen. His consular returns show the arrival of as many as a dozen American vessels each month, almost all whalers, for periods averaging about three weeks. He complained in his dispatches of the high desertion rate of American seamen, attributing the problem to the beauty of Tahiti, the appearance of an easy life, and the absence of any means of punishment, since there was no place of confinement for wrongdoers. He pleaded several times with the local government to build a jail; the Tahitians promised action but failed to perform.[21] A later dispatch revealed another side of the problem: Moerenhout blamed desertions on the unscrupulous methods used to recruit whaler crews in the United States. The system, he explained, put seamen in debt by selling them clothing and supplies when they signed on, after which unethical captains overcharged them for provisions while at sea. The heavily indebted seamen thus had a strong incentive to desert. Moerenhout reported, for example, that when the whaler *Rose*, out of Nantucket, reached Tahiti after thirty-three months at sea, the crew was virtually naked and heavily in debt despite nearly three years of work. In desperation, the crew had mutinied. Moerenhout investigated and had six men taken ashore and confined in a native house. Using his powers as consul, he turned the ship over from the captain to the first mate for the voyage home.

By the end of his first year as consul, Moerenhout found himself embroiled in more serious problems. Two American seamen were attacked by armed "savages," who beat them with clubs and took their boat. The perpetrators were apprehended but given a light sentence. Moerenhout complained to Queen Pomare, threatening her with the unhappiness of the U.S. government. He implied that a U.S. warship might come to seek reparations, a common enough practice of the British and French in the Pacific. Although the United States also followed this approach in some instances— recall the USS *Potomac*'s attack on Qualah Battoo, as well as Capt. David Porter's 1813 attack on the Typees of Nookaheeva, not far from Tahiti—American naval visits to the South Pacific were a rarity; the largely uninterested U.S. government would have been highly unlikely to send a warship. Nevertheless, Pomare yielded to the threat and called another trial. She asked Moerenhout to name the sentence and agreed to banish the guilty parties, a punishment regarded by the islanders as the severest of penalties. Although the case was resolved, it would resurface.

Almost exactly a year after taking up his duties, Moerenhout became involved in an international incident that was to change the course of events in the South Pacific. Unwittingly or otherwise, the American consul intervened in the growing British-French rivalry in the region, siding squarely with the French. The crisis unfolded over the arrival of Catholic missionaries. With the encouragement of the French government, which hoped to mimic Britain's success in gaining influence through its missionary presence, the newly established Catholic Society of Picpus sent missionaries to Tahiti and Hawaii. Both island groups were already firmly Christian, suggesting that France's missionary zeal was aimed more at curbing Protestant and British gains than at converting islanders who had never heard the Gospels. The first two Catholic missionaries—François Caret and Louis Laval—landed in Tahiti in 1836, bearing a letter of introduction from the apostolic vicar to Moerenhout, who provided them with lodgings in a small building on the grounds of his residence.

The British Protestant missionaries lost no time in quashing the threat to their congregation posed by the newly arrived papists. Using their influence with Queen Pomare, the British promptly arranged for the expulsion of the Catholic fathers, who were unceremoniously removed from Moerenhout's guest bungalow and sent packing on the first available ship. To prevent a recurrence, Pritchard arranged for the promulgation of a new law forbidding any foreigner to land in Tahiti without government permission, clearly aimed at Catholic missionaries.

Moerenhout, of course, saw the incident from a different perspective. He was furious both at the violation of his consular premises and at the expulsion of the Catholic missionaries. He complained directly to the queen, appealed for religious tolerance, and railed at a public meeting against what he described as an insult to the United States. When he did not receive satisfaction, Moerenhout took what was considered drastic action for a consul: he struck his flag and announced that he would not raise it again until an American warship arrived to reinstate him.[22]

Moerenhout had opened a religious and political can of worms. Moreover, he had either misjudged the support he would receive from Washington or wrongly believed his threats alone would once again frighten the Tahitian government into meeting his demands. The State Department, however, turned a deaf ear to Moerenhout's protests. Worse, it seemed to take Pritchard's side. Pritchard, in fact, wrote directly to Secretary of State Forsyth on behalf of Queen Pomare and the principal chiefs, requesting that the American government "take into consideration the propriety of selecting a more suitable person to act as consul among this people."[23] Among other complaints, Pritchard asserted that although Moerenhout had struck his flag, he continued to perform consular duties and to collect fees from visiting American vessels. Almost simultaneously with his complaint to Washington on behalf of the queen, Pritchard was appointed British consul to Tahiti, a role he had been performing informally for some time.

Shortly after Pritchard's complaint reached Washington, the State Department appointed Samuel Blackler, a resident of Buffalo, New York, as the new American consul for Tahiti and the Society Islands, replacing Moerenhout. The Department, however, neglected to inform Moerenhout of this development. Although little is known of Blackler's life prior to his selection as consul, it is clear from his lack of regional or consular experience that he owed his appointment by President Andrew Jackson to the spoils system.

Father Caret returned to France to complain of his mistreatment by the Tahitian authorities. Moerenhout, receiving no positive response from Washington, wrote to the closest French official, the chargé d'affaires in Valparaíso, his former home, with dire warnings of the need for stern action if Frenchmen were ever again to be safe in Tahiti. The chargé forwarded Moerenhout's letter to Paris, where it contributed to a decision to send a warship to Tahiti to seek redress. At the time, there were very few French citizens in Tahiti and negligible commercial interests, none of which had been threatened.

Both the British and the French—as well as the less interested Americans—misread the larger implications of the situation. The British admiral closest to the scene judged wrongly that Moerenhout was trying to provoke a quarrel that would allow the United States to annex Tahiti. The French misread Prichard's zeal to keep Tahiti Protestant as an insult to the French nation.

Nonetheless, France dispatched a warship to Tahiti under Capt. Abel Aubert Du Petit Thouars, who had been instrumental in the French conquest of Algiers in 1830. Du Petit Thouars reached Tahiti in August 1838. After consulting with Moerenhout, who was still the American consul pending Blackler's arrival, the French captain issued an ultimatum to the Tahitians, demanding an apology for the treatment of the priests, permission for any Frenchman to settle in Tahiti, most favored nation treatment for France, and a relatively modest cash indemnity. Faced with the threat of the imminent bombardment of Papeete, Queen Pomare accepted the terms. Pritchard put up the money for the indemnity. Du Petit Thouars sailed away. The American consul, whose actions had prompted the entire chain of events, was satisfied with the outcome. France had made its presence felt in a way that foreshadowed even sterner action ahead.

Moerenhout's dispatches became less frequent over the next two years, while he remained consul pending Samuel Blackler's arrival. Blackler was unable to locate a passage to Tahiti for almost a year following his appointment and then sailed by the long eastern route around Africa, not arriving until March 1839. He carried with him Moerenhout's letter of recall, dated July 1837. Moerenhout, however, had heard rumors of his impending replacement and had accepted an offer from Du Petit Thouars to become the first French consul to Tahiti.

In the interim, Moerenhout had suffered a terrible personal tragedy that highlighted the dangers of service in the South Pacific. On the night of Sunday, June 9, 1838, Moerenhout was awakened by a noise outside his house. When he lit a candle and opened his door, he was immediately struck in the face by an axe. He fell helpless to the floor while his assailant continued to beat him. His wife ran to his aid, but she too was beaten with the axe. The commotion attracted some Tahitians, and the attackers fled. Moerenhout was left with twelve axe wounds, including two serious head injuries. His wife's skull was fractured; she clung tenuously to life for several weeks before passing away. The assailants were a Mexican and an Englishman, both deserters from American whalers, intent on robbery. Moerenhout bitterly blamed his plight on lack of support by the U.S. government. The repeated failure to send a warship, he reasoned, had reduced U.S. prestige to a point where its representatives could be attacked with impunity. Lawless, American-based desperadoes could roam the island without fear.[24] Little wonder that Moerenhout, his loyalties divided from the start, should readily accept Du Petit Thouars's offer two months later to become the French consul. Little wonder also that he should advocate a strong Western hand against local authorities, whom he saw as unwilling or unable to maintain public order. When Samuel Blackler arrived in Tahiti, Moerenhout set sail for France to deliver his motherless daughter to be raised by relatives. Moerenhout would return, however, to play a role in the events to come.

Judging from the preponderance of contemporary accounts, Samuel Blackler, the first American citizen to represent his country in Tahiti, was a scoundrel or worse. Blackler was thirty-two years old at the time of his nomination. He regarded his office primarily as an opportunity to enhance his finances. Blackler put enormous stock in the symbols of his office and the personal prestige he derived as American consul. In the absence of any serious official U.S. interest in South Pacific affairs, Blackler's high-handed approach and his preoccupation with the perquisites of his office set the tone for U.S. policy in Tahiti at the most critical moment of its history.

In his first substantive dispatch to the State Department, Blackler made clear his views on how best to deal with the Tahitians. He praised the action of the French government in demanding indemnity for the expulsion of the Catholic fathers. The United States, he believed, should adopt the same approach in dealing both with the Tahitians and with renegade American seamen: "Nothing but the dread of naval force will be effectual, both in correcting reckless habits of the seamen and the abuses under which they occasionally suffer."[25] The only prudent course for the United States, he urged, was to station a warship in the South Pacific.

Blackler's first year in Tahiti passed quietly. He established himself as a merchant, opened a store in partnership with an island trader named Hall, and hired Americans as clerks. His consular business was active but largely routine. In a fairly typical three-month period he reported the arrival of twenty-nine American ships—mainly whalers—with 763 seamen and cargoes valued at more than a million dollars. The volume of American shipping at Papeete far exceeded that at many European and Latin American cities. From every American ship that entered port, the U.S. consul collected a fee of four dollars, in addition to fees for any special services he might render.

With the whalers came familiar problems: attempted mutinies, desertions, a captain killed by a whale, unruly seamen illegally discharged in Tahiti by their captains, a seaman gone insane, and the return to the United States of American seamen charged for crimes. The problem of criminals was particularly irksome to Blackler. Despite the Tahitian government's promises to Moerenhout, there was still no prison in Tahiti. Islanders convicted of serious offenses were generally sentenced to construct a length of road, and as a result, by the end of Blackler's tenure, a well-kept highway circled much of the island. European and American prisoners were more of a problem. The Tahitians would not pay for their upkeep, and those confined in designated dwellings would generally be released or make an uncontested escape after a few days. The mild punishment encouraged further desertions and lawlessness. Blackler wrote bitterly to Secretary of State Forsyth that "the total inefficiency and duplicity of the Tahitian government, added to their evident incapacity to govern white men, renders it impossible to answer for the security of prisoners landed here."[26] Blackler's proposed solution to this problem was predictable: send a U.S. warship to visit or, preferably, station one in Tahiti. The State Department did not reply to his pleas. In fact, communications from Washington were so infrequent and so slow in arriving that Blackler was left almost entirely to his own devices. In December 1839, for example, Blackler acknowledged with no hint of surprise or dismay his recent receipt of consular instructions dated December 1837![27]

Although Blackler's consular dispatches projected a sense of business as usual, his various activities in Tahiti were bringing him into conflict with Queen Pomare and her missionary-backed government. On an official basis, Blackler continued to underscore supposed U.S. unhappiness at the removal of the French fathers from the consular premises more than three years earlier, as well as reviving complaints about the 1836 incident in which two U.S. seamen were attacked, although that issue had been resolved by Moerenhout before Blackler's arrival. On a private basis, he was involved in much more questionable practices.

The visit to Tahiti of the U.S. Exploring Expedition under Lt. Charles Wilkes sheds considerable light on Blackler's attitudes and activities. The long-planned Exploring Expedition, which had finally come to fruition, was the first American naval squadron in years to anchor in Tahiti. Blackler was elated. He visited Wilkes in Matavai Bay and requested his help in remedying American grievances, real and imagined. Blackler pressed for a show of force that would cow the Tahitian government into respect for the United States and its citizens.

Wilkes was not a man who was inclined to go easy on local populations. On the contrary, he believed that the success of his mission required him to demonstrate American power and military superiority. In his memoirs, Wilkes recounted an incident in the Tuamotu group, immediately before his arrival in Tahiti, in which he ordered a shotgun to be fired at the legs of a group of islanders, because "it was necessary to show our power."[28] Wilkes used much greater force whenever he felt his men were threatened or to rectify wrongs to Americans. He took Blackler's complaints seriously and resolved to look into them.

Wilkes, however, was also a man of moral principle, who quickly took offense at some of Blackler's doings. Wilkes had his first indication of foul play when one of his men reported for duty drunk despite the prohibition of liquor on Tahiti. Wilkes had heard rumors that Americans were involved in smuggling and illicit sales of alcohol. He decided to consult Blackler to discover the wrongdoers. To Wilkes's surprise, however, his men pointed to the consul's residence as the source of the spirits. Wilkes gave the following account:

I immediately interrogated him [Blackler] as to the truth of the assertion. He denied all knowledge of it and at once offered to permit his premises to be searched. This, somewhat to his surprise, I acted upon and ordered the search to be made. When it was discovered he had a large store of gin in jugs under his bed, amounting to some six or seven dozen, which he had been selling for four dollars a jug, I felt greatly shocked at this discovery and still more so at his prevarication which he attempted to excuse. He said he had come out to this Consulate to make money and intended to make it, and attempted to excuse himself for this desecration of our flag and the honor of our country. . . . He remarked to me that he could not live, even in Tahiti, on what was allowed him, that . . . he had been compelled to resort to making money where and when he could. It was not worth his while to remain unless he could make some money, and by his illicit traffic he had made a comfortable support.[29]

In fact, in this instance Blackler had landed seventy cases of gin, telling the local authorities that it was for the use of the Exploring Expedition and that it would not be sold on the island.[30] Wilkes's shock at discovering the U.S. consul was a bootlegger prompted him to look more deeply into Blackler's activities. He found, to his further dismay, that Blackler had taken to severely punishing crewmen for minor offenses reported by their captains. In one instance, Blackler had personally administered a flogging to an American seaman, contrary to U.S. law and certainly beyond the official duties of a consul. Wilkes recommended to Washington that Blackler be removed from office. Washington, typically, took no action.[31]

Whatever his misgivings about Blackler, Wilkes convened a council of chiefs to look into American grievances. The meeting was opened by British consul George Pritchard, who was still acting as the queen's advisor and with whom Wilkes was much impressed. Wilkes did not allow Blackler to speak, much to the latter's annoyance. Wilkes presented the U.S. grievances, including the violation of the consulate during the Catholic missionary incident (denied by the Tahitians) and the 1836 outrage on two American seamen (explained away by the Tahitians as action taken against two seamen caught in the act of abducting an islander). He also raised the need to provide a piece of land for a new consulate (agreed) and the need to build a prison for deserters (also agreed). To Blackler's consternation, Wilkes accepted the Tahitian explanations, considered the matters settled, and distributed presents.

Blackler's long-desired naval visit had failed miserably to yield the stern results he wanted . Blackler complained for years afterward that the Wilkes visit had seriously undermined American interests and prestige. Wilkes had good intentions, Blackler later reported to the State Department, but erred in accepting the meaningless promises of the Tahitians. Wilkes's reluctance to give stern warnings or to use force, Blackler asserted, convinced the Tahitians they had nothing to fear from the Americans.[32] Subsequent events reinforced Blackler's convictions. In the months to come he reported a long list of "outrages" against Americans by islanders and of American claims that went unfulfilled.

Blackler also inveighed to the State Department against Pritchard, asserting that his hand was behind every act of Queen Pomare and her government. Blackler saw Pritchard and the growing British influence on the island as a threat to Tahiti's independence and to

American interests. Moreover, Blackler considered Pritchard personally responsible for Queen Pomare's request years earlier that Moerenhout be removed as U.S. consul. Blackler foresaw a similar plot against himself.[33]

The anticipated complaint was not long in coming. In a letter to President Martin Van Buren, certified by George Pritchard, the Tahitian government requested Blackler's recall. The American consul, the Tahitians alleged, repeatedly violated local laws prohibiting the sale of liquor. He constantly circumvented government regulations limiting seamen's stay ashore. He protected American lawbreakers rather than helping bring them to justice. Finally, he was an adulterer and a fornicator, both in violation of law. "Should not the President be ashamed?" asked the Tahitians.[34] If President Van Buren was ashamed, he took no action to demonstrate it. Contrasting to the Tahitian complaints, the U.S. diplomatic archives also contain a few letters from American sea captains commending Blackler's performance as consul.

Blackler was continuously dismayed by waning U.S. influence in a port where American shipping predominated. He chafed at the ability of his British and French counterparts to call in naval power when they deemed it necessary, while his government was silent in the face of his pleas. In his consular returns for 1840, Blackler reported that seventy-nine American ships visited Tahiti, compared with twenty British vessels and only one French ship.[35] Yet three of the British visitors were warships, while no American naval vessels visited. British influence and prestige in the islands was expanding, while Americans, he believed, were treated with contempt.

Blackler's worst fears were soon borne out by an incident that was to preoccupy him for the remainder of his career. On Monday morning, May 13, 1841, he was standing outside the consulate yard in conversation with several visiting sea captains when a group of island constables attempted to arrest two American seamen standing nearby. Blackler quickly intervened, telling the men to run into his office. Blackler followed immediately behind. The constables gave chase and caught up with Blackler a few feet from his office door. When he protested, the constables hit him, knocked him to the ground, and then carried off the seamen from inside the office. According to American witnesses, Blackler did not strike a blow even in self-defense. Blackler normally carried a walking stick, but that morning he had left it in his office. The brief altercation left Blackler with a bloody face and bruised body, but his physical wounds were small compared with the blow to his dignity. Blackler reported the incident to Washington as an unforgivable "assault upon the Consular person." The only remedies, he railed in a dispatch to Secretary of State Daniel Webster, would be either for the United States to take control of Tahiti or to establish a permanent naval station on the island.[36] Blackler struck his flag, as Moerenhout had done four years earlier, following the violation of his residence. Like Moerenhout, Blackler continued to exercise consular functions and collect fees, despite having lowered his flag.

One of Queen Pomare's chiefs, Paraita, wrote directly to the American president with the Tahitian version of the incident. Paraita regretted the altercation with Blackler and had punished the constables involved, but alleged that Blackler had unjustly sought to protect individuals possibly associated with a murder. He reiterated numerous complaints about Blackler: he did not obey laws, he persisted in selling liquor, he drew his sword against government officials, and he committed adultery "before our eyes, without shame, and in defiance of us." Worst of all, the Tahitians reported, Blackler had arranged, in violation of government orders, for the anchoring in Papeete of an American vessel known to be infected with smallpox. He had landed goods from the ship and sold them. Now, Chief Paraita reported, the disease was starting to take hold on the island; three people had already succumbed.[37] Within a month smallpox was ravaging Tahiti. The disease spread to a fearful extent, almost every infected inhabitant died, and ships avoided the island.[38]

It was many months before either version of the incident reached Washington, which, as usual, made no reply. Fortuitously, however, an American warship, the *Yorktown*, under Cdr. John Aulick, arrived in Papeete just a few months later. Aulick listened to Blackler's complaint but seemed more amused than concerned by Black-ler's pompous description of "the outrage upon his Consular person." Still, Aulick called the chiefs together and conducted an investigation. The result, he reported, "satisfied my mind that the action and general conduct of our Consul towards these people have been both injudicious and undignified—that he is in the habit of paying very little respect to either the laws or authorities of the island—is dictatorial and overbearing in his official intercourse, and consequently extremely unpopular with them."[39] Blackler proposed to Aulick that to atone for the outrage against him, the Tahitians should appropriate land and build on it a permanent American consular residence. Aulick regarded this suggestion as highly dishonorable and rejected it out of hand. Since Blackler would not consent to any other solution, Aulick left the affair as he found it. For the second time in as many years, Blackler had been let down by a visiting U.S. Navy captain.

Unlike the Americans, other powers showed little reluctance to intervene politically in the islands. The British, through Pritchard, were indirectly controlling Tahiti. In addition, the British settlement in Australia was by this time thriving and making its influence felt through much of the South Pacific. In 1839, through the Treaty of Waitangi, the British annexed New Zealand.

France, meanwhile, viewed with alarm the growing British predominance in the Pacific. As early as the 1820s the French began to consider ways to counter British influence. Official backing for Catholic missionaries was one means, but this yielded little progress. By the late 1830s the French leaned toward more direct action. The government supported an attempt to colonize New Zealand, but this was thwarted by poor execution and the British annexation. French warships began to ply the South Seas more systematically, intent on demonstrating French power. In sharp contrast to the American unwillingness to send warships even to remedy grievances, in 1838 the French ordered one of their captains to sail to Tahiti and Hawaii to ascertain whether there were any grievances and, if so, to stay until he had obtained indemnity and demonstrated French power to the inhabitants.

Attempts by France to expand its influence in the South Pacific were consistent with its emerging policy elsewhere in the world. During the same period, France occupied Algeria, expanded its presence in West Africa and Madagascar, and increased its share of the China trade. With the appointment of Moerenhout as consul in Tahiti, France joined Britain and the United States as the only countries with official representatives in the Pacific islands. By 1840 Moerenhout was complaining to the French government that British preponderance in Tahiti and Pritchard's dual role as consul and advisor to the queen were resulting in Frenchmen being subject to ill treatment.[40] In 1841, while Pritchard was away from Tahiti on leave, Moerenhout organized an appeal from several prominent Tahitian chiefs, rivals of Queen Pomare, for another French warship to visit and look into problems on the island.

By this time the French were already on the move in nearby islands. Du Petit Thouars, by now promoted to admiral, had orders to take control of the Marquesas, a nearby island group in which no Western country had a notable presence or interests. The French move in the Marquesas caught the Americans and British by surprise. Samuel Blackler sent the first word from Tahiti in June 1842, based on the account of a visiting American whaler, that a frigate under the command of Du Petit Thouars had landed a military force, constructed a fort, and taken possession of the islands.[41]

Well before Blackler's report reached Washington, Du Petit Thouars arrived back in Papeete. Moerenhout met with him on his arrival and complained that Frenchmen in Tahiti continued to suffer mistreatment. With some justification, Moerenhout reported that the government of Tahiti was breaking down and that feuding between Pomare and her principal chiefs had resulted in more than the usual amount of government indolence and capriciousness. Still, the list of grievances conveyed by Moerenhout to Du Petit Thouars and thence to Queen Pomare has been described as "astonishingly out of proportion" to the interests of the tiny French community on Tahiti.[42] There were only about a dozen Frenchmen living on the island.

Du Petit Thouars offered the Tahitians two alternatives: either pay 10,000 piasters in compensation for past abuses and as a guarantee of future good behavior, or grant permission for France to occupy all strategic points on the island pending a decision from Paris on next steps. Du Petit Thouars trained the guns of his flagship, the *Reine Blanche*, on Papeete and demanded an answer within forty-eight hours. He invited Blackler to take refuge on his ship in case bombardment became necessary. Pritchard was still away from Tahiti, and his stand-in, Samuel Wilson, was not up to dealing with the situation. Queen Pomare was also away on a neighboring island awaiting the birth of a child.

The Tahitians gave in. At a late night meeting at Moerenhout's residence, four principal chiefs (three of whom had signed the appeal a year earlier for the visit of a French warship) signed a document asking France to assume protection over Tahiti. Pomare later added her signature to the request. The document, as translated by Blackler, states, "Because we cannot govern our government in present circumstances so as to harmonise with foreign governments, and lest our land and our government and our liberty become another's, . . . the Queen and . . . the high chiefs of Tahiti write you asking that the King of the French may protect us." The document put several limits on French protection, including that the queen and chiefs would retain their authority, that all Tahitians would retain their land without foreign interference, that people would be allowed to worship as they wished, and that British missionaries would not be molested. However, "all affairs relative to foreign governments and concerning foreigners resident at Tahiti shall be with the French."[43] Blackler's report to Washington added that the queen and high chiefs would receive a "yearly allowance sufficient to maintain the dignity of their rank."[44] With this, Du Petit Thouars accepted in the name of King Louis Philippe the Tahitian "request" for French protection.

The American consul was fully attuned to the probable consequences of these momentous events. He was in close personal contact with both Moerenhout and Du Petit Thouars. He remained preoccupied, however, with his personal dignity. On September 10, 1842, while the chiefs were signing Tahiti over to France, Blackler penned a letter of protest to Du Petit Thouars. Blackler's protest was not against the French takeover, however. Rather, it appraised Du Petit Thouars of Blackler's claim "on behalf of the United States against the Tahitian Government for full and ample satisfaction for an outrage committed by the authorities of this soil on the person and premises of the Consul of the United States at a previous date."[45] Perhaps, Blackler fancied, Du Petit Thouars might assist him where his own government had not. Blackler ultimately made a deal with the French admiral: he would provisionally raise the American flag over the consulate (which had not flown since he struck it over a year earlier) in return for a 21-gun salute from Fort Moutou Outa, in Papeete Harbor, which was now under the flag of the French protectorate. The salute would demonstrate Tahitian remorse for the "outrage" and signal respect for the United States and its consul. Blackler then penned a second letter to Du Petit Thouars, congratulating him on having peacefully settled the French-Tahitian difficulties and assuring him of "my cheerful cooperation in maintaining harmony and peace, where hitherto disorder and confusion have been predominant."[46] The French were the big winners in this exchange, for in raising his flag and having it saluted, Blackler had offered tacit American recognition and approval of the French takeover.

Blackler was not blind to what he was doing. Even beyond the question of restoring his personal dignity, he wholeheartedly supported the French takeover and was anxious to proffer his recognition. Blackler justified his action to the State Department by explaining that with the protectorate, tranquility and order had finally come to Tahiti. The new administration would make it easier to protect American seamen. And the French were, after all, a friendly government. The same could not be said of the British, whose influence in Tahiti Blackler believed to be at the root of many of the problems there. The primary policy reason to support the French action, Blackler argued, was to avoid a likely British takeover, which would result in an "exclusive system" to the detriment of American whalers and traders. On the latter point, Blackler may have been on the mark; British practices following the annexation of New Zealand had effectively shut those islands off to Americans.

One of the most interesting aspects of the establishment of the French protectorate was that Blackler could easily have prevented it, had he wished. The means were simple and well within his power. Blackler reported to Secretary of State Webster that the guarantee demanded by Du Petit Thouars—10,000 piasters—was sufficiently small that he could have put it up from his own pocket.[47] Pritchard would certainly have provided the funds if he had been in Tahiti, just as he had put up the previous guarantee demanded by Du Petit Thouars a year earlier. Blackler, however, reasoned that since the United States would not occupy Tahiti, French occupation was preferable either to a British takeover or to continued Tahitian independence.[48] As usual, the State Department did not take the time to respond to dispatches from its consul in Tahiti.

While these events unfolded, Blackler's dispatches confirmed that he remained pompously preoccupied with his personal status. In addition to his long-festering resentment over the Tahitian outrage on his consular person, Blackler had developed a semiofficial feud with Moerenhout.

As it turned out, the American seamen arrested inside the U.S. consulate on the day of the outrage had been involved in a serious altercation between a resident American hotel and pool hall operator and a group of visiting seamen from Chile. The Chilean seamen were in Tahiti to deliver a cargo of horses to Moerenhout, part of his lucrative private business. Following the altercation Moerenhout attempted to have the Americans charged and punished, while Blackler sought to defend them. If we are to believe Blackler's version of events, this confrontation led Moerenhout to slander Blackler's reputation in an effort to have him recalled. It was Moerenhout, Blackler alleged, who drew up the letter from Queen Pomare to the president impugning Blackler's character and falsely accusing him of misdeeds.[49] In support of this contention, Blackler produced an affidavit from Acting British Consul Samuel Wilson.

Blackler also presented these charges to Du Petit Thouars. After some discussion, Blackler and the admiral agreed to leave matters to their governments, a tacit acknowledgment by Blackler that Du Petit Thouars had taken Moerenhout's side in the dispute.[50] Nevertheless, in anticipation that Washington might finally take his complaint seriously, Blackler asked the State Department to raise with the French government both the problem of the "outrage" and the question of Moerenhout's slanderous intriguing. If Washington showed any interest in Blackler's charges, there is no record of it.

The story was not quite over, however. A protectorate is not a colony, and France had yet to win international recognition for its action, beyond Blackler's personal and provisional recognition. In fact, the French government did not even learn of the establishment of the protectorate until six months later. When word reached Paris, the cabinet quickly endorsed Du Petit Thouars's action. With this approval, Tahiti briefly became an area of sharply increased British-French tension.

The British, of course, did not approve of the French protectorate. When George Pritchard returned to Tahiti early the next year aboard the British frigate *Vindictive*, Queen Pomare immediately issued a declaration announcing her preference for British over French protection. The *Vindictive* remained in Papeete for six months, refusing to recognize French suzerainty. Blackler characterized this British action as "unparalleled interference" in Tahitian affairs by the British, a rather odd conclusion considering his support for the actions of Du Petit Thouars.[51] Pritchard not only continued to recognize the queen's complete independence but even provided her with a new flag, which British warships saluted in preference to the protectorate flag. At one point French and British warships faced each other across Papeete Harbor, producing a threat of imminent hostilities.

As in each of the two previous years, the situation came to a head with the return of Du Petit Thouars, who arrived in November 1843, carrying his government's official ratification of the protectorate. Pomare took refuge in Pritchard's home and raised her British-provided flag. Du Petit Thouars, always the man of action, landed three hundred men, constructed new fortifications, and declared the queen deposed. Pritchard struck his flag, a last futile gesture, reminiscent of Moerenhout's and Blackler's earlier actions, and with an equal absence of results. Blackler, for his part, blamed Pritchard directly for bringing about the French occupation by pursuing a "policy as imbecile as it was unjustifiable" in opposing the protectorate.[52] In coming months Pritchard's actions and attitudes so offended the French administration that he was eventually detained and then expelled.

As the French solidified their occupation, the British representatives on the spot found themselves abandoned by their government. The *Vindictive* sailed away. Pritchard was transferred to Samoa, which he found "barbarous" in comparison to Tahiti.[53] France did eventually offer an apology and indemnity for its treatment of the British consul. Not until 1847 did the British fully accept the French occupation, to the lasting chagrin of Queen Pomare. The mood in London, however, did not allow for a British confrontation with France over Tahiti. The recent annexation of New Zealand had satisfied for the moment British territorial ambitions in the South Pacific.

In contrast, Tahiti served only to whet the French appetite. By the end of 1844 France had established protectorates over the islands of Wallis, Futuna, New Caledonia, and the Gambiers. The original protectorate over Tahiti was extended to include all of the Society and Georgian Islands.

When the protectorate was established over Tahiti, Moerenhout and two lieutenants from the *Reine Blanche* were named by Du Petit Thouars as a provisional advisory council. A year later, with annexation, Moerenhout became a royal commissioner, second only to governor in the French administration. He remained in Tahiti until 1846, taking an active part in the colonial government. According to Herman Melville, Moerenhout was "bitterly detested" by the islanders.[54] Whatever his popularity, the onetime American consul was certainly as responsible as anyone for the French acquisition of Tahiti.

With the French in control, Tahiti rushed into the modern era. By 1844 the French had established a telegraph line across the island. The ability to send messages across Tahiti in a flash stood in stark contrast to the many months it still took for letters to travel between Papeete and Paris or Washington. Within a few years, however, American consular reports note the arrival of the first steamships in Papeete Harbor.

Amid this political turmoil and economic transformation, Samuel Blackler fell ill and passed away in September 1844, at the age of thirty-nine. Throughout this period, American ships retained their predominance as commercial and whaling visitors to Tahiti. Over the next decade, however, the number of visiting American ships began to decline sharply, first because of the depletion of the Pacific whaling grounds and then as new French regulations and fees began to make Hawaii a more attractive port of call.

The American government had difficulty in finding a replacement for Blackler. For several years the position was filled by a succession of acting consuls of questionable distinction. More than a decade later it seems that the quality of U.S. representation on Tahiti was not much improved. The *Boston Daily Journal* of October 29, 1858, reported on a U.S. consul at Tahiti who appears to have been a successor worthy of Blackler: "He is drunk a large portion of the time, and has repeatedly been picked up in the streets intoxicated, even in his Consular uniform, and carried home. Lately in one of his drunken sprees, he fell from a bridge into a gutter, and striking his face upon a stone, was picked up not only dripping with filth, but with a broken nose. On another occasion some sailors found him in a taro patch and carried him to the calaboose as a 'drunk.' He however was not confined as the French officer recognized in him the Consul of the United States."[55]

Meanwhile, Jacques-Antoine Moerenhout went on to a distinguished career in the French consular service. In 1846 Moerenhout left Tahiti for Monterey, to become the French consul in what was then Mexican California. In California, however, center stage belonged to a different consul, Thomas Larkin, whose story is told in the next chapter.

# EIGHT

# The Land of Gold

*Thomas Larkin, William Leidesdorff,*
*and the Americanization of California*

While American envoys were establishing outposts in countries from Turkey to Tahiti, Americans at home were starting to look west. Settlers were beginning to push across the Mississippi River in increasing numbers. The Missouri Territory won statehood in 1821, becoming the second state west of the Mississippi, after Louisiana. Arkansas was next, in 1836, the year that Edmund Roberts died in Macao and Jacques-Antoine Moerenhout raised the American flag in Tahiti. In April of the same year, American settlers defeated a Mexican army at San Jacinto, winning independence for the Republic of Texas.

Still, the vast American west was largely unknown territory. A few expeditions had explored parts of the interior, most famously Lewis and Clark and Zebulon Pike. Small numbers of American fur trappers traveled overland as far west as Oregon. A handful of intrepid mountain men reached Mexican California, notably Jedediah Smith in 1826. These journeys, however, just scratched the surface of a still mysterious continent.

While the American interior remained little known, a few Americans reached the Pacific coast by sea and began to establish themselves there in a very small way. The American vessel *Columbia* reached Oregon in 1788, back in the times of Samuel Shaw and the early days of the Northwest-China trade. John Jacob Astor's Pacific Fur Company set up a short-lived American fur trading post at the mouth of the Columbia River. The post was occupied by the British during the War of 1812 but was returned to the United States at the war's end. Borders were ill defined between the small Russian settlements in the north and the British and American traders in

Oregon. There was no clear northern boundary of California, which remained Spanish territory until Mexico's independence in 1821.

When the time came for the United States to resume possession of the former Astor trading post on the Columbia River, the task was entrusted to John Prevost, the U.S. consul in Lima, Peru. Prevost was the stepson of Aaron Burr and had been a judge in New Orleans before the War of 1812, where he almost certainly would have known Daniel Clark and David Porter. Although Lima was five thousand miles from Oregon, Prevost was the closest U.S. representative, an indication of how remote the American Northwest was at the time, and how tenuous American links were. It could still take well over a year for a ship to make the journey from the east coast of the United States around Cape Horn to Oregon and back. Prevost traveled from Lima to Oregon on a British warship, evidence that although the United States was becoming an economic power in the Pacific, it had few official or naval resources there to draw on. Prevost stopped in California, still a Spanish territory at the time. He wrote to Secretary of State John Quincy Adams that "the port of St. Francis is one of the most convenient, extensive, and safe in the world, wholly without defense, and in the neighborhood of a feeble, diffused, and disaffected population. Under all these circumstances, may we not infer views to the early possession of this harbor, and ultimately to the sovereignty of entire California?"[1] Prevost may thus have been the first American diplomat officially to urge the acquisition of California. He would not be the last.

By the 1830s, just a handful of Americans had arrived in California by sea, integrating themselves into the small Mexican settlements there. Almost all took up Mexican citizenship, which made them eligible for large land grants. California at the time was a sparsely populated expanse of wilderness, punctuated with Catholic missions and dotted with huge cattle ranches. There were no more than 10,000 people of European origin in the entire province, and only twice as many Native Americans. Skilled Mexican horsemen were famous for lassoing grizzly bears that invaded the ranches. Population centers were so far away that there was no market for the beef raised in California; the cattle were slaughtered for hides and tallow, which could be shipped more easily. This pastoral existence had been largely undisturbed for decades. Even the independence of Mexico from Spain in 1821 had little immediate effect on far-away California. But quiet times were rapidly approaching their end.

Onto this stage in 1832 sailed a young man named Thomas Oliver Larkin. As the first and only American consul in California, Larkin would play a pivotal role in the coming upheavals.

Larkin was born in Charlestown, Massachusetts, in 1802. His father died when he was a child, followed by his mother when he was fifteen. Thomas received limited formal schooling; later in life he regarded his lack of education as an embarrassment. He compensated by becoming a voracious reader and eventually a prolific writer. At age fifteen, his love of books led him to try out a career as a bookbinder, but he soon decided that bookbinding was unlikely to bring him the wealth and success he craved. He moved to Wilmington, North Carolina, where he found employment variously as a clerk, a storekeeper, a postmaster, and a justice of the peace, none of which brought him much fortune or happiness. In 1831, therefore, Larkin accepted an unexpected offer from his half-brother, John Cooper, to travel to distant Monterey, California, to assist in his trading business with Mexico and the Sandwich Islands (Hawaii).

Larkin's passport described him as twenty-nine years of age, five feet seven and a half inches tall, with a dark complexion, dark eyes, and black hair. A contemporary later described him as "dark and thin . . . with a slight stoop to his shoulders. . . . He appeared to be a little deaf, and held one of his hands back of his ear when he saw that you were disposed to speak to him."[2]

Larkin sailed on the ship *Newcastle* in September 1831. He had scraped together his meager life savings and borrowed money from friends and relatives to purchase some goods for sale on his own account, looking ahead to starting a business. Monterey was so far away that he was unsure whether he would ever see his native land again. It took seven months to make the arduous journey, sailing south around Cape Horn. Larkin spent his days at sea learning Spanish. He had the enjoyable company of just one other passenger: Rachel Hobson Holmes, a young woman on her way to join her husband, who was a ship captain and trader in the Pacific. Rachel and Larkin began an illicit romance while aboard the ship.

The *Newcastle* finally reached the coast of California in April 1832. It stopped first at Yerba Buena, a tiny hamlet of adobe houses that would later be renamed San Francisco. It then sailed on to Monterey, the administrative center of California and the only legal port of entry along the coast. Monterey was larger than Yerba Buena, but not by much; it had just a few dozen buildings. There was no wharf or customs house. Monterey's residents included about a dozen Americans and other foreigners, all of them men and most naturalized as Mexican citizens.[3] Several owned ranches outside of town. Larkin was welcomed by his half-brother. Rachel became their houseguest, since there were no hotels in Monterey and her husband was away at sea. She was the first American woman to settle in California.

By summer it was clear that Rachel was pregnant with Larkin's child. This was a grave development for both of them. Rachel was married to another man, whom she had not seen for at least two years. Divorce was out of the question in Catholic California. Larkin, for his part, could have faced criminal charges and deportation. Fate saved them from further scandal when news arrived in the fall that Rachel's husband had died at sea. Baby Isabel was born in January and was baptized by a Catholic priest.

Still, Thomas and Rachel did not marry until the following summer. Ostensibly, as Protestants, they did not want to be married in the Catholic Church, the only venue for legal marriage in California. Their wedding was held on June 10, 1833, on board the *Volunteer*, a visiting American ship. The ceremony was performed by the ship's captain, John C. Jones, who was also the U.S. commercial agent in Honolulu. Larkin later said that he had the idea "that consuls can perform the ceremony of marriage between their countrymen in any port of the world if on board an American ship."[4] He was wrong on two counts: American consuls had no authority to perform marriages, and Jones was not a consul at all but a U.S. commercial agent.[5] After discovering his mistake, years later

Thomas and Rachel were remarried in a Catholic ceremony, still the only type of wedding permitted in California. Baby Isabel, who was the first child ever born of two American parents in California, died less than a month after the first wedding.

Larkin worked briefly for his half-brother, then started his own business as a general merchant and trader. Initially he traded in hides and tallow, the main products of California. The hides were usually shipped by way of the Sandwich Islands to Boston for its growing shoe industry. Business flourished. Larkin soon opened a general store, began to manufacture soap from tallow, and supplied the whalers and other ships that sometimes called at Monterey. He began an expanding trade in hardware, cloth, furs, liquor, and any other product that could turn a profit, shipping to and from the Sandwich Islands, Mazatlán, and other Mexican ports. Before long, Larkin owned and operated one of the largest businesses in California.[6] As he grew more prosperous, Larkin began offering lines of credit in what was effectively the first banking operation in California.

The Larkins built a house in Monterey that still stands as a historic monument. Larkin House was the first New England–style, two-story house in California. The family lived upstairs, while Larkin had his store and business on the ground floor. Over the years Thomas and Rachel would have eight more children. To educate their growing family, Larkin established the first English-language school in Monterey. With their growing prosperity, the Larkins became one of Monterey's leading couples, known as great hosts and entertainers.

Meanwhile, a few settlers continued to make their way to California by sea. Among these was John Sutter, a Swiss German immigrant who arrived in 1839, fleeing from creditors. Sutter became a Mexican citizen and claimed to have been given the rank of captain in the Mexican army.[7] He received a 40,000-acre land grant near present-day Sacramento, where he established a small, fortified outpost that he named "New Helvetia" after his native Switzerland. Another early American settler was William Leidesdorff, a trader and ship's captain from New Orleans who arrived in Yerba Buena in 1841. Both Sutter and Leidesdorff would play important parts in

Larkin's future. Settlers also began to arrive in California overland in miniscule numbers beginning in 1841, with the opening of the Oregon Trail. A few settlers broke off from the Oregon wagon trains and went south to California, usually arriving first at Sutter's establishment, where they were welcomed. The U.S. Exploring Expedition also reached San Francisco Bay in 1841, where it surveyed the coast and parts of the interior, but the glum description of California in the expedition's official narrative did little to encourage new settlers.

While the Larkins prospered in sleepy Monterey, several world powers were beginning to take an interest in California. The British and French were engaged in a colonial rivalry in the Pacific and elsewhere, as we have seen in Tahiti. Warships from both countries made occasional stops in California, while adventurers and politicians in both countries eyed California as a largely undefended territory, ripe for the picking. British businessmen in Mexico, in particular, saw British acquisition of California as a solution to the problem of Mexican debts.

Some Americans also began to advocate the purchase of California. In 1842 Secretary of State Daniel Webster raised the possible purchase of San Francisco with the Mexican minister in Washington.[8] As American settlers began to make their way to Oregon, tensions arose between the United States and Great Britain over the border between Oregon and Canada. More ominously, rumors of imminent war between the United States and Mexico were constantly in the air following the independence of Texas in 1836.

The situation was further complicated by the often-turbulent relationship between California and its distant government in Mexico City. The Californians regularly ousted governors and other senior officials sent from the capital and quarreled among themselves. California was simply too vast, too sparsely populated, and too distant to be effectively controlled from Mexico City. A few Californians began to think about the possibility of independence.

The extent of tensions was brought sharply into focus in 1842. In the spring of that year, Cdre. Thomas ap Catesby Jones—the same Jones who had signed the first U.S. treaty of commerce and amity with Tahiti sixteen years earlier—arrived in the eastern Pacific to take command of the U.S. Pacific Ocean squadron, consisting of five ships. The British and French fleets in the area were far stronger. Arriving on the west coast of Mexico, Jones learned that the French fleet had sailed from Chile for an unknown destination. Recalling the French annexation of Tahiti, Jones feared a similar move in California. Meanwhile, the British fleet in the area suddenly sailed under secret orders, further raising Jones's suspicions. At about the same time, Jones received a letter from the U.S. consul in Mazatlán, John Parrot, suggesting that war between the United States and Mexico over Texas might break out at any moment. Parrot's letter enclosed a New Orleans newspaper report that Mexico had sold California to England for $7 million.[9]

With all this alarming information, Jones set sail immediately for California, arriving off Monterey on October 18, 1842. He was relieved to see that neither the British nor the French navies had arrived, but he was still worried that the United States and Mexico were at war. Fearing that the British might arrive at any moment to take possession, or that a Mexican force might arrive to reinforce defenseless Monterey, Jones decided to act. He demanded the surrender of the town. The governor, with no defenses of consequence, yielded and sent a team on board to negotiate the terms of surrender. Thomas Larkin went along to act as interpreter. On October 20, the few Mexican troops in Monterey marched out of their small fort. U.S. Marines went ashore to take possession and raise the American flag.

Once ashore, the American forces found private letters and newspapers in the governor's office showing that relations were still amicable and that the rumor of a British purchase was unfounded. Jones, belatedly realizing his mistake, hastily lowered the Stars and Stripes, contacted the Californian officials, and restored their city to them. All this was accomplished with the greatest courtesy. The American ships saluted the Mexican flag as it was raised. The officials of both countries exchanged visits. Jones remained in the area for several months, staying on friendly terms with local officials.

While Jones's exploits apparently did not much disturb local feelings in California, they caused outrage in Mexico City and consternation in Washington. The Mexicans filed a sharp protest. The State Department assured them that the commodore's actions were unauthorized. Jones was relieved of command and called home to face an inquiry and a possible court-martial. Communications between Washington and the Pacific were so slow, however, that Jones's replacement did not arrive off Peru until the middle of 1843, and Jones himself did not make it back to the east coast until 1844, two years after his short-lived occupation of Monterey.

Meanwhile, in a demonstration that Jones's fears were not entirely far-fetched, a British man-of-war seized the Kingdom of Hawaii with meager justification just four months later. Jones learned of this while still in Monterey. He sailed immediately for the Sandwich Islands, where the British ended their occupation shortly after his arrival.

The growing tensions between Mexico and the United States helped persuade the State Department of the need for an American representative in California. As the department considered its choices in 1842, Larkin seemed an obvious candidate. The department had previously appointed other individuals to serve in California, but for various reasons, none of them made the trip.

By this time Larkin was almost certainly the best-known American in California and among the wealthiest. He was one of very few Americans in California who kept his U.S. citizenship rather than being naturalized as a Mexican. Ships' captains, naval officers, and other travelers were willing to recommend him. An officer of the U.S. Exploring Expedition who had stayed with Larkin in Monterey, for example, wrote: "He is a gentleman of property, much respected both by foreigners & natives, & bearing, so far as my knowledge extends, an irreproachable character. He is, beyond question, the principal American merchant resident at Monterey. He speaks the language fluently."[10]

On May 1, 1843, Secretary of State Daniel Webster appointed Larkin as U.S. consul in Monterey. News of the appointment took most of a year to reach Larkin. It was April 1844 by the time his appointment was officially recognized by the Mexican and Californian authorities and he formally assumed office. Larkin asked for and received permission to fly the American flag, a privilege not granted to other consuls. He wrote to the State Department that there were unopened packages in Monterey addressed to the previously appointed consuls who had never arrived, and he asked permission to open them.[11] Acknowledging that he knew little of what was expected of him as consul, Larkin wrote both to the Department and to the closest American consulates, in Oahu and Mazatlán, asking for books and guidance. Both the consuls answered promptly. Among other information, John Parrott, the consul in Mazatlán, advised that if a sailor were found guilty of robbery on the high seas, "the captain should inflict the punishment allowed by law, one dozen lashes with a rope's end."[12]

Larkin ordered a military-style consular uniform of the type American consuls of the day were expected to wear to meetings with local officials and on other appropriate occasions. The uniform included a blue coat with a cape, embroidered with gold, a cocked hat with gold tassels and black cockade, a small sword, and shoes with gold buckles.[13]

Although Larkin's position as consul did not provide a salary, it worked very much to the benefit of his expanding business interests. Being named consul conferred a prestige that made visiting ship captains and merchants turn first to him for their needs. Many of Larkin's letters on consular business also touch on private commercial matters, a conflict of interest that was not regarded as inappropriate at the time. His consular title also gave him reason to increase his already active role as a host, both to visitors and to the local population.

Like other American consuls, Larkin had a wide range of duties and responsibilities. All American ships had to submit their papers to him upon entering port. He also had duties regarding sales of ships, shipwrecks, and caring for ill or destitute seamen. As consul, Larkin had responsibility for the estates of Americans who died in his district, for issuing passports, and for protecting the rights of Americans before the local authorities. He was also required to report from time to time to the State Department on commercial and political developments. By the 1840s, consular instructions required a report at least once every three months, if only to confirm that he was still at his post. Consuls were also cautioned "to abstain from all participation whatever, direct or indirect, in the political concerns of the countries to which they are appointed" and not to give "publicity, through the press or otherwise, to opinions or speculations injurious" to those countries.[14] An earlier special instruction to consuls in Mexico—which, of course, included Larkin—warned that because of the "disturbed and unsettled conditions" there, they should "forbear intermeddling . . . in the smallest degree whatever."[15]

Larkin dutifully dealt with all kinds of problems relating to Americans, intervening with local authorities on behalf of Americans in trouble, administering wills and estates, issuing passports, and even being called on to give advice on marital problems. He settled disputes between captains and their crews. He was especially attentive to sick seamen, usually put ashore by the New England whalers that were beginning to call more frequently in Monterey. The 1840s were the peak of the American whaling industry. Many of the crew members suffered from scurvy after years at sea. There were so many such cases that Larkin established a small hospital to accommodate them, where they received a bunk, food, and simple treatment. In an 1845 letter, a crewman from a whaler certified that he "received from March 10 to July 1, 1845, from the Consulate of the United States in this Port, board, lodging, clothes and medical assistance, this day being cured, am discharged from this Consular Hospital by my own request."[16]

On the other hand, Larkin largely disregarded his instructions to stay out of political affairs. From the start he engaged in an active campaign to bring California peacefully into the United States, a cause that was already gaining popularity in the east. Larkin's effort was multipronged. He sought to encourage American acquisition through dispatches to the secretary of state that continually touted the riches of California, its tenuous ties with Mexico, and the threat of a British or French takeover. He promoted American immigration through a steady stream of letters published in East

Coast newspapers extolling California's virtues. Larkin foresaw that unless some unexpected event intervened—such as a British takeover—the arrival of American settlers would soon lead to the province's effective Americanization. Larkin also worked tirelessly and with considerable success to persuade the Mexican Californians that their future lay with the United States. He was convinced that given the right encouragement, the Mexican Californians would soon opt to separate from Mexico and join the United States. These efforts dominated his life over the next several years.

Larkin's letter writing was so prolific that one historian has called him a "one-man publicity bureau."[17] His letters began to have a significant impact on American public opinion. He corresponded especially with the *New York Herald* and the *New York Sun*, both of which welcomed his letters and asked for more. To the *Herald*, he wrote, for example, that "Solomon, in all his glory, was not more happy than a Californian."[18]

Larkin's output was particularly noteworthy in light of his sensitivity over his limited education. His letters are replete with mistakes. Recognizing this deficiency, Larkin wrote at one point to the editor of the *Sun* commenting that "the letters I may send will require your carfull correcting in stile or grammer."[19]

In contrast, Larkin's frequent official dispatches to the secretary of state were well written. For these, he employed a consular clerk at his own expense, since the State Department would not honor his expense claim. One of his clerks, William Swasey, recalled that Larkin "would embody his views in rough notes, and hand them to me, from which I would compose and write his dispatches and communications to the Department of State."[20]

About 250 American settlers reached California overland in 1845, more than in any previous year. It was still a tiny number, but in sparsely populated California it signaled the beginning of a demographic shift. Most arrived first at John Sutter's New Helvetia, which had grown to include a small fort and a dozen adobe houses. Sutter had again fallen deeply into debt. His creditors included Thomas Larkin.

Most of the new American settlers were illegal immigrants to California. Mexico officially restricted new arrivals, perhaps recalling its unhappy experience with American immigrants in Texas. The settlers were nonetheless well treated. Larkin arranged passports for those who wished to remain Americans, although many took up Mexican citizenship because it entitled them to land grants.

Politically, tensions continued to increase. Three American warships visited Monterey during Larkin's first year as consul. While the visits were friendly, they served as a reminder that war between the United States and Mexico—over the future of the Republic of Texas—remained a distinct possibility. Each naval visit caused the townspeople to remember Commodore Jones's ill-fated occupation of Monterey. Larkin, in fact, took time to assure the State Department that the general feeling of the population was still friendly toward America, despite the Jones incident.

The year 1844 also saw another small-scale, unsuccessful revolt by Californians against Mexico. Many foreigners were involved in the brief uprising, including some with Mexican citizenship such as John Sutter, who was imprisoned briefly. There was yet another revolt early in 1845, during which California governor Pío Pico and Gen. José Castro, commander of California's military, drove away troops dispatched from Mexico City. Having asserted their power, however, Pico and Castro stopped short of a break with Mexico. Larkin described the end of the revolt in an amusing letter to the *New York Sun*: "The last battle between the Mexicans and Californians was fought in February with cannon on each side and plenty of small arms. The loss—four horses killed. The men were wiser keeping out of the way of cannon ball and grape—they only like the latter when distilled."[21]

The short revolts were part of a long string of such power struggles between Californian officials and Mexico City. For Larkin, however, the revolts provided further evidence that California would eventually separate itself from Mexico, without the need for U.S. intervention. When it did, Larkin was sure, it would inevitably come into the U.S. orbit, provided the British or French did not intervene first.

The British and the French, like the Americans, had consular representatives in California. The French had an acting consul, Louis Gasquet, in Monterey starting in November 1843. The British had a vice consul in Yerba Buena, who also served as head of the British Hudson Bay Company there. The presence of these officials left Larkin deeply suspicious of their governments' intentions. Although the British and French representatives had essentially the same official responsibilities as Larkin—protection and assistance to their citizens—Larkin considered that British and French interests in California were not sufficient to merit consulates. He wrote to the State Department: "These consuls have nothing to do, apparently; why they are in service their governments best know, and Uncle Sam will know to his cost." The British vice consul had, in fact, supplied arms to the rebels during the 1844 revolt and had joined them in the field. A French newspaper reported that the British were about to buy California.[22]

Secretary of State James Buchanan shared Larkin's suspicions. He replied to Larkin that the presence of the consuls "produce[s] the impression that their respective governments entertain designs on that country. . . . On all proper occasions you should not fail prudently to warn the govt and people of Cal. of the danger of such an enterprise to their peace and prosperity . . . and to arouse in their bosoms that love of liberty and independence so natural to the American continent."[23] The fear of French and British designs on California remained as a constant undercurrent in American policy. Buchanan's instruction to Larkin was sharply at odds with the standing instructions to consuls in Mexico "to forbear intermeddling."

In July 1845 Larkin received an alarming report that the Mexican government was assembling troops to send to California. This report, which would have been distressing to Larkin under any circumstances, was even more disturbing because the British were said to be financing the deployment. He immediately forwarded the news to the State Department.[24] By coincidence, a French warship was visiting Monterey at the time, reinforcing Larkin's suspicions of European meddling. In fact, neither the British nor the French governments planned to occupy California, although neither Larkin nor the State Department could have known this. Still, even if London and Paris were not officially scheming to acquire California, locally based officials of both governments did favor action, and it would not have been unusual for a French or British naval captain to take the initiative to seize territory, as Commodore Jones had done in Monterey a few years earlier and as the French did in Tahiti and the British had recently done in Hawaii. To Larkin and to the State Department, it seemed that the growing British-French colonial rivalry could easily spill over into California.

By this time, James K. Polk had been elected president on an expansionist platform that advocated annexing Texas and expanding American territory in Oregon. Polk also hoped for an opportunity to purchase California, although this was lower on his list of priorities. Since Polk did not take office until March 1845, however, Larkin did not yet have any guidance or instructions from the new administration; letters from Washington were still taking five months or more to reach Monterey. By the same token, Larkin would not have known that Congress approved the annexation of Texas the same month that Polk took office. Texas officially became a state in December 1845.

The overriding significance of Texas for Larkin and other residents of California was that Mexican officials had made it clear that American annexation of Texas would lead to war with the United States. Throughout 1845 and 1846, the prospect of war was a constant issue of discussion in Monterey. Still, there was no firm news from either Mexico City or Washington. In fact, Larkin wrote to his friend William Leidesdorff in Yerba Buena in June that "Texas is acknowledged by the Mexicans as an Independ state, guaranteed by the English and French that the Yankes will never take it in to the Union."[25]

The growing American tensions with Mexico and the perceived threat of British or French interference in California prompted President Polk to adopt a more active role on the ground in California. Secretary of State Buchannan wrote to Larkin in October 1845: "In addition to your consular functions, the President has thought proper to appoint you a confidential agent in California and you may consider the present despatch as your authority for acting in this character. The confidence which he reposes in your patriotism and discretion is evidenced by conferring upon you this delicate and important trust."[26]

The essence of the appointment, Buchanan explained, was to thwart any British or French designs and to support the Californians if they should choose to assert their independence. By Californians, Buchanan meant the Mexican Californians who still dominated the territory both demographically and politically. There was no thought yet in Washington that the tiny colony of Americans in California might launch a revolt against Mexico, as the Americans in Texas had done a decade earlier. Larkin was one of the few who did foresee this as a distinct possibility in the near future, as numbers of immigrants increased. For the moment, however, Larkin—and Washington—believed that a more likely scenario was for the Mexican Californians themselves to declare independence. Larkin was already encouraging them to move in this direction, believing that once they separated from Mexico, it would not be long before they freely opted to join the United States.

Although Larkin was appointed special diplomatic agent on October 17, 1845, the word of the appointment did not reach him for another six months. Because the appointment was confidential, delivery of the news was entrusted to a lieutenant in the U.S. Marines, Archibald Gillespie, who traveled from Washington to the east coast of Mexico and then overland on horseback to Mazatlán. Gillespie also carried new orders for Cdre. John Sloat, head of the American squadron in the Pacific.

Gillespie's mission was regarded as so sensitive that he posed as a traveler visiting Mexico for health reasons. In Mazatlán Gillespie delivered the instructions to Sloat, then took passage on an American warship to Monterey, by way of the Sandwich Islands. He arrived in Monterey on April 17, exactly six months after the date of Larkin's commission. This delay highlights the extent to which Larkin and others in California continued to operate without a clear or timely understanding of events elsewhere.

In October 1845 Larkin took it upon himself to appoint a vice consul in Yerba Buena, the future San Francisco. American consuls at that time were permitted to appoint vice consuls to assist them with their duties. Yerba Buena was still more a village than a town, with fewer than fifty buildings and fewer than two hundred residents. Nonetheless, Larkin reasoned that having a vice consul there would both reduce his own workload and provide better services to American ships arriving in that small port. Yerba Buena was also closer to John Sutter's New Helvetia, where most of the new American settlers were arriving. Another consideration was that the British vice consul was resident in Yerba Buena, so having an American equivalent there might help Larkin keep abreast of what the British were up to. Finally, Larkin considered that having a vice consul in Yerba Buena would be an advantage in the event of a political upheaval.

For the position of vice consul, Larkin turned to his friend and business partner William Leidesdorff, a man who holds his own niche in American diplomatic history. Leidesdorff's appointment made him the first person of African American heritage to serve as an American consular officer. Leidesdorff was the illegitimate son of a Danish sugar planter and a mixed-race mother. He was born in St. Croix, in what was then the Danish West Indies, in 1810 and educated in Denmark. As a boy, he was informally adopted by an Englishman, who took him to New Orleans to learn the cotton trade. At the age of twenty-four he was naturalized as an American citizen. As master of his own ship trading between New Orleans and New York, he took the title "Captain Leidesdorff." When his foster father died, he inherited a thriving business.

Leidesdorff was sufficiently light-skinned to pass as white in New Orleans. Larkin's consular clerk years later described him as "a man of fine appearance and pleasing address, of a swarthy complexion, denoting a tropical descent."[27] According to some accounts, a romance with a New Orleans belle broke up over rumors about his family background.[28] Seeking a new start, Leidesdorff sailed his ship, the *Julia Ann*, around Cape Horn to Yerba Buena, where he established himself and began a trading business between California and the Sandwich Islands. His business thrived and branched out into other enterprises, including establishing Yerba Buena's first small hotel. By 1845 he was the largest merchant in Yerba Buena, not an enormous distinction given the town's small size, but significant in the local context.[29]

Leidesdorff was naturalized as a Mexican citizen in 1844. This enabled him to receive a large land grant adjoining Sutter's New Helvetia, where he started to raise cattle. Following his naturalization, he sometimes signed his name Guillermo Leidesdorff. At the time, as we have seen, foreign nationality did not disqualify an individual from becoming an American consular officer. Despite his new Mexican citizenship, Leidesdorff's sympathies lay strongly with the United States and, like Larkin, he looked forward to the eventual American acquisition of California. An eminent California historian noted wryly that for a Danish Mexican, Leidesdorff was intensely American.[30]

Larkin called Leidesdorff "active, bold, honorable, passionate, and liberal. A linguist of medium talents, formerly Sea Captain of New York. . . . Decidedly partial to the United States."[31] Swasey, Larkin's consular clerk, wrote that "Captain Leidesdorff was in the strongest sense a man of public spirit and was prominently identified with every enterprise tending to advance the interests of the community. He was . . . a man . . . of great energy and enterprise, of an impetuous and rather irascible temperament, but not at all implacable."[32] Another description called him "an intelligent man of fair education, speaking several languages; active, enterprising and public-spirited; honorable for the most part in his transactions; but jealous, quick-tempered, often quarrelsome and disagreeable."[33] Leidesdorff's written English was poor, even compared with Larkin's.

One of Leidesdorff's better-known enterprises was bringing the first steamboat to San Francisco Bay in 1847. He procured the boat from Russian traders in Sitka, Alaska. Named the *Sitka* and later rechristened the *Rainbow*, the boat was an underpowered side wheeler just thirty-seven feet long. The *Sitka* was so slow that on its maiden voyage up the Sacramento River, a bystander reportedly bet a side of bacon that he could make faster progress on foot. The *Sitka* chugged for six days up river, traveling a distance of just eighty miles. The bystander won his side of bacon with three days to spare.³⁴ The *Sitka*'s historic first voyage is commemorated on the State Seal of California. Leidesdorff is also credited with some other San Francisco firsts: the first horse race, the first house with a flower garden, the first commercial shipping warehouse, and the first public school.

Leidesdorff accepted Larkin's offer to become vice consul and began immediately with his duties, which were similar to Larkin's. Larkin sent him instructions, passports, and other materials. Leidesdorff was not officially recognized by the Mexican authorities or by the British vice consul, which caused him considerable angst. Larkin reassured him that it didn't matter; Americans would recognize him and in a year or so Washington would formally acknowledge his appointment. Meanwhile, he should do the best he could and, if necessary, conduct his business aboard American ships.

During the final months of 1845 and the early months of 1846, political events took an increasingly ominous turn. In December Texas was admitted as a state, heightening fears of war with Mexico. Meanwhile, President Polk reasserted a very broad American claim to all of Oregon. Polk had run for office on the bellicose campaign slogan "54–40 or fight!" reflecting U.S. territorial claims to the entire west coast of North America up to the border of Russian Alaska at latitude 54°–40´. This expansive claim to Oregon would have cut Canada off entirely from the Pacific Ocean. It raised a very real specter of war between the United States and Great Britain.

At the same time, a series of events started to unfold in California that would have a profound impact on the future of the territory. In early December 1845, John Frémont, a captain in the army's topographical corps, stumbled cold and hungry into New Helvetia after a cross-country mapping expedition. Frémont had set out from the lower Missouri River the previous May on an official expedition to chart the American west. Frémont, it may be recalled, had begun his career as a protégé of Joel Poinsett, who sent him on his first exploring mission in 1838 to Wisconsin. In the intervening years, Frémont had made a name for himself as "the Pathfinder" on two previous mapping expeditions to Oregon. Frémont was accompanied by about sixty armed men, as was regarded necessary for a long expedition through dangerous and unexplored territory. Frémont's party was not, however, a military force; all of his men were civilians. One member of the team was the famous frontiersman Kit Carson. With winter setting in, the expedition ran short of supplies in the mountains and sought temporary shelter in California, which, as Mexican territory, was beyond Frémont's terms of reference.

John Sutter welcomed Frémont and his men. Leaving his men in New Helvetia, Frémont headed south to Monterey to find Thomas Larkin, the only official American in California, and to seek his help. Larkin received Frémont warmly, arranged to send him supplies and funds, and introduced him to local officials. Larkin accompanied Frémont to his meetings, where Frémont assured local authorities that his expedition was geographical and scientific and that his men were civilians. With this assurance of peaceful intentions, Frémont was given permission to winter in California, with the caveat that he should make camp in the countryside and stay away from populated areas. Larkin mentioned Frémont's visit in a dispatch to the secretary of state, saying, "He is now in this country surveying, and will be again at this consular house during this month. . . . To this gentleman is due, from the government, unqualified praise for the patience, industry, and indefatigable perseverance in attaining the object he is engaged in."[35]

There is little doubt that at this stage Frémont intended to head on to Oregon and then back east with the spring thaw. In January he wrote his wife, Jessie, "So soon as the proper season comes, and my animals are rested we turn our faces homeward."[36]

Frémont, however, soon ran afoul of local authorities. Contrary to his agreement, he moved his camp to within a day's march of Monterey. This alarmed the local officials, who on March 3 served him with orders to leave California. By this time, spring was already in the air. While snow still blocked the mountain passes to the east, there was nothing to prevent Frémont from starting to move north toward Oregon. The impetuous Frémont, however, took offense at the expulsion order and decided to defy it. He led his men to Pico Gavilan (Hawk Hill), where he built a makeshift fortification of logs, raised the Stars and Stripes, and announced that he would fight rather than flee. General Castro, the military commander of California, issued a pompous ultimatum and began to assemble troops to oust Frémont.

Larkin was appalled by this turn of events. His goal was still the peaceful acquisition of California by the United States, which he believed was within his grasp. Frémont's hotheaded actions were alienating the very California officials that Larkin was wooing to the U.S. banner. Over the next several days Larkin worked feverishly to prevent a military confrontation. He warned Frémont that his action was unnecessarily endangering American citizens in California.[37] He urged Castro to stand down and avoid hostilities.

By March 9 Castro had assembled a force of three to four hundred men and three artillery pieces for an attack on Pico Gavilan. Frémont wrote to Larkin, "If we are unjustly attacked, we will fight to extremity and refuse quarter, trusting to our country to avenge us. . . . We will die, every man of us under the flag of our country."[38] That very night, however, Frémont abandoned his position and began to move north. Castro jubilantly declared that his forces had repelled the invaders.

As a practical matter, Frémont seemed to have had little choice. Staying to fight would have been at odds with the purpose of his topographical expedition and risked making him the cause of a war with Mexico. Frémont was not averse to a fight, but realized that he needed political cover that was not yet available at the time. Within a few months, the situation would change.

Frémont and his party made their way slowly north to Sutter's fort. From there, they headed to Oregon. Frémont sent a letter to Larkin on March 25, indicating he was leaving California behind to continue his explorations.[39] Larkin wrote to a friend the next day, "All troubles have passed over. Capt Fremont is quietly pressing his way to the Oregon or elsewhere according to his instructions from home."[40] Larkin remained on good terms with Frémont despite his disquiet at the latter's actions. Following the Pico Gavilan incident,

Larkin sent dispatches to the secretary of state praising Frémont's courage in the affair.[41] Frémont had left the scene, but his role in the story was far from over.

The next month saw another significant political event that showed the extent to which Larkin still carried influence with a broad range of Californians. A *junta* of prominent citizens—primarily Mexican Californians—gathered in Monterey to discuss declaring California independent from Mexico. The meeting was hosted by Larkin at his home. There was general agreement that if the Californians were to declare independence, they would need to seek the protection of a major power. Participants disagreed, however, whether they should turn to France, Britain, or the United States. The question was left hanging, but in Larkin's view, events were moving in the right direction.

It was amid this tumult, in mid-April 1846, that Lieutenant Gillespie, who was carrying word of Larkin's appointment as special diplomatic agent, finally reached Monterey. Gillespie wrote to the secretary of the navy, "I am happy to inform the Department, that I find our Consul, a gentleman entirely different from what I anticipated and every way worthy of the confidence reposed in him; and occupies a position here, which has enabled him to protect the interest of our Countrymen with all the zeal his patriotism inspires, and his good judgement would dictate. I am sorry however to learn, that he thought of resigning the Consulship, in consequence of his bills having been protested, and the allowance made to him by the Department being so small, as to subject him to serious loss."[42] Before long, Gillespie and Larkin would cease to see eye to eye.

Unlike his unpaid consular appointment, Larkin would receive a salary of six dollars a day as special diplomatic agent. This is exactly the same salary Edmund Roberts received when he was made special diplomatic agent ten years earlier. To Larkin, this must have appeared to be a nice gesture, but it was insignificant compared with his business income. Larkin was scrupulous in guarding the secrecy of his confidential appointment; his role did not become public for another forty years.[43]

Gillespie also left a brief description of Monterey as he found it in 1846: "The town of Monterey is small, containing not over one hundred houses, built upon streets running back from the beach, but are in some cases far apart. Everything about the town has a primitive appearance, and nothing is to be met with, that will remind the traveler of the refinements of long settled countries."[44] Gillespie's impression serves as a good reminder of how small the California settlements still were. At this point, tiny Monterey was still the capital and the most important town in California.

Larkin dispatched Gillespie north to find Frémont and inform him of developments. He wrote to Leidesdorff in Yerba Buena, introducing Gillespie and asking Leidesdorff to provide him with accommodation and whatever assistance he required. He warned Leidesdorff that events seemed to be reaching a climax. "There is a prospect of highly exciting times. . . . in all likelihood the States have declared War against M. . . . the pear is near ripe for falling."[45]

Meanwhile, Larkin wrote to Buchanan accepting his new appointment as special diplomatic agent "with unfeigned satisfaction." He advised Buchanan again that the Mexican leaders of California had no great affection for Mexico and would take the plunge and declare independence "if their salaries were secured to them."[46] With this, Larkin was suggesting a specific step to promote separation, without war and at a minimal cost. By the time his dispatch reached Washington, however, it was too late.

Frémont had gone north weeks ahead of Gillespie. It took almost a month for Gillespie to catch up with him at Klamath Lake in Oregon, after a dangerous and arduous journey during which he was attacked by hostile Indians and reduced to eating nothing but horsemeat. Gillespie wrote to Larkin, once he was safely back at Sutter's, that he had informed Frémont of developments. Gillespie ended his letter to Larkin with the words, "He [Frémont] now goes home from here."[47]

Historical controversy has raged over what message Gillespie actually delivered to Frémont, and whether Frémont's subsequent actions were taken on his own initiative or under instructions from Washington delivered by Gillespie. Larkin's consular secretary, William Swasey, wrote in his memoirs that Larkin's message from Buchanan included an instruction to tell Frémont to remain in California and, in the event of a movement by American settlers to block a British or French takeover, "Frémont was at liberty to cooperate with them *in his private capacity*."[48] Frémont later wrote that the instructions conveyed by Gillespie "had for their principal object to ascertain the disposition of the California people, to conciliate their feelings in favor of the United States, and to find out, with a view to counteracting, the designs of the British Government upon that country."[49] Frémont's instructions were almost certainly in line with those given to Larkin and to Commodore Sloat: to remain vigilant, to stand against a takeover of California by any foreign power, and to support Californian independence if the Mexican Californians made a move in that direction. In other words, Frémont's instructions were to follow the same policy Larkin was already pursuing.

Not long after meeting Gillespie, however, Frémont reinterpreted his instructions as a justification for "taking possession of California."[50] Frémont later confirmed he had "acted solely on my own responsibility, and without any expressed authority from the Government to justify hostilities."[51] President Polk wrote in his diary that Frémont had no authority to initiate hostilities in California.[52] At that point, Polk still hoped to purchase California; he did not want events there to precipitate a war with Mexico or to interfere with the peaceful acquisition of Texas. Whatever the thinking in Washington, by the end of May Frémont and his men were back at New Helvetia.

While Gillespie was pursuing Frémont, other significant political events were under way in California. As news of the latest change of power in Mexico City reached Monterey, Commander Castro and Governor Pico took different sides. Each was raising troops, and Castro was making preparations to march against Pico, who had based himself in Los Angeles. Hostilities appeared imminent. In an effort to avoid civil war, Pico called for an assembly in Santa Barbara, with the goal of declaring California independent and seeking the protection of a foreign power.[53] This is exactly what Larkin had been encouraging and anticipating. Larkin made preparations to attend. The captain of the USS *Cyane*, a sloop of war visiting Monterey, offered to take him there, but Larkin believed this might alarm the Californians and that he would be more effective if he didn't arrive in an American warship. In the end, however, the assembly was not held.

As word of these events reached Mexico, Sir George Seymour, commanding the formidable British naval forces in the eastern Pacific, sailed north for Monterey, an ominous sign for the Americans. Another alarming development was the arrival in Monterey in early June, aboard a British naval vessel, of Father Eugene Mac-Namara, an Irish Catholic priest with a plan to bring ten thousand Irish settlers to California. The Mexican government had approved the proposal and awarded MacNamara a huge land grant. With millions of Irish at risk of starvation from the devastating potato famine, the project seemed credible. Irish immigration on this scale would dwarf the American-origin population of California, which at this point was still only a few hundred. MacNamara met Larkin in Monterey and asked whether, in the event of an American take-over, the United States would recognize his land grant. Larkin replied that the grant was far too large to be legal even under Mexican law.[54]

Meanwhile, the American naval squadron in the Pacific, under Commodore Sloat, recognizing that important events were afoot, sailed from Mazatlán for California. Sloat's standing orders, dating from a year earlier, were that he should attempt to seize California only when he "learned beyond a doubt that the Mexican government has declared war against us."[55] These strict limits recalled the occupation of Monterey by Commodore Jones three years earlier; Sloat was not to provoke a similar, embarrassing incident.

June 1846 therefore saw impending dangers facing California from many directions. An internal civil conflict between Governor Pico and General Castro was threatening. War between the United States and Mexico seemed imminent, as it had for months. A separate U.S.-British conflict loomed over the Oregon border. A British fleet was nearing Monterey with uncertain instructions. A massive immigration of Irish settlers seemed to be in the offing.

An American naval squadron was also on the way. And Frémont had returned to California with intentions that remained unclear. Larkin, for his part, continued to try to steer events toward a peaceful acquisition by the United States. Within a few days, however, events would spin out of control.

Amid this jumble of confusion and high expectation, Frémont was the first to make a dramatic move. On June 10 he and his followers seized almost two hundred horses that General Castro was assembling for his intended march against Governor Pico. Ostensibly Frémont wanted to ensure that Castro's troops and horses would not be used against American settlers. To Castro, however, Frémont's action was at best large-scale horse rustling and at worst an incipient insurrection led by a man he recently claimed to have ousted from California. Larkin was distraught at the idea of a violent and unnecessary conflict between Americans and Californians. He immediately wrote to the local authorities to offer his good offices to have the horses returned.[56]

Before Larkin's offer could be accepted, the other shoe dropped. On June 14, a group of thirty or forty American settlers, either inspired or instigated by Frémont, marched into the sleepy town of Sonoma, occupied the town's official buildings, and made prisoners of eighteen leading citizens. Among the captives were Mariano Vallejo, a pro-American former military commander of California and his brother Salvador, who was one of the founders of California's wine industry, as well as Jacob Leese, an American who was one of Larkin's many business partners. The prisoners were taken off to be held at Sutter's fort. The settler band in Sonoma elected William Ide as its leader. Then, reportedly fortified by Vallejo's excellent California brandy, the attackers raised a flag featuring a grizzly bear and the words "California Republic."[57] Thus was born the short-lived "Bear Flag Republic" of California.

Ide wrote to the nearest U.S. Navy officer, Cdr. John Montgomery of the uss *Portsmouth*, anchored off Yerba Buena, asking for supplies and ammunition and making known he wanted to join his "republic" with the United States. Montgomery, who served under Commodore Sloat, had orders not to intervene in California except in case of war between the United States and Mexico. He refused Ide's requests.

It took some days for word of these events to reach other parts of California. On June 17 Leidesdorff heard of the Sonoma incident. He immediately wrote to Larkin, "This is to inform you of what has taken place in Sonoma, it appears that on the 14th instant about forty men, said to be Americans, entered the town of Sonoma and took charge of the arsenal (if it may so be cald) a person by the name of Ive is in command and they have taken as prisoners" several prominent citizens.[58]

Within two days, Leidesdorff had developed a good deal more information and was enthusiastic about the events. He wrote Larkin on June 19 that "'Sonoma' was surprised on Sunday morning last by 34 men—their present force it is impossible to give as no one pretends to know how many they now have at their camp on the Sacramento and in the surrounding country. . . . There is no doubt that the most *determined* and chivalric spirit actuates the men now under the command of Ide, as their elected Chief, and that they are actuated by a spirit which forbids them to commit any act of violence, or injury upon any one. . . . I think the Proclamation will call many to the 'Banner,' which is a white 'field' with a red 'border,' a large 'Star' and a Grisly Bear! Such is the flag of 'Young California.' . . . Hoping there is not so much excitement with you as we have here."[59] Leidesdorff added that the men were well armed and would be hard to dislodge.

Rumors of the Sonoma incident reached Larkin in Monterey even before he received Leidesdorff's letters. Larkin's first goals were to get more information and to try to prevent any bloodshed. On June 18, before receiving Leidesdorff's letters, he wrote to Leidesdorff: "I can hardly believe it and do not understand the affair." In regard to the origins of the takeover, Larkin mused, "There is a supposition that this affair is started by Frémont and G. [Gillespie] and that I was aware of it. I knew nothing and don't believe they do. . . . I hope the persons taken will be well used."[60] Larkin also wrote immediately to Washington reporting the incident.

Almost two weeks passed before Larkin had full details. By that time, there were indications that the Bear Flag revolt was spreading, still bloodlessly, to other settlements in northern California. Larkin understood that the movement was likely to burgeon among the American settlers. His main concern was still to prevent violence, both to leave open the possibility for reconciliation between the American settlers and the Mexican Californians, and to avoid any action that might give the British an excuse to intervene. Larkin feared that the affair in Sonoma could lead Governor Pico to seek British protection, bringing about his worst-case scenario. In fact, one of the Sonoma incident's immediate effects was to cause Pico and General Castro to set aside their differences and join together against the American insurrection.

By this point, Larkin realized that his hope of a peaceful and orderly transition to American rule was fading fast. He was convinced that given a little more time—perhaps a year at the most—the Mexican Californians would have rallied on their own to the American banner, avoiding a legacy of bloodshed and ethnic division. Larkin wrote to Buchanan regretting "that a farther time could not be had to produce our flag in this country in another form."[61] Beyond this, the affair also put Larkin himself in danger as the American consul and a well-known proponent of merging California with the United States. It would have been a natural presumption that he supported and perhaps even instigated the Sonoma rebels. Eventually Larkin came to blame Frémont and Gillespie for undermining what he considered excellent prospects for a peaceful American annexation.

An interesting footnote on the Bear Flag incident is that the flag was designed by a settler named Todd, a nephew of Mary Todd Lincoln. Ironically, that same year Abraham Lincoln was elected to his first term in the U.S. House of Representatives, where he opposed war with Mexico. As for the flag itself, the takeover of Sonoma was so hastily undertaken that the paint on the flag was said to still be wet when it was raised in Sonoma's expansive central plaza. Legend has it that the red stripe at the bottom of the flag was fashioned from a woman's petticoat.

The bloodless takeover of Sonoma has inspired generations of historians to dispute whether the occupation was an impulsive action by settlers or something better planned. Also at issue is whether Frémont was involved in the planning or if he seized on events instigated by others. Whatever the truth, within about ten days, Frémont arrived in Sonoma and took charge of the town, renaming the occupying force the "California Volunteers."

In the midst of these confused events, Commodore Sloat sailed into Monterey on July 2 aboard his flagship, the 64-gun frigate *Savannah*. Four ships of the U.S. Pacific squadron were now in California. The U.S. sloops of war *Cyane* and *Levant* were also in Monterey, while the *Portsmouth* under Commander Montgomery was still off Yerba Buena. Sloat was much relieved to find that no British warships were in port. He was unsure, however, what to do next. He had written Larkin a few weeks earlier asking him to "consult, and advise with me on the course of operations I may be disposed to make on the coast of California."[62] On arrival in Monterey, Sloat's first move was to summon Larkin. The two men met repeatedly over the next several days.

To show his peaceful intentions, Sloat offered to salute the Mexican flag at Monterey's presidio, but there was no flag to salute; it had been missing for two months. The missing flag was one more indication of how ill-equipped Monterey was. It was virtually defenseless and would easily have fallen to any invading force.

Larkin counseled Sloat to be patient. A little more time, he urged, and the Mexican Californians might yet ask the United States to intervene and take possession. He believed this could happen in as little as two or three weeks.[63] He had already written to Pico and Castro urging them to move.[64] On July 4 Larkin wrote to the American consul in the Sandwich Islands that he still hoped to convince the Californians to "call on the Commodore for protection, hoist his Flag & be his Countryman, or the Bear may destroy them."[65] This was the last chance to bring California peacefully into the United States.

Sloat hesitated. Larkin's advice was consistent with his orders. There was still no definitive word of war between Mexico and the

United States. The memory of Commodore Jones's recall for prematurely seizing Monterey must have weighed heavily on his mind. On the other hand, Sloat's officers, eager for action and glory, urged him to seize the town. Sloat knew that Frémont was involved in some sort of military activities in Sonoma. Although the details were still vague, it was clear that the Bear Flag revolt was gaining momentum in the north. Most worrying, though, was the knowledge that Sir George Seymour and the British fleet might arrive at any moment.

On July 5 Sloat informed Larkin that he had decided to act. Larkin, despite his preference for restraint, accepted Sloat's decision and worked with him to put it into effect. They spent July 6 laying plans and drafting a proclamation to be issued the following day.

July 7, 1846, according to Larkin's consular secretary, William Swasey, "dawned most auspiciously; the sky was without a cloud, and the day without a ripple; the sun shone serenely, and all nature seemed to have donned her loveliest garb to welcome in an event that would be fraught with consequences of scarcely less importance than any that have occurred in the history of our country during the present century."[66]

At about 7:00 a.m., Captain Mervine came ashore from the squadron and, together with Larkin, visited Comandante Silva to demand the surrender of Monterey. Silva replied sardonically that he had nothing to surrender; he had no troops, no arms—even the flag was missing. By 9:00 a.m., most of Monterey's small population had gathered near the customs house, watching the boats from the U.S. squadron as they were loaded with men and arms. The boats rowing ashore were "a magnificent sight," according to Swasey. Two officers hoisted the American flag, which "gracefully rose and the gentle breeze revealed its lustrous stars and luminous stripes, amid the booming of cannon and strains of martial music."[67] Monterey was in American hands.

The proclamation drawn up the previous day by Sloat and Larkin was read aloud and posted. Under its terms, the United States took possession of all of California. The proclamation promised freedom from governmental vexations, reductions in burdensome customs duties, protection of personal rights, and "a great increase in the value of real estate and the products of California." Sloat also issued a general order to U.S. forces that it was "of the first importance to cultivate the good opinion of the inhabitants," that the navy would be "eternally disgraced . . . by indignity offered to a single female," and that "plunder of every sort is strictly forbidden" under severe penalties.[68]

A sour note was sounded by the French consul, Louis Gasquet, who vigorously protested the American occupation or, as Swasey put it, "opened an annoying correspondence" with Sloat.[69] Gasquet, who had arrived in Monterey about a year earlier, was a strong proponent of French occupation of California. His hopes were dashed by Sloat's action.

Larkin remained the principal American ashore for all nonmilitary matters. He wrote immediately to William Ide, the Bear Flag leader in Sonoma, to inform him of the American occupation of Monterey. He also sent messages to Governor Pico and General Castro, on Sloat's behalf, still hoping to persuade them to welcome the American takeover. Pico and Castro, however, refused.

Sloat, meanwhile, ordered Commander Montgomery of the *Portsmouth* to take possession of Yerba Buena; this was accomplished on July 9 with no resistance. Leidesdorff translated Sloat's proclamation into Spanish for the benefit of the local residents. Lt. James Revere of the *Portsmouth* traveled inland to Sonoma, where he oversaw the replacement of the Bear Flag with the Stars and Stripes. The "California Republic" had come to an end, just four weeks after it began. Riders were dispatched to take the word to Sutter's fort, where the American flag was also raised. Frémont and the California Volunteers were sworn into the U.S. military. Frémont left for Monterey, where he was received coolly by Sloat and Larkin.[70]

By a curious coincidence, at this point Larkin received a letter from Capt. Thomas ap Catesby Jones reporting that a board of inquiry in Washington had finally issued its report on Jones's occupation of Monterey three years earlier. The board had exonerated Jones of all charges against him.[71]

On July 16, just nine days after the occupation of Monterey, the British squadron under Sir George Seymour sailed into the harbor to find the American flag flying ashore. Seymour's flagship, the HMS *Collingwood*, was a ship of the line with as much firepower as the entire U.S. squadron. It was a critical moment. Sloat ordered all men to their stations and had the decks of the U.S. squadron cleared for battle.

The British, however, did not want to fight. The *Collingwood* offered courtesy salutes to the American ships, which returned the honors. Sir George and Commodore Sloat exchanged dinners aboard their flagships. Reportedly, the first thing Seymour said to Sloat when they met was, "Sir, if your flag was not flying on shore, I should have hoisted mine there."[72] Although the British saluted the American ships, they refused to salute the American flag ashore, thus withholding British recognition of the American occupation. Larkin took some comfort, however, in Sir George's apology that he could not offer Larkin a consular salute since, if the Americans were in possession of California, Larkin's position as consul would lapse. Larkin regarded this as a tacit acknowledgment by the British of the American position.[73] After a week in Monterey, Sir George sailed away, leaving California to its fate.

Throughout this period, Larkin remained at the center of events not just politically but also socially and commercially. Larkin and his wife, Rachel, stepped up their already busy entertaining calendar, acting as hosts for officers of the U.S. squadron. The *Savannah*'s chaplain, Walter Colton, was among many who praised "the magnificent hospitalities of T. O. Larkin Esq., which reach every officer of the squadron." Larkin also took full commercial advantage of the situation, becoming the main supplier for the squadron. He wrote to his contacts in the United States that if California remained American, "business will increase astonishingly."[74]

State Department records show that Larkin continued to serve officially as consul for another year, until 1848. However, his consular duties effectively ended when Sloat claimed California as U.S.

territory. A week after the Stars and Stripes was raised in Monterey, he wrote to Leidesdorff that both their offices were at an end.

Larkin's role as confidential special agent, however, continued. Larkin wanted to travel to Washington and report directly to Buchanan on developments in California. He was afraid that the United States might relinquish California as part of a peace agreement, and he wanted to be on hand in Washington to ensure this did not happen. Commodore Sloat, however, insisted that his services were still needed in California and asked him to stay.

Since he couldn't go to Washington, Larkin reverted to trying to build U.S. public opinion for annexation through letters to the major eastern newspapers. To James Gordon Bennett, owner of the *New York Herald*, he pleaded: "Our own flag waves over California, and I am in the U.S.A. as well as yourself, therefore you must come to the rescue. Your paper is a host and I want its service." Bennett, already a strong proponent of annexation, replied that Larkin need not fear: "We will take care of California."[75] Larkin had a similar exchange with the *New York Sun*.

The State Department, for its part, also wanted Larkin to stay in California and continue his official work. As soon as Secretary of State Buchanan learned of the American occupation of Monterey, he wrote to Larkin, on January 13, 1847, confirming that "you shall continue, at least for the present, as Confidential Agent in the Californias. . . . Your services in this character have heretofore been valuable & are justly appreciated; and they may be of great consequence hereafter."[76] Larkin's hard work and good service notwithstanding, Buchanan continued, the State Department was rejecting his claim for expenses in hiring a consular secretary, which had not been authorized. Swasey would have to go, or Larkin would have to foot the bill himself. Swasey, however, had already left to join Frémont and the volunteers.

Unbeknownst to anyone in California, the long expected hostilities between the United States and Mexico broke out along the Texas border in April 1846. Mexico declared war a month later. The United States followed with its own declaration of war on May 13,

1846. This was a month before the Bear Flag incident and almost two months before the Stars and Stripes was raised in Monterey.

With war now officially under way, the War Department ordered Brig. Gen. Stephen Kearny and the First Dragoons to move west overland from their base at Fort Leavenworth to Santa Fe and then onward to California. It would take six months for Kearny to complete the journey.

In another major development, on June 15 the United States and Great Britain signed a treaty establishing the border between the United States and British Canada at 49° north latitude, where it remains today. This was hundreds of miles further south than President Polk had promised during his presidential campaign. The treaty ended the long-festering threat of war between the United States and Britain over the Oregon Territory and freed the United States to concentrate on war with Mexico. Neither Commodore Sloat nor Sir George Seymour was aware of this agreement when their warships faced each other in Monterey Harbor a month later.

Back in California, a change in military leaders portended a new direction for American policy. On July 23 the aging and ailing Commodore Sloat turned over command of the U.S. Pacific squadron to a newly arrived commodore, Robert Stockton. Sloat headed home, carrying with him a gift from Larkin to Buchanan, a magnificent sea otter pelt, the kind that had for years fueled the Northwest-China trade. By this time, sea otters had been hunted close to extinction.

Unlike the cautious Sloat, Stockton was anxious for action. He regarded his command of the Pacific squadron at this crucial moment as an opportunity to win glory and the laurels of war. In this respect, Stockton had much in common with Frémont, who saw developments in California in much the same way. As just one example of the changed approach, on Stockton's first day of command he placed French consul Louis Gasquet under arrest. Sloat, in contrast, had tolerated the consul's continuing protests of the U.S. occupation. Gasquet was confined under house arrest for the next seven weeks.

Although the U.S. flag flew in Monterey, Yerba Buena, and New Helvetia, the more populated areas of southern California were still under Mexican control. Larkin advised Stockton that the most prudent course would be to go to Los Angeles to seek the support of Governor Pico and Commandante Castro for the U.S. occupation. If successful, this might still result in a bloodless transfer of California from Mexico to the United States with the support of the Mexican Californians, even at this late date. Stockton, however, chose instead to issue a bellicose proclamation accusing Castro of "wicked intent."[77] Larkin nonetheless tried to open a dialogue with Pico through contacts in Los Angeles. Not surprisingly, the effort came to naught.

This difference in approach did not sour relations between Larkin and Stockton. Larkin remained strongly supportive of the U.S. acquisition and was prepared to back the U.S. military commander, even if he did not always agree with specific decisions. Stockton, for his part, continued to seek Larkin's advice—even if he didn't always follow it—and used Larkin as both an intermediary and an interpreter. In mid-August, Stockton appointed Larkin as U.S. Navy agent for California "until the President of the United States shall otherwise direct."[78] Larkin's main role as agent was to ensure supplies for the Pacific squadron. As the largest businessman in Monterey, he would have been a natural choice for the position even without his political connections. The appointment provided yet another boost for his personal business.

In August Stockton sent Larkin to Los Angeles to pave the way for the U.S. occupation of the town. Larkin arrived on August 12 and was greeted peacefully by the populace. The following day, a combined force of marines and volunteers arrived and took possession. Five days later, official word finally arrived in California that war had broken out between the United States and Mexico.

Commodore Stockton believed his work was complete. On August 22 he reported to the Navy Department that the flag of the United States was flying at every commanding position and California was effectively in the military possession of the United States.[79] Stockton appointed Archibald Gillespie as military commandant of southern California and John Frémont as military commandant in the north. Stockton's failure to placate the Mexican Californians, however, together with his choice of Gillespie to administer the south, would have serious consequences.

Gillespie did not share Larkin's view of the need for American conciliation with the local population, instead instituting a heavy-handed administration. According to a letter from Larkin to his wife, Gillespie fined and imprisoned whomever he pleased, without legal hearings. By late September, the population had had enough. Gen. José María Flores led an uprising that drove Gillespie and his troops out of Los Angeles. Thus began the military conflict that Larkin had worked so hard to avoid. The fighting spread through southern California and into the north. Larkin placed the blame directly on Gillespie. He wrote to Buchanan that "had the officers left in command in the different towns in the Country had the kind and friendly, yet firm manner of Comm. Stockton, I am firm in the opinion that the people would not have arisen."[80]

The conflict was low in intensity, and from a military standpoint the fighting in California was a sideshow in the Mexican War, with no more than a few hundred men involved. Still, there were numerous engagements with dozens killed on each side. The situation was sufficiently dangerous, especially in the south, that Larkin sent Rachel, who was once again pregnant, and their children to live in Yerba Buena, which was further removed from the fighting.

As an interesting aside, in October a new French consul arrived in Monterey, replacing the troublesome Gasquet. The new arrival was none other than Jacques-Antoine Moerenhout, who had been the first American consul in Tahiti and later oversaw the French annexation of the kingdom. If France had any serious designs on California, as Larkin and others feared, Moerenhout would have been a good man to put them into effect. As it was, he arrived too late. Moerenhout found himself in an awkward position, representing France in a territory that was still legally part of Mexico but occupied by the United States. He kept his head down and avoided offending the Americans.

The fighting, meanwhile, put Larkin in personal danger once again. In mid-November, while en route to Yerba Buena to visit Rachel, Larkin was taken captive by Californians supporting General Flores's revolt. Fortunately for him, his captor was an old friend, Manual Castro, a former prefect of Monterey, who ensured his safety during his early days of captivity. Still, it was an arduous and dangerous period for Larkin. He feared that he might be summarily executed or sent to an uncertain fate in Mexico City. Larkin was taken south to Santa Barbara, then to Los Angeles. On the way, he witnessed the defeat of American forces in a clash at Natividad, one of several American reverses on the battlefield.

Generally Larkin was treated well while in captivity. After his release months later, he wrote to Leidesdorff, "I am again at home. I've had, as you may imagine, some ups and downs. Twice aimed at to be shot. . . . I was closely confined . . . but had never less than 4 or 5 meals sent to me a day, 4 or 5 courses each meal. Shirts, Stockings, Hkfs. &c, even money offered me by [General José María] Flores. The Mexicans & C. [Castro] appeared [desirous] to out do each other in obtaining my good will. . . . I was liable to be marched for Mexico each day."[81]

The last significant engagement of the war in California took place at La Mesa General on January 9, 1847. General Flores sent for Larkin, who was brought to the battlefield, where he was threatened by some of the Mexican Californian soldiers. In the end, the American forces won the day. Flores fled to Mexico. Two days later, the Americans retook Los Angeles and Larkin was freed. On his release, several of his erstwhile captors asked him to help ensure the safety of their families after the American takeover; he did what he could. Larkin had been a prisoner for almost two months. On his release Larkin learned of the death from fever of his daughter Adeline, "my favourite child."[82] The birth of Larkin's last child while he was a prisoner did not ease the pain.

On January 13, 1847, Governor Pico and John Frémont signed the Treaty of Cahuenga, a cease-fire ending the conflict in California, while the war between Mexico and the United States continued. The terms were mild. The defeated army had to surrender its artillery and promise to abandon the revolt. With that, the Californian soldiers were allowed to return peacefully to their homes. Stockton asked Frémont to function as governor of occupied California.

Many historians have been critical of American actions, which in retrospect appeared to spark an unnecessary conflict. The prominent California historian Hubert Howe Bancroft holds Frémont and Gillespie "largely accountable for all the blood that was spilled throughout the war."[83] Another leading California historian, Josiah Royce, went further and wrote that "no drop of blood need have been shed in the conquest of California, no flavor of the bitterness of mutual hate need have entered . . . had Larkin been left to complete his task."[84]

The war with Mexico dragged on until September 1847, eight months after hostilities ended in California. It took several more months to conclude the peace agreement. The U.S. peace negotiator was Nicholas Trist, the second-ranking official in the State Department, who was sent by President Polk to Mexico to conclude a peace treaty at the most propitious moment. Polk later had second thoughts and sent a message recalling Trist. By the time the message reached Mexico, however, Trist had nearly concluded the negotiations and decided to ignore it. The agreement ending the Mexican War, the Treaty of Guadalupe Hidalgo, was signed on February 2, 1848, and approved by the Mexican congress on May 24. Under its terms, Mexico ceded California and most of New Mexico and Arizona to the United States. For winning Mexican approval to cede these vast territories, Trist was sacked by Polk, who railed that he was an "impudent and unqualified scoundrel."[85] Nonetheless, Polk submitted Trist's treaty to the Senate, which ratified it. News of the treaty reached California three months later, late in the summer of 1848.

In the interim, the American occupation of California remained peaceful. Among the victorious Americans, however, a vicious bureaucratic struggle began between Commodore Stockton and John Frémont, on the one hand, and Brig. Gen. Stephen Kearny, on the other. Frémont had become Stockton's right-hand man, assuming the rank of lieutenant colonel in charge of the California Volunteers and commandant of land forces under Stockton's authority. Brigadier Kearny, it will be recalled, had set out from Ft. Leavenworth at the outset of the war with orders to seize Santa

Fe and then move on to California. After an arduous march across the continent, Kearney finally reached California in December 1846, at the head of a small number of troops mounted on mules, in time to participate in a few of the final battles of the California campaign.

Kearny held orders from Washington to organize a government in California after he had completed the conquest. Commodore Stockton, however, considered that California was under his effective control long before Kearney's arrival and that he had already established a legitimate civil administration with Frémont as military commandant. Frémont was caught in the middle, owing his position to Stockton but clearly ranking lower in the army than Kearny. Frémont refused to yield to Kearny, telling him that he had to work out a solution with Stockton. Stockton and Kearney exchanged heated correspondence without resolving their differences.

In early spring, Stockton received orders from Washington, dispatched months earlier, telling him to yield command of land operations and civil government to Kearny. This finally resolved the controversy, but it did not soothe Kearny's feelings for Frémont. In June 1847 Kearny ordered Frémont to accompany him back overland to the United States. On arrival at Ft. Leavenworth in August, he had Frémont arrested and charged with mutiny, disobedience of orders, and misconduct. A military tribunal in Washington found Frémont guilty and ordered him discharged from the army. President Polk commuted the penalty and asked Frémont to return to duty. Frémont, however, realized that his prospects for a successful military career were over. He chose instead to resign his commission.

Frémont organized another mission of exploration to California, this time by way of the upper Rio Grande. The expedition was a disaster; a third of the men and all the animals perished from hunger and cold in the mountains. Some of the group was driven to cannibalism to survive. By the summer of 1849, the survivors staggered into the Sacramento valley. Despite Frémont's ordeals, his connection with California—and his mark on U.S. history—was far from over.

Larkin continued in his official capacities with the State Department until almost the end of 1848. His work as naval agent and storekeeper continued even after that. Long before his official duties ended, however, Larkin had begun to look ahead to what an American California would mean to him, his family, and his business interests. With the expected increase in immigration, the future looked bright. But even the optimistic Larkin could never have imagined what the next few months would bring.

By the end of 1847, Larkin was planning a move from Monterey north to San Francisco, as Yerba Buena had been renamed in January of that year. The town had grown to about five hundred inhabitants, making it one of the largest towns in California, another reminder of how small the population of California remained at the time. Larkin had already acquired a substantial amount of property in San Francisco, as well as in other parts of California.

William Leidesdorff, who had relinquished his office as vice consul, was prospering in San Francisco. By early 1847 Leidesdorff, perhaps with Larkin's help, had secured contracts to supply U.S. naval ships in San Francisco, in addition to his other booming business interests. Leidesdorff was one of the town's most prominent and respected citizens. His house was among the finest in San Francisco and was the site of lavish entertaining, including a reception for Commodore Stockton.[86] When San Francisco's first "city" council was elected in October 1847, Leidesdorff was among its members and served as town treasurer.

Sadly, Larkin and Leidesdorff fell out with each other in October 1847. The dispute centered on whether Leidesdorff had paid for goods sent to him by Larkin. Leidesdorff insisted that he had. The disagreement ended their long and productive friendship. They had little contact for the remainder of Leidesdorff's short life.

By January 1848 the United States had been occupying California for a year, but the war with Mexico was not yet officially over. Just one week before the peace treaty was signed came an event that would forever change the history of California.

On the banks of the American River, in the wilderness about forty miles from John Sutter's New Helvetia, James Marshall was building a sawmill for Sutter. On the morning of January 24, 1848, a sparkle in the millrace caught his eye. He bent over, picked up some mineral flakes, and shouted to his companions, "Boys, by God I believe I have found a gold mine!"[87] California would never be the same.

The word of Marshall's discovery—on Sutter's land—took some time to circulate, and its significance took even longer to set in. There had been small gold finds in California before; Native Americans, in particular, had made small discoveries in the riverbeds from time to time. Larkin had mentioned gold as one of California's resources in a consular dispatch as early as 1846.[88] Up until now, however, gold finds had been small, isolated, and not commercially viable. The discovery on Sutter's land looked much more promising, but it was not immediately recognized as viable and certainly not as a bonanza.

Sutter didn't advertise the discovery, either from a sense of caution or because he was not sure of its value. One person he did confide in was William Leidesdorff. In March 1848 Sutter wrote Leidesdorff asking for large quantities of supplies on credit and offering him a share in the new gold mining enterprise. "My sawmill in the mountains is now completed," wrote Sutter. "We intend to form a company for working the Gold mines, which prove to be very rich. Would you not take a share in it? So soon as if it would not pay well, we could stop it at any time."[89] Two months after Marshall's discovery, Sutter was still not sure about its commercial viability.

In April, spurred both by Sutter's offer and increasing reports of new gold discoveries in the interior, Leidesdorff hired a team to travel to his ranch on the upper Sacramento River to investigate whether he might also be sitting on a gold mine. The reports back were encouraging: "Some more recent discoveries on the upper part of your ranch prove that the gold washing could be pursued with much profit. . . . Gold has been found within ten miles of your house, and I am certain that it is still nearer. I do not write from mere conjecture, but from facts which I have proven. . . . the gold region on your land covers the whole of the Eastern part of the ranch."[90]

By spring, word of the discovery was beginning to circulate in the towns. Californians began to explore other creek beds or to head for unclaimed land in the interior to see for themselves if the stories of a rich gold strike were true. As more discoveries were reported, more people headed for the interior. A trickle soon turned into a flood. By May, gold fever had begun to take hold of California.

Larkin, still serving as confidential agent, reported the discovery of gold in an official dispatch to Secretary of State Buchanan on June 1, 1848:

Sir:

I have to report to the State Department one of the most astonishing excitements and state of affairs now existing in this country that perhaps has ever been brought to the notice of the Government. On the American fork of the Sacramento and Feather River, another branch of the same, and the adjoining lands, there has been within the present year discovered a Placer, a vast tract of land containing gold, in small particles. This gold, thus far, has been taken on the bank of the river, from the surface to eighteen inches in depth, and is supposed deeper, and to extend over the country.

. . . [T]he people have, up to this time, only gathered the metal on the banks, which is done simply with a shovel, filling a shallow dish, bowl, basket, or tin pan, with a quantity of black sand, similar to the class used on paper, and washing out the sand by movement of the vessel. It is now two or three weeks since the men employed in those washings have appeared in this Town with gold, to exchange for merchandise and provisions. I presume near twenty thousand dollars (20,000$) of this gold has as yet been so exchanged. Some two or three hundred of the men have remained up the river or are gone to their homes, for the purpose of returning to the Placer, and washing immediately with shovels, picks, and baskets—many of them for the first few weeks depending on borrowing from others. I have seen the written statement of the work of one man for sixteen days, which averaged twenty-five (25$) dollars per day; others have, with a shovel and pan, or wooden bowl, washed out ten dollars to even fifty dollars in a day. There are now some men yet washing who have five hundred to one thousand dollars. As they have to stand two feet deep in the river, they work but a few hours in the day, and not every day in the week.

. . . I am confident that this town [San Francisco] has one-half of its tenements empty, locked up with the furniture. The owners—storekeepers, lawyers, mechanics, and labourers all gone to the Sacramento with their families. Small parties, of five to fifteen men have sent to this town and offered cooks ten to fifteen dollars per day for a few weeks. Mechanics and teamsters, earning the year past five to eight dollars per day, have struck and gone. Several U.S. volunteers have deserted. U.S. barque *Anita*, belonging to the Army, now at anchor here, has but six men. One Sandwich Island vessel in port lost all her men; and was obliged to engage another crew at fifty dollars for the run of fifteen days to the Islands.

. . . Common spades and shovels, one month ago worth 1 dollar, will now bring ten dollars, at the gold regions. I am informed fifty dollars has been offered for one. Should this gold continue as represented, this town and others would be depopulated. Clerks' wages have risen from six hundred to one thousand per annum, and board; cooks, 25 dollars to 30 dollars per month. This sum will not be any inducement a month longer, unless the fever and ague appears among the washers. . . . A merchant, lately from China, has even lost his China servants. Should the excitement continue through the year, and the whale-ships visit San Francisco, I think they will lose most all their crews. . . . I have seen several pounds of this gold, and consider it very pure, worth in New York 17 dollars to 18 dollars per ounce; 14 dollars to 16 dollars, in merchandise, is paid for it here. What good or bad effect this gold mania will have on California, I cannot fore tell. It may end this year; but I am informed that it will continue many years. . . . I have seen some of the black sand, as taken from the bottom of the river . . . containing many pieces of gold; they are from the size of the head of a pin to the weight of the eighth of an ounce. I have seen some weighing one-quarter of an ounce (four dollars). Although my statements are almost incredible, I believe I am within the statements believed by every one here. Ten days back, the excitement had not reached Monterey. I shall, within a few days, visit this gold mine, and will make another report to you. In closed you will have a specimen.

I have the honour to be, very respectfully,

Thomas O. Larkin.

P.S. This placer or gold region is situated on public land.[91]

Larkin did indeed visit the goldfields several days later. A few weeks touring the gold country swept away any doubts he may have had and convinced him that his earlier report, as wild as it seemed at the time, had underestimated both the size of the gold deposits and the effect the discovery would have on California. Larkin wrote again to Buchanan from Monterey on June 28 reporting that the gold finds were even more fabulous than the rumors he had heard. Larkin recounted that he himself had tried panning for gold and, standing at the edge of the water, he washed out two or three dollars worth of gold dust in just half an hour; he enclosed the gold dust in his letter to Buchanan. At a time when a typical workman on the East Coast might make a dollar a day, this was fantastic wealth.

In a period of just four weeks, Larkin wrote, the search for gold had become a stampede. Three-fourths of the population of San Francisco had left for the goldfields. People in Monterey—where the news arrived later—were starting to decamp for the north. Laborers and ranchers were leaving their work. A large number of the California Volunteers had deserted. More ships' crews were deserting for the goldfields. Both of San Francisco's newspapers had stopped publishing as their staffs left to hunt for gold.

Larkin wrote also to the eastern newspapers to report the discovery of gold and even sent a sample of gold dust to James Gordon Bennett of the *New York Herald*. Bennett wrote him back, "Your letters have been read like fury."[92] Larkin's letters to Buchanan also made their way into the press and helped launch the great California gold rush of 1849.

Others also visited the goldfields and wrote accounts that contributed to gold fever. Among them was Jacques-Antoine Moerenhout, the French consul in Monterey. Like Larkin, Moerenhout reported to his foreign minister in May that gold had been discovered and was causing great excitement. Although Moerenhout had seen enough new gold in circulation to give some credence to the amazing stories coming down from the hills, he considered that "some reports which are being passed around are certainly either false or exaggerated, and until I can myself go over the ground where these mines are, or until I receive reports from trustworthy persons, I believe that I should limit myself to informing Your Excellency that they have been claimed and that it is probable that they exist."[93]

Moerenhout visited the goldfields shortly thereafter, at the same time as Larkin. And, like Larkin, after his return Moerenhout reported to his minister that where he had previously assumed the reports must be exaggerated, "this discovery seems on the contrary to be surpassing all that was said of it then. . . . the proofs are too positive now to leave any doubt as to the extreme richness of this deposit. Some of those who worked there have made three to five hundred francs per day."[94] Moerenhout also repeated Larkin's tales of the panic that the discovery of gold was causing. He estimated that more than two-thirds of the population of San Francisco had left for the goldfields. Most of the town's military garrison had deserted, taking their arms and equipment with them. All the ships in port had lost their crews, and there was not a workman left to perform the slightest task. The movement was spreading to San Jose, Santa Cruz, and Monterey. Most Frenchmen in California had also joined the stampede. Moerenhout added that political grievances between American and Mexican Californians were being forgotten as gold fever engulfed both populations.

Accounts such as those written by Larkin and Moerenhout of the fabulous wealth lying along the riverbanks, free for the taking, sparked thousands to leave their homes in the east—and in Europe—and head for California. The 49ers, as those who participated in the gold rush came to be called, faced daunting hardships in trekking across the continent or in long sea voyages to their destination. Only a tiny proportion would strike it rich. Most of the best lands were claimed long before the first 49ers even began their journeys. Still, they set out for California by the tens of thousands to join in the hunt for riches. Many stayed and made permanent homes in California.

Larkin tried briefly to set up a gold mining enterprise, using hired labor. The attempt was a failure, not because they couldn't find gold, but because the men were unwilling to stay and work for wages once they reached the goldfields. Nonetheless, the gold rush contributed greatly to Larkin's growing fortune. As one of California's largest retailers and wholesalers, he made enormous profits, importing ever-greater quantities of goods to feed California's boom. He continued also to speculate in real estate, often successfully, buying extensive properties in San Francisco, Sacramento, and elsewhere. Despite his personal success and prosperity, however, he sometimes could not help being nostalgic for the "old" California. He wrote to his friend Isaac Sterns in 1856 that "I begin to yearn after the times prior to July, 1846."[95]

The gold rush changed California in many ways. The rapid rise in population led to a political transformation and a demand for statehood. In September 1849, even before most 49ers arrived, a constitutional convention convened in Monterey to draft a state constitution. Monterey was already dwarfed by burgeoning San Francisco, which had grown to more than six thousand inhabitants and was increasing geometrically as 49ers poured in; it would soon pass one hundred thousand. Thomas Larkin was among the forty-eight delegates elected to the statehood convention. Many friends and associates urged him to run for statewide office as well, but he was not interested. Within a year, California was admitted as the thirty-first state of the United States.

Some fared well in the new California, while others did not. John Sutter, the Swiss immigrant and onetime Mexican army officer whose fort at New Helvetia once welcomed new settlers from the United States, seemed to be best placed of all to reap a personal bonanza from the gold rush sparked by the discovery on his land. Sutter, however, was no match for the tidal wave moving in his direction. He could not keep control of his land in the face of an onslaught of squatters. Sutter, who was once among the most powerful men in California, spent the rest of his life in a vain effort to win U.S. government compensation for his losses. He died in Washington DC in 1880. Today California's capital, Sacramento, sprawls on land that was once part of Sutter's wilderness settlement of New Helvetia.

Alexander Leidesdorff, the former New Orleans cotton trader who became the first African American vice consul, died in the spring of 1848, just days after learning that gold was discovered on his ranch. Leidesdorff contracted meningitis, then commonly known as "brain fever," and succumbed quickly. He was just thirty-eight. His death was considered a tragedy in San Francisco, where he had become one of the city's leading citizens. An obituary in the *California Star* reported:

> One of the largest and most respectable assemblages ever witnessed in this place, followed the deceased from his late residence to the place of interment. . . . All places of business and public entertainment were closed, the flags of the garrison and shipping were flying at half-mast, and minute guns were discharged. . . . In private life he was social, liberal, and hospitable to an eminent degree. . . . As a merchant and a citizen, he was prosperous, enterprising, and public-spirited and his name infinitely identified with the growth and prosperity of San Francisco. It is not injustice to the living, or unmeaning praise for the dead, to say that the town has lost its most valuable resident.[96]

Leidesdorff left no immediate heirs. His sizable estate provoked a controversy that dragged through California's courts for more than fifty years. In 2004 the California legislature named a state highway after Leidesdorff, claiming in its resolution, inaccurately, that Leidesdorff "was an active leader in the Bear Flag Revolt."[97] There is also a street in San Francisco named in his honor.

John Frémont, the fiery explorer and topographer whose military action helped spark the U.S. conquest, continued to make history in California and beyond. He was elected one of California's first two senators, but served only briefly. He became an outspoken opponent of slavery, leading to his nomination for president by the newly formed Republican Party in 1856. He lost the election to Secretary of State James Buchanan. At the outbreak of the Civil War, Frémont returned to military service and was named military governor of Missouri. There, he sparked another of the controversies for which he was so well known, issuing a decree freeing the slaves of all persons in rebellion. President Lincoln, not yet ready for such a bold move against slavery, ordered him to withdraw the decree. Frémont refused and was relieved of duty. After the war, Frémont returned to California and launched several unsuccessful business ventures, forcing him back into government service to earn a living. In 1878 he was named governor of the Arizona territory. He outlived many of his contemporaries, dying peacefully in 1890. Controversy followed Frémont in death as it did in life; historians continue to debate whether his role in the U.S. acquisition of California was a positive one.

Lt. Archibald Gillespie, the U.S. Marine who carried Larkin his commission as special diplomatic agent in 1846 and later served as commandant of the U.S. forces in southern California during the Mexican War, returned east with Commodore Stockton. He was promoted to captain for his service in California and participated as a witness in Frémont's court-martial. Gillespie left the Marines a few years later—apparently under a cloud—and returned to California as a civilian. He opposed Frémont's run for president and wrote articles sharply disparaging Frémont's courage as a soldier and his role in the American acquisition of California. Gillespie died in obscurity in San Francisco in 1873.

Jacques-Antoine Moerenhout, the French consul in Monterey and former American and French consul in Tahiti, remained at his post in Monterey until 1859. His dispatches to the French foreign minister were later published as *The Inside Story of the Gold Rush*. As a final twist to his long career, he opened the first French consulate in Los Angeles in 1859. There, the erstwhile U.S. consul represented France in the United States for twenty years, until his death in 1879.

Thomas Larkin, the first and only American consul in California, continued to prosper as a trader, merchant, and real estate magnate. He remained one of the richest and best-known figures in California and was said to own a quarter million acres of land. In 1856 he supported Frémont's bid for the presidency. Larkin contracted typhoid fever and died in San Francisco in 1858. By that time San Francisco was America's fourth largest city, a far cry from the tiny village of Yerba Buena where he had first set foot in California a quarter century earlier. Larkin was widely eulogized by his contemporaries. His former consular secretary, William Swasey, commented sadly that "none ever lived and died more respected by all who knew him."[98] Larkin himself would have been most pleased with the epitaph written by historian Josiah Royce, who called him in "every way by far, the foremost among the men who won for us California."[99]

NINE

# Shimoda and the Shogun
*Townshend Harris and the Opening of Japan*

A merica's westward vision did not end with the conquest of California. Some Americans were already looking even further west, across the Pacific Ocean. This was not entirely new, of course. From the earliest days of the new nation, Samuel Shaw and other daring merchants made their way across the Pacific to China. Official envoys such as Edmund Roberts broke down diplomatic barriers and raised the Stars and Stripes in distant countries of Asia. Thomas Larkin and other businessmen enjoyed success in Pacific trading ventures. Countless New England whalers were also making their way across the Pacific. The whaling grounds were no longer centered in the South Pacific, as they had been in the time of Samuel Blackler and Jacques-Antoine Moerenhout; intrepid whalers in their tiny ships now ranged across the entire ocean as far as northern Japan. American missionaries, following in the wake of the Portuguese, Spanish, French, and British, were establishing themselves around the Pacific. Although most Americans did not yet realize it, the United States was becoming a Pacific Ocean power.

As Americans widened their gaze, some looked with interest at Japan as a tantalizingly mysterious closed empire and an untapped potential trading partner, a prospective market with a population larger than the United States. Japan, however, was a closed country that for more than two hundred years had prohibited the entry of foreigners. Japan's tenuous contacts with the West were entirely in the hands of the Dutch, who since 1790 had been permitted to send just one trading ship a year and only to the port of Nagasaki.

A few Americans had actually managed to visit Japan during the Napoleonic Wars, when Dutch shipping was disrupted by the British, and the Dutch chartered neutral American vessels to make the annual trip to Nagasaki on their behalf. In 1815, as described in an earlier chapter, Cdre. David Porter proposed a U.S. naval visit to Japan, but it never took place. Two decades later, in 1835, Edmund Roberts was commissioned to negotiate a treaty with Japan, but he died en route. The U.S. Exploring Expedition under Lt. Charles Wilkes was instructed to include a visit to Japan as part of its work surveying the Pacific, but the four-year expedition never entered Japanese waters.

Several other failed efforts followed. In 1844 Caleb Cushing, who negotiated America's first treaty with China, was commissioned to negotiate with Japan, but he never made the trip. The next envoy, Alexander Everett, fell ill en route to the Far East and had to abandon his voyage. Everett delegated Cdre. James Biddle, who was taking him to the Far East, to go to Japan and "test the sentiments" of the government, while being careful not to "excite a hostile feeling."[1] Biddle, in his younger days, had served as a junior officer on the *Philadelphia* when it ran aground during the war with Tripoli in 1803; he was among those held prisoner there for nineteen months, with David Porter and hundreds of other crewmen. Biddle sailed two U.S. warships into Yedo Bay (now Tokyo Bay) in 1846. His ships were surrounded by the Japanese and towed out to sea, a humiliating end to his efforts.

The next American mission came in 1849, when Cdr. James Glynn was ordered to Nagasaki to retrieve the stranded crew of the American whaler *Lagoda*. The Japanese were happy to be rid of the castaway Americans, since foreigners were not welcome in Japan. To Glynn's surprise, the Japanese turned over not only the crew of the *Lagoda* but also another American that Glynn did not even know was there. This was Ranald MacDonald, a remarkable adventurer from Oregon who had developed such an intense interest in the closed Empire of Japan that he paid a captain to cast him adrift off its shores, hoping that as a stranded sailor he would be able to visit the country. MacDonald was quickly apprehended and confined in Nagasaki. While he didn't get to see much of the country, the Japanese quizzed him about life in the West and sent a few officials to learn English from him.

By this time, American leaders, notably President Millard Fillmore and Secretary of State Daniel Webster, were becoming increasingly attracted to the idea of opening relations with Japan. The sudden settlement of California after 1849 and the advent of transoceanic steamships, among other developments, suggested there would be a much larger American role in the Pacific in years to come. Some members of Congress and private Americans were beginning to agitate for opening Japan. In 1851 President Fillmore chose Cdre. John H. Aulick to lead a new expedition that would include well-armed steamships, in hopes that a show of power would impress the Japanese and facilitate an agreement. The mission, however, turned into a fiasco, with Aulick relieved of command by the time he reached Hong Kong. The mission was abandoned, one more in the long list of American failures to open contact with Japan.

Fillmore next turned to Cdre. Matthew Perry, who was designated "special diplomatic agent," the same title borne by Edmund Roberts, Thomas Larkin, and others. Fillmore wrote to the emperor of Japan, "I have no other object in sending him to Japan, but to propose to your Majesty that the United States and Japan should live in friendship and commercial intercourse with each other."[2] Fillmore stressed that the expedition was "to be of a pacific character" and that Perry was not to "resort to force unless in self defence."[3] Perry had instructions from both the secretary of state and the secretary of war, reflecting his dual role as a diplomat and a naval officer.

American interest in Japan was so great by this time that dozens of civilians applied to join Perry's mission. Perry refused virtually all of them, fearing that civilians would bristle under naval regulations and might be reluctant to obey his commands. One of those he refused was a Far East trader named Townsend Harris, who would go on to make his own indelible mark on the history of U.S.-Japan relations.

The mission to Japan had taken on such importance in Washington that Perry was given command of a dozen ships, both steam and sail, a substantial portion of the U.S. Navy. It took almost a year to assemble and outfit the ships and to gather presents for the emperor. After endless delays and a seven-month sail halfway across the world, Perry entered Yedo Bay on July 8, 1853, with just four ships, two of them steamers.

The Japanese were not as surprised to see Perry as the Americans thought they would be. Although Japan was officially closed to the outside world, Japanese officials made it a point to keep up with international developments. Through the Dutch trading post at Nagasaki, the Japanese learned of Western incursions into China and were even aware of American conquests during the Mexican War. The Japanese officials who came aboard Perry's ships could point out New York and Washington on a globe and knew that one was the commercial center and the other was the political capital. They had learned through Western publications of innovations such as railroads and steamships. A few Japanese who met Perry had even learned some English from the castaway seaman Ranald MacDonald, although they did not reveal this.

It might be fair to say that the Japanese knew as much about the West as the West did about Japan. Americans had little understanding of Japan's complex system of government. Perry, for example, had a letter from the president to the emperor, but he believed the emperor to be the same as the shogun, a hereditary secular ruler who controlled the government administration. For more than two hundred years, Japan had been ruled by a shogun—also known as a *tycoon* in Japan and a *ziagoon* in the West—of the Tokugawa dynasty. The title "shogun" originally meant "barbarian-subduing generalissimo" (*sei-i tai shogun*).[4] The emperor, or mikado, had a strictly limited political role and was largely confined to the imperial city of Kyoto. The mikado was described in a contemporary British account as "the spiritual emperor of Japan. . . . In many respects his functions seem very similar to those of the Pope."[5]

By the time of Perry's arrival, the Tokugawa dynasty was already in decline. The administration was weak, and the treasury was empty. Although most of the Japanese nobility clung tenaciously to the old ways and were committed to Japan's policy of excluding foreigners, a number of shogunate officials were aware that Japan could not win a military contest against the West. They knew that the British had recently won a war against China, while Russia had already begun to encroach on northern islands that were once fully within Japan's sphere of influence.

Perry's expedition had been so well publicized and had taken so long to get organized that the Dutch in Nagasaki warned the Japanese three times of the impending American visit. Still, the "black ships," as the Japanese dubbed the smoke-belching steamers, caused intense excitement and angst. They did well to worry; Perry's arrival marked the beginning of the end for the old order.

Japan had made just one preparation for Perry's arrival: as soon as he dropped anchor, a boat came alongside his flagship and delivered a scroll of paper with an order, written in French, telling him to go away.

Perry decided well before his arrival that he would refuse to take "no" for an answer. He anchored in Yedo Bay with his decks cleared for action and bristling with armaments, placed in full view to make an impression on the Japanese. He refused repeated orders, and then supplications, to retire to Nagasaki. He issued threats, telling his reluctant hosts that he had only friendly intentions but was determined to deliver the president's letter. He was prepared, if necessary, to "go on shore with a sufficient force and deliver them in person, be the consequences what they might."[6] Perry never seemed to grasp the irony between his pretensions of friendship and his threats of force, nor was he bothered that his instructions were to resort to force only in self-defense.

His tactics, however, succeeded. After getting assurances that he would leave if they accepted the president's letter, the Japanese arranged a ceremony for Perry to make the presentation. On July 14 he went ashore near Uraga, at the mouth of Yedo Bay, accompanied by 250 officers and men and two ship's bands, to present the letter to Japanese officials, in a building specially erected for the purpose. Two Japanese nobles solemnly accepted the letter without a word, bowed formally, and withdrew.

The American squadron sailed away after just eight days in Yedo Bay. Not only did Perry want the Japanese to have a chance to deliberate over the president's letter. He was also short on supplies and was still awaiting the rest of his squadron, which was carrying presents for the Japanese. He told the Japanese to expect his return in the spring with a larger force.

After Perry's departure, the shogun's government took an unprecedented step: it consulted the *daimyos*, or feudal lords, about what to do when Perry returned. The shogun did not normally consult the daimyos before making decisions. Seeking their views was a groundbreaking change in procedures, highlighting the extent to which Perry's arrival created an internal crisis. The leaders of the shogunate knew they could not hope to resist Perry militarily, but they did not feel secure enough to meet his demands without solidifying internal support.

The shogun's decision to seek their views backfired. Most of the daimyos were intent on maintaining the policy of exclusion. Seeking their views emboldened them to speak out in a way that would have been unthinkable just a few weeks earlier. Some of those in opposition to opening Japan began to rally around the mikado as a new center of political power. This internal turmoil would continue to bubble for years, beginning a process that would fatally undermine the shogunate. Although the Americans did not realize it, internal politics would color every aspect of the upcoming negotiations. Because of internal pressures, even the most outward-looking Japanese officials were determined to yield as little as possible to the barbarians at the gate.

Despite the daimyos' opposition, a number of Japan's great lords saw the writing on the wall. Among them were Lord Abe, the president of the ruling council, Lord Ii, and Lord Hotta, all of whom would play a further role in opening Japan. The council, under Abe's leadership and on the shogun's authority, issued an order that if the Americans returned, they were to be dealt with peacefully. This fateful decision implied that the shogun, the "barbarian-subduing generalissimo," was no longer up to the task.

While the Japanese pondered their reaction, Perry steamed back into Yedo Bay in February 1854, months earlier than he had told the Japanese to expect him. He had heard rumors that Russian and French fleets were planning visits to Japan, and he did not want them to claim the honor of the first treaty. This time Perry's squadron boasted eight ships, including three steamers. The ships' decks were once again "cleared for action, the guns placed in position and shotted, . . . preparations made, usual before meeting an enemy."[7] Not surprisingly, the Japanese doubted that Perry's intentions were peaceful.

The goal of Perry's first visit to Japan had been to deliver the president's letter; this time the goal was to obtain a treaty. What the Americans hoped for was a treaty similar to the U.S.-China treaty of 1844, including provisions opening several ports to free trade, allowing permanent residence by Americans, and granting privileges such as extraterritoriality—exempting resident Americans from Japanese law. Perry carried with him a draft treaty which, according to the official account of his expedition, "in all its essential features, is identical" with the China treaty.[8] The Japanese goal was to yield the minimum concessions needed to make Perry go away.

Over several days of polite discussions, punctuated by more veiled threats from Perry, the outlines of an agreement were hammered out. Perry asked that five ports be open to free trade. The Japanese agreed to open two ports, one immediately and another after a year, where American ships could obtain water, coal, and supplies. However, Americans would not be allowed to establish residence, and visiting seamen would not be allowed to travel more than a few miles from the city centers. As the two ports, Japan proposed the small port of Shimoda, not far from Yedo by sea, and Hakodate, on Japan's northern island, which might be convenient for whalers. Perry accepted after sending one of his ships to examine Shimoda, which reported that it was "suitable in every respect." The official records noted, however, that Japanese opposition to free trade "put an end to all prospect of negotiating a 'commercial treaty.'"[9] Throughout the discussions, Perry alternately styled himself "ambassador" and "admiral," although neither title was authorized by his government. The highest American naval rank at the time was commodore, and the highest diplomatic rank was minister.

Perry won one more important point: the United States would have the right to appoint a consul resident in Japan. This caused great anxiety for the Japanese, who had trouble understanding either the role of or the need for a consul. In the face of further threats, however, the Japanese yielded and agreed to an American consul at Shimoda, not to be appointed for at least eighteen months.

The treaty was signed on March 31, 1854, with great pomp, ceremony, and an exchange of presents. The Japanese gifts of lacquer ware and other local products became the first Japanese items in Joel Poinsett's new United States National Museum, which was eventually subsumed by the Smithsonian Institution.

With the treaty completed, the American squadron sailed away and disbanded. Perry was followed to Japan within a few months by the British and the Russians, who obtained similar treaties. The Perry expedition was an important turning point in history, marking the beginning of the reopening of Japan to the outside world. The treaty itself, however, was a disappointment to most Americans. Its provisions fell far short of the earlier treaty with China. It was called a "shipwreck convention," providing for little more than the protection of stranded American seamen. Diplomatic relations were not formally established. Just two isolated ports were opened for American ships to resupply. Supplies could be purchased only from official Japanese government agents. Any other sort of business was left vaguely to future "careful deliberations between the parties." Americans would not be allowed to live in Japan, and visiting Americans would be severely restricted in their movements. Worst of all, the treaty contained no provisions for trade. Even Perry's official account conceded that the treaty did not provide "much ground for congratulation."[10]

Perry had hammered a wedge into Japan's closed door, but it still remained to pull the door open. This task, ironically, was left to a man Perry had refused to take with him to Japan: Townsend Harris.

Harris was born in Sandy Hill, New York, in 1804. The youngest of six children, he received only a limited education at the village school before being taken, at age thirteen, to begin work in a dry goods store in New York City. His mother taught him "to tell the truth, fear God, and hate the British," things he did all his life. Taking her third injunction to heart, he refused even to use a Sheffield knife or to wear English cloth.[11] Despite his lack of formal education, he read voraciously and managed to learn French, Spanish, and Italian by speaking with his store's customers. Reading newspapers sparked an early interest in foreign affairs.

As Harris grew to adulthood, he became a successful businessman, civic leader, and active member of the Democratic Party. Perhaps because of his own lack of formal schooling, he took a special interest in education, winning election to the New York City Board of Education and serving for a time as its president. He championed the idea of free higher education for poor boys and was a founder of the New York Free Academy, which later became the City College of New York.

In 1848, at age forty-four, Harris, determined to fulfill a dream of seeing the world, sold his New York business interests, used the proceeds to buy cargo and a schooner, and sailed for California. His timing couldn't have been better. After a six-month voyage around the tip of South America, he arrived in San Francisco during the early days of the gold rush. His cargo sold for profits beyond his wildest expectations. He sailed north to Oregon to procure a cargo of furs, then he headed for the Far East. For the next four years, Harris wandered the Pacific and Indian Oceans in his own ship, trading at ports from New Zealand to Ceylon to China. He loved to tell tales of his travels, especially of an evening he spent with a cannibal chief in a hut decorated with human skulls.

In 1853 he decided to base his business in China, settling initially in Hong Kong. There he learned about the planned Perry mission to Japan, which he tried and failed to join. Nonetheless, Harris set his sights on Japan, reasoning that if Perry's mission were successful, Japan would be open to American traders and others. He decided to return to the United States to seek an official American position in Japan.

Harris steamed into New York in July 1855 after an absence of seven years. Within days, he was in Washington lobbying to be named the first U.S. consul in Japan. Through his contacts in the Democratic Party, he arranged an interview with Secretary of State William Marcy. Marcy was quite taken with Harris, writing to a friend that "I had a short interview with Mr. Harris yesterday and he dined with me to-day. He is evidently a man of high character, and his large intelligence derived both from books and observation impresses me forcibly. . . . I shall appoint him at once and think he had better sail as soon as possible."[12]

Harris was delighted to find himself appointed consul general, a rank above consul, although he was well aware that he was headed for a difficult situation. He knew enough about Japan to expect that he would not be welcome and that he would likely be living in isolation for a long period of time, both from the Japanese and from his own countrymen. Harris also knew, however, that his assignment was historic and that it was an unprecedented opportunity to participate in one of the great events of his day. He began immediately to make preparations for his departure, purchasing presents for Japanese officials, in particular alcoholic beverages, which he had learned from the Perry expedition were especially welcome. He also sought out information on Japan, which was scarce; one of the best sources available was Engelbert Kaempfer's *History of Japan*, dating from 1690. Harris arranged to hire a Dutch-speaking interpreter, since Dutch was the only Western language the Japanese admitted to knowing. For this key position he took the recommendation of friends in New York and hired a young man named Henry Heusken, who would become his close friend and colleague.

Shortly before his departure, Harris was given a second, unexpected assignment. On his way to Japan, he was to stop in Bangkok to negotiate a new commercial treaty with Siam in order to update the twenty-year-old Edmund Roberts treaty. The British had recently obtained an improved treaty, and the United States wanted to do the same.

The State and Navy Departments arranged for the steam frigate *San Jacinto* to convey Harris to Siam and then Japan. The *San Jacinto* was an entirely new kind of steamer, using a screw propeller instead of paddle side wheels. In theory, it was supposed to be far more efficient than the older models; in practice, the new technology had not yet been perfected. The ship was slow and broke down constantly, greatly delaying Harris's arrival in Japan. One of the ship's company described it as "a clumsy, black-looking vessel, with a smoke stack protruding from her deck and guns projecting from her sides."[13]

Harris's voyage, beginning in October 1855, took him briefly to London, where he called on the American minister, James Buchanan, later to become the fifteenth U.S. president. The next stop was Paris, where "I ordered some properly ornamented clothes to wear at the Court of Bangkok." His new outfit was the standard State Department consular uniform, including a blue coat embroidered with gold, gold knee buckles, white silk stockings, gold shoe buckles, and a cocked hat.

On reaching Penang, on the Malaysian peninsula, Harris wrote to Secretary of State Marcy informing him of his arrival and letting him know that he had appointed Henry C. J. Heusken to be his Dutch interpreter. Heusken was to receive a salary of $1,500 a year, but payment would not begin until his arrival in Japan, meaning he would go most of a year without pay. Harris advanced him half a year's salary and arranged free transport for him aboard the *San Jacinto*.

Heusken was just twenty-three years old. He was born in Amsterdam and emigrated to the United States in 1853, about the time of Perry's visit to Japan. As a recent immigrant, Heusken was having trouble finding work and making ends meet. He had, however, impressed some prominent New Yorkers, who recommended him to Harris. Heusken has been described as "brave, capable, enthusiastic, and scholarly."[14] Whereas Harris tended to be quiet and reserved, Heusken was outgoing and made friends easily. The two men maintained a formal relationship in the style of the era—they were always "Mr. Harris" and "Mr. Heusken" to each other—but they would grow close through their many years of isolation together in Japan.

Heusken would face his own challenges, as well as grave dangers, in Japan. The first challenge was that the form of Dutch used in

Japan was a two-century-old patois that even native Dutch speakers had trouble understanding. Many Western concepts did not have Japanese equivalents, so the interpreter's job was also one of explaining and teaching. Moreover, many Japanese officials did not fully grasp the concept behind foreign languages; when negotiating documents, they sometimes insisted that the Dutch version have each word in exactly the same order as the Japanese, which would have resulted in a nonsensical document. Eventually Heusken became fluent in Japanese. His services were much sought after by later visitors to Japan.

It was April 1856 when Harris finally arrived in Siam to begin his treaty negotiations. The 1833 Roberts treaty had set the foundation for free trade and protection for Americans in Siam, but it did not allow for the appointment of a U.S. consul, and its rates of duty turned out to be too high to make Siam an attractive trading partner. The United States had tried and failed to improve on the Roberts treaty; as recently as 1851 a diplomatic mission had come away empty-handed.

But times had changed. In 1851 King Rama IV (now known as King Mongkut) ascended the throne of Siam. The new king had spent more than twenty-five years as a monk-scholar, during which time he sought out Western knowledge and even learned English. Rama IV is popularly known in Western culture as the Siamese king of *Anna and the King of Siam* and *The King and I*, who hired Anna Leonowens, among other westerners, to tutor his children. He realized that Siam would have to change if it were to remain independent. Rama felt threatened by the British, who in 1852 annexed part of neighboring Burma. In 1855 he concluded a new commercial treaty with Great Britain. Harris's task was to secure the same terms as the British.

Harris was received in Siam politely and with great ceremony, but he was forced to wait to begin his treaty negotiations. Anxious to get on to Japan, he chafed under the delay. Still, he wrote philosophically in his journal: "It is an old saying that those who come here for business should bring one ship loaded with patience, another loaded with presents."[15]

After what seemed to Harris an interminable wait—in fact, it was only a little over two weeks—he received his audience with Rama IV, recording his name as "King Somdet Phra Paramendr Maha Mongkut." Harris's procession to the royal palace had all the same pomp and ceremony accorded to Roberts more than twenty years earlier. Like Roberts, he was aghast to see nobles crawling on their hands and knees in the royal presence. Unlike in Roberts's time, the king spoke English, although with amusing and disconcerting quirks, such as saying "good-bye" as a greeting instead of "hello." The king served him dinner in the Western style and later met with him socially several times.

On the substance of a treaty, Harris found the Siamese willing to give the Americans all they had given the British and even more. With little difficulty, he won protection for missionaries, a sharp reduction in tariffs, and extraterritoriality for Americans in Siam. The Siamese were clearly anxious to win American friendship as a counterweight to Great Britain. On May 29, 1856, the treaty was signed to the echo of a 21-gun salute. The negotiations had seemed endless to Harris but had taken only two weeks, an extraordinarily short time to negotiate a treaty in any day or age.

The *San Jacinto* left Siam for Hong Kong two days after the treaty was signed. The engines were up to their old tricks, however, and could barely power the ship along at five knots an hour, an excruciatingly slow pace. There was more bad news in Hong Kong; it would take three weeks to repair the engine. Harris used the time to hire Chinese servants to take with him to Japan: a "butler/head boy" for $16 a month, a cook and his assistant at $16 a month for the pair, and a tailor and washman for $14 a month each. Harris was to furnish their food and pay their way back to Hong Kong after a year unless they wanted to stay longer with him. The tailor immediately absconded with three months' advance pay, but he was quickly found and delivered to the ship, "bound hand and foot."[16] Harris also purchased furniture and supplies, which were duly loaded on board. Among the many ships in Hong Kong's harbor, Harris noted, was the British vessel *Minden*, the ship on which Francis Scott Key wrote the "Star Spangled Banner" during the bombardment of Baltimore in 1814. The *San Jacinto* finally got under way for Japan in July, but broke down again after just one mile. The ship returned to Hong Kong for yet another month of repair work.

When the *San Jacinto* finally steamed into Japanese waters in late August, two years had passed since Perry's departure. During that time, several American ships had visited Japan. They were treated politely, but the Japanese would neither trade with them nor allow them to take up residence, since the Perry treaty did not provide for this.

Within Japan, internal dissention continued over how to deal with foreigners. In August 1855 Lord Hotta, backed by Lord Ii, assumed the leadership of the shogun's council. The same year, the shogunate established an "Institute for the Investigation of Barbarian Books" to learn more about Western technology and military might. The arrival of an American consul sparked a new series of crises for the Japanese. Their goal was to limit the damage of the Perry treaty and to keep the consul as isolated as possible. His goal, in contrast, was to open Japan.

Townsend Harris, like the officials of the shogunate, was looking ahead. He was acutely aware of his potential place in history as the first official American to reside in Japan. As he approached Shimoda, he wrote in his journal: "I shall be the first recognized agent from a civilized power to reside in Japan. This forms an epoch in my life and may be the beginning of a new order of things in Japan. I hope I may so conduct myself that I may have honorable mention in the histories which will be written on Japan and its future destiny."[17]

The *San Jacinto* finally arrived at the small port of Shimoda on August 21, 1856. One of the ship's company wrote that "as the ship ran into the harbor, its picturesque beauties called forth general admiration. The bay, bounded by a chain of pointed mountains, clothed with vegetation to their very summits, and the steep plains and valleys running up between these mountains are neatly cultivated in terraces or shelves." To the amazement of all those aboard, a boat with the American flag approached them from the shore bringing a harbor pilot, who presented a commission given to him by Commodore Perry to guide American ships. The pilot wore straw sandals, "with a separate place for the great toe," a curiosity the Americans had never seen before. Although the pilot spoke no English, "the Captain and he carried on an animated conversation in gestures which employed both of their bodies and all their limbs, and took up half the poop deck."[18]

Once ashore, Harris's real problems began. The governor of Shimoda declined to meet him. When the governor eventually did agree to meet, his first request was for Harris to depart immediately, or as Heusken put it, "They would be delighted if His Excellency, the Consul-General, didn't mind leaving and coming back in a year or two. . . . His Excellency, a title they never missed repeating at every moment—their dear, dear friend, the Consul-General whom they were so glad to see and whom they would be so glad to see returning to the United States."[19] After some argument, the governor produced a copy of the Perry treaty, which, in his version, said that a consul would be appointed to Shimoda if *both* governments considered it necessary, while the American version said if *either* government considered it necessary. The Japanese then argued that they could not afford to maintain Harris; he replied that he would cover his own expenses. Next, they pointed out that Shimoda had recently been hit by an earthquake and tidal wave—which was true—so there were no appropriate facilities where Harris could live. Harris politely turned aside all of their objections.

This discussion continued through a long series of meetings, each one conducted with great ceremony and courtesy. Harris would leave the *San Jacinto* each day to a salute of thirteen guns, the designated salute for a consul, accompanied by ship's officers in their dress uniforms. The Japanese would receive them in the town's principal hall. Inevitably, the meeting would begin with the governor asking after the health of the consul general; his inquiry was translated by his interpreter into Dutch, and then translated again by Heusken from Dutch into English. The response was conveyed back in the same manner. The question was then repeated in regard to the captain and then in regard to the rest of the ship's company. These cumbersome formalities could last for hours. The Japanese interpreter was a man named Moriyama Takichiro, himself a senior official, who had assisted during Commodore Perry's negotiations. Moriyama was one of the Japanese who had learned English from the castaway American adventurer Ranald MacDonald, though he gave no hint of this to the Americans. This subterfuge gave the Japanese the slight advantage of knowing what the Americans said to each other in unguarded moments. Moriyama did not reveal his secret to Harris for almost two years.

At the meetings, the Japanese always served refreshments to the visitors, with chopsticks as utensils, and "were amused at our awkwardness, and very kindly offered to show us the mode of using these novel tools."[20] Overall, Harris was impressed with his hosts, writing, "We were all much pleased with the appearance and manners of the Japanese. . . . They are superior to any people east of the Cape of Good Hope."[21]

Eventually the Japanese agreed to let Harris stay "temporarily." For a residence, they offered him a small Shinto temple and its compound five miles around the bay from Shimoda. Harris acknowledged that the temple was a far nicer building than anything in Shimoda, with large, clean, and spacious rooms where "a person might stay . . . for a few weeks in tolerable comfort."[22] He was concerned, however, that the choice was a deliberate attempt to keep him isolated from Shimoda. He agreed to stay there "temporarily" until a proper house could be erected in Shimoda; in the end, such a building never materialized, and the temple remained his residence. The governors insisted that three rooms be reserved for Japanese officers who would serve as an "honor guard." The Americans, however, thought that "the temple was to be our prison and the helpful officers our wardens, placed here to observe our slightest move and to prevent any communication between us and the people."[23] Harris refused to give up three rooms but compromised and agreed to let the guards stay in another building on the compound. The first night at the temple, Harris and Heusken discovered it had other occupants: bats, large rats, hungry mosquitoes, and spiders that measured more than five inches across.

Harris's first purchase was a forty-eight-foot wooden spar, which the ship's carpenter fashioned into a flagpole and installed in his front yard. He raised the Stars and Stripes over the new consulate and flew the flag when foreign ships were in port and on Sundays and holidays, including Japanese holidays. There were thirty-one stars on the flag, reflecting California's recent statehood. On September 4, at 2:30 in the afternoon, he wrote proudly, "I hoist the 'First Consular Flag' ever seen in this Empire." His flag turned out to be so poorly made that within a few days it was fraying in the wind. Harris commissioned another flag to be made by a local seamstress, a Japanese Betsy Ross.

A British visitor to Shimoda two years later described his first view of the temple from the bay. It was clearly a religious center, he could tell, situated in a pleasant grove of trees and so isolated that "had one wished to retire altogether from the cares and anxieties of this troublesome world, it would be difficult to conceive a retreat more perfectly adapted for the purpose." When the visitor went ashore to visit Harris, he found "a well-stored library, and a few rooms comfortably fitted up, [which] gave an agreeable air of civilization to the establishment; but what can compensate for two years of almost entire isolation and banishment from communion with one's fellow-men?"[24]

After thirteen days, the *San Jacinto* sailed off, leaving Harris and Heusken alone and unwelcome in a strange land. As recorded by a member of the ship's company, the Japanese "did not regard him as a very acceptable addition to the empire, yet we left him and his flag successfully planted on the beach at Shimoda."[25] Harris could tell that he would have a difficult struggle ahead. He sent a letter to Secretary of State Marcy with the ship, saying he had decided to let a few weeks lapse before trying to open treaty negotiations, in order to give the Japanese time to recover from the unhappy shock of his arrival and to convince them of his friendly disposition.

Harris thus spent his first few weeks settling quietly into his new home and exploring Shimoda and its environs. He unpacked his belongings, including books, furniture, and four pairs of pigeons that would soon be eaten by his cat. The town itself turned out to be a poor place, made all the worse by the recent earthquake and tidal wave. The disaster, Harris wrote, came when a nearby volcano erupted and "a mighty wave rolled in on Shimoda, encountering as it entered a flourishing town of some eight thousand to ten thousand souls. When the wave receded, it left only fourteen houses standing." The rebuilt houses were clean and dry. Shimoda was primarily a fishing village. The people were poor, but appeared well fed, and there was none of the squalor Harris expected to see. The crops, mainly rice, were rich and well tended, covering every available inch of flat ground as well as terraces cut into the mountains. The country exuded calm and good order. "In no part of the world," he wrote, "are the laboring classes better off than at Shimoda."[26] The surrounding countryside rose steeply into majestic, terraced mountains, dotted with attractive temples.

A contemporary British visitor gave a more negative view: "Simoda is a mean place compared with Nagasaki, and it is difficult to conceive why Commodore Perry should have fixed upon it as a port. . . . The town . . . is . . . composed of a few mean streets, running at right angles to each other, and contains, probably, from three to four thousand inhabitants. . . . The houses are all built of wood, many of them only of one story. The shops are poor and thinly supplied. Here, as at Nagasaki, the poorer classes are but lightly clad, the men having little on besides a loincloth, and the women being generally uncovered above the waist."[27]

Despite the positive first impression, it didn't take Harris long to realize that the Japanese had outwitted Perry in convincing him to accept Shimoda as the American port. It was small, poor, and isolated. It was not one of Japan's commercial centers. While the harbor was large, it offered little protection from the frequent violent storms. Although Shimoda was not far from Yedo by sea, it was isolated on a rocky peninsula surrounded by mountains rising 6,000 feet, virtually cutting it off from the rest of the country. Some of the mountain passes were too steep to cross on horseback. It took five days for a letter to go overland from Shimoda to Yedo.

In short, it was a perfect place to keep the Americans isolated from the rest of the country. Harris decided that once he began his negotiations, one of his goals would be to open more and better ports for American ships.

The Japanese, however, were not even thinking of further negotiations. They had already gone further than they wanted in opening Japan. The appearance of an American consul was one more irritating complication. Harris would have his work cut out for him. He set three objectives: first, to open discussions aimed at easing some of the restrictions included in the Perry treaty; second, to obtain an audience with the shogun; and third, to secure a new treaty that established formal diplomatic relations and opened Japan to American trade. These were daunting goals for a solitary American in an isolated port of an unwelcoming empire.

To achieve any of his objectives, Harris knew he would have to establish a constructive dialogue, and even a friendship, with Japanese officials. This would be a slow and difficult process. Harris soon discovered how little he really knew about Japan. It turned out that Shimoda had not one governor but two, who were sometimes there together but usually alternated with each other six months at a time. He sent each of them gifts of champagne, brandy, whiskey, cherry bounce, and anisette. He called on them regularly to discuss minor issues: his Chinese servants were not being allowed to purchase supplies in town; this would be fixed, he was told. He and Heusken were being followed every time they left the compound; this was for their protection. He wanted to engage some Japanese servants; this would have to be referred to Yedo. He wanted the Japanese guards to leave his residence; this wouldn't be possible. He asked to buy a horse; this was a problem, since the governor was responsible for Harris's safety and would have to perform hara-kiri if a vicious horse killed Harris.

While these were minor points and he made little progress, he was opening a dialogue. He decided to raise his first real substantive issue: his American silver dollars were being exchanged for only one-third of their weight in Japanese silver coins. Perry, for whatever reason, had accepted this exchange rate. Harris realized that this unreasonable practice would pose a grave barrier to trade. It was also a serious personal problem, since everything was costing him three times as much as it should.

Harris refused to meet with any officials ranking lower than the governors themselves, leaving Heusken to deal with all others. His objective was to convey a sense that a consul general was a high-level officer deserving of great respect; an appreciation of this would be essential if he were to have any hope of meeting the shogun. As a matter of principle, Harris also steadfastly refused to conduct any kind of business on Sundays. This at first baffled the Japanese, but they soon grew accustomed to it.

The weeks dragged on with little change and little progress. The isolation took its toll. Harris's spirits dimmed, and he began to suffer from depression and loss of appetite. Life in Shimoda was pleasant enough, but both he and Heusken longed for company and for news of the outside world. They grew miserably homesick.

As the time passed, however, the Japanese seemed to be getting friendlier and less suspicious. Harris decided it was time to ask formally for a visit to Yedo. The purpose of the visit would be to present his credentials and to deliver a letter from the president to the emperor (the letter was addressed from President Fillmore to the emperor, a sign of continuing American confusion over the difference between the shogun and the mikado). Harris wrote a formal letter to the foreign minister requesting him to make the necessary arrangements. He did not expect a quick response, nor would he receive one.

Harris achieved a minor breakthrough at the end of October, when the two governors agreed to visit his house. He noted gleefully in his journal: "This will be remembered as an important day in the history of Japan. The laws forbidding the Imperial Governor of a city to visit any foreigner at his residence is to-day to be broken." The governors arrived with a large suite of followers, whom Harris happily entertained. This was his first purely social interaction with the Japanese; the ice was starting to thaw. When the governors asked why Commodore Perry had sent longboats from his ships to survey the bays of Shimoda and Yedo, Harris used the question to begin an education on Western ways. To the governors' astonishment, he explained that the harbors of all Western countries were surveyed in order to draw charts, which were then made freely available to navigators of all nations. Harbor entrances were marked with lighthouses and buoys to encourage ships to visit. All Western nations supported trade in these and other ways, since trade made them rich and powerful. Japan, too, could enjoy these benefits. The governors seemed astounded and clearly wanted to hear more. In regard to the harbor surveys they were much relieved, telling Harris they had been concerned that they might have to "perform the *hara-kiri*, or 'happy dispatch,'" if such surveys resumed. At the end of the evening, Harris presented one of the governors with a Colt five-shot pistol, which seemed to please him greatly.[28]

More weeks crawled by. By the end of the year, Harris had lost forty pounds. He took long walks every day to try to keep up his energy, and he gave up smoking. On Christmas Day he wrote: "I am sick and solitary, living as one may say in a prison—a large one it is true—but still a prison." On New Year's Day he added: "I am very low spirited from ill health and from the very slow progress I am making with the Japanese."[29]

The governors were always polite, but there was little change in conditions. Harris decided the time had come to make a stand. At his next meeting with the governors he changed his previous polite tone and instead demanded the immediate removal of the guards from his home. If this wasn't done, he warned, he would consider himself a prisoner and inform his government that he was being ill-treated. He then launched into a litany of old and new complaints, from being followed by police every time he left his residence, to being shunned by the townspeople, to the continued harassment of his servants, to Japanese refusals to accept his invitation to visit him on New Year's Day. His changed demeanor startled his hosts. The discussion continued for four hours. When he returned home, the guards were packing up to leave.

Slowly things began to change. The governors brought him gifts of food, exotic birds, and pigeons to replace the ones his cat had eaten. They presented him with two special dogs, a mark of respect. He was given a fine sword from Yedo, with an explanation that no foreigner had ever before owned one. Policemen stopped trailing ostentatiously behind him. Townspeople no longer closed their shutters at his approach. Heusken, who was already learning a bit of Japanese, was able to strike up conversations with villagers who had previously shunned him. Harris finally got the horse he had requested months earlier. A few weeks later Heusken was able to buy one as well. For Heusken, who had recently escaped poverty in New York, the purchase of a horse—for $27.41—was a symbol that his ship had finally come in. He gloated in his journal: "Here I am now the owner of a horse! If I go on this way why shouldn't I maintain my own carriage and ask in marriage the Emperor's only daughter?"[30] The horses wore straw sandals, which wore out so quickly that they were almost useless. Years later, Harris had a ship's blacksmith put iron shoes on his horse. This innovation so amazed the Japanese that the prime minister asked to borrow the horse and had his own mount shod the same way; this was the beginning of horseshoes in Japan.[31]

In February there was another social breakthrough: he was invited to dinner at the governors' home. His relationship was slowly turning into a friendship. Among the fine dishes served, Harris noted with distaste, was *raw* fish, making him perhaps the first American to be served sushi. They also served sake, "a drink distilled from rice." Harris, who drank very little in any circumstances, declined for health reasons, but Heusken felt that courtesy required him to drink the toasts, "although the drink is detestable . . . my palate suffers unbearable tortures."[32]

A few days later the Japanese agreed to Harris's request to fire a salute of honor on George Washington's birthday. They did this on two small brass howitzers "exactly copied in every respect from one Commodore Perry gave them; every appointment about the gun, down to the smallest particular, was exactly copied."[33] Harris's and Heusken's journals separately attest to this remarkable feat of reverse engineering, although the official list of gifts from the Perry expedition makes no mention of howitzers. The Japanese claimed to have made one thousand copies; Harris was not sure whether to believe them.

Harris used the improved atmosphere to press his diplomatic agenda. He wrote again to the foreign minister asking for an invitation to visit Yedo to present his credentials and deliver the president's letter. This time he hinted that dire calamities were facing Japan from other countries—not the United States—and that he wanted to confer with them about how to avoid the impending dangers. The response, when it arrived more than a month later, was on a sheet of paper five feet long. It said that all business should be conducted with the governors of Shimoda. Harris continued to press for a visit, but he also began to discuss with the governors some of the points he wanted to include in a new treaty.

Thus began months of negotiations. The lack of progress sometimes drove Harris to despair. In March he bemoaned in his journal that "I am really ill, yet I am forced day after day to listen to useless debates, on points that have been exhausted, and are only varied by some new phase of falsehood!" In April, echoing the sentiments of earlier U.S. consuls in many countries, he added, "If I had a vessel of war here, I should have speedy answers to my demands."[34] But there was no man-of-war. The *San Jacinto*, which had promised to return within six months, was nowhere to be seen.

In June Harris achieved his first notable success. On the seventeenth, he and the governors signed the Convention of Shimoda, a short but highly significant agreement. The convention granted ordinary Americans the right to reside at Shimoda and Hakodate beginning one year later, a major breakthrough. It established extra-territoriality for Americans in Japan; they would be subject to an American consular court rather than to Japanese law. One of the most important points was the currency exchange question; after seemingly endless arguments, Harris won Japanese agreement to accept American silver dollars for equal weights of Japanese silver coin, granting the Japanese a 6 percent fee for "recoinage," or the costs of melting down American coins to mint new Japanese coins. The two currencies were now virtually on par. This not only eliminated a major obstacle to trade—once trade was permitted—

but would immediately benefit any American ships arriving to purchase coal or other supplies. Another clause specified the rights of the American consul to travel in Japan and to make purchases without government intervention. Finally, the convention formalized an American right to obtain supplies at Nagasaki, in addition to the two ports opened by Perry.

Heusken was elated and penned in his journal, "Great victory!"[35] Harris's reaction was more sober. He knew the convention was a major achievement, but he did not expect to get much credit at home for his efforts. "Am I elated by this success?" he asked himself. "Not a whit. I know my dear countrymen but too well to expect any praise for what I have done, and I shall esteem myself lucky if I am not removed from office" for not achieving enough.[36]

The Convention of Shimoda was signed ten months after Harris's arrival. It stood as a monument to his skill and perseverance. Unlike previous agreements, it was not backed by a naval squadron. Harris had worked entirely on his own. Since his arrival in Shimoda, not a single American naval vessel had visited, nor had he received any further instructions or guidance from the State Department. It was a promising start, but Japan still was not open.

While the negotiations dragged on, Harris tried to learn more about Japan and assiduously recorded his impressions. He worked at learning some Japanese words, picking up at least enough to communicate with his servants. Heusken, in contrast, made rapid progress in learning the language. When Harris was well, the two of them meandered on long walks, at least five or six miles a day, to enjoy the surrounding countryside, with views "of the most picturesque kind. . . . A walk here is a thing to be desired and long remembered. . . . Every new walk I take shows me more and more of the patient industry of the Japanese, and creates new admiration of their agriculture, while the landscape from the top of the hills, overlooking the terraces rising one above another like the steps of a giant staircase and running over the rich fields of the valley and terminating with a glimpse of the blue water of the sea, forms a series of charming landscapes which are well worthy of the pencils of able artists."[37]

Japanese houses were extremely plain inside, almost totally lacking in furniture except for a few chests and mats on the floors. The houses were clean because the Japanese always removed their shoes before entering. There were no displays of wealth, even at the homes of the governors, leading Harris to conclude that the Japanese were among the world's most frugal people. "I do not hesitate to say that the house of a Prince of the Empire does not contain half the value of furniture that you will find in the house of a sober, steady mechanic in America."[38]

Japanese dress was also plain. Curiously, there were fixed days on which, by law, the entire population changed from winter to spring clothes and then to summer clothes and "no inclemency of weather can postpone the change."[39] Heusken was amazed by the degree of regimentation in this and all other activities. By law, he wrote, all people in Japan must do all the same things at the same time. "They take their breakfast, lunch and dinner all exactly at the same hour. They change clothes four times a year on the same day. One day everybody is busy drying fish; another day is to dry fabrics woven by the women. Apparently they go even further, for today everybody without exception has a cold, certainly by order of the government."[40]

The Japanese were also meticulously clean, Harris noted. "Everyone bathes every day. . . . There are many public bathhouses in Shimoda. . . . The wealthy people have their baths in their own houses, but the working classes all, of both sexes, old and young, enter the same bathroom and there perform their ablutions in a state of perfect nudity. I cannot account for so indelicate a proceeding on the part of a people so generally correct. I am assured, however, that it is not considered as dangerous to the chastity of their females."[41] The Japanese, for their part, were surprised to learn that Harris bathed in cold water, even in the winter.

Harris was able to uncover frustratingly little about Japan's government. "Their great object appears to be to permit as little to be learned about their country as possible; and, to that end, all fraud, deceit, falsehood and even violence is justifiable in their eyes. It is true that this is the most difficult country in the world to get information; no statistics exist; no publications are made on any subject connected with industry."[42] Harris still had no idea of the internal turmoil wracking the country's leadership since Perry's visit, now heightened by his own presence. The government seemed to him to be a rigid despotism, with inflexible laws. At the same time, however, he was impressed with the social protections the government had in place, which were far stronger than those in the United States: destitute parents were given an allowance to care for their children, and paupers were placed with relatives and given an allowance for their upkeep. As for religion, Harris commented that he had never seen a country with so many temples where the people seemed so indifferent to religion, to the point that he judged most upper-class Japanese to be atheists.

Shimoda itself didn't hold much in the way of attractions. There was little to buy in the market, and prices were exorbitant. Many people had asked him to buy Japanese goods for them, but he found little worth buying. The Japanese themselves had few possessions and almost no luxuries. He thought that westerners, with their penchant for acquisition, might learn a valuable lesson from the Japanese on this score. The one aspect that disturbed him was that children didn't seem to have any toys: "no hoops, no skip ropes, no marbles, no tops, and, I fear, nothing else."[43] He was delighted one blustery May day to see a group of boys flying kites, the first time he had seen children at play.

Throughout the long months of 1857, Harris suffered almost continually from ill health. He couldn't eat. He vomited blood. By the Fourth of July, he was too ill even to attend a salute to the American flag that he had arranged for the occasion. Heusken donned a dress uniform and went in Harris's place. By the end of August, the undiagnosed ailments turned the once-stout Harris into a skeleton of his former self; he weighed just 130 pounds.

Adding to the misery was the extended isolation. Harris and Heusken felt abandoned. Very few Western ships called at Shimoda. Soon after their arrival, Shimoda was visited by a Dutch ship and then by an American vessel seeking to sell rifles, which was turned away. A Russian man-of-war called at Shimoda, and the captain told Harris that a Russian consul would join him there in the spring; the consul never arrived. After that, there was not another ship for months. Finally, in March, an American barque out of Boston stopped in Shimoda; it was their first contact with Americans in six months. There was no mail aboard, but they reveled in reading the few old newspapers it carried. Harris learned that James Buchanan, the U.S. minister in London with whom he had met on his way to the Far East, had been elected president.

Still, there was no official visit. The *San Jacinto* had promised to return by March. They expected it every day, but to no avail. In April Harris despaired in his journal that he hadn't had a letter from the United States in over a year and that his last instructions from the State Department were eighteen months old. He desperately wanted a naval visit for the news, reassurance, and medical advice that it was sure to bring. April dragged into May and then June. Where was the *San Jacinto*? For that matter, where were the British and French fleets that were expected to follow the United States to Japan? Where was the Russian consul? "I am only nine days from Hong Kong," wrote Harris, "yet I am more isolated than any American official in any part of the world." The State Department, which had promised him that a navy ship would visit every three months, seemed to have totally abandoned him. He had important news to send to Washington about the new convention he negotiated, but he had no way to communicate. What good was his new agreement with Japan if no one knew about it? In July a signal gun finally boomed from a mountaintop above Shimoda, announcing the approach of a ship. Heusken immediately ran up the mountain to check who the visitor might be, only to see the sails receding into the distance; the ship did not pull into Shimoda.

One evening when Harris was having dinner at the governors' house, his hosts began to quiz him about Western women. "I was asked a hundred different questions about American females, as whether single women dressed differently from the married ones, etc., etc.; but I will not soil my paper with the greater part of them, but I clearly perceived that there are particulars that enter into Japanese marriage contracts that are disgusting beyond belief. Bingo-no-Kami [one of the governors] informed me that one of the Vice-Governors was specially charged with the duty of supplying me with female society, and said if I fancied any woman the Vice-Governor would procure her for me, etc., etc., etc."[44] This reference in Harris's journal is the only tantalizing hint in the American historical record of a story that has grown and prospered, the tale of Okichi-san.

According to the Japanese legend, the governors presented Harris with a young woman named Kichi, variously described as a geisha, a courtesan, a concubine, or a prostitute. In the most dramatic version, Kichi is a beautiful girl of seventeen, forced to abandon her love for Tsurumatsu, a ship's carpenter, in order to satisfy the American barbarian, Harris. Poor Kichi is then unfairly stigmatized and shunned by the townspeople for her forced association with a foreigner. After Harris's departure from Shimoda, Kichi turns to drink and eventually, like Madame Butterfly, takes her own life, drowning in a river.

Other versions of the story add further embellishments. One variation has Heusken, as well as Harris, receiving a mistress. Some suggest that Kichi may have been a servant girl on Harris's staff in Shimoda and that in itself was enough to start local tongues wagging. In another popular rendering, Okichi-san (the honorifics "O" and "san" were added to Kichi's name as the story grew) was returned by Harris almost immediately after she was sent to him because she had a skin infection; her shame and humiliation were thus on account of being rejected by a foreigner, not from being his lover. In yet another adaptation, Okichi-san is a Japanese Mata Hari, sent to spy on Harris. Adding an odd twist, Okichi-san's suicide is usually said to have occurred decades after her supposed liaison with Harris, when she was in her fifties, prompted not by the agony of her relationship with him but by the failure of a restaurant she eventually established.

The appealingly tragic story has taken on a life of its own, appearing over the years in poetry, songs, and books. At least five plays are based on the legend. In 1958 Hollywood took on the story, with John Wayne starring as Townsend Harris in a little-acclaimed film, *The Barbarian and the Geisha*.

In the little town of Shimoda, the story has become the basis of a flourishing tourist industry featuring shrines, her grave, her failed restaurant, and museums with illustrations of her in provocative poses. There is even a line of Okichi-san merchandise for tourists.

While the details of the story remain shrouded in legend and the fog of history, official Japanese records provide some basic facts. Okichi was in fact a prostitute working with Shimoda's fishermen. She was provided to Harris under the guise of a "nurse" after he made a request for female companionship (another woman was procured for Heusken). Japanese officials arranged the transaction despite her initial reluctance. Okichi's remuneration, paid by Harris, was far higher than the going rate. The records indicate that Harris quickly tired of her and terminated the relationship after three visits to his residence.[45]

The story was not popularized until the 1920s, when the first of the Okichi-san plays was produced, amid anti-American sentiment after the United States banned immigration from Japan. Ironically, Harris may be better known as the villain of the Okichi-san saga than for his groundbreaking work to open U.S.-Japanese relations.

With the signing of the Convention of Shimoda in June, Harris had met his first objective, making improvements to Perry's treaty. He now began to press harder on his second goal, permission to visit Yedo and meet with the shogun. That, he believed, would put him in position to tackle the third and final goal, the hardest of all: a new treaty that would really open Japan.

About a week after signing the Convention of Shimoda, the governors produced an imperial mandate commanding them to receive the president's letter from Harris. They were dumbfounded when he refused to hand it over. Harris continued to insist that he personally had to hand the letter to the shogun.

More weeks dragged by. There was still no news of the *San Jacinto*, and no other ship visited. Harris's health continued to decline. In late August the governors offered another major concession that might have cheered Harris but did not: he could travel to Yedo and be received by the shogun's High Council but not by the shogun himself. Harris refused, maintaining that it would dishonor the United States if Japan's most senior leader did not receive him. The governors were anguished. They told him that meeting his demands would cause an uprising in the empire. Harris refused to budge.

Harris's fortunes changed suddenly on September 7, 1857. The governors met him again, saying they "were ordered to inform me that I was to proceed to Yedo with every honor: that on my arrival I was to have an immediate interview with the Prime Minister; and, on the first ensuing fortunate day, I should have a public audience of the Ziogoon, and, at that audience, I should deliver the President's letter."[46] Under a compromise arrangement, Harris would not hand the president's letter directly to the shogun, but hand it to the chairman of the High Council, Lord Hotta, in the presence of the shogun. One year and four days after he bid farewell to the *San Jacinto*, Harris had won his second major diplomatic victory. He would be the first westerner received by a shogun since 1638.

His joy increased when the signal gun boomed from the hilltop that very afternoon, announcing the approach of a ship. From shore, they could tell it was a sailing ship, not a steamer, but they could not make out its flag. The winds shifted, and the ship was unable to approach the port, but it fired a gun, announcing its intention to land. Heusken couldn't contain himself. He paid a group of Japanese boatmen to row him out to the ship, which still lay ten miles offshore.

The visitor turned out to be the American sloop of war *Portsmouth*, the same ship that had stood in the harbor of Yerba Buena during the Bear Flag revolt and had refused to assist the American insurrectionists. The ship made its way into the harbor the next morning. Harris went on board to the usual salute of thirteen guns. The ship had not expected to visit Japan, so it did not bring mail or any new word from the State Department. Still, Harris and Heusken were overjoyed to have American visitors with news of the outside world. They learned from the captain why the *San Jacinto* had never returned: a new war had broken out between the British and French and the Chinese (the "Second Opium War"), and the U.S. Pacific squadron had to remain in China to help protect westerners. The war was still under way, which explained why the Europeans, as well as the Americans, had not arrived in Japan as expected. Japan was spared, at least for the moment.

Harris gratefully accepted the captain's hospitality and was embarrassed that he could not reciprocate adequately, since his stores were reduced to fish, rice, and tough chickens. He was doubly grateful that the ship was willing to sell him much needed supplies, including lard, hominy, smoked tongues, and Virginia hams. Harris was relieved finally to be able to send news to the State Department—a copy of the Convention of Shimoda and dispatches explaining all he had done during a year in Japan.

Although the *Portsmouth* did not bring mail, it carried the first newspapers Harris had seen in months. He stayed up all night reading. One article of particular interest was the happy news that the Senate had ratified his treaty with Siam. The *Portsmouth* stayed only a few days in Shimoda before sailing south, leaving Harris and Heusken once again in isolation.

The next two months were consumed with preparations for the visit to Yedo. There was a great deal of back and forth about the specific arrangements, including a half-hearted effort by the Japanese to get Harris to agree to bow to the shogun on his knees and "knock-head" to the ground. Harris refused in a huff. He did agree to make three bows at the waist, as he would do if he were meeting a European monarch. He also agreed to put on a new pair of shoes as he entered the palace; a shoe-bearer thus became part of his retinue. He selected presents for the shogun and the senior ministers at Yedo: "champagne and sherry, wines, cordials and cherry brandy; books of natural history, richly illustrated; telescope; barometer; rich astral lamp; richly cut decanters; preserved fruits, etc., etc."[47] The Japanese for the first time informed him that the proper title of their ruler, the shogun, was "tycoon."

Harris was still "wretchedly ill" during most of this period. On October 4 he remarked in his journal that it was his fifty-third birthday and "My lease is rapidly running to its close. . . . Shall I ever see New York and my dear American friends again? Doubtful."[48]

Heusken, meanwhile, had his own small worries to contend with. He had taken a tumble while out riding his much prized horse and suffered a gash on the top of his head. He had to shave a spot of hair to clean the wound. To his distress, the shaved patch was "precisely at the same spot where the Catholic clergy wear the tonsure." Knowing of Japanese persecution of Catholic missionaries, Heusken feared that when he got to Yedo, he might be mistaken for "a Jesuit or a Franciscan in disguise." He lamented to himself, only half-jokingly, that "if they don't cut off your head immediately, the alarmed authorities of Japan will lock you up in a cage for the rest of your days!"[49]

The trip to Yedo was a grand ceremonial event with every aspect meticulously planned and the same level of pomp accorded to a Japanese prince. Harris warmed immediately to the ceremonial aspects. He decided that the more he surrounded himself with accouterments of grandeur, the more respect he would win from the Japanese. He began to call himself "ambassador," although the United States would not confer that title on an envoy until 1893.[50] His retinue would include a large contingent of guards and servants. Each guard would be armed with two swords, like samurai, and would wear an American coat of arms on his chest, in the same manner that samurai wore the emblems of their lords. Harris would pay for his personal guards, bearers, and grooms so they would be fully under his control, but the Japanese would pay for the "coolies" to transport the baggage.

The procession finally set out for Yedo on November 23, 1857. It was led by men waving bamboo poles with strips of paper attached, who ran ahead yelling, "Kneel down," which the Japanese did as the procession went past. The criers continued their yells even "in the remotest parts of the forests or on the tops of the mountains where there was no one, as if the trees and plants should pay homage" to the American envoy.[51] Behind the criers came a Japanese military officer, followed by an American flag, guarded by two men with American emblems on their breasts. Then came Harris on horseback, with six armed guards wearing American coats of arms. These were followed by Harris's *norimon* (palanquin, or traveling chair) with twelve bearers. Harris hated the small and uncomfortable norimon, which was designed so the rider had to sit on his knees, with his feet behind him. Although Harris much preferred to walk or ride his horse, he used the norimon when passing through towns because this was the custom of Japanese nobility—walking or riding a horse would have signaled that he was a lower-level official and engendered less respect for the United States. Behind the norimon walked Harris's shoe-bearer, umbrella-carrier, and other personal attendants. Then came Heusken on horseback or in his own norimon, with his guards and bearers. Next was a long line of bearers carrying bedding, equipment, chairs, food, trunks, and presents. Following behind were Harris's cook and his other servants. Behind Harris's entourage came other Japanese officials with their guards, retainers, and servants. In all, there were some 350 people in the parade, which stretched out for half a mile along the road.

The cumbersome procession traveled slowly, making only a few miles a day. The trip afforded Harris his first view of Japan outside the narrow confines of Shimoda. He found the countryside beautiful and well tended. The people all seemed to be well clad, well fed, and content, leading him to muse privately that "I sometimes doubt whether the opening of Japan to foreign influences will promote the general happiness of the people."[52] Not long after leaving Shimoda, they got their first view of the snowcapped "Mountain Fusi Yama," which Harris found "grand beyond description" and Heusken described as the most beautiful vista he had ever witnessed. The paths through the mountains were extremely difficult and steep, giving Harris and Heusken their first real sense of how isolated Shimoda was from the rest of Japan.

News of the caravan spread far and wide. Crowds of curious onlookers gathered by the roadsides, dressed in their holiday best, hoping to catch a glimpse of the foreigners. Harris's Japanese escort told him that some people had walked a hundred miles to see him pass. The crowds increased as he approached Yedo. As Harris rode by, they knelt, looked down, and remained silent and motionless. In every town, senior officials saluted him by "knocking head" on the ground. Each village and resting place along the route was festooned with bunting and decorations. The roads were swept clean and closed to other travelers on the days Harris was to pass.

One night they broke their journey in Kanagawa, near where Commodore Perry had negotiated his treaty. Harris was surprised to see three European ships in the harbor, two schooners and a steamer. As he puzzled over the idea of other westerners in Kanagawa, he was told that the ships were in fact Japanese, purchased from the Dutch. Just four years after Perry's first visit, Japan was already beginning to develop a modern navy.

The journey to Yedo took eight days; they entered the city on November 30, 1857. The road into Yedo was level and well tended; they judged that it would have been good for carriages, although carriages were not yet used in Japan. Enormous numbers of people lined the streets, no longer on their knees as in the countryside, but always quiet and respectful. Heusken thought that there must have been a million onlookers; Harris estimated a more modest but still huge 185,000. His hosts told him there would have been millions more, but they had closed the roads to Yedo. The city was divided into walled-off neighborhoods, each separated from the other by a stout gate, about 120 yards apart. As they passed each gate, the neighborhood officials would kneel and "knock head." Harris was well aware that his entry into the capital was a historic moment: "It will form an important epoch in my life, and a still more important one in the history of Japan. I am the first diplomatic representative that has ever been received in this city."[53]

In Yedo they were housed on the grounds of the Imperial Castle. The Japanese had built Western furniture for them, including chairs, tables, and beds. Each of them was provided with a separate bathroom. On arrival, they were introduced to eight senior nobles who had been assigned as "Commissioners of the Voyage of the American Ambassador to Yedo." The commissioners appeared with hundreds of retainers and welcomed them with great ceremony. Amusingly for the Americans, the chief commissioner kept changing places as he spoke to them, standing in one spot when he spoke in the name of the shogun and moving to a different side of the room when he spoke in his own name. Harris had to keep changing places with him. After the ceremony, Harris penned a formal letter to Lord Hotta, who served as the equivalent of both prime minister and foreign minister, to inform him officially of his arrival. He proudly headed the message "U.S. Legation, City of Yedo," the first ever such letter. The day ended with a present from the tycoon, a seventy-pound box of Japanese sweets and bonbons. Heusken recorded that "there was enough to fill the shop of a confectioner and make ill an infinite number of children."[54]

A few days later Harris called formally on Lord Hotta, who Heusken described as "a man of most charming manners. He has a very gentle countenance and he smiles with a great deal of charm. He is 45 yrs old. He stammers a little when speaking, and seemed a little ill at ease." If Hotta was ill at ease, his aides were far more nervous. "The agitation of the Japanese interpreter is beyond anything I ever saw,—he trembled all over his body as though he had an ague fit, while large drops of perspiration stood like beads on his forehead."[55] The meeting went well, however, and Harris's audience with the tycoon was set for December 7, ironically, a day that would later live in infamy as Pearl Harbor Day.

On the appointed day, Harris was carried to his audience in his norimon, accompanied by his procession of guards and followers. He wore his diplomatic dress uniform, and Heusken wore a navy uniform, as authorized by the State Department. Before entering the palace, Harris was handed clean shoes by his shoe-bearer. While the Western dress certainly looked curious to the Japanese, Harris and Heusken found the Japanese court dress to be equally odd. The nobles wore breeches "of yellow silk, and the legs are some six to seven feet long! Consequently, when the wearer walks, they stream out behind him and give him the appearance of walking on his knees, an illusion which is helped out by the short stature of the Japanese."[56]

Outside the reception room, Harris and Heusken passed six or seven hundred court nobles on their knees. Once inside, Harris was asked to enter the inner chamber to rehearse for the meeting. To the consternation of his hosts, he declined, saying no rehearsal was necessary. The inner chamber, where he would meet the tycoon, was divided from the rest of the hall by a sliding paper door so that those outside could hear but not see the conversation. At the appointed hour, the court nobles accompanying Harris fell to their knees and crawled toward the door of the inner chamber. As Harris entered, standing erect, a chamberlain cried out, "Embassador Merrican!"

The tycoon sat on a platform two feet higher than the rest of the room. He wore a silk outfit with a little gold woven in, "but it was as distant from anything like regal splendor as could be conceived. No rich jewels, no elaborate gold ornaments, no diamond hilted weapon appeared, and I can safely say that my dress was far more costly than his."[57] Harris later described the tycoon as a "wretchedly-delicate-looking" old man.[58]

As agreed, Harris bowed at the waist three times and then addressed the tycoon briefly, offering the president's wishes for the emperor's health and happiness and for the prosperity of the empire. Harris spoke for just a minute or two, stressing his desire for a firm friendship between Japan and the United States. The Japanese told him afterward that they were surprised he did not tremble before the tycoon, as they had expected. After Harris's remarks, the tycoon spoke two sentences, which were translated by Heusken: "Pleased with the letter sent with the Ambassador from a far distant country, and likewise pleased with his discourse. Intercourse shall be continued for ever." [59]

After the tycoon's remarks, Heusken advanced from the back of the room carrying the president's letter in a box covered with red and white striped silk. As he walked forward slowly, he couldn't help thinking to himself about the Japanese exclusion edict—still officially in force—which proclaimed death for anyone carrying a letter from abroad. The letter was actually addressed to the emperor rather than the shogun and was signed by President Pierce, who had been replaced almost a year earlier by President Buchanan. Neither side allowed these details to spoil the ceremony. Lord Hotta stood and took the letter, placed it on a table, then prostrated himself again. The meeting was over.

The audience with the tycoon marked a watershed for Harris. He had been officially received in the capital, at the highest level, with full honors, as a diplomatic representative. He was opening doors that had been tightly shut for hundreds of years. And he had achieved this through patience and discussion, without gunboats in the harbor.

Harris knew, however, that his work was not over. He still needed to begin negotiations on a new treaty that would really open Japan. He made his move in a long, pivotal meeting with Lord Hotta and the council on December 12. He began by describing the dangers facing Japan from imperialist powers, primarily the British. Foreign fleets were certain to visit Japan soon, and they would make demands far beyond what the United States had asked. Harris had plenty of examples to draw on, most convincingly the ongoing war in China, where the British and French were running roughshod over that once powerful nation. The British were also busy colonizing India and other parts of Asia. Russia posed yet another threat. Japan's policy of exclusion was no longer viable, he argued; it would lead to ruin and destruction. But Harris also offered a way out: the Japanese government could save face by reaching a peaceful agreement with him rather than one dictated by a foreign fleet. Other Western nations, Harris said, would be satisfied with whatever the United States negotiated, whereas if there were no agreement, they would demand much more. Harris stressed that the United States, unlike Britain, France, and Russia, had no territorial ambitions. Unlike the British, the United States would be willing to prohibit the importation of opium. Unlike the Spanish and Portuguese, the United States was not bent on religious conversion of the Japanese. In short, he was offering the best deal they were likely to get.

The United States, he said, wanted three things from Japan: permanent diplomatic representation at Yedo, freedom for Americans to trade without government interference, and the opening of additional ports. Harris also explained at great length the potential benefits Japan could reap from free trade, especially the revenue the government could expect from import and export duties. Most of these arguments were not new to the Japanese. This was the first time, however, that the most senior Japanese officials had ever heard such a reasoned and detailed exposition from a westerner of what lay ahead. It had a powerful effect. Lord Hotta was impressed with the arguments and assured Harris that they would be carefully considered. The negotiation had begun.

Harris remained in Yedo for months, holding more than twenty laborious negotiating sessions. He acted as professor as well as negotiator, tutoring the Japanese on concepts that were new to them, including aspects of international law, trade, tariffs, and diplomacy. Many terms did not exist in Japanese, further complicating the talks and posing a challenge especially for Heusken to explain. Harris faced endless questions: What would be the duties, ranks, and privileges of diplomatic envoys? Would they have to reside at Yedo, or could they be based elsewhere? What did he mean by government interference in trade? What were trade regulations, and how did they work? What Japanese products were wanted in the West? Could certain exports—rice, for example—be excluded from trade? Could the importation of armaments be prohibited? Would Americans have the right to move freely around the cities, or could their movements be limited? And the most difficult questions: which cities would have to be opened, when, and what exactly did "open" mean?

All of this required enormous patience. The talks sometimes drove Harris to despair. To facilitate the discussion, he put forward a model treaty, which he explained article by article. Often they agreed with a point one day, only to withdraw agreement the next. In addition there were "many absurd proposals made by them, without the hope, and scarcely the wish, of having them accepted." The rule of Japanese diplomacy, he wrote in his journal, is that "he who shows the greatest absurdity . . . is most esteemed." At one point Harris remarked wryly, "They were so unreasonable and so inconsistent that I could not help suspecting the champagne which I sent to them had not operated favorably."[60] By year's end, Harris was discouraged. He was again seriously ill. On January 1, 1858, he mused in his journal that he might never see the start of another new year.

As the negotiations lagged, Harris decided to create a crisis, as he had done in Shimoda a few months earlier with positive results. On January 9 he told the chief Japanese negotiator that he had had enough. Unless the Japanese showed they were serious about a treaty,

he would return immediately to Shimoda and leave them to negotiate with others, who would use cannon balls as their arguments. It
was a high-risk strategy. If he didn't get a positive answer, he would
have no choice but to break off the talks. His mission would end in
failure. Harris nervously awaited the Japanese response.

The answer from Lord Hotta came a few days later: Japan agreed
to each of his three main points. They just needed to work out the
details. With this agreement in principle, it took only a few more
weeks to negotiate a draft treaty.

It was during this period that Harris finally began to understand
more clearly the intricacies of the Japanese government and the
internal obstacles to concluding a treaty. He was surprised to hear
his counterparts speak "almost contemptuously of the Mikado, and
[they] roared with laughter when I quoted some remarks concerning the veneration in which he is held by the Japanese."[61] Particularly troubling to Harris, however, was his growing understanding
of the depth of opposition to a treaty among most of the nobles, as
well as within the army and even inside the tycoon's Council. Several points in the draft treaty, Harris was told repeatedly, could lead
to internal upheaval and bloodshed. As Heusken put it, "Japan is
in a dangerous position. On the one hand, she is threatened with
war and conquest if she does not grant certain privileges. On the
other, her people will revolt if she does grant these privileges."[62]

Harris found that he himself was also in danger; the commissioners told him they had broken up a plot to murder him. Three
*ronin*—or rogue samurai—were captured and had confessed. The
plot against Harris later became the basis of a popular play in Japan.

Throughout the weeks of negotiations, Harris and Heusken had
barely left the tycoon's compound. Their hosts asked them not to
wander the streets, since it could be dangerous or might spark
embarrassing incidents that would complicate the negotiations.
Harris insisted that they at least be given someplace to exercise, so
the Japanese set aside a military parade ground where they could
walk or ride their horses each afternoon.

The draft treaty was completed in mid-February. It included virtually everything Harris initially wanted, plus more. An American

minister would be permitted to reside in Yedo and would be free to travel throughout Japan. Other Americans could reside permanently at open ports in Japan and could lease land and erect buildings. Americans would enjoy extraterritorial rights. They would be free to practice their religion and to build houses of worship. A depot could be established for American naval stores. Japanese and American coinage of equal weight would be exchanged with no commission. Most important, however, the draft treaty established free trade without government interference. It provided for detailed trade regulations and duties low enough to encourage both exports and imports. Finally but not least, six ports would be opened to Americans within a period of two years after the treaty's ratification.

To Harris's great pleasure, the Japanese asked to send a diplomatic mission to the United States. He happily agreed and modified the draft treaty to set Washington as the venue for the exchange of ratifications. This request confirmed that Japan's door was really swinging open. Just months earlier, no Japanese could leave the country on pain of death. Now a group of senior officials was planning to visit the United States.

More trouble lay ahead, however. As word of the treaty's provisions began to circulate among the nobles, internal opposition increased. The vast majority of nobles disapproved of the treaty. Those who backed it, such as Lord Hotta and the powerful Lord Ii, did so more out of a sense of necessity than enthusiasm. Meanwhile, the treaty issue was caught up in what seemed to the Japanese to be an even more pressing internal issue: the shogun's health was failing, and he had no son, so a succession struggle was brewing.

The Japanese explained these problems to Harris only in general terms. In order to overcome internal opposition, they informed him, signing the treaty would have to be delayed while they obtained approval from the emperor, the mikado. This mystified Harris. Just days before, they had belittled the mikado; now they wanted his approval. Japanese politics were still impenetrable to an outsider. What if the mikado didn't approve? The Japanese replied that they would not take "no" for an answer. In addition, they intimated, large sums of money were being distributed to the mikado's retainers to enlist their support. The Japanese said they would need two months to overcome internal opposition. Harris reluctantly agreed.

At this point Harris's health took another downturn, so severe that it threatened his life. By late February he was too weak to move from his bed. Worried that his death would undo everything he had achieved, Harris had Heusken prepare the treaty in final form and then signed two copies. The Japanese could sign later, if necessary, even after his death. He had a copy of the signed treaty delivered to the Japanese and in return was given a letter pledging they would sign by April 21. With this promise in hand, he decided to return to Shimoda, where he might be more comfortable waiting in his own home. The Japanese sent their only steamer to take him back, saving him the arduous overland trip.

In Shimoda, Harris's condition went from bad to worse. By March 10 Heusken recorded, "Last night, Mr. Harris moaned horribly. He fell from his bed this morning and could not get up. . . . The doctor comes [and says] it will be difficult to cure him. Mr. Harris scarcely recognizes me" and cannot hear me when I speak. The next day, brown and purple spots began to appear on his body. The doctors said the end was at hand. Harris awoke only intermittently over the next two days to tell Heusken, "You are a good boy and a true friend. I leave the care of my soul to you." And "I want you to write to the President that, if he approves of my conduct here, he exhibit me as minister upon my return."[63]

Over the next few days, to the amazement of the doctors, Harris woke from his delirium and began slowly to recover. He sat in a chair for part of each day. He smoked opium to cope with the lingering pain. By late March the danger had passed, and he was anxious to return to Yedo. Throughout his illness, the Japanese had been extremely solicitous. The tycoon himself had sent the doctors to tend him, as well as kind messages and presents.

On April 15 Harris, still not fully recovered, was carried on board the Japanese steamer for the trip back to Yedo. He anticipated that the treaty would be signed within a week. It was not to be. The mission to seek the mikado's endorsement had ended in failure, as too many members of the imperial court opposed opening Japan. In fact, the request to the mikado had backfired: his refusal marked the beginning of what would become a political resurgence for the mikado. A second mission also failed. The first signs of a power struggle between the shogun and the mikado were emerging; the treaty became a weapon for the mikado's followers to use against the shogun.

At this point, the ailing shogun gave Lord Ii the powers of regent, tipping the internal power balance in Yedo in favor of the treaty, even though the majority was still opposed.

Ii understood the need for the treaty and was committed to it, but he first needed to settle the succession question to ensure a new shogun who would support his decisions. Ii needed time. He sent Lord Hotta to tell Harris he would have to wait.

Harris, who had waited in Yedo six more weeks beyond the promised date, had begun to understand how difficult the internal situation really was. He knew that anti-treaty lords had called for Hotta's death and his own. Anti-treaty forces were rallying under the slogan "honor the emperor and expel the barbarians."[64] Harris did not want to precipitate a civil war, but he was certain that the failure of the treaty would lead to an international war. He walked a fine line, avoiding threats, but cautioning again about the dangers ahead if Japan did not sign the treaty before the British and French fleets appeared. Hotta assured him it was just a question of time. He gave Harris a written pledge that Japan would sign by September 4, a delay of more than four months, together with a friendly letter from the tycoon to the president—the first letter from the tycoon to a foreign leader in more than two hundred years. At Harris's request, Hotta added a commitment that Japan would not sign a treaty with any other government until at least thirty days after signing the American treaty. With these in hand, Harris agreed to return to Shimoda and resume his wait.

Six weeks later, at the end of July, the U.S. warships *Mississippi* and *Powhatan* arrived in Shimoda with news that the war in China was over. The foreign fleets would soon arrive in Japan. Harris wrote immediately to Lord Hotta to say time was up; the treaty had to be signed "without the loss of a single day."[65] Harris set off for Yedo at once, arriving on July 27. The Japanese were in a quandary. Opposition to the treaty was still running high. The mikado still had not approved. But the wolf was at the door. Hotta sought one last concession. Would Harris pledge that the British and French would accept the U.S. treaty as the basis for their own and, if not, would Harris act as a mediator with them? Harris could not make a pledge on behalf of another country, but he did put in writing for the Japanese his conviction that they would accept and his pledge to act as a friendly mediator if necessary. With this last assurance in hand, Lord Ii took the responsibility upon himself and made the fateful decision. The Japanese commissioners went aboard the *Powhatan* on July 29 and signed the treaty. The flags of both countries were hoisted to a 21-gun salute. The saga was over; Japan was open.

It had taken almost two years of often agonizing work for Harris to complete the treaty. He was elated to achieve his goal and even more so that he did it peacefully. He had developed a deep respect for the Japanese. He was convinced that the treaty was in their interest as well as American interest. He was fully aware what a momentous achievement it was. On August 2 Harris wrote gleefully to his friend Sir John Bowring, the British consul general in Hong Kong, that the British and French envoys en route to Japan "will find their work all done . . . when they arrive, and that a large fleet was not required as a demonstration."[66]

Within the next two weeks the foreign fleets did arrive, first the Russians, followed closely by the British, the Dutch, and then the French. By one account, they "were amazed to find that the lonely American consul-general had won, unsupported, all that they well could ask."[67] The British ships stopped first at Shimoda, where they "experienced great civility and kindness from Mr. Harris . . . but were more especially indebted to him for the liberality with which he supplied a most important deficiency, in placing at Lord Elgin's disposal the services of his excellent Dutch interpreter, Mr. Hewsken." They were astonished to find that after two years of "exile" in hostile Japan, Harris had a high regard for the Japanese and their "amiable qualities and charming natural dispositions." The British were also impressed with the U.S. treaty.[68] Within a few weeks, Japan had signed treaties with the Dutch, Russians, and British, all nearly identical to the U.S. treaty.

In mid-August, as the European fleets arrived, the old shogun died. Lord Ii was able to have his favorite, still a boy, installed as the new shogun. Ii dismissed the faithful Lord Hotta because of differences over the succession question. Several years later Hotta's political enemies got further revenge, having him sentenced to house arrest for life for his role in opening Japan.[69] The Japanese kept the shogun's death a secret from the foreigners for more than a month. The European squadrons came and went with their new treaties in hand and with virtually no understanding of the changes under way in Japan. Only Harris remained in the country.

With the field to himself and an eye toward his treaty's place in history, Harris persuaded the Japanese to sign another agreement that they would exchange instruments of ratification with the United States before doing so with any other country. Washington would be the first capital visited by a Japanese envoy. The Japanese were still planning to send a mission to Washington with the ratified treaty, but this would take a year to get organized.

In May 1859 Harris took his first break from Japan in more than two and a half years. When the *Mississippi* arrived back in Shimoda, Harris, who had been ill again, put himself under the care of the ship's surgeon. He decided to spend a few weeks in China to relax and recuperate. While in Shanghai, Harris learned that he had been promoted; in January the Senate had confirmed his appointment as the first U.S. resident minister in Japan.

Harris returned to Japan in June. He moved the American consulate from Shimoda to Kanagawa, one of the newly opened towns, raising the flag there on the Fourth of July. This was the town on Yedo Bay where Perry had signed his treaty. The Japanese were busily developing a new port for foreign trade at the nearby village of Yokohama, where they were building piers, landing places, a customs house, and homes for consuls and traders. Harris objected to this as an effort to isolate westerners, as had been done in Nagasaki. He and other foreign representatives insisted on placing their consulates in Kanagawa, three miles away, in accordance with the treaties. The foreign traders, however, were pleased with the facilities in Yokohama and happily settled there; the consulates eventually followed in their wake.

On July 7, 1859, Harris raised the Stars and Stripes over the first American legation in Japan, situated in a former Buddhist temple in Yedo.

Harris remained in Japan for three more years. In some ways, life settled into a diplomatic routine. As the longest serving and best-connected foreigner in Yedo, he often had deeper insights into Japanese politics than the other envoys who increasingly made their way to Japan. He began to discern the growing strength of the mikado and had a better understanding of the internal disputes dividing the country. Harris won substantial respect from both his colleagues and the Japanese. Heusken, too, was much happier in Yedo, away from the social isolation of Shimoda. He was popular in the small Western community, admired for his fluent Japanese, and regarded as one of the best-informed foreigners in the country. His name is mentioned with affection in many travel accounts published by westerners about Japan. Heusken was also promoted, moving beyond his duties as interpreter to become a diplomatic officer of the American legation. His future looked bright.

One of the highlights of these years was the Japanese mission to the United States. The delegation included seventy-one people. They traveled in early 1860 aboard the *Powhatan* to San Francisco and then to Panama, where they crossed the isthmus and then were conveyed on another American warship to Washington. The delegation was welcomed enthusiastically in the United States, entertained by President Buchanan, and feted in several East Coast cities. Gold medals were struck in honor of the visit. The Americans were amused to find their visitors constantly stopping to sketch points of interest, foreshadowing, perhaps, the camera-packing tour groups of the next century. The mission was a great success, helping to solidify the warm ties Harris had worked so hard to launch.

Overshadowing other issues, however, was an increasingly dangerous security situation for foreigners in Japan. Groups of ronin were outraged at the presence of foreigners and began to take their revenge, both against the foreigners and against the government. The first assassinations took place almost immediately after the opening of the new Western consulates and legations. In August 1859, three Russian sailors were cut down in Yokohama. The Japanese government forestalled the kind of reprisals often taken by Western fleets by quickly expressing its regrets, executing the culprits, and dismissing the governor of Yokohama.

More assassinations followed: a Chinese employee of the French consulate, a Japanese interpreter of the British legation, and two Dutch merchants. The Japanese offered protection for the consulates and legations, but the westerners initially declined, fearing a Japanese ruse to isolate them. Most foreigners began to arm themselves, even wearing weapons in diplomatic meetings with the Japanese. Harris and Heusken were exceptions, refusing to carry arms.

In March 1860 Lord Ii was cut down by sword-wielding assassins just outside the shogun's palace. It was a tragedy of major proportions, which finally convinced the doubting westerners that the Japanese truly faced a serious internal threat.

A few months later, tragedy struck again. Henry Heusken had been helping a newly arrived Prussian delegation negotiate a treaty with Japan. He had taken to spending the evenings with friends at the Prussian residence and returning to the American legation after dark. The ronin attacked Heusken on the evening of January 14, 1861. He was severely wounded with several cuts from the assassins' samurai swords. The attackers then melted into the night and disappeared. Heusken was carried to the American legation, where British and Prussian doctors attended him. It was no use. He died a few minutes after midnight, just two days short of his twenty-ninth birthday.

Harris was heartbroken. He wrote to the secretary of state a few days later: "It is my melancholy duty to inform you of the death of Mr. Henry C. J. Heusken, the able efficient and faithful Interpreter of this Legation. . . . I am suffering deeply from this sudden and awful catastrophe. Mr. Heusken was associated with me over five years, and he was the companion of my long solitude at Simoda. Our relations were rather those of father and son, than *chef* and *employe*."[70] Harris arranged an elaborate funeral, which was attended by senior Japanese officials, an unusual sign of respect. Heusken was interred in a Buddhist cemetery. His aging tombstone still stands outside a temple in Tokyo.

On April 12, 1861, in the harbor of Charleston, South Carolina, Brig. Gen. P. T. G. Beauregard of the Confederate States of America gave the order to open fire on Fort Sumter. The Civil War had begun.

About the same time, but well before the news reached Japan, Harris submitted his resignation to the new president, Abraham Lincoln. Harris cited his advancing age—he was fifty-six—and his continuing ill health. With the opening of Japan, Harris had completed his greatest achievement. He was tired. He had been in Japan for five years with only one short break. He had been back to the United States only once in eleven years, the brief trip in 1855 when he was appointed consul general. It was time to go home.

When the Japanese learned of Harris's plan, they sent Secretary of State Seward a letter "testifying to his ability, knowledge of the country, and friendly attitude, and begging that he be allowed to remain."[71] Seward, in turn, wrote Harris, "I regard your retirement from the important post you have filled with such distinguished ability and success as a subject of grave anxiety, not only for this country, but for all the Western nations."[72] Harris was determined, however, and by the fall Lincoln had accepted his resignation with "profound regret."[73] Harris agreed to remain in Yedo until a replacement could be named.

Harris's able successor, Robert Pruyn, arrived in Japan on April 25, 1862. The next day, Harris made his farewell call on the shogun. He left Japan on May 8 and returned to the war-torn United States. He lived his remaining years quietly in a boarding house in his beloved New York City. At the war's end, he sent General Grant the ceremonial sword presented to him by the shogun at his farewell call, as a token of thanks for saving the Union. He resumed his civic activities, joining scholarly societies and helping found the New York Society for the Prevention of Cruelty to Animals. He traveled a bit, including to Europe with members of his family. Harris died in 1878 at the age of seventy-four. His grave at Greenwood Cemetery in Brooklyn is marked by a Japanese stone lantern and a cherry tree.

In Japan, internal troubles mounted, breaking into open conflict by 1864. In early 1868, forces loyal to the mikado overthrew the shogun and claimed political power for the first time in seven hundred years. Ironically this upheaval, which began on a demand to expel the barbarians and maintain Japan's isolation, promptly reversed itself and became the country's great modernizer. Within a single generation, Japan transformed itself into one of the world's great powers. Throughout this period, the Harris treaty and others modeled on it remained the basis of Japan's foreign relations.

American influence in Japan and elsewhere in Asia declined as a result of the Civil War. Harris did win some praise at home for his work in Japan, but by the time he returned, Americans were focused firmly on the war, and developments in Asia were no more than an afterthought. The magnitude of Harris's achievements was never fully understood or appreciated by the American public. He remains far better remembered in Japan than in the United States.

# Afterword

**M**ost of the diplomatic cast of characters that first raised the Stars and Stripes in faraway corners of the globe have been long forgotten. Their statues do not adorn city squares; their names and exploits are seldom mentioned, even in textbooks on diplomatic history. Some of their stories died with them; others remain buried in dusty archives, waiting to be unearthed.

For all their anonymity, however, the influence of these early envoys was profound. Their stories help explain how the United States, even in its formative years, began to shape today's world. Their activities also highlight the impact that individual diplomats have had on some of the most significant events of American history. Most of all, their work illustrates the often-overlooked importance of U.S. diplomacy in achieving American goals, spreading American influence, and advancing American interests.

In many instances, it was also the diplomats who brought knowledge of the world home to the public and inspired the great events that followed. Samuel Shaw's letters sparked direct trade with China, launching a thousand ships to the Orient. Thomas Larkin's tireless efforts helped inspire a popular perception of California as a utopia, contributing to a burgeoning wave of American settlers moving west and in the process tipping the demographic balance toward acquisition. Joel Poinsett's *Notes on Mexico* was the first American book to provide a serious description of our neighbor to the south, shaping public images that lasted for generations. Edmund Roberts, David Porter, and Jacques-Antoine Moerenhout published books opening new vistas on little-known countries and whetting American interest in the world.

America's early envoys lived and worked in a world on the cusp of monumental change. By the eve of the Civil War, new technologies were beginning to transform communications and transportation in ways that would forever alter the conduct of diplomacy. Regular steamship service between the United States and a few foreign ports was starting to break down barriers of time and space. In 1866 the first successful transatlantic telegraph cable was laid, providing instantaneous, although not yet reliable, communications between the United States and Europe. In 1869 the transcontinental railroad was completed, linking California with the eastern states and reducing travel time across North America from as long as six months to as little as a week. Leaders in Washington could maintain better contact with many American envoys and closer control over them. The days of isolated diplomats and consuls forced to act on their own instincts, without guidance or instructions, would soon come to an end. Most post–Civil War envoys would operate in a very different environment.

The accounts in this book represent just a few of the countless stories of courage, hardship, innovation, and adventure faced by the many extraordinary individuals who represented the United States abroad during the country's formative years. These stories just scratch the surface. Dozens more envoys planted the flag for the first time in other countries around the world. Thousands more contributed to the panoply of foreign affairs, establishing relations, deepening cooperation, building peace, defending American interests and values, developing commerce, and protecting citizens. Each diplomatic venture held—and continues to hold—its own dangers, its own promise, and its own rewards or tragedy. Later American envoys would continue to experience their own travels, troubles, and adventures, many of them every bit as exotic, extraordinary, and influential as the ones recounted here. Those tales, however, are for another day.

# Notes

## Introduction

1. For a fuller description of American diplomatic and consular titles, duties, and prerogatives, see Eicher, ed., *"Emperor Dead" and Other Historic American Diplomatic Dispatches*, 7–16.

2. Smith, *America's Diplomats and Consuls of 1776–1865*, 8.

## 1. For Tea and Country

1. Shaw, *Journals*, 10.

2. Shaw, *Journals*, 58.

3. Shaw, *Journals*, 61–62.

4. Shaw, *Journals*, 38; Smith, *Empress of China*, 60.

5. Shaw, *Journals*, 110–11.

6. The Society continues to exist, with impressive headquarters at Anderson House on Massachusetts Avenue in Washington DC. It has sometimes been criticized as elitist or aristocratic, since membership is generally limited to direct descendants of officers who served the American cause in the Revolution. The Society's current missions are patriotic, historical, and educational.

7. Wang, "Benjamin Franklin and China," 8, referring to *Pennsylvania Gazette*, March 17 and 21, 1738.

8. Fairbank, *The United States and China*, 132.

9. Ledyard, *The Last Voyage of Captain Cook*, 46.

10. Smith, *Empress of China*, 7–8.

11. Armstrong, "Opening China."

12. "Wildlife Trade, Traditional Chinese Medicine," 2016. https://web.archive.org/web/20041102011243/http://www.worldwildlife.org/trade/tcm.cfm.

13. Wang, "Benjamin Franklin and China," 32.

14. Smith, *Empress of China*, 38–42.

15. Smith, *Empress of China*, 61.

16. Smith, *Empress of China*, 67–69.

17. Smith, *Empress of China*, 70.

18. Shaw, *Journals*, 112.

19. Shaw to Jay, May 19, 1785, in *The Diplomatic Correspondence of the United States of America, from the Signing of the Definitive Treaty of Peace, 10th September 1783, until the Adoption of the Constitution, March 4, 1798* (hereafter *Diplomatic Correspondence*), 7:337.

20. Green, *A Journal of an Intended Voyage*, 79.

21. Shaw, *Journals*, 134.

22. Smith, *Empress of China*, 254.

23. Shaw, *Journals*, 134–36; Smith, *Empress of China*, 255.

24. Shaw, *Journals*, 142, 138.

25. Green, *A Journal of an Intended Voyage*, 108.

26. Green, *A Journal of an Intended Voyage*, 159.

27. Armstrong, "Opening China."

28. *Modern Gazetteer* 2 (1799): 192.

29. Shaw, *Journals*, 163.

30. Smith, *Empress of China*, 152.

31. Shaw to John Jay, December 31, 1786, in *Diplomatic Correspondence*, 460–61.

32. Shaw, *Journals*, 176.

33. Smith, *Empress of China*, 182.

34. Armstrong, "Opening China."

35. Shaw, *Journals*, 172.

36. Shaw, *Journals*, 179.

37. Fairbank, Reischaur, and Craig, *East Asia*, 73.

38. "Platter, Order of the Cincinnati, c. 1785."

39. Shaw, *Journals*, 199.

40. "Society of the Cincinnati Chocolate Pot and Two-Handled Mugs, ca. 1790."

41. Shaw to Jay, May 19, 1785, *Diplomatic Correspondence*, 432.

42. Shaw to Jay, May 19, 1785, 433.

43. Shaw, *Journals*, 190.

44. Shaw to Jay, May 19, 1785, *Diplomatic Correspondence*, 434.

45. Shaw, *Journals*, 195.

46. Shaw, *Journals*, 210.

47. Winsor, *Memorial History of Boston*, 204.

48. Shaw to Jay, May 19, 1785, *Diplomatic Correspondence*, 434–35.

49. Jefferson to the Count de Vergenes, October 11, 1785, *Diplomatic Correspondence*, 707.

50. Jay to Shaw, June 23, 1785, *Diplomatic Correspondence*, 437.

51. Armstrong, "Opening China," 249. John Green was once again recruited as captain. Within a few years the ship was starting to decay. She sank off Dublin Harbor in 1791.

52. Shaw, *Journals*, 114.

53. John Jay to the President of Congress, January 20, 1786, *Diplomatic Correspondence*, 439–40.

54. John Jay to Samuel Shaw, January 30, 1786, *Diplomatic Correspondence*, 440.

55. John Jay to Samuel Shaw, January 30, 1786, *Diplomatic Correspondence*, 440–41.

56. Shaw to Jay, January 30, 1786, *Diplomatic Correspondence*, 441–42.

57. Shaw, *Journals*, 220.

58. Shaw, *Journals*, 221.

59. Morison, *Maritime History of Massachusetts*, 66.

60. Shaw to Jay, December 31, 1786, *Diplomatic Correspondence*, 465.

61. Shaw to Jay, December 31, 1786, *Diplomatic Correspondence*, 452.

62. Shaw to Jay, December 31, 1786, *Diplomatic Correspondence*, 463.

63. Shaw to Jay, December 31, 1786, *Diplomatic Correspondence*, 462.

64. Shaw to Jay, December 31, 1786, *Diplomatic Correspondence*, 462.

65. Shaw, *Journals*, 195–97.

66. Shaw, *Journals*, 238.

67. Fairbank, Reischaur, and Craig, *East Asia*, 131.

68. Shaw, *Journals*, 183.

69. Shaw, *Journals*, 248–49.

70. Shaw, *Journals*, 250.

71. Winsor, *Memorial History of Boston*, 208.

72. Morison, *Maritime History of Massachusetts*, 66.

73. "Object of the Month: The Columbia and Washington Medal."

74. Morison, *Maritime History of Massachusetts*, 67.

75. Winsor, *Memorial History of Boston*, 207.

76. Paine, *The Old Merchant Marine*, 82–84.

77. Barnes and Morgan, *The Foreign Service of the United States*, 32.

78. Bemis, *A Diplomatic History of the United States*, 342.

79. Samuel Shaw to George Washington, December 7, 1790, *Diplomatic Correspondence*, 473–74.

80. Paine, *The Old Merchant Marine*.

81. *The Writings of Thomas Jefferson*, ed. Lipscomb, 49–50. A surety bond is a guarantee intended to ensure the honesty and faithful performance of people appointed to positions of public trust.

82. Lay, *The Foreign Service of the United States*, 10.

83. Shaw, *Journals*, 124.

84. Morison, *Maritime History of Massachusetts*, 45.

85. Dennett, *Americans in Eastern Asia*, 63.

86. The Convention on International Trade in Endangered Species lists American ginseng as protected and strictly regulates its international trade.

87. U.S. Fish and Wildlife Service, "Sea Otters and the Endangered Species Act."

88. "1790 Northwest China Trade."

## 2. To the Shores of Tripoli

1. *Modern Gazetteer* 2 (1799): 552, 556.

2. De la Croix, *Géographie du Monde*, 322.

3. Cooper, *History of the Navy*, 168.

4. Cathcart, *The Captives*, 5. Some accounts have misnamed the ship the *Dolphin*.

5. Cathcart Family Papers, biographical sketch, New York Public Library Rare Books and Manuscripts Division.

6. Cathcart, *The Captives*, 7–8.

7. Cathcart, *The Captives*, 12.

8. Cathcart, *The Captives*, 26.

9. Baepler, *White Slaves, African Masters*, 83.

10. Cathcart, *The Captives*, 31.

11. Cathcart, *The Captives*, 116.

12. David Humphreys to Robert Montgomery, December 1, 1793, in *"Emperor Dead,"* 51, ed. Eicher, 51.

13. Cathcart, *The Captives*, 149.

14. Cathcart, *The Captives*, 137.

15. John Adams to John Jay, January 27, 1787, *Diplomatic Correspondence*, 2:694. Barclay suffered his own difficulties after his return to France, ending up arrested for debt despite his consular status. Jefferson, with difficulty, arranged his release. Barclay would return to Morocco as consul in 1791.

16. Notes on a letter from Mathew Irwin to George Washington, July 9, 1789, Papers of George Washington, https://founders.archives.gov/documents/Washington /05–03–02–0079–0001.

17. Cathcart, *The Captives*, 137–38.

18. Todd, *Life and Letters of Joel Barlow*, 116.

19. Cooper, *History of the Navy*, 171.

20. Irwin, *Diplomatic Relations of the United States with the Barbary Powers*, 70.

21. *Historical Statistics of the United States, Colonial Times to 1970*, part 2, 1:106.

22. Cooper, *History of the Navy*, 172.

23. Baldwin, *Joel Barlow*, 421.

24. Douty, *Hasty Pudding and Barbary Pirates*, 33, 96.

25. Cathcart, *The Captives*, 173, 182–85.

26. Cooper, *History of the Navy*, 174, 176.

27. Baepler, *White Slaves, African Masters*, 98–99.

28. Todd, *Life and Letters of Joel Barlow*, 125–26, 130.

29. Todd, *Life and Letters of Joel Barlow*, 126–27.

30. On its way back to Algiers, the ship was seized as a prize by the British. The owners, the same Jewish bankers who had lent Barlow the money to free the prisoners, sent Barlow a bill for forty thousand dollars for the ship, which Barlow agreed to pay.

31. Cathcart, *The Captives*, 218, 269.

32. Todd, *Life and Letters of Joel Barlow*, 138.

33. Miller, *Treaties and Other International Acts of the United States of America*, 364–66.

34. Minnigerode, *Lives and Times*, 58.

35. Irwin, *The Diplomatic Relations of the United States with the Barbary Powers*, 100–101.

36. Cooper, *History of the Navy*, 215.

37. Minnigerode, *Lives and Times*, 61.

38. Cathcart to Eaton, August 8, 1799, *Letter Book*, 59.

39. Cathcart to Eaton, July 7, 1799, *Letter Book*, 59.

40. Cathcart to Eaton, July 7, 1799, *Letter Book*, 59.

41. Cathcart to Pickering, June 9, 1799, *Letter Book*, 51.

42. Cathcart to Eaton, November 9, 1799, *Letter Book*, 91.

43. Secretary of the Navy to Commodore Dale, May 20, 1801, *American State Papers*, 359.

44. Irwin, *The Diplomatic Relations of the United States with the Barbary Powers*, 98.

45. Cathcart to Madison, May 16, 1801, in *"Emperor Dead,"* ed. Eicher, 58.

46. Cathcart to Madison, July 2, 1801, *American State Papers*, 699.

47. Eaton to Madison, September 3, 1801, *American State Papers*, 699.

48. Cathcart to Madison, August 25, 1802, *American State Papers*, 700.

49. Madison to Cathcart, August 22, 1802, *American State Papers*, 701.

50. Cooper, *History of the Navy*, 232.

51. Cooper, *History of the Navy*, 121.

52. Minnigerode, *Lives and Times*, 63.

53. Madison to Cathcart, April 9, 1803, *American State Papers*, 701.

54. Irwin, *The Diplomatic Relations of the United States with the Barbary Powers*, 129.

55. Irwin, *The Diplomatic Relations of the United States with the Barbary Powers*, 135.

56. Secretary of the Navy R. Smith to Eaton, May 30, 1804, *American State Papers*, 702.

57. Irwin, *The Diplomatic Relations of the United States with the Barbary Powers*, 145.

58. Irwin, *The Diplomatic Relations of the United States with the Barbary Powers*, 145.

59. Secretary of State to Lear, June 6, 1804, *American State Papers*, 701–2.

60. Robinson, "The Rise and Fall of Tobias Lear."

61. Rodd, *General William Eaton*, 161, 175.

62. Convention between the United States and His Highness Hamet Caramanly, Bashaw of Tripoli, *American State Papers*, 706.

63. Eaton to Secretary of the Navy, February 13, 1805, *American State Papers*, 704.

64. Eaton to Secretary of the Navy, February 13, 1805, *American State Papers*, 704.

65. Rodd, *General William Eaton*, 202.

66. Felton, "William Eaton," 140.

67. Felton, "William Eaton," 143.

68. Felton, "William Eaton," 149–51.

69. Barron to Eaton, March 22, 1805, *American State Papers*, 707–8.

70. Eaton to Barron, April 29, 1805, *American State Papers*, 709.

71. Eaton to Barron, May 1, 1805, *American State Papers*, 710.

72. Eaton to Barron, May 1, 1805, *American State Papers*, 710.

73. Bainbridge to Barron, March 16, 1805, *American State Papers*, 704.

74. Lear to Secretary of State, July 5, 1805, *American State Papers*, 717.

75. Barron to Lear, May 18, 1805, *American State Papers*, 710–11.

76. Barron to Lear, May 18, 1805, *American State Papers*, 711.

77. Lear to Barron, May 19, 1805, *American State Papers*, 711.

78. Lear to Secretary of State, July 5, 1805, *American State Papers*, 718.

79. Irwin, *The Diplomatic Relations of the United States with the Barbary Powers*, 153.

80. Rodd, *General William Eaton*, 257–58.

81. Eaton to Rodgers, June 12, 1805, *American State Papers*, 716.

82. Hamet to Eaton, June 29, 1805, *American State Papers*, 716.

83. Rodd, *General William Eaton*, 272.

84. Lear to Madison, July 5, 1805, *American State Papers*, 716.

85. Eaton to Cdre. John Rodgers, June 13, 1805, *American State Papers*, 716.

86. Irwin, *The Diplomatic Relations of the United States with the Barbary Powers*, 154.

87. Minnigerode, *Lives and Times*, 93.

88. "Arlington Oaks History."

### 3. Diplomacy in New Orleans

1. Harmon, *The Famous Case of Myra Clark Gaines*, 53.

2. See Clark to Ellicott, August 8, 1798, State Department Consular Dispatches, New Orleans.

3. Clark to Ellicott, March 14, 1798, and March 15, 1798, Clark to Pickering, March 17, 1798, State Department Consular Dispatches, New Orleans.

4. Clark to Ellicott, August 8, 1798, State Department Consular Dispatches, New Orleans.

5. John Pintard to the Secretary of the Treasury, September 14, 1803, *Territorial Papers of the United States*, vol. 9, *The Territory of Orleans, 1803–1812*, 52.

6. Clark to Pickering, June 14, 1798, State Department Consular Dispatches, New Orleans.

7. Jones to Madison, May 15, 1801, in "Documents: Dispatches from the United States Consulate in New Orleans, 1801–1803," part 1, 813.

8. Daniel Coxe to Timothy Pickering, December 2, 1797, State Department Consular Dispatches, New Orleans.

9. Ellicott and Guion to Clark, March 2, 1798, State Department Consular Dispatches, New Orleans.

10. Harmon, *The Famous Case of Myra Clark Gaines*, 275, quoting Belchasse.

11. Wilkinson to Jefferson, July 1, 1804, *Territorial Papers*, 253.

12. Benjamin Morgan to Chandler Price, August 7, 1803, August 18, 1803, *Territorial Papers*, 7–9.

13. Harmon, *The Famous Case of Myra Clark Gaines*, quoting Laussat, 54; Whitaker, *The Mississippi Question*, 245.

14. Wilkinson to Jefferson, July 1, 1804, *Territorial Papers*, 55.

15. Cox, "Daniel Clark," 125; Harmon, *The Famous Case of Myra Clark Gaines*, 22.

16. Good contemporary descriptions of New Orleans can be found in *An Account of Louisiana, Being an Abstract of Documents, in the Departments of State and of the Treasury* and in Morse, *The American Gazetteer, exhibiting a full account of the Civil Divisions, Rivers, Harbors, Indian Tribes, &c. of the American Continent.*

17. Whitaker, *The Mississippi Question*, 102–75.

18. Clark to Daniel Coxe, April 18, 1798, State Department Consular Dispatches, New Orleans.

19. Clark to Pickering, November 18, 1799, State Department Consular Dispatches, New Orleans.

20. Lyon, *Louisiana in French Diplomacy*, 136.

21. Clark to Madison, April 27, 1803, in "Documents: Dispatches from the United States Consulate in New Orleans, 1801–1803," part 2, 335.

22. Madison to Clark, July 20, 1803, *Territorial Papers*, 61.

23. Clark to Madison, September 29, 1803, State Department Consular Dispatches, New Orleans.

24. Clark to Madison, March 18, 1803, State Department Consular Dispatches, New Orleans.

25. Clark to Madison, March 24, 1803, State Department Consular Dispatches, New Orleans.

26. Gayarré, *History of Louisiana*, 473.

27. Jefferson to Livingston, April 18, 1802, in *The Writings of Thomas Jefferson*, ed. Lipscomb, 143.

28. Clark to Madison, March 18, 1803, State Department Consular Dispatches, New Orleans.

29. Clark to Madison, April 27, 1803, State Department Consular Dispatches, New Orleans.

30. Clark to Madison, August 18, 1803, State Department Consular Dispatches, New Orleans.

31. Clark to Madison, April 27, 1803, "Documents: Dispatches from the United States Consulate in New Orleans, 1801–1803," part 2, 339.

32. Jefferson to Clark, July 17, 1803, in *The Writings of Thomas Jefferson*, ed. Lipscomb, 10:406.

33. Clark to Madison, August 12, 1803, "Documents: Dispatches from the United States Consulate in New Orleans, 1801–1803, II," part 2, 346.

34. Jefferson to Secretary of the Treasury Gallatin, November 9, 1803, and Madison to Clark, October 12, 1803, *Territorial Papers*, 100–101, 78–79.

35. Clark to Madison, March 18, 1803, "Documents: Dispatches from the United States Consulate in New Orleans, 1801–1803," part 2, 335.

36. Clark to Madison, April 27, 1803, "Documents: Dispatches from the United States Consulate in New Orleans, 1801–1803," part 2, 342–43.

37. Clark to Madison, May 13, 1803, "Documents: Dispatches from the United States Consulate in New Orleans, 1801–1803," part 2, 343.

38. Clark to Madison, May 3, 1803, State Department Consular Dispatches, New Orleans.

39. Clark to Madison, October 20, 1803, "Documents: Dispatches from the United States Consulate in New Orleans, 1801–1803," part 2, 349, and Clark to Jefferson, n.d., *Territorial Papers*, 29–47.

40. Clark to Claiborne, November 23, 1803, *Territorial Papers*, 121.

41. Madison to Clark, September 16, 1803, *Territorial Papers*, 54.

42. Madison to Clark, October 31, 1803, *Territorial Papers*, 95.

43. Clark to Madison, November 7, 1803, "Documents: Dispatches from the United States Consulate in New Orleans, 1801–1803," part 2, 350.

44. Clark to Claiborne, November 11, 1803, *Territorial Papers*, 102.

45. Clark to Madison, October 4, 1803, State Department Consular Dispatches, New Orleans.

46. Clark to Madison, November 29, 1803, *Territorial Papers*, 354–55.

47. Whitaker, *The Mississippi Question*, 247–48.

48. Clark to Claiborne, November 23, 1803, *Territorial Papers*, 121.

49. Clark to Madison, July 21, 1803, and October 20, 1803, "Documents: Dispatches from the United States Consulate in New Orleans, 1801–1803," part 2, 345–46.

50. Clark to Claiborne, November 23, 1803, *Territorial Papers*, 121.

51. Lyon, *Louisiana in French Diplomacy*, 240.

52. "Documents: Dispatches from the United States Consulate in New Orleans, 1801–1803," part 2, 356n43.

53. Whitaker, *The Mississippi Question*, 251.

54. Lyon, *Louisiana in French Diplomacy*, 246.

55. Wilkinson to Secretary of War, n.d., *Territorial Papers*, 138.

56. Clark to Madison, June 3, 1804, Claiborne to Jefferson, November 19, 1804, and Claiborne to Madison, November 5, 1804, *Territorial Papers*, 242, 334, 320.

57. Jefferson to Claiborne, August 30, 1804, *Territorial Papers*, 282–83.

58. Clark to Wilkinson, June 16, 1806, in *Territorial Papers*, 660.

59. Claiborne to Jefferson, June 1, 1807, in *Territorial Papers*, 742.

60. Harmon, *The Famous Case of Myra Clark Gaines*, 73.

61. Claiborne to Jefferson, June 28, 1807, in *Territorial Papers*, 743.

62. Harmon, *The Famous Case of Myra Clark Gaines*, 91.

63. Jefferson, Special message to Congress of January 20, 1808, *Writings of Thomas Jefferson*, ed. Lipscomb, 3:458.

64. Claiborne to Madison, April 5, 1808, in *Official Letter Books of W.C.C. Claiborne*, ed. Rowland, 4:168.

## 4. Inventing Interventionism

1. Stillé, "The Life and Services of Joel R. Poinsett," 144.

2. Stillé, "The Life and Services of Joel R. Poinsett," 150.

3. Smith, *America's Diplomats*, 207.

4. Secretary of State Robert Smith to Poinsett, June 28, 1810, in *Diplomatic Correspondence*, ed. Manning, 1:7.

5. Putnam, *Joel Robert Poinsett, a Political Biography*, 24.

6. Parton, "The Diplomatic Career of Joel Roberts Poinsett," 4.

7. Poinsett, *Journal to Rio Janeiro, Buenos Ayres, and Chile*. Neither Poinsett's *Journal* nor his other unpublished reports from the Library of Congress collection have page numbers. They were all handwritten originals.

8. Poinsett, *Journal to Rio Janeiro, Buenos Ayres, and Chile*.

9. U.S. Minister in Brazil Thomas Sumter to Secretary of State Robert Smith, February 25, 1811, *Diplomatic Correspondence*, ed. Manning, 673.

10. Poinsett, *Journal to Rio Janeiro, Buenos Ayres, and Chile*,

11. U.S. Minister in Brazil Thomas Sumter to Secretary of State Robert Smith, February 25, 1811, *Diplomatic Correspondence*, ed. Manning, 672.

12. Rippy, *Versatile American*, 38.

13. Poinsett, *United Provinces of the River Plate*,

14. Junta of the Provinces of the Rio de la Plata to President Madison, February 13, 1811, *Diplomatic Correspondence*, ed. Manning, 320–21.

15. Poinsett, *Journal to Rio Janeiro, Buenos Ayres, and Chile*.

16. Poinsett, *Buenos Ayres Revolution, 1810–1812*,

17. Poinsett, *Journal to Rio Janeiro, Buenos Ayres, and Chile*.

18. Rippy, *Versatile American*, 38.

19. Secretary of State James Monroe to Joel Poinsett, April 30, 1811, *Diplomatic Correspondence*, ed. Manning, 11.

20. Parton, "The Diplomatic Career of Joel Roberts Poinsett," 25.

21. Poinsett, Report to Secretary of State John Quincy Adams, November 4, 1818, *Diplomatic Correspondence*, ed. Manning, 463.

22. Poinsett, *Journal to Rio Janeiro, Buenos Ayres, and Chile*.

23. Poinsett, *United Provinces of the River Plate*.

24. Poinsett, *Journal to Rio Janeiro, Buenos Ayres, and Chile*.

25. Poinsett, Report to Secretary of State John Quincy Adams, November 4, 1818, *Diplomatic Correspondence*, ed. Manning, 461.

26. Poinsett, *United Provinces of the River Plate*.

27. Poinsett, *United Provinces of the River Plate*.

28. Poinsett, *United Provinces of the River Plate*.

29. Poinsett, *United Provinces of the River Plate*. Twenty-five years later, traveling on much the same route, Charles Darwin would write: "At night I experienced an attack (for it deserves no less a name) of the *Benchuca*, a species of Reduvius, the great black bug of the Pampas. It is most disgusting to feel soft wingless insects, about an inch long, crawling over one's body. Before sucking they are quite thin, but afterwards they become round and bloated with blood, and in this state are easily crushed." See Darwin, *Voyage of the Beagle*, 28.

30. Poinsett, *United Provinces of the River Plate*.

31. Poinsett to Secretary of State James Monroe, February 20, 1813, *Diplomatic Correspondence*, ed. Manning, 897–98.

32. Rippy, *Versatile American*, 47.

33. Putnam, *Joel Robert Poinsett, a Political Biography*, 33.

34. Rippy, *Versatile American*, 56.

35. Parton, "The Diplomatic Career of Joel Roberts Poinsett," 27.

36. Porter, *Journal of a Cruise*, 101.

37. Parton, "The Diplomatic Career of Joel Roberts Poinsett," 33.

38. Stillé,"The Life and Services of Joel R. Poinsett," 154–55.

39. Stillé, "The Life and Services of Joel R. Poinsett," 26.

40. Poinsett, *Chile, Kingdom of, 1812–1814.*

41. Poinsett, *Chile, Kingdom of, 1812–1814.*

42. Poinsett, Joel, *Chile, Kingdom of, 1812–1814.*

43. Poinsett report of November 4, 1818, to Secretary of State John Quincy Adams, *Diplomatic Correspondence*, ed. Manning, 1011.

44. Poinsett, *Chile, Kingdom of, 1812–1814.*

45. Rippy, *Versatile American*, 54.

46. Poinsett to Secretary of State James Monroe, June 14, 1814, in *Diplomatic Correspondence*, ed. Manning, 1:335.

47. Rippy, *Versatile American*, 55.

48. Parton, "The Diplomatic Career of Joel Roberts Poinsett," 38.

49. Parton, "The Diplomatic Career of Joel Roberts Poinsett," 42.

50. "Joel Roberts Poinsett," *Masonic Trowel.*

51. Monroe communication to Congress, March 8, 1822, *Diplomatic Correspondence*, ed. Manning, 1:147.

52. Poinsett, *Notes on Mexico, Made in the Autumn of 1822*, 1.

53. Poinsett, *Notes on Mexico, Made in the Autumn of 1822*, 16.

54. Poinsett, *Notes on Mexico, Made in the Autumn of 1822*, 15.

55. Poinsett, *Notes on Mexico, Made in the Autumn of 1822*, 16.

56. Poinsett, *Notes on Mexico, Made in the Autumn of 1822*, 27–29.

57. Poinsett, *Notes on Mexico, Made in the Autumn of 1822*, 37, 132, 154.

58. Poinsett, *Notes on Mexico, Made in the Autumn of 1822*, 139–42.

59. Poinsett, *Notes on Mexico, Made in the Autumn of 1822*, 39, 191–93.

60. Poinsett, *Notes on Mexico, Made in the Autumn of 1822*, 45–46.

61. Poinsett, *Notes on Mexico, Made in the Autumn of 1822*, 48.

62. Poinsett, *Notes on Mexico, Made in the Autumn of 1822*, 83.

63. Poinsett, *Notes on Mexico, Made in the Autumn of 1822*, 119.

64. Poinsett, *Notes on Mexico, Made in the Autumn of 1822*, 146.

65. Poinsett, *Notes on Mexico, Made in the Autumn of 1822*, 71.

66. Poinsett, *Notes on Mexico, Made in the Autumn of 1822*, 68.

67. Poinsett, *Notes on Mexico, Made in the Autumn of 1822*, 68, 205.

68. Rippy, *Versatile American*, 102.

69. Secretary of State Henry Clay to Poinsett, March 26, 1825, *Diplomatic Correspondence*, ed. Manning, 1:229–33.

70. Poinsett to Secretary of State Clay, October 12, 1825, *Diplomatic Correspondence*, ed. Manning, 1:639.

71. Rippy, *Versatile American*, 108.

72. Poinsett to Secretary of State Clay, October 12, 1825, *Diplomatic Correspondence*, ed. Manning, 1:636–38.

73. Poinsett dispatches to Secretaries of State Clay and Van Buren, June 1825–October 1829, *Diplomatic Correspondence*, ed. Manning, 1:612–627, 640, 656, and 704.

74. Putnam, *Joel Robert Poinsett, a Political Biography*, 79.

75. Rippy, *Versatile American*, 114.

76. Secretary of State Martin Van Buren to Poinsett, August 25, 1829, State Department Diplomatic Instructions.

77. Rippy, *Versatile American*, 114–15.

78. Poinsett to Secretary of State Van Buren, March 10, 1829, *Diplomatic Correspondence*, ed. Manning, 1:679.

79. Poinsett to Secretary of State Clay, October 12, 1825, *Diplomatic Correspondence*, ed. Manning, 1:638–39.

80. Poinsett to Secretary of State Clay, July 8, 1827, in *Diplomatic Correspondence*, ed. Manning, 1:663.

81. Rippy, *Versatile American*, 124.

82. Poinsett to Secretary of State Van Buren, March 10, 1829, *Diplomatic Correspondence*, ed. Manning, 1:681.

83. Poinsett to Secretary of State Van Buren, March 10, 1829, *Diplomatic Correspondence*, ed. Manning, 1:682.

84. Bazant, *A Concise History of Mexico*, 43.

85. Poinsett to Secretary of State Van Buren, August 7, 1829, *Diplomatic Correspondence*, ed. Manning, 1:685.

86. Putnam, *Joel Robert Poinsett, a Political Biography*, 101–2.

87. Putnam, *Joel Robert Poinsett, a Political Biography*, 101.

88. Putnam, *Joel Robert Poinsett, a Political Biography*, 102.

89. Morison, *The Oxford History of the American People*, 186.

90. "Joel Roberts Poinsett," *Masonic Trowel.*

91. Bazant, *A Concise History of Mexico*, 50–51.

92. Philbrick, "The United States Exploring Expedition, 1838–1842."

93. John Charles Frémont to Poinsett, June 8, 1838, September 5, 1838, and January 3, 1840, Poinsett Papers, Library of Congress.

94. Bazant, *A Concise History of Mexico*, 57.

## 5. Cochin China, Siam, and Muscat

1. Paine, *The Ships and Sailors of Old Salem*, 379–405.

2. Andrew Jackson, State of the Union address, December 6, 1831.

3. Roberts, *Embassy to the Eastern Courts of Cochin-China, Siam, and Muscat*, 6.

4. Foster, *American Diplomacy in the Orient*, 140.

5. Roberts and Ruschenberger, *Two Yankee Diplomats in 1830s Siam*, 12.

6. Secretary of State Edward Livingston to Roberts, January 27, 1832, quoted in Douglas and Martinez, "Nineteenth-Century American Merchants in the Indian Ocean."

7. Ticknor, *The Voyage of the Peacock*, 337–38.

8. Livingston to Roberts, January 27, 1832.

9. Livingston to Roberts, January 27, 1832.

10. Carronades were short, light iron cannons.

11. Ruschenberger, *A Voyage round the World*, 13.

12. Ticknor, *The Voyage of the Peacock*, 307.

13. Ticknor, *The Voyage of the Peacock*, 10, 66, 211, 337.

14. Roberts, *Embassy to the Eastern Courts*, 6.

15. Reynolds, *Voyage of the United States Frigate* Potomac, 104–22.

16. Ticknor, *The Voyage of the Peacock*, 99.

17. Roberts, *Embassy to the Eastern Courts*, 32.

18. Woodbury to Downes, July 16, 1832, in Reynolds, *Voyage of the United States Frigate* Potomac, 116–17.

19. Andrew Jackson, State of the Union address, December 12, 1832. http://odur.let.rug.nl/usa/P/aj7/speeches/ajson4.htm.

20. Ticknor, *The Voyage of the Peacock*, 209.

21. White, *A Voyage to Cochin China*, 246–47.

22. Roberts, *Embassy to the Eastern Courts*, 172.

23. Ticknor, *The Voyage of the Peacock*, 200.

24. Roberts, *Embassy to the Eastern Courts*, 175.

25. Roberts, *Embassy to the Eastern Courts*, 182.

26. Roberts *Embassy to the Eastern Courts*, 184.

27. Roberts, *Embassy to the Eastern Courts*, 220–21.

28. Ticknor, *The Voyage of the Peacock*, 220, 222.

29. Ticknor, *The Voyage of the Peacock*, 206, 209.

30. Roberts, *Embassy to the Eastern Courts*, 189.

31. Roberts, *Embassy to the Eastern Courts*, 198.

32. Roberts, *Embassy to the Eastern Courts*, 204. The full text of the letter was:

> President Andrew Jackson, President of the United States of America, to his majesty the emperor of Cochin-China: Great and good friend—This will be delivered to your majesty by Edmund Roberts, a respectable citizen of these United States, who has been appointed special agent, on the part of this government, to transact important business with your majesty. I pray your majesty to protect him in the exercise of the duties which are thus confided to him, and to treat him with kindness and confidence; placing entire reliance upon what he shall say to you in our behalf, especially when he shall repeat the assurances of our prefect amity and good will towards your majesty. I pray God to have you, great and good friend, under his safe and holy keeping. Written at the city of Washington, the twentieth day of January, AD 1833, and in the fifty-sixth year of independence. Your good and faithful friend, Andrew Jackson.

33. Roberts, *Embassy to the Eastern Courts*, 204.

34. Roberts, *Embassy to the Eastern Courts*, 208.

35. Roberts, *Embassy to the Eastern Courts*, 210.

36. Roberts, *Embassy to the Eastern Courts*, 216.

37. Roberts, *Embassy to the Eastern Courts*, 6, 225, 282.

38. "History of a Missed USA-Vietnam Draft Trade Agreement since over 170 Years Ago."

39. Ticknor, *The Voyage of the Peacock*, 229.

40. Roberts, *Embassy to the Eastern Courts*, 229, 231.

41. Roberts, *Embassy to the Eastern Courts*, 248, 264.

42. Roberts, *Embassy to the Eastern Courts*, 231–35.

43. Roberts, *Embassy to the Eastern Courts*, 262.

44. Roberts, *Embassy to the Eastern Courts*, 232, 262.

45. Roberts, *Embassy to the Eastern Courts*, 236–38.

46. Roberts, *Embassy to the Eastern Courts*, 238–39, Ticknor, *The Voyage of the Peacock*, 255.

47. Ticknor, *The Voyage of the Peacock*, 242.

48. Roberts, *Embassy to the Eastern Courts*, 247, 285, 284.

49. Ticknor, *The Voyage of the Peacock*, 260.

50. Roberts, *Embassy to the Eastern Courts*, 246–47.

51. Roberts, *Embassy to the Eastern Courts*, 319.

52. "A Historical Perspective on Gifts to the United States of America."

53. Roberts, *Embassy to the Eastern Courts*, 234, 243.

54. Roberts, *Embassy to the Eastern Courts*, 285, 240; Ticknor, *The Voyage of the Peacock*, 252.

55. Roberts, *Embassy to the Eastern Courts*, 248.

56. Roberts, *Embassy to the Eastern Courts*, 233.

57. Roberts, *Embassy to the Eastern Courts*, 253–54.

58. Roberts to Secretary of State Livingston, June 22, 1833, Roberts Papers, Library of Congress.

59. Roberts, *Embassy to the Eastern Courts*, 6.

60. Roberts, *Embassy to the Eastern Courts*, 255–58.

61. Roberts, *Embassy to the Eastern Courts*, 257–59.

62. Roberts, *Embassy to the Eastern Courts*, 320.

63. Fairbank, Reischaur, and Craig, *East Asia*, 451.

64. Bemis, *A Diplomatic History of the United States*, 344.

65. Roberts, *Embassy to the Eastern Courts*, 320.

66. Ticknor, *The Voyage of the Peacock*, 328.

67. Ticknor, *The Voyage of the Peacock*, 107–8.

68. Roberts, *Embassy to the Eastern Courts*, 352.

69. Roberts, *Embassy to the Eastern Courts*, 353.

70. Roberts, *Embassy to the Eastern Courts*, 361–62.

71. Roberts, *Embassy to the Eastern Courts*, 352, 360.

72. Ticknor, *The Voyage of the Peacock*, 297.

73. Roberts, *Embassy to the Eastern Courts*, 361.

74. Ticknor, *The Voyage of the Peacock*, 305, 301.

75. Foster, *American Diplomacy in the Orient*, 52.

76. Roberts, *Embassy to the Eastern Courts*, 360.

77. Smith, *America's Diplomats*, 262; Ticknor, *The Voyage of the Peacock*, 355.

78. Roberts, *Embassy to the Eastern Courts*, 353.

79. Ticknor, *The Voyage of the Peacock*, 296, 353.

80. Ticknor, *The Voyage of the Peacock*, 355.

81. Cotheal, "Treaty between the United States of America and the Sultan of Maskat," 358.

82. Ticknor, *The Voyage of the Peacock*, 300.

83. Roberts, *Embassy to the Eastern Courts*, 430.

84. Cotheal, "Treaty between the United States of America and the Sultan of Maskat," 346.

85. Cotheal, "Treaty between the United States of America and the Sultan of Maskat," 365.

86. Cotheal, "Treaty between the United States of America and the Sultan of Maskat," 399.

87. Andrew Jackson, State of the Union address, December 5, 1836.

88. Ticknor, *The Voyage of the Peacock*, 9–10.

89. Ticknor, *The Voyage of the Peacock*, 6.

90. Roberts to Secretary of State Forsyth, October 23, 1835, in Douglas and Martinez, "Nineteenth-Century American Merchants in the Indian Ocean."

91. Ruschenberger, *A Voyage round the World*, 303.

92. Ruschenberger, *A Voyage round the World*, 319–20.

93. Ruschenberger, *A Voyage round the World*, 342, 344.

94. "1804 Draped Bust Silver Dollar-Class I, the 'King of Siam' Specimen."

95. Ruschenberger, *A Voyage round the World*, 349.

96. Fairbanks, Reischaur, and Craig, *East Asia*, 439.

97. Ruschenberger, *A Voyage round the World*, 372–73.

98. Taylor, *A Voyage round the World, and Visits to Foreign Countries*, 295.

## 6. The Commodore as Diplomat

1. Porter, *A Memoir of Commodore David Porter*, 72.

2. Eviline Anderson to Andrew Jackson, November 29, 1828, in *The Papers of Andrew Jackson*, ed. Moser and Clift, 6:625.

3. Porter, *A Memoir of Commodore David Porter*, 212.

4. Porter to his wife Evelina Porter, December 15, 1828, Porter Papers, Library of Congress.

5. Porter to his wife Evelina Porter, December 15, 1828, Porter Papers, Library of Congress.

6. Rhind to Secretary of State Martin Van Buren, March 26, 1830, State Department Diplomatic Dispatches, Constantinople.

7. Porter, *Constantinople and Its Environs*, 1:19–20.

8. Porter, *Constantinople and Its Environs*, 1: 22.

9. Navoni to Secretary of State Livingston, October 25, 1831, State Department Diplomatic Dispatches, Constantinople.

10. Porter to Secretary of State Livingston, September 13, 1831, State Department Diplomatic Dispatches, Constantinople.

11. Navoni to Secretary of State Livingston, October 25, 1831, State Department Diplomatic Dispatches, Constantinople.

12. Porter, *Constantinople and Its Environs*, 2:49–51.

13. Andrew Jackson, State of the Union Message, December 6, 1831.

14. Porter, *Constantinople and Its Environs*, 2:20–21.

15. Porter to Secretary of State Livingston, September 26, 1831, State Department Diplomatic Dispatches, Constantinople.

16. Porter, *Constantinople and Its Environs*, 1:76–77.

17. Porter to Secretary of State Livingston, September 26, 1831, State Department Diplomatic Dispatches, Constantinople.

18. Porter to Secretary of State Livingston, January 4, 1833, State Department Diplomatic Dispatches, Constantinople.

19. Porter to Secretary of State Livingston, October 5, 1831, State Department Diplomatic Dispatches, Constantinople.

20. Secretary of State Livingston to Porter, March 23, 1832, State Department Diplomatic Instructions, Constantinople.

21. Secretary of State Livingston to Porter, April 3, 1832, State Department Diplomatic Instructions, Constantinople.

22. Porter, *Constantinople and Its Environs*, 1: 111.

23. Porter, *Constantinople and Its Environs*, 2: 297.

24. Porter, *Constantinople and Its Environs*, 2:161–68; 1:39–41.

25. Porter, *Constantinople and Its Environs*, 2:313.

26. Porter, *Constantinople and Its Environs*, 2:9–10.

27. Porter, *A Memoir of Commodore David Porter*, 401.

28. Porter, *Constantinople and Its Environs*, 2:316–18.

29. Porter to Secretary of State Livingston, January 4, 1833, State Department Diplomatic Dispatches, Constantinople.

30. Porter, *Constantinople and Its Environs*, 2:293–94.

31. Porter to Secretary of State Livingston, January 20, 1834, State Department Diplomatic Dispatches, Constantinople.

32. Porter to Secretary of State Livingston, March 27, 1833, State Department Diplomatic Dispatches, Constantinople.

33. Porter to Secretary of State Livingston, May 10, 1833, State Department Diplomatic Dispatches, Constantinople.

34. Churchill to Secretary of State Livingston, August 10, 1833, State Department Consular Dispatches, Constantinople.

35. Secretary of State McLane to Porter, October 10, 1833, State Department Diplomatic Instructions, Constantinople.

36. Secretary of State Forsyth to Porter, September 15, 1835, State Department Diplomatic Instructions, Constantinople.

37. Porter to Secretary of State McLane, May 12, 1834, State Department Diplomatic Dispatches: Constantinople.

38. Secretary of State Forsyth to Porter, September 10, 1835, State Department Diplomatic Instructions, Constantinople.

39. Porter to Secretary of State McLane, June 5, 1834, State Department Diplomatic Dispatches, Constantinople.

40. Porter, *Constantinople and Its Environs*, 2:307.

41. Porter, *A Memoir of Commodore David Porter*, 406–8.

42. Porter, *A Memoir of Commodore David Porter*, 408–11.

43. Porter to Secretary of State Forsyth, August 2, 1839, State Department Diplomatic Dispatches, Constantinople.

44. State Department Log, Summary of Dispatches from Constantinople, September 1839, State Department Diplomatic Dispatches: Constantinople, emphasis in original.

45. Secretary of State Forsyth to Porter, August 17, 1840, State Department Diplomatic Instructions, Constantinople.

46. Porter, *Constantinople and Its Environs*, 2:11.

47. John Porter Brown to Secretary of State Webster, March 6, 1843, State Department Diplomatic Dispatches, Constantinople.

### 7. Adventures in Paradise

1. Murray, *The Encyclopedia of Geography*, 158.

2. Melville, *Omoo*, 66, 68.

3. Moerenhout, *Travels to the Islands of the Pacific Ocean*, 104.

4. Bennett, *Narrative of a Whaling Voyage*, 81.

5. Charles Darwin, *The Voyage of the Beagle*, 13.

6. Moerenhout, *Travels to the Islands of the Pacific Ocean*, 108–10.

7. The first European to visit Tahiti was Pedro Fernandez de Quiros, a Spanish explorer, in 1606.

8. *The Christian Watchman*, Boston, June 12, 1824, in Ward, ed., *American Activities in the Central Pacific, 1790–1870*, ed. Ward, 7:8.

9. Hiroa, *Explorers of the Pacific*, 105.

10. Russell, *Polynesia*, 114.

11. Melville, *Omoo*, 127.

12. Bennett, *Narrative of a Whaling Voyage*, 73.

13. Moerenhout to Forsyth, May 4, 1836, State Department Consular Dispatches, Tahiti.

14. *General Instructions to Consuls*, 9–10, 22, 25–26.

15. Moerenhout to Forsyth, January 11, 1836, State Department Consular Dispatches, Tahiti.

16. Moorehead, *The Fatal Impact*, 107.

17. Bennett, *Narrative of a Whaling Voyage*, 75–77.

18. Moerenhout to Forsyth, January 11, 1836, State Department Consular Dispatches, Tahiti.

19. Pritchard to Forsyth, December 31, 1836, State Department Consular Dispatches, Tahiti.

20. Moerenhout to Forsyth, February 15, 1836, State Department Consular Dispatches, Tahiti.

21. Moerenhout to Forsyth, May 4, 1836, State Department Consular Dispatches, Tahiti.

22. Moerenhout to Pomare, December 4, 1836, and Moerenhout to Forsyth, December 24, 1836, State Department Consular Dispatches, Tahiti.

23. Pritchard to Forsyth, December 31, 1836, State Department Consular Dispatches, Tahiti.

24. Moerenhout to Forsyth, June 28, 1838, State Department Consular Dispatches, Tahiti.

25. Blackler to Forsyth, April 14, 1839, State Department Consular Dispatches, Tahiti.

26. Blackler to Forsyth, October 31, 1840, State Department Consular Dispatches, Tahiti.

27. Blackler to Forsyth, December 2, 1839, State Department Consular Dispatches, Tahiti.

28. Wilkes, *Autobiography*, 423.

29. Wilkes, *Autobiography*, 426.

30. Stann, "Charles Wilkes as Diplomat," 212.

31. Wilkes, *Autobiography*, 426–27.

32. Blackler to Forsyth, October 31, 1840, State Department Consular Dispatches, Tahiti.

33. Blackler to Forsyth, October 31, 1840, State Department Consular Dispatches, Tahiti.

34. Secretary of Government of Tahiti to President of the United States, January 20, 1841, State Department Consular Dispatches, Tahiti.

35. Blackler to Forsyth, March 11, 1841, State Department Consular Dispatches, Tahiti.

36. Blackler to Webster, June 5, 1841, State Department Consular Dispatches, Tahiti.

37. Paraita to President of the United States, August 18, 1841, State Department Consular Dispatches, Tahiti.

38. "Small Pox at Tahiti," *Mercantile Journal*, Boston, January 11, 1842, in *American Activities in the Central Pacific*, ed. Ward, 7:29.

39. Aulick to Navy Department, October 13, 1841, State Department Consular Dispatches, Tahiti.

40. Brookes, *International Rivalry in the Pacific Islands*, 107.

41. Blackler to Webster, June 23, 1842, State Department Consular Dispatches, Tahiti.

42. Brookes, *International Rivalry in the Pacific Islands*, 109.

43. Blackler to Webster, September 10, 1842, State Department Consular Dispatches, Tahiti.

44. Blackler to Webster, September 10, 1842, State Department Consular Dispatches, Tahiti.

45. Blackler to Du Petit Thouars, September 10, 1842, State Department Consular Dispatches, Tahiti.

46. Blackler to Du Petit Thouars, September 13, 1842, State Department Consular Dispatches, Tahiti.

47. Blackler to Webster, September 26, 1842, State Department Consular Dispatches, Tahiti.

48. Blackler to Webster, September 10, 1842, State Department Consular Dispatches, Tahiti.

49. Blackler to Webster, September 10, 1842, State Department Consular Dispatches, Tahiti.

50. Blackler to Du Petit Thouars, September 25, 1842, State Department Consular Dispatches, Tahiti.

51. Brookes, *International Rivalry in the Pacific Islands*, 139.

52. Blackler to Webster, November 23, 1843, Department of State Consular Dispatches, Tahiti.

53. Brookes, *International Rivalry in the Pacific Islands*, 171.

54. Melville, *Omoo*, 128.

55. "Disgraceful Conduct of the U.S. Consul at Tahiti," *Boston Daily Journal*, October 29, 1858, in *American Activities in the Central Pacific*, ed. Ward, 7:175. It is not clear if the consul in question was William H. Kelly, Henry Owner, or Vicesimus Turner, all of whom served terms as consul between 1857 and 1858.

## 8. The Land of Gold

1. Prevost to Adams, November 11, 1818, in *"Emperor Dead,"* ed. Eicher, 81.

2. Hague and Langum, *Thomas O. Larkin*, 37.

3. Underhill, *From Cowhides to Golden Fleece*, 11.

4. Underhill, *From Cowhides to Golden Fleece*, 41.

5. Smith, *America's Diplomats*, 181.

6. Underhill, *From Cowhides to Golden Fleece*, 10–12.

7. Bancroft, *History of California*, 449.

8. Bancroft, *History of California*, 299.

9. Bancroft, *History of California*, 302.

10. Hague and Langum, *Thomas O. Larkin*, 103.

11. Larkin to Secretary of State Buchanan, April 11, 1844, State Department Consular Dispatches, Monterey.

12. Underhill, *From Cowhides to Golden Fleece*, 90.

13. *General Instructions to the Consuls and Commercial Agents of the United States* (1838), 39.

14. *General Instructions to the Consuls and Commercial Agents of the United States* (1838), 9–28.

15. *General Instructions to Consuls, &c.* (1834), 26.

16. Underhill, *From Cowhides to Golden Fleece*, 88.

17. Underhill, *From Cowhides to Golden Fleece*, 92.

18. Hague and Langum, *Thomas O. Larkin*, 109.

19. Hague and Langum, *Thomas O. Larkin*, 17.

20. Swasey, *The Early Days and Men of California*, 40.

21. Underhill, *From Cowhides to Golden Fleece*, 49.

22. Bancroft, *History of California*, 591, 594.

23. Bancroft, *History of California*, 591.

24. Larkin to Secretary of State Buchannan, July 10, 1845, State Department Consular Dispatches, Monterey.

25. Hawgood, *First and Last Consul*, 23; Larkin's spelling.

26. Buchanan to Larkin, October 17, 1845, Diplomatic Instructions, National Archives.

27. Swasey, *The Early Days and Men of California*, 155.

28. Palgon, *William Alexander Leidesdorff*, 8–11.

29. Swasey, *The Early Days and Men of California*, 155.

30. Bancroft, *History of California*, 711.

31. Larkin, "Description of California prior to the Year 1846," State Department Consular Dispatches, Monterey.

32. Swasey, *The Early Days and Men of California*, 155.

33. Bancroft, *History of California*, 711.

34. Palgon, *William Alexander Leidesdorff*, 54.

35. Larkin to Buchanan, March 6, 1846, State Department Consular Dispatches, Monterey.

36. Swasey, *The Early Days and Men of California*, 105.

37. Larkin to Frémont, March 8, 1846, State Department Consular Dispatches, Monterrey.

38. Frémont to Larkin, n.d., State Department Consular Dispatches, Monterey.

39. Underhill, *From Cowhides to Golden Fleece*, 108.

40. Hawgood, *First and Last Consul*, 53.

41. Swasey, *The Early Days and Men of California*, 110.

42. Hawgood, *First and Last Consul*, xxxv.

43. Hague and Langum, *Thomas O. Larkin*, 129.

44. Hague and Langum, *Thomas O. Larkin*, 126.

45. Hawgood, *First and Last Consul*, 56.

46. Hague and Langum, *Thomas O. Larkin*, 116.

47. Underhill, *From Cowhides to Golden Fleece*, 111.

48. Swasey, *The Early Days and Men of California*, 52.

49. Henry, *The Story of the Mexican War*, 109.

50. Henry, *The Story of the Mexican War*, 111.

51. Hague and Langum, *Thomas O. Larkin*, 129.

52. Hague and Langum, *Thomas O. Larkin*, 259.

53. Henry, *The Story of the Mexican War*, 111–12.

54. Hague and Langum, *Thomas O. Larkin*, 143–44.

55. Henry, *The Story of the Mexican War*, 111–12.

56. Hague and Langum, *Thomas O. Larkin*, 136.

57. Henry, *The Story of the Mexican War*, 114.

58. Palgon, *William Alexander Leidesdorff*, 33.

59. Underhill, *From Cowhides to Golden Fleece*, 275–76.

60. Hawgood, *First and Last Consul*, 73, 75.

61. Hague and Langum, *Thomas O. Larkin*, 138.

62. Hague and Langum, *Thomas O. Larkin*, 118.

63. Hawgood, *First and Last Consul*, xxxvii.

64. Underhill, *From Cowhides to Golden Fleece*, 121.

65. Hague and Langum, *Thomas O. Larkin*, 141.

66. Swasey, *The Early Days and Men of California*, 61.

67. Swasey, *The Early Days and Men of California*, 61.

68. Henry, *The Story of the Mexican War*, 117.

69. Swasey, *The Early Days and Men of California*, 40.

70. Hawgood, *First and Last Consul*, 84

71. Underhill, *From Cowhides to Golden Fleece*, 122.

72. Swasey, *The Early Days and Men of California*, 60.

73. Underhill, *From Cowhides to Golden Fleece*, 130.

74. Underhill, *From Cowhides to Golden Fleece*, 125, 127.

75. Underhill, *From Cowhides to Golden Fleece*, 129.

76. Secretary of State Buchanan to Larkin, January 13, 1847, State Department Diplomatic Instructions.

77. Hague and Langum, *Thomas O. Larkin*, 144–45.

78. Underhill, *From Cowhides to Golden Fleece*, 131.

79. Henry, *The Story of the Mexican War*, 120.

80. Underhill, *From Cowhides to Golden Fleece*, 142, 149.

81. Hawgood, *First and Last Consul*, 88–89.

82. Hawgood, *First and Last Consul*, 89.

83. Bancroft, *History of California*, 98.

84. Royce, *California*, 161–62.

85. Eicher, ed. *"Emperor Dead,"* 116.

86. Palgon, *William Alexander Leidesdorff*, 51.

87. Rohrbough, *Days of Gold*, 7.

88. Underhill, *From Cowhides to Golden Fleece*, 179.

89. Hawgood, *First and Last Consul*, 95.

90. Hawgood, *First and Last Consul*, 95–96.

91. Larkin to Secretary of State Buchanan, June 1, 1848, Department of State Consular Dispatches, Monterey.

92. Underhill, *From Cowhides to Golden Fleece*, 193.

93. Moerenhout, *The Inside Story of the Gold Rush*.

94. Moerenhout, *The Inside Story of the Gold Rush*.

95. Hawgood, *First and Last Consul*, 104.

96. Palgon, *William Alexander Leidesdorff*, 96.

97. Palgon, *William Alexander Leidesdorff*, 90.

98. Swasey, *The Early Days and Men of California*, 107.

99. Royce, *California*, 127.

## 9. Shimoda and the Shogun

1. Hishida, *The International Position of Japan as a Great Power*, 107.

2. Hashida, *The International Position of Japan as a Great Power*, 108.

3. Treat, *The Early Diplomatic Relations*, 13.

4. Fairbank, Reischaur, and Craig, *East Asia*, 202–3.

5. Oliphant, *Narrative of the Earl of Elgin's Mission*, 349.

6. Hawks, *Narrative of the Expedition of an American Squadron*, 273.

7. Treat, *The Early Diplomatic Relations*, 26–27.

8. Hawks, *Narrative of the Expedition of an American Squadron*, 409.

9. Hawks, *Narrative of the Expedition of an American Squadron*, 440, 447.

10. Hawks, *Narrative of the Expedition of an American Squadron*, 304.

11. Griffis, *Townsend Harris*, 4.

12. Griffis, *Townsend Harris*, 11.

13. Wood, *Fankwei*, 12.

14. Griffis, *Townsend Harris*, 20.

15. Harris, *Complete Journal*, 90.

16. Harris, *Complete Journal*, 186–87.

17. Harris, *Complete Journal*, 196.

18. Wood, *Fankwei*, 299–302.

19. Heusken, *Japan Journal*, 84–85.

20. Wood, *Fankwei*, 312.

21. Harris, *Complete Journal*, 208.

22. Harris, *Complete Journal*, 203.

23. Heusken, *Japan Journal*, 86.

24. Oliphant, *Narrative of the Earl of Elgin's Mission*, 344–45.

25. Wood, *Fankwei*, 319.

26. Harris, *Complete Journal*, 244, 258.

27. Oliphant, *Narrative of the Earl of Elgin's Mission*, 346, 354.

28. Harris, *Complete Journal*, 253, 255.

29. Harris, *Complete Journal*, 293–94.

30. Heusken, *Japan Journal*, 99.

31. Fortune, *Yedo and Peking*, 200–201.

32. Heusken, *Japan Journal*, 99.

33. Harris, *Complete Journal*, 310; Heusken, *Japan Journal*, 99.

34. Harris, *Complete Journal*, 327, 350.

35. Heusken, *Japan Journal*, 101.

36. Harris, *Complete Journal*, 347.

37. Harris, *Complete Journal*, 244–48.

38. Harris, *Complete Journal*, 360.

39. Harris, *Complete Journal*, 353.

40. Heusken, *Japan Journal*, 119.

41. Harris, *Complete Journal*, 252.

42. Harris, *Complete Journal*, 363.

43. Harris, *Complete Journal*, 360.

44. Harris, *Complete Journal*, 308.

45. Statler, *Shimoda Story*, 383–86, 449.

46. Harris, *Complete Journal*, 386.

47. Harris, *Complete Journal*, 400.

48. Harris, *Complete Journal*, 398.

49. Heusken, *Japan Journal*, 119.

50. Heusken, *Japan Journal*, 119.

51. Heusken, *Japan Journal*, 134.

52. Harris, *Complete Journal*, 429.

53. Harris, *Complete Journal*, 437.

54. Heusken, *Japan Journal*, 143.

55. Heusken, *Japan Journal*, 142; see also Harris, *Complete Journal*, 462.

56. Harris, *Complete Journal*, 472.

57. Harris, *Complete Journal*, 479.

58. Oliphant, *Narrative of the Earl of Elgin's Mission*, 460.

59. Heusken, *Japan Journal*, 149.

60. Harris, *Complete Journal*, 505, 533.

61. Harris, *Complete Journal*, 518.

62. Heusken, *Japan Journal*, 173.

63. Heusken, *Japan Journal*, 196–200.

64. Heusken, *Japan Journal*, 109.

65. Griffis, *Townsend Harris*, 319.

66. Griffis, *Townsend Harris*, 321.

67. Treat, *The Early Diplomatic Relations*, 116.

68. Oliphant, *Narrative of the Earl of Elgin's Mission*, 355, 345.

69. Satoh, *Lord Hotta, the Pioneer Diplomat of Japan*, 107.

70. Heusken, *Japan Journal*, 223, 226.

71. Treat, *The Early Diplomatic Relations*, 189.

72. Griffis, *Townsend Harris*, 324.

73. Treat, *The Early Diplomatic Relations*, 188.

# Bibliography

### Archives

Library of Congress
> Poinsett, Joel. Papers, 1810–21. Correspondence, journals, notes, and memoranda, as well as four special reports to the Department of State:
>> *Buenos Ayres Revolution, 1810–1812*
>> *Chile, Kingdom of, 1812–1814*
>> *Journal to Rio Janeiro, Buenos Ayres, and Chile*
>> *United Provinces of the River Plate*
>
> Porter Family Papers. Papers of David Porter (1780–1843) and his son, David Dixon Porter (1813–1891) relating to their naval careers and families.
> Roberts, Edmund. Papers, 1832–36. Diplomatic documents, correspondence, journals, manuscript drafts.

Louisiana Digital Library
> Papers relating to Daniel Clark, 1800–1814. Business transactions, land purchases papers, legal papers. http://cdm16313.contentdm.oclc.org/cdm/search/searchterm/daniel%20clark%20land/order/nosort.
> Papers relating to Zulime Gardette (wife of Daniel Clark and mother of Myra Clark Gaines). Donaldsonville LA: *Le Vigilant*, n.d. http://cdm16313.contentdm.oclc.org/cdm/compoundobject/collection/lwp/id/3147/rec/14.
> Stokes, C. J., and Aimee Linn. 1861. "Description of the Life and Legal Cases Surrounding Myra Clark Gaines." http://cdm16313.contentdm.oclc.org/cdm/compoundobject/collection/lwp/id/7358/rec/2.

National Archives
> State Department General Records
>> Consular dispatches and instructions: Algiers, Monterrey, New Orleans, Tahiti, Tripoli, and Tunis.
>> Diplomatic dispatches and instructions: Constantinople and Mexico City.
>> Diplomatic instructions, 1829–1845.
>> Larkin, Thomas. "Description of California prior to the Year 1846."
>> Poinsett, Joel. 1822. "The Present Political State of Mexico."
>
> Founders Online
>> Papers of George Washington relating to the Barbary regencies. https://founders.archives.gov/about/Washington.

New York Public Library Rare Books and Manuscripts Division
> Cathcart Family Papers. Correspondence of James Leander Cathcart, 1785–1816, and biographical sketch.

State Department, Ralph J. Bunche Library

    *An Account of Louisiana, Being an Abstract of Documents, in the Departments of State and of the Treasury.* Washington DC: Department of State, 1803.

    *General Instructions to Consuls, &c.* 1834.

    *General Instructions to the Consuls and Commercial Agents of the United States.* Washington DC: Blair and Rives, 1838.

University of Virginia

    Papers of George Washington, digital edition.

    George Washington and the Barbary Coast Pirates. http://gwpapers.virginia.edu/history/topics/gw-and-the-barbary-coast-pirates/.

**Published Works**

"1790 Northwest China Trade." Boston Innovation, 2005. https://web.archive.org/web/20070710041905/http://bostoninnovation.org/pdf/1790_nw_China_Trade_10.12.05.pdf.

"1804 Draped Bust Silver Dollar—Class I: The 'King of Siam' Specimen." *Coin Facts.* http://www.coinfacts.com/silver_dollars/1804_dollars/king_of_siam_1804_silver_dollar.htm.

*American State Papers, Documents, Legislative and Executive of the Congress of the United States.* Washington DC: Gales and Seaton, 1832.

"Arlington Oaks History." Arlington Oaks, 1999. https://web.archive.org/web/20000418154431/http://arlingtonoaks.com/history.htm.

Armstrong, Oscar V. "Opening China." *American Heritage* 33, no. 2 (February–March 1982). http://www.americanheritage.com/content/opening-china.

Baepler, Paul, ed. *White Slaves, African Masters: An Anthology of American Barbary Captivity.* Chicago: University of Chicago Press, 1999.

Baldwin, A. C. *Joel Barlow.* 1873. University of Michigan Press, 2005.

Bancroft, Hubert Howe. *History of California.* 7 vols. San Francisco: History, 1886.

Barnes, William, and John Heath Morgan. *The Foreign Service of the United States.* Washington DC: Department of State, 1961.

Bazant, Jan. *A Concise History of Mexico from Hidalgo to Cárdenas, 1805–1940.* Cambridge: Cambridge University Press, 1977.

Bemis, Samuel Flag. *A Diplomatic History of the United States.* New York: Henry Holt, 1936.

Bennett, Frederick Debell. *Narrative of a Whaling Voyage round the Globe from the Year 1833 to 1836.* London: Richard Bentley, 1840.

Brookes, Jean Ingram. *International Rivalry in the Pacific Islands, 1800–1875.* Berkeley: University of California Press, 1941.

Cathcart, James Leander. *The Captives: Eleven Years a Prisoner in Algiers.* Compiled by his daughter, J. B. Newkirk. La Porte IN: Herald Print, 1899.

———. *The Diplomatic Journal and Letter Book of James Leander Cathcart, 1788–1796.* Worcester MA: Davis Press, 1955.

———. *Tripoli: First War with the United States. Inner History. Letter Book Compiled by His Daughter, J. B. Newkirk.* La Porte IN: Herald Print, 1901.

Clark, Daniel. *Proofs of the Corruption of Gen. James Wilkinson and of His Connexion with Aaron Burr.* 1809. Honolulu: University Press of the Pacific, 2005.

*Compilation of Treaties in Force, Prepared under Resolution of the Senate.* Washington DC: Government Printing Office, 1904.

Cooper, J. Fenimore. *History of the Navy of the United States of America.* Paris: Baudry's European Library, 1839.

Cotheal, Alexander I. "Treaty between the United States of America and the Sultan of Maskat: The Arabic Text." *Journal of the American Oriental Society* 4 (1854): 341–56.

Cox, I. J. "Daniel Clark." In *Dictionary of American Biography*, vol. 7, ed. Dumas Malone. New York: Charles Scribner's Sons, 1936.

Darwin, Charles. *The Voyage of the "Beagle."* Raleigh: Hays Barton Press, 2007.

De la Croix, l'Abbé Nicolle. *Géographie du Monde.* Paris: Imprimerie d'Auguste Delalain, 1817.

Dennett, Tyler. *Americans in Eastern Asia.* New York: Macmillan, 1922.

*The Diplomatic Correspondence of the United States of America, from the Signing of the Definitive Treaty of Peace, 10th September 1783, until the Adoption of the Constitution, March 4, 1798.* Washington DC: Francis Preston Blair, 1834.

"Documents: Dispatches from the United States Consulate in New Orleans, 1801–1803." *American Historical Review* 32, no. 4 (1927) and 33, no. 2 (1928).

Douglass, Susan L., and Aisa Martinez. "Nineteenth-Century American Merchants in the Indian Ocean: Voyage of the *Peacock* and the Treaty of Friendship with the Sultan of Muscat." Washington DC: Sultan Qaboos Cultural Center, 2009. http://docplayer.net/9022076-The-united-states-in-global-history.html.

Douty, Esther. *Hasty Pudding and Barbary Pirates: A Life of Joel Barlow.* Philadelphia: Westminster Press, 1975.

Eicher, Peter D., ed. *"Emperor Dead" and Other Historic American Diplomatic Dispatches.* Washington DC: Congressional Quarterly Press, 1997.

Eilts, Hermann F. *Early American Diplomacy in the Near and Far East: The Diplomatic and Personal History of Edmund Q. Roberts (1784–1836).* Washington DC: New Academia, 2012.

Fairbank, John King. *The United States and China.* Cambridge: Harvard University Press, 1972.

Fairbank, John K., Edwin O. Reischauer, and Albert M. Craig. *East Asia: The Modern Transformation.* Boston: Houghton Mifflin, 1965.

Felton, Cornelius C. "William Eaton." In *American Biography*, vol. 2, edited by Jared Sparks. New York: Harper Brothers, 1902.

Fortune, Robert. *Yedo and Peking: A Narrative of a Journey to the Capitals of Japan and China.* London: John Murray, 1863.

Foster, John W. *American Diplomacy in the Orient.* Boston: Houghton Mifflin, 1903.

Gayarré, Charles. *History of Louisiana.* New York: William J. Widdleton, 1866.

Gedalecia, David. "Letters from the Middle Kingdom: The Origins of America's China Policy." *Prologue Magazine* 34, no. 4 (Winter 2002). http://www.archives.gov/publications/prologue/2002/winter/gedalecia-1.html.

Green, John. *A Journal of an Intended Voyage on Board the Ship "Empress of China" Bound from New York to Canton in India, John Green, Commander.* In *The Empress of China*, by Philip Smith. Philadelphia: Philadelphia Maritime Museum, 1984.

Griffis, William Elliot. *Townsend Harris: The First American Envoy in Japan.* Boston: Houghton, Mifflin, 1895.

Hague, Harlan, and David J. Langum. *Thomas O. Larkin: A Life of Patriotism and Profit in Old California*. Norman: University of Oklahoma Press, 1990.

Harmon, Nolan B. *The Famous Case of Myra Clark Gaines*. Baton Rouge: Louisiana State University Press, 1946.

Harris, Townsend. *The Complete Journal of Townsend Harris: First American Consul General and Minister to Japan*. Edited by Mario Emilio Cozena. Garden City NY: Published for the Japan Society by Doubleday, Doran, 1930.

Hawgood, John A., ed. *First and Last Consul: Thomas Oliver Larkin and the Americanization of California. A Selection of Letters*. Palo Alto: Pacific Books, 1970.

Hawks, Francis L., comp. *Narrative of the Expedition of an American Squadron to the China Seas and Japan, 1852, 1853, and 1854, under the Command of Commodore M. C. Perry, United States Navy, by order of the Government of the United States. Compiled from the original notes and journals of Commodore Perry and his officers at his request and under his Supervision*. Washington DC: B. Tucker, 1856.

Hawkes, James A. (writing as "a citizen of New York"). *Retrospect of the Boston Tea-Party, with a Memoir of George R. T. Hewes, a Survivor of the Little Band of Patriots Who Drowned the Tea in Boston Harbor in 1773*. New York: S. S. Bliss, printer, 1834.

Henry, Robert Selph. *The Story of the Mexican War*. New York: Da Capo Press, 1989.

Heusken, Henry. *Japan Journal, 1855–1861*. Translated and edited by Jeannette C. van der Corput and Robert Wilson. New Brunswick: Rutgers University Press, 1964.

Hiroa, Te Rangi (Buck, Peter H.). *Explorers of the Pacific: European and American Discoveries in Polynesia*. Honolulu: Bishop Museum, 1953.

Hishida, Seiji G. *The International Position of Japan as a Great Power*. New York: Columbia University Press, 1905.

"A Historical Perspective on Gifts to the United States of America." Smithsonian Institution, 2013. http://www.mnh.si.edu/treasures/frame_exhibit_gallery1_main.htm.

*Historical Statistics of the United States, Colonial Times to 1970*. Washington DC: Bureau of the Census, 1975.

"History of a Missed USA–Vietnam Draft Trade Agreement since over 170 Years Ago." Vietnam Union of Science and Technology Associations, 2012. http://www.vusta.vn/en/news/International-Events/History-of-a-missed-USA-Vietnam-Draft-Trade-Agreement-since-over-170-years-ago-8385.html.

Irwin, Ray W. *The Diplomatic Relations of the United States with the Barbary Powers, 1776–1816*. Chapel Hill: University of North Carolina Press, 1931.

Jackson, Andrew. State of the Union Address, December 6, 1831. http://www.thisnation.com/library/sotu/1831aj.html.

———. State of the Union Address, December 12, 1832. http://odur.let.rug.nl/usa/P/aj7/speeches/ajson4.htm.

———. State of the Union Address, December 5, 1836. http://stateoftheunion.onetwothree.net/texts/18361205.html.

"Joel Roberts Poinsett." The Masonic Trowel, 2012. http://www.themasonictrowel.com/masonic_talk/stb/stbs/84-12.htm.

Lay, Tracy Hollingsworth. *The Foreign Service of the United States*. New York: Prentice-Hall, 1925.

Ledyard, John. *The Last Voyage of Captain Cook: The Collected Writings of John Ledyard*. Edited by James Zug. Washington DC: National Geographic Society, 2005.

Lipscomb, Andrew A., ed. *The Writings of Thomas Jefferson*. Library ed. Washington DC: Thomas Jefferson Memorial Association, 1903.

Lyon, Wilson. *Louisiana in French Diplomacy.* Norman: University of Oklahoma Press, 1934.

Manning, William R., ed. *Diplomatic Correspondence of the United States Concerning the Independence of the Latin American Nations.* 3 vols. New York: Oxford University Press, 1925.

Melville, Herman. *Omoo.* New York: Dodd, Mead, 1924.

Miller, Hunter, ed. *Treaties and Other International Acts of the United States of America.* Washington DC: Government Printing Office, 1933.

Minnigerode, Meade. *Lives and Times: Four Informal American Biographies.* New York: G. P. Putnam's Sons, 1925.

*Modern Gazetteer.* Perth: Morison and Son, 1799.

Moerenhout, Jacques-Antoine. *The Inside Story of the Gold Rush.* Translated and edited by Abraham P. Nasatir, in collaboration with George Ezra Dane. San Francisco: California Historical Society, 1935. https://cdn.loc.gov//service/gdc/calbk/018.pdf.

———. *Travels to the Islands of the Pacific Ocean (1837).* Translated by Arthur R. Bordon. Lanham MD: University Press of America, 1993.

Moorehead, Alan. *The Fatal Impact: The Invasion of the South Pacific, 1767–1840.* New York: Harper and Row, 1966.

Morison, Samuel Eliot. *The Maritime History of Massachusetts.* Boston: Houghton Mifflin, 1921.

———. *The Oxford History of the American People.* New York: New American Library, 1972.

Morse, Jedidiah. *The American Gazetteer, exhibiting a full account of the Civil Divisions, Rivers, Harbors, Indian Tribes, &c. of the American Continent: also of the West-India and other appendant Islands, with a Particular Description of Louisiana.* Boston: Thomas & Andrews, 1810.

Moser, Harold, and J. Clift, eds. *The Papers of Andrew Jackson.* Vol. 6. Knoxville: University of Tennessee Press, 2002.

Murray, Hugh. *The Encyclopedia of Geography, Comprising a Complete Description of the Earth, Physical, Statistical, and Political; Exhibiting Its Relation to the Heavenly Bodies, Its Physical Structure, the Natural History of Each Country, and the Industry, Commerce, Political Institutions, and Civil and Social State of All Nations.* Philadelphia: Lea and Blanchard, 1842.

"Object of the Month: The Columbia and Washington Medal." Massachusetts Historical Society, 2004. https://web.archive.org/web/20160226201751/http://www.masshist.org/object-of-the-month/objects/the-columbia-and-washington-medal-2004-05-01.

Oliphant, Laurence. *Narrative of the Earl of Elgin's Mission to China and Japan in the Years 1857, '58, '59.* New York: Harper & Brothers, 1860.

Paine, Ralph D. *The Old Merchant Marine: A Chronicle of American Ships and Sailors.* New Haven: Yale University Press, 1919. http://www.fullbooks.com/The-Old-Merchant-Marine-A-Chronicle-of1.html.

———. *The Ships and Sailors of Old Salem.* Chicago: A. C. McClurg, 1912.

Palgon, Gary Mitchell. *William Alexander Leidesdorff, First Black Millionaire, American Consul, and California Pioneer.* Self-published, 2005.

Parton, Dorothy M. "The Diplomatic Career of Joel Roberts Poinsett." PhD diss., Catholic University, Washington DC, 1934.

Philbrick, Nathaniel. *Sea of Glory, America's Voyage of Discovery: The U.S. Exploring Expedition, 1838–1842.* New York: Penguin Books, 2003.

———. "The United States Exploring Expedition, 1838–1842." Smithsonian Institution Libraries Digital Collection, 2010. http://www.sil.si.edu/DigitalCollections/usexex/learn/Philbrick.htm.

Pitot, James. *Observations of the Colony of Louisiana from 1796 to 1802.* Baton Rouge: Louisiana State University Press, 1979.

"Platter, Order of the Cincinnati, c. 1785." Dietrich American Foundation, 2011. http://earlyamericanart.org/source/mainplate.html.

Poinsett, Joel R. (writing as "A Citizen of the United States"). *Notes on Mexico, Made in the Autumn of 1822.* Philadelphia: H. C. Carey and L. Lea, 1824.

Polk, James K. State of the Union Address, December 5, 1848. http://www.presidency.ucsb.edu/ws/?pid=29489.

Porter, David (writing as "an American"). *Constantinople and Its Environs, in a Series of Letters, by an American Long Resident at Constantinople.* 2 vols. New York: Harper and Brothers, 1835.

———. *Journal of a Cruise to the Pacific Ocean by Captain David Porter in the United States Frigate "Essex," in the Years 1812, 1813 and 1814.* New York: Wiley and Halsted, 1822.

Porter, David Dixon. *A Memoir of Commodore David Porter of the United States Navy.* Albany NY: J. Munsell, 1875.

Putnam, Herbert Everett. *Joel Roberts Poinsett: A Political Biography.* Washington DC: Mimeoform Press, 1935.

Reynolds, Jeremiah N. *Voyage of the United States Frigate "Potomac," under the Command of Commodore John Downes, during the Circumnavigation of the Globe, in the Years 1831, 1832, 1833, and 1834.* New York: Harper & Brothers, 1835.

Rippy, J. Fred. *Joel R. Poinsett, Versatile American.* Durham: Duke University Press, 1935.

Roberts, Edmund. *Embassy to the Eastern Courts of Cochin-China, Siam, and Muscat; in the U.S. Sloop-of-War "Peacock," David Geisinger, Commander, during the Years, 1832–3–4.* New York: Harper and Brothers, 1837.

Roberts, Edmund, and W. S. W. Ruschenberger. *Two Yankee Diplomats in 1830s Siam.* Edited by Michael Smithies. Bangkok: Orchid Press, 2002.

Robinson, J. Dennis. "The Rise and Fall of Tobias Lear." 2013. https://web.archive.org/web/20121114113022/http://www.seacoastnh.com/Famous_People/Tobias_Lear/The_Rise_and_Fall_of_Tobias_Lear/.

Rodd, Francis Rennell. *General William Eaton: The Failure of an Idea.* New York: Minton, Balch, 1932.

Rohrbough, Malcolm J. *Days of Gold: The California Gold Rush and the American Nation.* Berkeley: University of California Press, 1997.

Rowland, Dunbar, ed. *Official Letter Books of W.C.C. Claiborne, 1801–1806.* Jackson MS: State Department of Archives and History, 1917.

Royce, Josiah. *California, from the Conquest in 1846 to the Second Vigilance Committee in San Francisco: A Study of American Character.* Boston: Houghton, Mifflin, 1886.

Ruschenberger, William Samuel Waithman. *A Voyage round the World; Including an Embassy to Muscat and Siam, in 1835, 1836, and 1837.* Philadelphia: Carey, Lea & Blanchard, 1838.

Russell, M. *Polynesia; or, Account of the Principal Islands of the South Sea, including New Zealand.* New York: Harper and Brothers, 1848.

Satoh, Henry. *Lord Hotta, the Pioneer Diplomat of Japan.* Tokyo: Hakubunkan, 1908.

Shaw, Samuel. *The Journals of Major Samuel Shaw, the First American Consul at Canton.* Edited by Josiah Quincy. Boston: Wm. Crosby and H. P. Nichols, 1847.

Shepard, Betty, ed. *Bound for Battle: The Cruise of the United States Frigate "Essex" in the War of 1812, as Told by Captain David Porter.* New York: Harcourt, Brace & World, 1967.

Shreve, Royal Ornan. *The Finished Scoundrel: General James Wilkinson, Sometime Commander-in-Chief of the Army of the United States, Who Made Intrigue a Trade and Treason a Profession.* Indianapolis: Bobbs-Merrill, 1933.

Smith, Philip Chadwick Foster. *The Empress of China.* Philadelphia: Philadelphia Maritime Museum, 1984.

Smith, Walter B., II. *America's Diplomats and Consuls of 1776–1865: A Geographic and Biographic Directory of the Foreign Service from the Declaration of Independence to the End of the Civil War.* Washington DC: Center for the Study of Foreign Affairs, Foreign Service Institute, 1986.

"Society of the Cincinnati Chocolate Pot and Two-Handled Mugs, ca. 1790." Knox Museum, 2011. http://knoxmuseum.org/portfolio-posts/3712/.

Stann, E. Jeffrey. "Charles Wilkes as Diplomat." In *Magnificent Voyagers: The U.S. Exploring Expedition of 1838–1842,* ed. Herman J. Viola and Carolyn Margolis. Washington DC: Smithsonian Institution, 1985.

Statler, Oliver. *Shimoda Story.* New York: Random House, 1969.

Stillé, Charles J. "The Life and Services of Joel R. Poinsett." *Pennsylvania Magazine of History and Biography* 12 (1888).

Swasey, W. F. *The Early Days and Men of California.* Oakland: Pacific Press, 1891.

Strauss, W. Patrick. *Americans in Polynesia, 1783–1842.* East Lansing: Michigan State University Press, 1963.

Taylor, Fitch W. *A Voyage round the World, and Visits to Various Foreign Countries, in the United States Frigate "Columbia."* New York: D. Appleton, 1845.

*Territorial Papers of the United States.* Edited by Clarence Edwin Carter. Washington DC: Government Printing Office, 1940.

Ticknor, Benajah. *The Voyage of the Peacock: A Journal by Benajah Ticknor, Naval Surgeon.* Edited by Nan Powell Hodges. Ann Arbor: University of Michigan Press, 1991.

Todd, Charles Burr, ed. *Life and Letters of Joel Barlow: Poet, Statesman, Philosopher.* New York: G. P. Putnam's Sons, 1886.

"Townsend Harris: America's First Consul to Japan." Consulate General of Japan in New York. http://www.ny.us.emb-japan.go.jp/150th/html/nyepiE2a.htm.

Treat, Payson Jackson. *The Early Diplomatic Relations between the United States and Japan, 1853–1865.* Baltimore: Johns Hopkins University Press, 1917.

Turnbull, Archibald Douglas. *Commodore David Porter, 1780–1843.* New York: Century, 1929.

Underhill, Reuben L. *From Cowhides to Golden Fleece: A Narrative of California, 1832–1858, Based upon Unpublished Correspondence of Thomas Oliver Larkin of Monterey, Trader, Developer, Promoter, and Only American Consul.* Stanford: Stanford University Press, 1946.

U.S. Fish and Wildlife Service. "Sea Otters and the Endangered Species Act." 2016. https://www.fws.gov/alaska/fisheries/mmm/seaotters/criticalhabitat.htm.

Versteeg, Clarence L. "Financing and Outfitting the First United States Ship to China." *Pacific Historical Review* 22, no. 1 (February 1953).

Wang, David. "Benjamin Franklin and China: A Survey of Benjamin Franklin's Efforts at Drawing Positive Elements from Chinese Civilization during the Formative Age of the United States." Benjamin Franklin Tercentenary, 2006. http://www.benfranklin300.org/_etc_pdf/franklinchina.pdf (site discontinued).

Ward, R. Gerard, ed. *American Activities in the Central Pacific, 1790–1870: A History, Geography, and Ethnography Pertaining to American Involvement and Americans in the Pacific Taken from Contemporary Newspapers, etc.* Ridgewood NJ: Gregg Press, 1967.

Whitaker, Arthur Preston. *The Mississippi Question, 1795–1803: A Study in Trade, Politics, and Diplomacy.* New York: D. Appleton–Century, 1934.

White, John. *A Voyage to Cochin China.* London: Longman, Hurst, Rees, Orme, Brown, and Green, 1824.

Wilkes, Charles. *Autobiography of Rear Admiral Charles Wilkes, U.S. Navy, 1798–1877.* Edited by William Morgan et al. Washington DC: Naval History Division, Department of the Navy, 1978.

Winsor, Justin. *The Memorial History of Boston: Including Suffolk County, Massachusetts, 1630–1880.* Vol. 4. Boston: James R. Osgood, 1881.

Wood, William Maxwell. *Fankwei; or, The San Jacinto in the Seas of India, China, and Japan.* New York: Harper & Brothers, 1859.

## Related ADST Book Series Titles

Charles T. Cross, *Born a Foreigner: A Memoir of the American Presence in Asia*

Peter D. Eicher, ed., *"Emperor Dead" and Other Historic American Diplomatic Dispatches*

Hermann F. Eilts, *Early American Diplomacy in the Near and Far East: The Diplomatic and Personal History of Edmund Q. Roberts (1784–1836)*

Stephen H. Grant, *Peter Strickland: New London Shipmaster, Boston Merchant, First Consul to Senegal*

Brandon Grove, *Behind Embassy Walls: The Life and Times of an American Diplomat*

Allen C. Hansen, *Nine Lives: A Foreign Service Odyssey*

Judith M. Heimann, *Paying Calls in Shangri-La: Scenes from a Woman's Life in American Diplomacy*

Michael P. E. Hoyt, *Captive in the Congo: A Consul's Return to the Heart of Darkness*

Richard L. Jackson, *The Incidental Oriental Secretary and Other Tales of Foreign Service*

Charles Stuart Kennedy, *The American Consul: A History of the United States Consular Service, 1776–1924*

Terry McNamara, with Adrian Hill, *Escape with Honor: My Last Hours in Vietnam*

Robert H. Miller, *Vietnam and Beyond: A Diplomat's Cold War Education*

William Morgan and C. Stuart Kennedy, *American Diplomats: The Foreign Service at Work*

David D. Newsom, *Witness to a Changing World*

Richard B. Parker, *Memoirs of a Foreign Service Arabist*

Nicholas Platt, *China Boys: How U.S. Relations with the PRC Began and Grew*

James W. Spain, *In Those Days: A Diplomat Remembers*

Jean Wilkowski, *Abroad for Her Country: Tales of a Pioneer Woman Ambassador in the U.S. Foreign Service*

Ginny Carson Young, *Peregrina: Unexpected Adventures of an American Consul*

For a complete list of series titles, visit adst.org/publications.